W9-CUQ-945

Project Evaluation: A Unified Approach for the Analysis of Capital Investments

J. Morley English

Macmillan Publishing Company
A Division of Macmillan, Inc.
NEW YORK
Collier Macmillan Publishers
LONDON

Macmillan Publishing Company
866 Third Avenue, New York, NY 10022

Collier Macmillan Canada, Inc.

Printed in the United States of America

printing number
1 2 3 4 5 6 7 8 9 10

Library of Congress Cataloging in Publication Data

English, J. Morley (John Morley), 1915–
 Project evaluation.

 Bibliography: p.
 1. Capital investments—Evaluation. 2. Economic
development projects—Evaluation. I. Title.
HG4028.C4E53 1984   332.63   84-11204
ISBN 0-02-949240-8

To Marva

Contents

Preface

This book represents a unique and different approach to the economic evaluation of investment alternatives. It is based on engineering and managerial economics but treats these from a somewhat different perspective than do traditional books on the subject. Time value of cash flows is usually evaluated by means of compound-interest relationships based on debt models. Here by contrast, the emphasis is on the perception of future values in continuous time rather than on debt. This may be more a philosophical point than it is a difference in technique but it is hoped that the reader will obtain new insights on the subject as a result.

As indicated by the title the book is based on a unified approach. A number of evaluation methods are in current use today. These have been developed and are used as if each were unique. In reality all are the same, provided that the underlying assumptions are consistent. That disparate conclusions seem to be reached by the different methods comes about because of hidden and unspecified assumptions that differ from one method to another.

This book is addressed to the professional reader who is interested more in understanding the fundamental ideas that must be considered in determining the suitability of a proposed investment, than he is in the detail that goes into an analysis. It is important for this reader to have questions raised concerning the efficacy and use of many well-accepted ideas and techniques in current use today. For example, the generally-used criterion of *return on investment* (ROI) is shown to have serious limitations.

A number of completely new ideas are presented. As one example, depreciation is shown to have relevance in accounting but is essentially extraneous in project evaluation. A generalized depreciation function is developed to show how depreciation is utilized for the performance measurement of an ongoing project. This is, of course, not relevant in the use of depreciation for determining optimal tax strategies. As a second example, risk is shown to be a function of the futurity of cash-flow components and, therefore cannot effectively be taken into account by increasing the desired rate of return. In fact, under certain circumstances the rate of return, when including risk, should be lowered rather than raised as is the common practice.

Because of these new and admittedly provocative ideas, this book should be suitable as a graduate or advanced text book as well as being of general interest to the professional reader. For both kinds of reader, no prior knowledge of economics is assumed. Two chapters are devoted to an elementary treatment of economic principles. A fairly extensive overview of macroeconomics and money is included, because the economic environment in which investment decisions are made requires some understanding of these subjects. This is particularly so for money (a widely misunderstood topic in economics) and its role in finance. Finance is included in the text because it addresses the question *how* to implement the chosen alternative investment.

While the book was not written as a first-course text (much of the material is too condensed for that purpose), its use would constitute a worthwhile challenge for senior students. However, the instructor who uses it for an introductory course should be prepared to add additional detail by drawing on his own experience or supplementing his lectures with notes. Furthermore, the problems at the end of each chapter will need to be supplemented. These problems may not appeal to, or be necessary for, the casual reader who desires to obtain an overview of the subject. They will be suitable for exercises, if the book is used in course work.

I have arrived at my present perceptions of a methodology of project evaluation as a result of an evolutionary process comprising 35 years of both consulting and teaching engineering economics. This has included lecturing in foreign countries where the basic and cultural background of the students was so different from those of American students, that I was forced to rethink my concepts from fresh perspectives.

I owe acknowledgments to so many students and colleagues that I could not conceivably list them. The one person whom I must identify and especially thank is my wife, Marva, whose editing help was so essential in making this a more readable book.

J. Morley English

○ CHAPTER ONE
○
○
○ *Framework for*
○ *Evaluation of Project*
○ *Investments*

Sustained economic growth and prosperity depend on expansion of capital investment. The impetus for the dynamic growth of the United States economy in the latter part of the twentieth century may well have been the result of the very high percentage of income devoted to investment during the latter part of the nineteenth and early part of the twentieth centuries. In contrast, the lag in investment in the 1970s and 1980s could have been responsible, in part, for recent underperformance of the economy. Revitalization of the economy will, in large measure, depend on sufficient saving for the creation of new capital investment.

While creation of capital is a necessary condition for renewal of prosperity, it is not a sufficient condition. Investments must be profitable. We cannot afford to squander our limited resources by making unwise investment decisions.

This book examines the methodology for evaluating investments to ensure successful investment decision making.

1

1.1 INVESTMENT NEEDS

Some characteristics of investment in today's environment, significantly different from those of the period following World War II, are:

1. *New technology.* While the rapidly developing information industry of the past is likely to continue its explosive growth, that growth is now built on a much larger base. It is widely believed that the success of the United States in competition with the rest of the world will depend on emphasizing investment in high technology.

2. *Modernization of basic industry.* Much of our industrial plant is obsolete and requires rebuilding. The steel and automobile industries, in particular, will have to be restructured to reduce labor intensities and to increase capital intensities. This will be accompanied by considerable labor shifting, with attendant structural unemployment.

3. *Large-scale systems.* We are in need of a number of new very large-scale systems today. Many of these will replace systems that have outgrown their usefulness. Energy is a notable example of this need to shift. Our society has been based on a petroleum energy economy. While periodic gluts may develop from time to time, the end of the oil era is in sight. Whether it is coal, nuclear power, or some other energy source that replaces oil, the scale of the changeover to a new energy supply system and the urgency for taking action are unprecedented. Large-scale systems require very long lead times, which in itself makes them long-term investments. In the past, we have not had satisfactory methods for evaluating very long-term projects.

4. *Infrastructure.* The underlying or foundation structures of society, such as harbors, roads, and water supply systems, are essential for all private-sector investments. In most part, infrastructure derives from government investment and is usually considered to be the responsibility of government. However there are also many private facilities that must be considered essential components of infrastructure—the rail-

way system, for example. The important point to be kept in mind is that infrastructure is a precondition for private investment. Obviously a company would not consider investing in a factory in a location not served by a highway.

1.2 EVALUATION TECHNIQUES

Any contemplated or proposed investment requires evaluation in order to ensure, with reasonable confidence, that prospective benefits outweigh costs. Whatever methodology is employed, certain basic principles must be recognized. These principles are valid whether the investment is for a new enterprise, the expansion of an existing facility, or the formation of a new corporate entity, and even for comparison of alternative ways of achieving a given objective. In this book we will identify principles, formulate a philosophical frame of reference for economic evaluation, and examine a general methodology for assessing the worth of any proposed capital investment.

1.2.1 Nature of the Investment Problem

Let us emphasize at the outset that we are concerned with *real investments* as contrasted with *financial investments*. A financial investment is one in which the investor allocates his resources to some form of financial instrument, such as stocks or bonds, which represent claims on real assets. Real investments are represented by the physical assets themselves. When an investor buys a share of stock he truly perceives that he is making an investment, but the person from whom he purchased that share of stock has, correspondingly, disinvested. A change of ownership took place, but from an overall perspective the investment was balanced by an equal disinvestment. By contrast, real investment takes place when new assets—new plant and equipment—are put in place.

The fundamental pattern of all investments is characterized by an initial commitment of resources, followed by a later payback. The simplest pattern is, as shown in Figure 1.1, a point outlay followed by a point return. More typically, investments and returns are characterized as flows spread out over time, the investment flow phase being followed by a return flow phase. This flow,

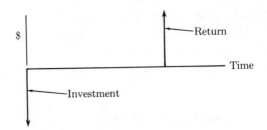

Figure 1.1 Point investment—point return.

which in terms of money value is a *cash flow*, is depicted in Figure 1.2. This cash-flow stream commences at a low level of expenditure for studies and engineering, builds up rapidly with construction, and eventually transitions to a net return-flow stream. This return-flow stream is the difference between revenues and operating expenditures.

The investment evaluation presupposes a decision to initiate this cash-flow sequence. The methodology for the evaluation requires:

1. Prediction of cash-flow stream.

2. Establishment of criteria for evaluation of cash flow.

3. Determination of how well the criteria are satisfied.

In addition, eight important considerations in evaluating the

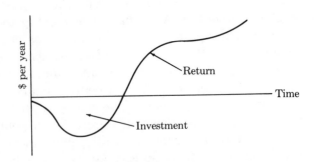

Figure 1.2 Typical investment cash flow.

investment decision are:

1. The value system.

2. The futurity of investment flows and return flows.

3. The economic context of the project.

4. Risk.

5. Inflation.

6. Finance (implementation).

7. Performance measurement (accounting).

8. The perspective of the investor (the point of view from which the investment is made).

1.3 THE VALUE SYSTEM

In general we will be concerned, in this book, with monetary values. However it is well to keep in mind that people are motivated by many things other than money, and that these other values necessarily influence their decisions. Often nonmonetary values will dominate a decision. These values are far less readily quantifiable and therefore are best left as separate assessments which can later be assigned appropriate weighting on the basis of the subjective judgment of the individual evaluator.

Monetary values are, essentially, indexed relative values of everything traded on the market, or for which relative values may be readily imputed. It should, however, be recognized that the market is basically a present-time mechanism for establishing relative value and does not function well in determining the relative value of anything a long time into the future. Therefore money measures by themselves may not be entirely satisfactory for establishing long-term value flows.

Finally, a most important consideration in the investment decision is the value of money with respect to time.

1.4 DEALING WITH FUTURITY

Investment decisions are made in the present, relative to *future prospects*. Difficult as it is to predict the future, there is simply no way to avoid the need to do so. In conventional methodology, this question is largely sidestepped by simply postulating future cash flows and then treating time-value relationships deterministically. Alternatively, we may extrapolate the experience of the past into the future and assume that this provides a best estimate of what will materialize. Such extrapolation of past data is properly called *forecasting*. We may use more sophisticated methods and infer from examination of many underlying political and economic forces what changes to expect. Such modification of a forecast involves *prediction*.

A fundamental problem with any forecast is that the greater the futurity, the greater will be the likely divergence between the forecast outcome and the actual outcome. This divergence (or variance, as defined in statistics) increases exponentially with the futurity of the forecast. It poses special problems for evaluation of long-term projects where the time pattern of the investment cash flow is very long and the return cash flow is delayed for many years. This problem of futurity may require substituting an *aspiration approach* in order to avoid direct dependence on prediction. This approach requires defining long-range objectives, or aspirations, and formulating the necessary plan for their achievement. In effect, an aspiration is in the nature of a self-fulfilling prediction. It overcomes the essential unpredictability of the future.

1.4.1 The Horizon Concept

It has been customary to introduce the notion of a *horizon time* in economic analyses. The notion of the horizon is simple and appealing. In the physical horizon there is a distance limit to visibility. Analogous with this, there is a time limitation to foresight. One can see only so far into the future. However, in the case of the physical horizon, one can navigate beyond the horizon with confidence. In economics, what might develop beyond the time horizon has, traditionally, been ignored. This has been justified, in practice, on the basis that any sum of money in the remote future, when discounted at market interest rates, becomes so small that it can be considered negligible. As will be demonstrated, this assumption is open to question. Unfortunately, while there is a limitation to visibility into the future, the horizon concept in economics does not provide much guidance for navigating beyond the horizon.

If the horizon concept is thus limited to a very few years, the question remains:

How should cash flows beyond the horizon be treated?

Clearly this is a problem to consider for the large-scale and long-range projects which are of such vital concern in the present-day economy. In many of these long-range investments, the return cash flow may not even commence prior to the horizon time.

1.5 CONTEXT OF THE INVESTMENT

An investment may be considered as being independent if it neither influences other investments nor is influenced by them. Under certain circumstances an investment may be treated as being entirely independent of all others. More generally, each investment is made in the context of an overall objective, of which it is only a contributing component. In a sense, each investment is a member of a *portfolio*. The investor is interested in the return on the entire portfolio. The returns on the individual investments that make up the portfolio are of interest only to the extent that they contribute to the larger objective.

In principle, each investment is complementary to others. There are varying degrees of complementarity of individual investments within a firm. Some are fully complementary. For example, a special process machine will not be profitable unless the firm is, as a whole, profitable. Other investments may be essentially independent of one another within the same corporate context. For example, a firm may be in a manufacturing business while at the same time investing in a hotel. The hotel will operate independently of the manufacturing operation. Nevertheless both will depend on the economy as a whole. Both the hotel business and the manufacturing operation may be expected to suffer in a recession, but not, perhaps, in exactly the same way.

These interdependencies must be examined for all proposed investments. Whenever we choose to examine an investment by itself, we should, at least, recognize that we are effectively assuming complete independence. However, as a matter of practice, we ought to identify the context of each investment both within a firm and within the general economy.

1.6 RISK

Risk can be thought of as probability of loss. It is, however, more than that. An investor undertakes an investment in anticipation of some expected gain. The probability of loss that he perceives as risk is, therefore, relative to expected gain. He might be willing to accept a given probability of loss, provided he can also anticipate a compensating probability of added gain. Thus the measure of risk is a function of the variance of the return.

All investments are risky because the return depends on an uncertain future. The nature of that risk depends on the variance of the cash-flow stream. The cash-flow stream will fluctuate as a manifestation of two separate effects—the variability innate in the investment itself and the variability that is induced by external influences. The degree to which an investment varies dependently with the firm or the economy is, in a sense, unrelated to the risk of the investment itself, but is nevertheless inseparable from it. For example, the output from a certain type of machine with a long and established record of performance may be virtually assured, but its risk will still be related to the variance of the manufacturing operation in which it is employed, and in which it is a complementary component.

1.7 FINANCE — IMPLEMENTATION OF THE INVESTMENT

The economic evaluation of a proposed investment is made to determine what investment should be undertaken. Having decided what the most desirable action is, it remains to answer the conditional question: Given the desirable investment, how can that investment be implemented?

In other words, how are the funds to be raised? Is the project financially feasible? These two questions—*what* and *how*—are not independent of each other, but they need to be separated, at least conceptually. All too often financial feasibility is determined without regard to the suitability of the investment in the first place. This can result in an investment being made when money is available and not because the investment is sound. Conversely, many investments that should be undertaken are rejected because of unfavorable funding prospects and/or lack of substantiation by means of an adequate economic evaluation.

Financing is drawn from two sources. Funds are generated internally from retained earnings (i.e. profits) and externally from new capital (i.e. stocks or bonds). The first source is constrained by the profitability of the firm; the second requires a conscious decision to alter the financial structure of the firm. For this latter type of financing, the point of view from which the evaluation is made must be altered. The reason the financing can change the point of view will be discussed in Section 1.9 below.

1.8 MEASUREMENT OF PROJECT PERFORMANCE — ACCOUNTING

It cannot be emphasized too strongly that economic evaluation is concerned with *future prospects*. Finance, too, is concerned with the future. On the other hand, accounting is retrospective. It is concerned with history.

After an investment has been made, it must be monitored to ensure that it performs as expected. This requires suitable means for measuring performance—a primary function of accounting. The accountant reports to management how well or how poorly the business has been doing. Accounting, as implied by the origin of the word, is oriented toward the past. Nevertheless, the accountant is still concerned with the future in one important respect. He must have a means for allocating past capital expenditures over future time. These allocations enter into the difference between revenues and expenses, including the allocated capital costs, thereby constituting a measure of current profitability. Such time-allocated costs are called *depreciation allowances.*

A depreciation allowance represents a recognition of the wearing out of an asset. However, in many ways this is an unfortunate choice of words. What is important is not the physical wearing out, but rather the time allocation of cost. It may be only of incidental interest that there is an approximate and implicit estimate of physical depreciation. This reasoning will be expanded in Chapter 6.

An important aspect of depreciation is that it comes into use in the formula for computing income taxes, which are a significant component of costs. Unfortunately, consequences of depreciation accounting for income-tax purposes have come to dominate operating practices and tend to obscure the fundamental accounting purpose for considering depreciation.

While the use of depreciation is important for making an estimate of last year's profits, annual depreciation allowances (except for their place in determining taxes) are irrelevant in determining correct investment decisions. The misconception that depreciation, in itself, is important is a persistent source of error in making investment evaluations.

This assertion may seem questionable at this point, but later it will be explained in depth. In the meantime it will be realized that depreciation is relevant when profitability is assessed for the immediate past time period in terms of the flow—dollars per unit of time (e.g., per year). But this is not the objective of investment evaluation. That objective is *the determination of profitability from beginning to end of the project.*

1.9 PERSPECTIVE OF THE INVESTOR

One of the first steps in an investment evaluation is the identification of the point of view from which the investment is to be made. In most textbooks, little or no emphasis is placed on exactly who is expected to profit from the investment. However, it is extremely important to consider this question and to identify the investor explicitly.

Whoever the investor is, all revenues accrue to him and all costs are charged to him. The difference between revenues and costs is his profit. This seems obvious, but by not identifying the investor explicitly we can fail to allocate revenues and costs properly. For example, in evaluating an investment for a firm, it is common practice to measure return on total capital, without regard to its source. This implies that the investment point of view is that of a joint venture. The investor in this case is, in reality, a coalition of stockholder and bondholder. The practice has been that, at the same time that we make the analysis from this joint-venture viewpoint, we also claim that the investment is in the interest of the owner (i.e., the stockholder). This is inconsistent. The same analyst, in assessing an investment in a home for himself, would not consider the amount provided by the bank as part of his investment. He would consider that his investment consisted of his down payment, coupled with whatever other expense he might have incurred, incidental to the purchase.

It is clear whose point of view is represented in the case of an individual investor. While it is not quite so clear when a corporation is considered, the proper viewpoint may still be readily delineated. A real problem arises, however, in the case of public investments. Some form of collective viewpoint is represented in public investments, but the diffused nature of the constituency, and the manner in which all individuals share fairly, makes for a great deal of vagueness in perspective, with corresponding difficulty in defining the point of view.

Finally, it should be recognized how the point of view of the investor in the stock of a company is manifested. It will be recalled that we are interested in real investments as contrasted with financial investments (such as the purchase of stock). However, there is a connection between the two. The stock market serves as a pricing mechanism for reflecting a collective view of the relative attractiveness of alternative opportunities. If the price of a stock drops on the market, the firm involved often finds itself unable to issue more shares or to borrow funds for what may otherwise seem to be attractive real investments.

1.10 TREATMENT OF SUBJECT MATTER

In recent years there has been a proliferation of textbooks on the subjects of engineering economics and managerial economics. Those on engineering economics have all been patterned after or built upon the pioneering work of Eugene L. Grant (1930). However, Grant's book was by no means the first. Arthur Wellington, a railroad engineer, wrote a classic book on the economics of railroads in 1879. The first textbook devoted exclusively to the subject may have been *Engineering Economics* by J. C. L. Fish in 1915. Managerial economics developed much later and began to be of significance subsequent to World War II.

In many respects engineering economics and managerial economics are similar in objectives and in the treatment of subject matter, but their emphasis differs. Both disciplines are concerned with investment evaluation and capital budgeting, but managerial economics is concerned largely with microeconomics and the workings of the market, whereas engineering economics is concerned more with the mathematics of finance (e.g., compound-interest relationships) and usually treats a number of seemingly different methods for analyzing investments.

This book differs from those in several important respects. The reader will become aware of these differences as he progresses through the text. In many ways these differences are philosophical in nature. Those readers who are familiar with the current literature may find it challenging to review the material from a new perspective. They may also wish to test their established concepts against the approach presented herein. For those studying the subject for the first time, difficulties that naturally arise when seeing things from an unfamiliar vantage point may never occur, because the first-time reader has not been preconditioned by earlier exposure to the subject.

The subject areas that have been treated from a somewhat different viewpoint are outlined in summary form below.

1.10.1 Concepts in Economics

In most texts no attempt is made to cover general economics. It is usually presupposed that the reader already has acquired some understanding of such basic concepts as supply and demand. Furthermore, while the techniques of investment evaluation may not require a great deal of knowledge of economics, economics is fundamental for an appreciation of some of the more subtle concepts of project evaluation. Many people fail to recognize these subtleties.

It is desirable that an investment analysis should be made with full cognizance of general economic conditions which, necessarily, have a bearing on success or failure. For this, it is essential to have a good grasp of the principles of general economics. For this reason these principles are covered in broad outline, in order to emphasize concepts without the distractions of the detail normally covered in texts on economics.

The coverage of economics includes the three principal categories

- Microeconomics.

- Macroeconomics.

- Money and banking.

Microeconomics is that subdivision of economics covering the basic relationships between individuals—largely as determined by the market. While microeconomics is the core of modern economics, it may be less important as a basis for investment analysis than is macroeconomics. The latter deals with measures of general economic activity and thus is important in assessing the investment environment. Related to macroeconomics, but an important subject in its own right, is money and banking. Money is perhaps the most difficult and least understood concept in economics. At the same time, monetary policy significantly influences the investment climate. Furthermore while monetary control with its effect on economic policy is controversial, its effect on inflation is unquestioned, and inflation is a very important consideration in economic evaluation. The basics of these subjects are covered in Chapters 2 and 3.

1.10.2   The Discounting Concept

The major consideration in all investment analysis is the treatment of projected cash flows, both revenue and expenditure streams. Briefly the basic concept is:

A prospective future dollar is not equivalent in value to a present dollar.

The process by which the equivalence between dollars at different points in time is established is the multiplication of the future amount by a factor

$$1/(1 + i)^{n},$$

where i is an interest rate and n is future time. This factor has been universally accepted as the appropriate one. Whether it is correct, or whether there may be some other factor which is more general will be examined below. The techniques for manipulating all future amounts in order to establish proper measures for comparing alternatives are developed in Chapter 4.

1.10.3   A Unifying Principle for Comparing Alternatives

Traditionally textbooks demonstrate a variety of methods for comparing alternatives. However, these numerous and apparently separate methods can be shown to be mathematically identical. Differences in the conclusions reached arise from the postulates employed, which are often left unstated. Therefore the reasons for the different conclusions tend to be concealed. In this book a unified method will be presented, which will encompass all the traditional methods.

This book is primarily concerned with the single independent project, which, by its nature, does not appear to be a case of comparing alternatives. However, the evaluation of a single project is implicitly a comparison of the proposed investment with some unspecified and undefined external investment alternative. This external investment, which provides a basis for comparison, is reflected in the concept of the *opportunity cost of capital* (OCC). The OCC is the rate of return realizable from an unspecified external opportunity in which the investment can be made as an alternative to the one proposed. As a minimum option one may always keep the money invested in a savings account. The opportunity-cost concept is a subtle one, as are so many of the concepts employed in economic evaluation. It will be covered in depth in Chapter 5.

1.10.4 Financing the Investment

Normally textbooks on project investment devote very little space to finance. In practice, however, it is surprising how often a financial feasibility study passes for an economic evaluation. For this reason it may be useful to restate the difference between project evaluation and project finance. The economic evaluation of a project is made in order to determine whether or not the project will be profitable over the long run. To reemphasize the point made earlier, a project evaluation is undertaken to answer the question:

> *What* project or investment alternative should be chosen?

Finance is concerned with quite a different question. This is:

> Given that the economic choice has been made, *how* can capital be managed to implement that choice?

The distinction is between "what" and "how".
The sources of capital for financing an investment are:

1. Internally generated funds from depreciation allowances and from reinvested profits.

2. Externally generated funds from the sales of new securities.

The various characteristics of securities, the working of financial markets, and the management of capital funding are discussed in Chapter 7.

1.10.5 Risk and a Portfolio Approach to the Investment Decision

Most elementary texts on engineering economics treat project evaluation deterministically. The early chapters of this book will adhere to this practice in order to keep discussion on the basic concepts of discounting as simple as possible. The inclusion of risk at this stage would introduce unnecessary complexities. However, all investment decisions are innately risky. The ultimate profitability of any investment depends on an unknown future. The essential risk in any venture arises from two sources, the external environment and the project itself. Risk in any investment cannot be changed. It is fixed by the conditions of the project and its environment. Nevertheless, a decision to accept or reject a proposed project depends on a careful assessment of the magnitude of the risk. There may be ways to shift risk or to share it between various participants in the venture.

As an illustration, the stockholder in a firm is more receptive to risk than is the bondholder. Thus the method of financing with respect to risk is an important factor in acceptance of a proposed project.

Project risk may also be more acceptable if it represents only a small portion of total invested capital of the enterprise, i.e., if it is a single element of a "portfolio" of investments. Portfolio theory provides insights into management of risk and can be an important tool in the methodology of project evaluation. For this reason it is accorded fairly extensive treatment in Chapter 9.

1.10.6 Treatment of Inflation

In early textbooks inflation was virtually ignored, because until recently it was not felt to be an important problem. At present, inflation is abating, but this abatement may ultimately prove to have been related more to economic recession than to a basic change in underlying inflation rates. Whether or not inflation has been controlled is questionable. Both its fluctuations and persistence may remain problems for some time to come. The most common treatment of inflation in project evaluation involves utilization of constant dollars. Unfortunately, this practice can lead to serious error.

The first requirement in dealing with inflation is prediction of its course. Therefore, some of the basic causes of inflation will be discussed in Chapter 8. A number of methods will be employed for treating the effects of inflation on cost and revenue estimates. These will be compared with the constant-dollar assumption.

1.11 COMPUTING CAPABILITY

Development of the techniques of evaluation will take advantage of modern computing capability. In the past a great deal of reliance has been placed on use of compound-interest tables. While limited interest tables are provided in Appendix D, they need only be used as checks on computations. The reader is expected to have a suitable hand calculator available. The modern programmable calculator is particularly useful. A good example is that of the Hewlett-Packard HP-12C, which has built into it all the compound-interest functions as well as others that make direct solution of many problems almost automatic. Some may wish to use a microcomputer instead. Familiarity with microcomputers is desirable, but lack of such familiarity will not be a handicap. Microcomputers all have useful software packages that make problem solution very easy. One such is VisiCalc, which has, as a standard feature, a net-present-value function. This permits direct solution of any cash-flow problem.

Some simple programs in BASIC for the Apple II+ are furnished in Appendix E.

1.12 COST ESTIMATION

Estimation of costs constitutes a major part of the detailed work required for an economic evaluation. Correct estimates of costs are essential for a successful outcome. Estimating involves skills and experience which are specific to the type of business or industry for which the project is proposed. Such techniques are extremely important, but they are not the subject of this book.

Nevertheless, a few points should be highlighted:

1. Careful attention to detail is needed in estimating the physical quantities of materials and supplies.

2. The labor time required to accomplish all the multiplicity of tasks must be calculated with due regard for the learning-curve effects.

3. Attention should be paid to identifying possible bottlenecks and delays.

4. Cost effects of change orders, which always seem to be greater than could be imagined, are one of the major sources of underestimation.

5. Some factor for overruns, in both time and money, should be assessed. Typically, large-scale projects tend to come in well above original estimates. Often overruns amount to a sizable fraction of the initial estimate.

6. Only after the estimates of physical quantities have been determined should these be priced. Pricing should be made with due regard to future price changes.

1.13 RECAPITULATION

This chapter has introduced and summarized the subject matter to come. A few basic concepts were introduced without elaboration. This will come later, but it is hoped that these ideas, even in preliminary form, will trigger both questions and reactions in the reader's mind. A few of these ideas are repeated below:

1. There are four areas of needed expansion of capital investment—new technology, modernization of basic industry, large-scale systems, and (above all) infrastructure.

2. The evaluation of projects requires the evaluation of the cash flows, as projected into the long-term future.

3. The horizon should be viewed as a limit of visibility but not as a limit for planning.

4. A project should not be considered in isolation, but rather in the context of a larger objective.

5. The evaluation of a proposed project determines "what" or "which", and the financial feasibility analysis determines "how".

6. It is important to identify and specify from whose point of view a project is to be evaluated.

7. General economics is a desirable background for the economic evaluation of projects. In particular, the projection of the economic environment in which the project will be expected to perform is important.

○

○

○

CHAPTER TWO

Economic Concepts

A broad understanding of economics is important in evaluating an investment, in order to assess influences that impinge on its successful outcome. One should have a grasp, at least, of basic economic principles and concepts. Some of the concepts are obvious but nevertheless can be illusive. As a consequence there is widespread misunderstanding of many basic ideas, and some misconceptions have persisted over the years.

The word "economics" derives from the Greek "oikos", meaning house, and "neimen", meaning distribution or management: thus literally, "household management". According to Webster, "Economics is the science that deals with the production, distribution and consumption of wealth, and the various related problems of labor, finance, taxation, etc."

Economists often refer to the purpose of their discipline as "the efficient allocation of resources". There are two distinctly different aspects of this problem. One is the allocation of resources as inputs into production. The other is the outputs from production which are the inputs into the consumption process. Human activity, as labor, is one of the major inputs into production, but human activity is also central to consumption.

Aside from questions of efficiency, which is an equivocal concept when used in connection with economics, economic activity may be viewed from two perspectives:

1. The physical activities of mining, transporting, transforming, and consuming material resources.

2. The exchange and allocation of resources among individuals in terms of their rights or claims to utilize them.

When we examine how economists analyze economic activity, we find them largely concerned with the second of these perspectives. The underlying first perspective is, more or less, implicit. People make exchanges in order to produce and consume more efficiently. While we may measure physical output—tons of steel, bushels of wheat, miles of travel, etc.—the only satisfactory way to measure economic activity is by means of values derived from the exchange process. Before examining the exchange process, let us first look at the underlying physical processes.

2.1 PRODUCTION AND CONSUMPTION

Seldom does nature furnish us with the resources we need for consumption in a form that is immediately useful. We must exploit our resources as we find them in nature and from them produce the things we need. We gather the natural resources (raw materials), and mine, smelt, bend, bond and otherwise process them in order to produce the final products we need. In short, the entire production process is one of creating a more ordered universe. It is a *negentropic* process.* Consumption is the reverse. Consumption is a process of taking the ordered arrangement of these resources and disordering them or producing waste. Con-

---

*Entropy is a measure of disorder. The concept of entropy originated in thermodynamics and was explained as the tendency, in closed systems, for molecules to become distributed in the most random arrangement. Energy dissipation involves an increase in entropy. The concept of entropy was extended to information theory by Claude Shannon of Bell Labs. Shannon defined the entropy of information with respect to randomness of transmitted messages.

sumption is an *entropic* process. Of course the two processes combined must satisfy the fundamental second law of thermodynamics, which states that in a closed system, entropy must always increase. Man's intervention, as with all living things, serves only as an accelerator in this basic process of nature. Thus the combined production–consumption process must be recognized as an entropy process.

It has been contended by Georgescu-Roegen (1975) that the basic model of economic systems should be an entropy model rather than a mechanistic model. The mechanistic model is the basis of present-day economic wisdom, but clearly it exhibits shortcomings in the explanation of economic phenomena. In the first place, economic phenomena are not reversible processes. We can never reverse an economic experiment but must always proceed from where we are. However, all mechanical models, that do not take account of the dissipation of energy (i.e., entropy) are reversible. Only by introducing entropy is it possible to properly consider irreversible systems.

Another vitally important fact to keep in mind is that production must always precede (lead) consumption. We must invest or, in effect, *lend* our work in the production process in anticipation of a later claim on the right to consume. Implicitly, consumption represents the repayment of the *debt* incurred by production.

This dual production–consumption process does not, in principle, require trading. An individual may produce for himself. He might plant a garden and enjoy the vegetables he grows without making any exchanges. Even without trades having taken place, the activity is still economic in nature. However, such self-satisfying activity does not represent the norm. Most economic activity comes about as a result of specialization of labor, which then necessitates trading goods and services. It is therefore natural to focus attention on the trading process as a proxy for examining economic activity. It should be noted that trades are made for the purpose of furthering both production and consumption. Values are associated with people's desires and motivations both in producing and, later, in consuming. These values may be inferred by observing how we trade, and therefore we must examine the nature of the trading process. To do this it is necessary to introduce the concept of *utility*, which is a personalized measure of worth, and *value*, which is determined by exchange.

2.2 UTILITY

Utility is a subjective measure of worth. It represents the satisfaction a person derives from the use or possession of a particular good or from the enjoyment of an activity. Because of its subjective nature there cannot be any absolute measure of utility. Under certain circumstances, an ordinal measure of utility may be inferred from observing how people behave. A functional relationship between utility and a quantity of a good can be derived for special situations to represent a cardinal measure. However, most economists find the concept of utility of tremendous conceptual value, although of little operational use.

A rational person may be expected to conform to a set of behavioral axioms. Some of these axioms and general characteristics of utility are:

1. Each individual's utility for a particular good is different from that of others and will vary in his own case from one time to another.

2. More of a good is always better than less.

3. Each additional increment of a good provides smaller increments of utility.

If we wish to define a function for utility in terms of the quantity of a good, we can satisfy the last two of these axioms by means of a function having its first derivative positive everywhere and its second derivative negative everywhere. This latter requirement is the principle of "decreasing marginal utility". Daniel Bournoulli, in the nineteenth century, suggested that such a function is, perhaps, reasonably represented by the logarithm. For practical purposes, a simple quadratic can serve, provided it is confined to the region where it is monotonically rising. A qualitative measure of utility is depicted in Figure 2.1 for a hypothetical good X.

Suppose a person enjoys ice cream very much. We can call ice cream X. The first serving would have a high utility, the second a great deal but a little less than the first, and so on for each successive serving. Eventually the utility of still one more serving would approach zero. It is even conceivable that a point would be

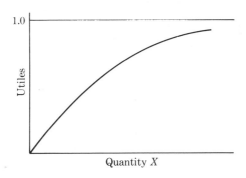

Figure 2.1 Utility function.

reached where one more serving would have a disutility. But this would violate the axiom that more is better than less. We could sidestep this important contradiction by assuming that any surplus could be sold. Our hypothetical individual certainly would not continue to consume more if he could not realize additional satisfaction.

The unit of utility, over an indefinable interval scale, is called a *utile*. Let us assign a value of zero utiles to the utility of $X = 0$. Under conditions of decreasing marginal utility, corresponding to the requirement that the second derivative must be negative, the utility function will be asymptotic to a limiting upper value, as X becomes very large. This asymptote may be assigned a value of unity, thus establishing a scale for utiles from 0 to 1. It must be emphasized that such a scale is arbitrary and is of conceptual value only.

2.2.1 The Utility Tradeoff

A second way to depict the notion of utility is by means of a tradeoff between the desirability of two goods. If a person must allocate his resources between two goods, he will be able to establish a locus of indifference for exchanging an increment of one for an increment of the other. Anywhere along that locus, the utility of a mix of X and Y will be equal, and the utility of a marginal change in X will equal the utility of a marginal change in Y. He will have such a tradeoff function for each level of utility. The further he can move from the origin, the higher will be his

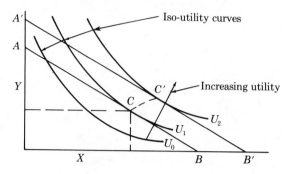

Figure 2.2 Utility tradeoff.

total utility for any combination of the two goods (X and Y). Thus there will be a family of tradeoff curves or loci of constant utility levels, called *iso-utility* curves, depicted in Figure 2.2.

These iso-utility curves are derived from the separate utility functions for the two goods being traded. However, these goods must not be complementary goods if the trade is to be a valid one. An example of complementary goods is bread and butter. Each has utility in its own right but the utility of the two combined is greater than the sum of the two taken separately.

In Figure 2.3, utility functions for two noncomplementary goods, X and Y, are shown in a three-dimensional coordinate system. Thus a mixture of X and Y will appear as a point on a utility surface. For any specified level of utility, U_1, an iso-utility curve

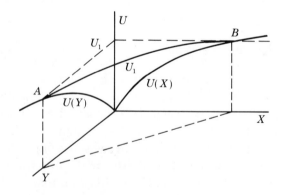

Figure 2.3 Utility for two goods.

will appear as a contour on a topographical utility map, such that

$$U_1 = U(X) = U(Y). \tag{2.1}$$

The constraint on how much the agent buys of the two goods, X and Y, is limited by his budget. If the size of his purchase is proportional to price (i.e., no price break for quantity purchase) then he can vary the allocation of his budget linearly between the two goods. Thus for a given budget W,

$$W = p_x x + p_y y, \tag{2.2}$$

where p_x is the price of X, x the quantity of X, p_y price of Y, and y the quantity of Y. We will arbitrarily establish the price of Y as unity, and thus the price of X will be in terms of the number of units of Y. Then equation 2.2 becomes

$$y = W - p_x x. \tag{2.3}$$

This function is called the budget line. Note that price is the slope of the budget line AB in Figure 2.4. If the economic agent, whom we will call Mr. Smith, starts out with an initial endowment W, he could raise the level of his utility by trading Δx for Δy in order to move along his budget line toward higher iso-utility contours on his utility map. The highest level of utility it is possible for him to attain is at point C (Figure 2.2), the point of tangency of the

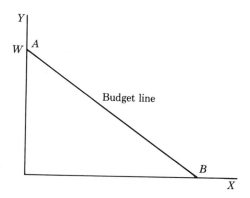

Figure 2.4   The budget constraint.

highest possible iso-utility curve with his budget line. Any point other than the tangent point would force him to a lower utility. Therefore this point of tangency represents the optimum allocation of his budget.

Should Smith's economic circumstances change, the implications for his choice between X and Y become clear by consideration of these diagrams. Suppose Smith were to become more prosperous and could thereby increase his budget to $A'B'$ (Figure 2.2). This new budget line is parallel to AB unless there is a price change; as you will recall, the slope is price. As a result of his improved circumstances, he would move to a new and higher iso-utility curve and thereby establish a new optimum allocation C'.

The increases in his demand for X and Y after the change, is not likely to be proportional to his original allocation. The path along which he would move, CC', determines the nature of the substitution. It is conceivable that he may actually reduce his total demand for one of the goods. This change, due to the ability to move to a higher iso-utility curve, is known as the wealth or income effect.

As an example, consider what a poor man might do if his budget for groceries were to rise dramatically. He may have been accustomed to allocating his budget for meat and bread in the ratio of one pound of meat to 10 pounds of bread. With a rise in his budget it is conceivable that he will raise his meat consumption to four pounds and reduce his bread consumption to 8 pounds.

Contrast this with what could happen if the price of one good, say X, were to change. Refer to Figure 2.5. Suppose the price of X were to drop by 50%, allowing the amount of X purchased to double for the same expenditure. This is the same as moving the budget line to AB'' and the allocation point to C''. The path C'' describes how the substitution between X and Y will change and therefore is known as the substitution effect. Note that it is possible that the agent will now buy less of Y than he did before the price decline, which incidentally raised his overall utility level. This example shows how a price rise of one commodity such as oil may result in significant readjustments of production and consumption of everything else as each agent, in maximizing his utility, brings about an overall change in demands.

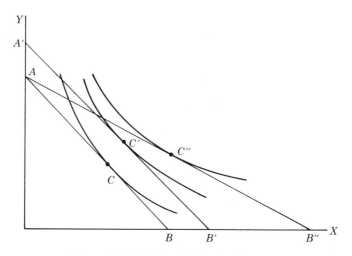

Figure 2.5 Wealth and substitution effects.

2.2.2 Trade between Individuals

Each person can be expected to act in such a way as to increase his utility if the opportunity arises. He does this by exchanging or trading with others, to their mutual gain. The budget line implies a monetary purchase of two goods up to the limit of a budget. The example simply demonstrates the allocation of this budget. However, let us consider how two people would negotiate a trade in such a way that each one would be able to increase his utility. In other words, they should both be better off after the trade than they were before it.

We will assume that in an exchange, the two parties start out with an initial endowment between them of the two goods in question. Before trading, the amounts held by both men will be such that each is removed from his maximum possible utility. Let Smith be the first man. The second, whom we call Brown, has an iso-utility map similar to that of Smith's already discussed above. He may be wealthier than Smith, so that his budget line is higher, but the slopes of each budget line will be the same, in order that the two men be confronted with the same price (i.e., slope is price). We will superimpose Brown's utility map on Smith's, but we will reverse it (Figure 2.6). The one will be the negative of the other, forming a box, called the Edgeworth box, after the British

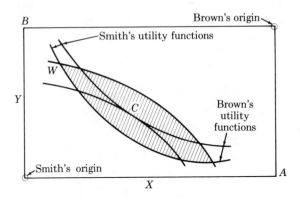

Figure 2.6 Edgeworth box.

mathematical economist who devised this representation. Assume the initial endowments are represented by point W. This point will lie on the intersection of a pair of their iso-utility curves. These overlapping iso-utilities will form end-to-end cusps (shaded). This represents the region in which it will be of mutual benefit to trade. However, since the price dictates that they can move only along the budget line, they will move to the point where their iso-utilities share a common tangent with the budget line at C.

2.2.3 Utility of Consumption versus Utility of Production

While the utility of consumption has been taken implicitly as the criterion governing economic decisions, utility is not related only to consumption. The primitive motivation of the individual to survive dictates that, up to a certain point, consumption must come first. However there is a point at which the desire to produce may take precedence over consumption.

Except for time to sleep and a moderate amount of time for relaxation, people are fully occupied in this joint production–consumption process. As soon as they are satisfied in terms of perceived consumption needs, they seek satisfaction from activity that is essentially productive in nature. Thus utility tradeoffs can be made between various goods, between opportunities to engage in some form of productive enterprise, or between goods and productive activity.

While this may seem reasonable, conventional books on economics all develop the theory of exchange from the viewpoint of utility associated only with consumption.

2.2.4 Tradeoff between the Present and the Future

The iso-utility tradeoff reasoning, exemplified in Figure 2.2, can be extended to establish the utility for a prospective interest rate on an investment. One may have an option to consume a good in the present or to postpone consumption in favor of investment, in order to have more consumption at a future time. This tradeoff is represented in Figure 2.7.

If we set present consumption equal to unity, then the ratio of future consumption OB to present consumption, OA, is

$$OB/OA = 1 + r, \tag{2.4}$$

where r is the rate of interest for the time period. This is seen to be the slope of the budget line, and so interest is recognized as the *price* for postponement of consumption for the period depicted. As before, the optimum point is the point of tangency, C. This establishes that from the current budget (income), DA would be spent and OD would be lent or invested in anticipation of future consumption.

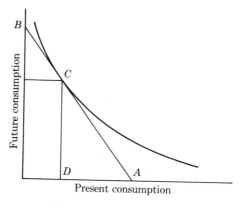

Figure 2.7 Time tradeoff.

2.3 VALUE

Value is one of those words with a multiplicity of popular meanings, but in economics it is confined to one: *the worth of a good in exchange*. Basically, value is a relative measure of worth, because a given amount of one good will be worth some relative amount of another in exchange. In order to establish a scale of value for the two goods, the quantities must be specified. The measure of value per unit of a good exchanged is its *price*.

2.3.1 The Economic Agent

Exchanges are made between individuals. In an economic sense, the individual need not be a person, but may also be a collection of people, a firm, or any organization that has an individual identity. In the interest of avoiding confusion, we refer to all such generic individuals as economic agents or simply as agents.

2.3.2 Exchange as a Basis for Value

Value arises from the fact that two agents, in endeavoring to increase their respective utilities, can make an exchange to the mutual benefit of each. In one sense, value is established in a measurable way only by recording what actually takes place when an exchange is made. Value is the relative measure of one good in terms of the other. If, for example, the trade is a loaf of bread for two pints of milk, then the unit value or price of a loaf of bread will be measured as equal to two pints of milk. In this way everything can be measured in prices relative to anything else. Conceivably we could, by common agreement, devise a system for selecting one good as a basis for referencing all others. Economists refer to such a hypothetical reference good as the *numeraire*. Indexing in this way makes it theoretically possible to measure relative values in units of a common standard measure, which we choose to call money.

2.3.3 Relevance of Money

So far in this chapter, the basic concepts of economics have been presented without reference to money. In this discussion, money is irrelevant and, in fact, probably does more to obscure than to illuminate economic concepts. This is not to say that money is unimportant. Indeed, to the individual, money is very important. The individual's perceptions are so steeped in the concept of value in terms of money that it is very difficult for him to think of value from the more fundamental viewpoint of relative worth of goods and services.

In order to understand economic principles it is essential to keep in mind that what is real is the exchange of goods and services produced, traded, and consumed. These real goods and services require some accountability mechanism for establishing entitlements to real things. Money is the system for accomplishing this objective. It was invented for facilitating the exchange process and, in itself, is only a *representation* of reality. Money is real to the individual because it is the most important system whereby he can exercise his claim to real goods and services.

Only after the concepts of *value in exchange* have been well understood should the role of money be introduced. Even then one must constantly remind oneself that money, as a concept, must never get in the way of realization of what is actually happening.

2.3.4 Money Value

Money and the related concepts, myths, and misunderstandings will be covered in Chapter 3. However for the purpose of examining value in terms of money, it is necessary to recognize a few basic facts about money.

As a practical necessity in any barter system, people have found it essential to trade the goods they have produced for some other good they may not really want, but which they know can be traded later for a mix of goods they do want. The good that acted as an intermediate trading device, or intermediate good, came to be called money. It served the purpose of conserving the value of goods foregone until that future time when the original supplier made up his mind what he wished to acquire. Hence it served as a mechanism for conserving value over time, i.e., a *store of value*. In order for such a good to be usable for this purpose, five essentials must obtain:

1. The good must be durable.

2. It must be readily divisible.

3. It must be easily stored and protected.

4. There must be a ready market available.

5. It must be valuable in its own right.

EXAMPLE: Exchange using an intermediate good

Let us postulate a hypothetical and highly idealized country which we will call Zog. In order to keep this example simple we will limit the population to four citizens. The people of Zog are fascinated by sand. One of their number is busy all his working hours processing (i.e., producing) it. Let us assume that sand is the intermediate good selected to serve as money by the citizens of Zog. Abel spends his time working in the sand pit; Bigger specializes in producing strawberries; Caspar concentrates his efforts on cabbage; and David thinks that the only thing worth doing is growing peanuts. Furthermore everything else is either so plentiful that no one needs to work for it and therefore it is free—or each man works individually to produce all other goods necessary for his own needs. No further specialization of labor is deemed desirable.

Bigger takes his strawberries to market early Monday morning after working all day Sunday in order to have fresh strawberries for market. He has not had time to consider what he would like in exchange and he cannot afford to take time out during the busy sales day to plan his purchases. Therefore he decides that he will accept sand in exchange for his strawberries. We will sidestep the question of why the others will happen to have sand to pay for the strawberries which they want.

Why would Bigger be willing to accept sand in exchange for his strawberries?

1. He is aware that tomorrow he can come back to the market and trade sand for cabbage and peanuts. There is a ready market for sand and from long experience he has learned that it holds its price well. Therefore it meets criteria 4 and 5 (marketability and value).

2. He finds sand preferable to other goods because it does not spoil. Cabbage is better than strawberries in this regard but not as good as peanuts. Sand is the best product for meeting criterion 1 (durability).

3. He does not have any idea of the quantities of peanuts and cabbage he will need or when he will need them, and therefore he wants the flexibility of subdividing his intermediate good as finely as possible. Sand meets this requirement also (criterion 2, divisibility).

4. Bigger knows from long experience that the other citizens of Zog are always prepared to buy sand. The supply seems to remain proportionate to the growth of supplies of other goods. The reason the other citizens want to acquire sand is much the same as his own. The demand for sand needed for the annual sand castle contest, a big event in Zog, does not impose a significant burden on the productive capacities of Zog. After all, the working time needed for Abel to produce the extra sand required for money represents something less than one-quarter of the GNP, a small societal price to pay for maintaining a steady and stable market for sand.

5. Actually sand does not fit criterion 4 ideally, only because it is bulky. In other respects it is relatively easy to store. It does not have to be sheltered from the weather; a simple storage yard should be sufficient. It is easy to guard but presents some difficulty in transportation. A good which was less bulky and so would command a higher price per pound would be somewhat better.

We have seen in this example that all the requirements for money as an intermediate good have been met. Clearly sand is a sensible form of money for the people of Zog. Strangely, no one in Zog raises the question: Why bother? Would it not be simpler to write on a piece of paper that Bigger is owed something for his strawberries, supposing that the other three, collectively, would be willing to recognize the existence of this debt? Consider how much time Abel could save. He could then grow potatoes and thereby expand the gastronomical horizons of the citizens of Zog.

Because, historically, gold fulfilled these five criteria for an acceptable intermediate good, understandably, it came to be accepted as money. However, such an intermediate good is neither necessary nor desirable in the modern world. As will be shown in Chapter 3, today the only practical money is credit or, in other words, a general recognition that something of equivalent value is owed for what has been surrendered. In the meantime, the use of the concept of an intermediate good for explaining value-in-exchange simplifies understanding of the exchange process.

2.3.5 The *Numeraire*

Logically the intermediate good, which we have labeled money, is the one we would choose to call the *numeraire*. At any given time, all the goods in the market will be changing hands. The exchange process is dynamic. However Leon Walras (1879), ignoring the essential dynamic nature of the process, developed a basic model of the market which he explained in terms of static equilibrium. He assumed that all agents had perfect information of all others' demands and supplies. However, it will be recognized that it would require infinite time for all agents in the market to gather perfect information. Nevertheless, assuming perfect information and instantaneous exchange, then for all the agents in the market, (i.e., nodes in the flow), there is a set of equations of the form

$$\sum_{j=1}^{n} x_j q_j = 0 \qquad \text{for} \quad j = 1 \text{ to } n \text{ goods,} \qquad (2.5)$$

where x_j is the quantity of good j, and q_j is the price.

The Walrasian equations were conventionally formulated to show that the summation of demands must equal the summation of supplies:

$$\sum_{j=1}^{n} x_j q_j = \sum_{j=1}^{n} y_j p_j \qquad \text{for} \quad j = 1 \text{ to } n \text{ goods,} \qquad (2.6)$$

where the $\{xq\}$ represent only the demand side and the $\{yp\}$ are the equivalent values on the supply side. However this is a matter of sign in the flow. If the supplies are taken as positive and the demands as negative, equation 2.6 is the same as equation 2.5.

The Walrasian equations comprise an indeterminate set with one more unknown than there are equations. This set of equations is, nevertheless, theoretically solvable in terms of any one chosen variable, the *numeraire*, to which a unit value can be assigned. Thus all prices are relative to the price of the *numeraire*.

Aside from the severe assumptions of perfect information and static equilibrium, there is an added difficulty in determining prices. Whatever good is chosen for the *numeraire*, it assumes speculative values in the market aside from its use as a commodity in its own right. This can have disturbing influences on other commodity prices simply because the value of the *numeraire* is fixed by definition.

It is interesting to note that the Walrasian equations are identical to those of Newtonian mechanics, or in electrical circuits, to Kirckhoff's node law: The sum of the forces or the sum of the currents must equal zero. It is also noteworthy that, while fundamental, neither of these physical laws is very useful until extended to include a storage term. In mechanics, the dynamics must be treated by introducing an equilibrating force in the form of an inertial term (i.e., force equals mass times acceleration). In electrical networks, dynamics is incorporated in the concept of inductance, an equivalent of inertia.

Furthermore, in both these physical analogies, a flow derives from a potential function. Force is a flow that is the derivative of a potential field (gravity). Current, also a flow, is the derivative of electrical potential. These energy-storage concepts are what enable us to treat physical systems in a dynamic way. Without something equivalent in economics, there is no satisfactory way to treat economic systems in a dynamic sense. Thus economic analysis is predicated on "comparative statics".

In economics, when an economist speaks of dynamics, he is usually thinking of how prices change over time in a kinematic sense and not in a dynamic sense. Kinematics is concerned with the description of change over time; dynamics encompasses the reason for change. This is clearly evident in the chapter on economic dynamics in the classic book, *Value and Capital*, by Sir John Hicks (1936). He includes a footnote on the first page of that section explaining his meaning of dynamics:

> The distinction between economic statics and economic dynamics has thus not much in common with the distinction between statics and dynamics in the physical sciences. One's justification for using the terms lies in the fact that they have a fairly well-established place in economic terminology; and if they have not acquired precise meanings, they have at least a series of meanings which seem to be converging upon something useful.

It may have been an unfortunate decision on his part not to make some attempt to be more precise, because the error in conception has persisted to this day.

2.3.6 Additional Comments on Value

Basically, although value derives from exchange, not all values can be determined by waiting for exchanges to take place. Value can be imputed by observing other transactions which occur under similar circumstances. Thus values are ascribed to assets that may never be traded. These values are imputed on the basis of small sample transactions. For example, the value of the IBM company may be quoted as being $57 billion because its stock traded on a certain day for $96 per share. However the value of IBM, as a company, can only be inferred from this kind of trade. Such a transaction may have represented a fraction of one percent of the total stock. It must be a false measure because, if a significant portion of the stock were to come to market at one time, the value so established would be markedly different. In spite of this shortcoming, the market mechanism is the most efficacious means for determining value. The point that must always be kept in mind is that value of a good, in an economic sense, is its worth in exchange.

In keeping with the economic definition of value, for a good to have value, it must be scarce. Scarcity, as a concept in economics, means a demand exists. In other words, for a good not to be scarce, it must be in such abundance that no one would be willing to sacrifice any other good in exchange for it. Scarcity is an essential ingredient of value. There is no such thing as value without scarcity.

People may still refer to a good as being valuable when they are actually using a different connotation or meaning from that established above for the economic definition. Often without realizing it, they are attaching to the good the concept of utility. This understandably leads to semantic problems and misunderstanding. Thus a good may have a high "value" in the sense of worth but be a "free good" in that it is not scarce—for instance, the air we breathe.

2.3.7 The Market Mechanism

The market is considered to be the best mechanism for establishing true value of goods, thereby leading to optimal allocation of goods among the members of society. While the market is the most effective allocation mechanism, the idealizations on which our model of it is based should be clearly understood. The degree to which these idealized postulates are approximated in the real world determines how well the market serves as a device for resource allocation.

These idealizations, including some that have already been mentioned, are:

1. Each supplier and each demander acts to maximize his utility.

2. Large numbers of essentially equal agents are competing in order to effect exchanges.

3. Each agent has perfect information about all supplies and demands.

4. The goods traded are continuously divisible.

5. Time is ignored. Transactions all occur instantaneously.

6. All goods are exclusive. That is, they are directly related to individual use, as opposed to collective goods, where the utility of all is enhanced by joint or cooperative use. A pair of shoes is a good example of an exclusive good; national defense is a collective good. It is inconceivable to imagine individuals competing in the market for purchase of their individual national defense needs.

7. No redistribution of wealth occurs. This means that the relative wealth of all individuals remains unchanged.

8. There is no entry or exit fee for privilege to trade in the market.

These conditions are only approximated in the real world, and economists refer to the deviations as market imperfections. In the case of natural monopolies, typified by public utilities, market idealizations cannot exist even in an approximate way and therefore pricing is regulated by fiat, based on relating price to cost of production. In actuality, the real world requires a spectrum of goods, ranging from totally collective goods at one extreme, to mutually exclusive goods at the other. The big problem is how to deal with conditions that fall somewhere between the extremes.

2.3.8 Monopoly, Monopsony, and Oligopoly

The principal deviations from the idealized competitive market are:

1. Monopoly—a single supplier with multiple agents competing against one another on the demand side. The single supplier can set the price which will maximize his profit. This price will be higher than that set by the competitive market and results in an inequitable distribution of the goods of society.

2. Monopsony—a single demander and multiple suppliers. This is exemplified by defense procurement. The government is the only customer and there are many firms competing for contracts. In effect, monopsony is monopoly on the demand side.

3. Oligopoly—a market typified by few suppliers and many agents on the demand side. In general the capital requirements needed to enter the market (i.e., the entry fee) limit the number of suppliers to a few large firms. The automobile industry is a good example of this.

Although the ideal market conditions are represented by free competition, the largest component of exchange is probably that characterized by oligopolistic markets. While a great deal of competition exists in oligopolistic markets, the competition may not be closely linked with price. Manufacturers tend to set prices based on their costs. The theory of free competitive markets calls for price adjustments to clear markets of over-supply. In fact, manufacturers resist downward adjustment of prices and rely on time to clear their excess inventory. Furthermore, it is likely that in oligopolistic markets, manufacturers will create demands which might never materialize in completely free markets. Such rigidities in pricing are usually referred to as market imperfections. The reality of real markets is that they are far from perfection.

2.4 SUPPLY AND DEMAND

Demand, as a function of price, is represented by the quantity of goods that will be removed from the market, or *demanded*, by means of exchanges from suppliers. Normally demand varies inversely with price. The lower the price of a good becomes, the greater the quantity of that good people will buy.

Supply also varies with price: as prices rise, suppliers will be anxious to produce greater quantities for the market. Those whose costs are already below the current price may expect to realize a greater profit. At the same time, the below-marginal producer may now find it profitable to enter the market. Considering the two functions separately, price determines quantity; therefore, for both supply and demand functions, price is the independent variable and might appear as in Figure 2.8A. When economists first developed supply–demand concepts, the functions were depicted as if quantity were the independent variable, and as a consequence the conventional diagram has always shown quantity on the horizontal axis, as in Figure 2.8B.

The intersection of the supply and demand curves represents the price at which the market will be cleared under conditions of static equilibrium, when supply and demand equate and there is no inventory remaining. Actually the market is dynamic, not static. However, time independence, a condition of the ideal market, is a valid assumption if the supplies and demands are considered as steady-state flows. In practice, flow is not steady-state and the variability of flow results in fluctuations of inventories and prices—demands and supplies do not equate, and the price is not an equilibrium price (Figure 2.9). If the price move-

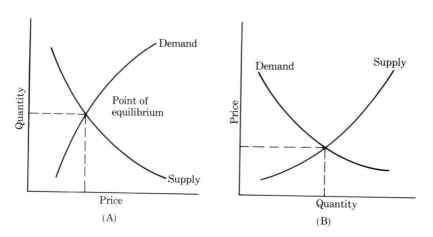

Figure 2.8 Supply and demand: (A) quantity versus price; (B) price versus quantity.

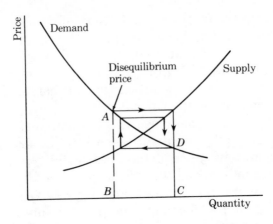

Figure 2.9 Disequilibrium supply and demand.

ment tends toward equilibrium, the price will follow a "cobweb" path as depicted.

If the price if actually established at point A, only an amount OB will be demanded. However, at that price, producers will want to supply the market with an amount OC. Thus there will be an oversupply, BC, which will in turn tend to cause prices to fall to D. Now an undersupply will occur, and demand will grow to OC. If no change in the demand–supply curves occurs, this process will continue until the price converges on the final equilibrium point at the intersection of the two curves.

2.4.1 Elasticity

Price is sensitive to demand, and economists refer to this sensitivity as the "price elasticity of demand". Likewise price is sensitive to supply, and this is described as the "price elasticity of supply". Mathematically, elasticity is defined as the slope of the curve at a defined point:

$$\text{elasticity} = \frac{dD}{dp} \times \frac{p}{D} \qquad \text{for demand,} \qquad (2.7)$$

$$\text{elasticity} = \frac{dS}{dp} \times \frac{p}{S} \qquad \text{for supply.} \qquad (2.8)$$

A steeply sloping demand (supply) curve indicates that demand (supply) is sensitive (i.e., elastic) to a change in price. The demand curve has a negative slope, and so the price elasticity of demand is often reported as a negative number. If the negative sign is omitted, the elasticity of demand is understood to be negative. In the special case of a demand function which is inversely proportional to price, the elasticity is unity. If the absolute value of elasticity is greater than one, the supply or demand is said to be *elastic*; if less than one, *inelastic*.

The use of the word "elasticity" may seem strange to the engineer. As a physical phenomenon, elasticity means a proportional stretching under the application of a force and a corresponding proportional restoration upon release of that force. Furthermore the distortion, except under extremely fast loading, is time-independent. In economics, the price movement is not linear, the return path is not the same as the loading path, and the movement is time-dependent. None of the requirements defining physical elasticity is satisfied. Nevertheless the term is universally used in economics to describe this phenomenon of price change, when what is really meant is *sensitivity*.

It should be recognized that time is an important variable in any consideration of elasticity. A commodity may be inelastic over a short run and quite elastic over a longer time frame. A good example of this may be seen in the way in which demand for oil responded to the fourfold increase in price resulting from the oil embargo in 1973. At first, demand seemed completely inelastic, but after people had time to adjust their lifestyles, demand slowly declined and continued to do so even after the price stabilized. Furthermore it would be highly unlikely for demand to follow the same path in reverse when prices decline as they did when prices were rising.

2.5 SUPPLY AS RELATED TO COST

The supply function depends on the willingness of suppliers to produce. They will produce as long as they can realize a price high enough to cover their costs. This means that they must generate enough revenue from sales to cover capital costs as well as all other costs. Capital costs include interest on debt as well as the economic interest on the equity capital invested in the business. The businessman recognizes economic interest as profit and distinguishes it from interest he pays on debt. Of course, he strives to increase profit beyond that minimum level, described as economic interest. However, the marginal producer will enter the market, or remain in it, at the point of zero profit. Therefore, supply is determined at the point where the difference between revenue and cost becomes zero. Revenue is the product of the quantity and price of the particular good delivered.

The market is assumed to operate on the basis of a large number of producers, competing to meet demands. Thus no single producer is large enough to command so large a share of the market that he, by himself, can influence price. This of course is an idealization that is not true in either monopoly or oligopoly. However, when this idealization is a reasonable approximation, each producer will face a constant price, unaffected by the quantity of supplies he contributes. For this reason his revenue will be a linear function of quantity (Figure 2.10).

Because the price is fixed, revenue follows a straight line, starting from the origin. On the other hand, the cost curve, also starting from the origin, is nonlinear. Typically it rises rapidly at the outset due to startup costs, which are more or less fixed, rises more slowly for a while, and eventually accelerates as the capacity limits of the firm are approached. Thus it is seen that profit, the difference between the revenues and costs, is initially negative, reaches a maximum at the point where the slopes of the revenue and cost curves are equal, and finally crosses into a loss region again.

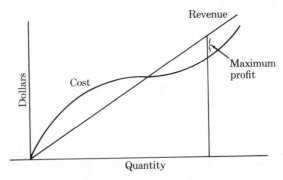

Figure 2.10 Total cost and revenue.

2.5.1 Average and Marginal Costs

We may determine an *average cost function* by dividing total cost by quantity (Figure 2.11). It is often convenient to consider costs in terms of average values. However, this can be misleading, and indeed a source of serious error in decision making. It is not uncommon to look for the lowest average cost as the basis for making a decision, but average cost is seldom, if ever, a valid criterion.

Marginal cost is a more meaningful function. The *marginal cost* is the slope (derivative) of the total-cost curve. It has the same dimensionality as average cost and is, in effect, the ratio of an incremental change in total cost for an incremental change in quantity.

The function representing average cost is

$$AC = \frac{TC}{Q}. \tag{2.9}$$

The marginal cost is the derivative of the total cost:

$$MC = \frac{d(TC)}{dQ}. \tag{2.10}$$

It will be noted that the point where marginal costs equal marginal revenues is the point of maximum profit.

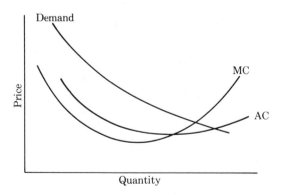

Figure 2.11 Marginal and average costs.

The demand curve is also shown in this diagram. Marginal revenue occurs at the intersection of the supply and demand curves. Profit reaches its maximum when marginal cost equals marginal revenue, at the point on the total-cost curve of Figure 2.10 where the slopes of revenue and cost curves are equal. Beyond this point, an incremental increase in supply can only occur at the expense of a decline in profits.

When we translate this to the demand curve (Figure 2.11), it will be recognized that the intersection of the marginal-cost curve with the demand curve holds special significance. The demand curve is, in effect, a marginal revenue function. The individual firm cannot influence the price it faces in the market, but that price does correspond with its marginal revenue, which we have already equated with its marginal cost for maximum profit. Therefore the intersection of the marginal-cost curve with the demand curve determines the optimum price.

2.5.2 Sunk Cost

In considering total cost, an important distinction must be made according to whether it is measured prior to startup of the production system, or is measured as the continuing cost of doing business after the business has been started. All costs in bringing a production system into being become *sunk costs* once they have been incurred. The only costs that are relevant in making a decision to increase supplies are those which vary with the quantity of output. Sunk costs are irrelevant. Such sunk costs are carried in the accounts of the firm and are averaged into the price the firm feels it should demand for its product. Clearly a firm will not enter the market if it cannot recover the costs of startup as well as the marginal costs associated with expansion of supply. However, once it has entered, such costs have no place in the determination of its marginal costs.

Economists tend to sidestep this issue by differentiating between what they refer to as long- and short-run marginal costs. The long-run marginal costs are assumed to take account of capital investments. However, this amounts to payment of an entry fee for getting into the market and, as such, is a violation of one of the basic tenets of market theory. And since this also corresponds to marginal cost, the intersection of the marginal cost function with the demand function establishes the optimum price. It should be observed that this does *not* yield the minimum average cost.

2.6 OPPORTUNITY COSTS AND SHADOW PRICES

One of the most important concepts needed in the evaluation of proposed investments is that of *opportunity cost*. An opportunity cost arises from the difference between accounting or market costs, given the decision to adopt the proposed investment, and the costs that would have been incurred if the investment had been rejected. Stated simply, what would the costs be with and without the project? Thus, opportunity cost is the cost of an opportunity foregone.

This principle applies equally well to income foregone. Whether considering incomes or outgoes, it is only the differences between adopting and rejecting a project or investment that are of importance. Therefore it can be reemphasized that the *only* cost that is of concern in evaluating an investment decision is opportunity cost.

Often it is desirable to treat unit opportunity costs. A unit opportunity cost is called a *shadow price*.

EXAMPLE: Opportunity cost of space utilization

A plant manager is considering utilizing a corner of his plant for expanding a product line. The accountant advises him that the rental cost of the space is $1000 per month, which is currently being charged to overhead.

The extra costs for materials and labor will be $600 per month, and the manufactured items will sell for $800 per month. Should he go ahead with the expansion?

SOLUTION

First we must exclude any alternative other than the one outlined. Having done that, we consider the opportunity costs.

The costs with the project in place will be shown in the accounts as

$$\$1000 + \$600 = \$1600.$$

The costs without the project would be $1000 (i.e., rent). The opportunity cost is the difference:

$$\$1600 - \$1000 = \$600.$$

Since the product can be sold for $800, the manager will make an effective profit of $200. However the accounting records will show a loss. This loss will be reported as $800 if the extra production is undertaken but $1000 if it is not. Clearly the firm is ahead by reducing the stated loss. The rental cost of the space is not recoverable in either event.

The reduction of loss is the same as a profit.

Perhaps the most important application of the opportunity-cost concept comes in considering the rate of return on an investment. Capital invested in one project must earn at least as much as it would have earned if employed in some alternative use. Failure to recognize this commonly leads to ignoring the true costs of investing capital.

EXAMPLE: Opportunity cost of interest

A man is considering buying a home for cash instead of taking out a mortgage for $100,000 at 10% interest. He remarks to his wife that by paying cash they will have a place to live which is much cheaper to own than to rent. After all, if they were to rent, all they would have to show for the money they spent would be rent receipts.

What he fails to consider is the opportunity cost of his capital. If his alternative is to invest that $100,000 in some other investment which could earn 12% interest, then his opportunity cost is

$$\$0 \quad \text{(i.e., interest if he uses his own \$)}$$
$$-(-\$12,000) \quad \text{(i.e., interest he foregoes)} = \$12,000.$$

He must compare this amount of interest with his cost of borrowing (i.e., $10,000).

Since his opportunity cost of borrowing is less than for owning, he should borrow. However, if he could earn only $8000 by investing, his opportunity cost in using his own money would be $8000. He can make that much by investing in his own home. Although he does not spend anything for interest, his interest cost still exists in the form of an opportunity cost.

Opportunity costs are always related to underutilization of resources. Whenever full utilization is reached, then market or accounting costs equal opportunity costs. If the plant manager, in the space-utilization example, could have used that plant space (on which he was paying rent) in some other way, then rental costs would have been an appropriate expense. However, even here, caution is in order. If there were a higher-use opportunity available and he did not take advantage of it, the rent, rather than being zero, would be the net income foregone by not making the best use of the space. It still would not have been the amount that the accountant charged.

Opportunity costs or shadow prices are very important in considering societal decisions such as development projects in developing economies. One of the most important of these is the shadow price for labor where unemployment or underemployment exists.

It is not uncommon, in estimating wage rates, to utilize the going market rate for labor. This is an invalid way of estimating labor costs. As long as that labor would otherwise remain unemployed, there would be a societal cost for unemployment compensation, welfare, social unrest, etc. For this reason the shadow price for labor—the difference between the actual market rate and the price of unemployment—would be the correct assessment of labor cost.

It should be noted that this issue of shadow prices comes into play from the point of view of a particular constituency. An individual firm will not be concerned with unemployment in the economy at large and cannot afford to consider societal shadow prices. Unless the firm can recover the difference between the shadow price and the market price by means of a subsidy, the market price should be used.

2.7 CAPITAL

Economic literature usually treats capital and interest together, because interest is the payment for the use of capital. Also, because capital is such a fundamental factor in production, it is usually considered in the context of production.

Capital may be defined as those goods allocated for the production of other goods.

This, however, is an oversimplification. As will be seen below, there is much more to the concept of capital than this definition implies.

2.7.1 Capital Value

Capital value should, of course, be established in the same way as value for any other good; under the workings of the market, its *worth in exchange* is determined by the price at which agents will buy or sell. Its value may be identified in money terms, like any other value. However, there are important differences between capital goods and other goods. Capital is not desired for itself, but rather for what it is capable of producing. Thus it derives its value from its potential for generating a flow of other values. It has the characteristics of a *potential function*, and because of this, one tends to think of it in terms of its monetary value rather than in terms of the real goods that create the possibility for production. People are inclined to look upon capital as dollars in a bank account or ownership of a stock certificate. These represent claims on resources and so are potentials for either consumption or other production. One may legitimately consider a bank account as capital, but there is at least a philosophical difference between the real potential represented by a physical system and the potential represented by claims or titles (e.g., stock certificates) to the use or ownership of that capital.

2.7.2 The Dynamics of Capital

Capital must be considered in relation to time associated with the processes of production and of consumption. It takes time to produce anything and subsequently to consume it. As has been noted earlier, production must lead consumption. Furthermore, production requires time for building the tools used to produce the end products desired for consumption. Consumption of those tools and of the various other materials utilized in the production process is, itself, part of the process of producing the final product. This "roundabout process" was recognized by Bohm-Bawerk (1891) and was, in his mind, the essence of capital.

In order to get a firm grasp on the concept of capital, it is well to contemplate the time-related phenomena of production and consumption. What takes place in these processes is a flow of resources in the endless ordering–disordering cycle—negentropy to entropy. This flow comprises a mixture of labor, materials, and energy, which together may be measured in money-value terms. The physical organization of these resources builds up the potential for producing the flow of end-use goods. The time lag between goods going into the production system, the wearing out or using up of some of them in production, and the finished products finally coming out of the system requires that there be storage of value in the system. This storage is capital.

There is even more to capital than just the dynamic storage of goods (i.e., a stockpile). The potential for generating a flow stems from the dynamics of organization as well as from the stockpile. In other words, the value of capital comes from the combined potential effect of a physical stock of capital goods and the ways in which this is organized and managed.

An analogy may be made between the production system and a mechanical or electrical system. In any physical system there must be a potential function that causes flow. In an electrical network the potential is voltage, deriving from a potential source in capacitance (i.e., static storage), or in inductance (i.e., dynamic storage). The flow is current. The same holds for a mechanical system. The flow (force) derives from the potential in the form of static storage of energy in a spring or from position of a mass in a potential field (i.e., gravity), or, in the case of dynamic storage, from the momentum of a flywheel.

In the economic system, capital is the potential function deriving from static storage of resources in the form of a stockpile, or from dynamic storage implicit in the going concern. Thus in a static sense, there is capital in a stockpile of steel, for instance, and in a dynamic sense, in the organization, people, machines, and inventory within a firm. The value of a stockpile of steel is determined by the market price of steel. The capital value of the firm may be assessed by the price of its securities on the market.

While value of capital may be market-determined in principle, the reason that a particular price is reached for that capital in the market must be based on the expectation of the future value flow that the capital will generate. A buyer or seller, contemplating an exchange, expects to pay or to receive the discounted value of the flow produced by the capital.

Capital is commonly visualized in connection with production because of the buildup of the potential needed to produce the return flow. As long as storage exists, the potential for generating a flow of value will apply. Thus it is perfectly rational to think of consumer capital as well as producer capital. The store of value in a home, for example, means that the home will continue to provide a flow of value as shelter for as long as that home exists.

2.7.3 Sources of Capital

An essential characteristic of capital is that it is created only by means of saving. Capital can be acquired by foregoing spending in anticipation of a potential for greater subsequent return. Saving is also implicit in the difference between inflow and outflow. As long as the value flow into the system exceeds the outflow, saving is occurring and capital value builds up accordingly.

There are three sources of savings for capital formation in society. The first source is the personal savings of individuals. The second is the savings of corporations. A corporation normally makes a profit which periodically must either be distributed as dividends or reinvested in the business. Reinvested profits are corporate savings. Dividends go to individuals, who make their own independent decisions to spend or save them.

The third source of savings is that part of taxes spent by government for capital investment. It is not as clear-cut as the other two, because government does not distinguish capital expenditures from operating expenses. Nevertheless, strictly speaking, all money spent by government on long-lived assets is capital. Those expenditures that go into such things as aircraft carriers are, technically, consumer capital. However, many government capital expenditures are truly for production capital. All those things that enhance the potential for production by the private sector fall into this category and are called *infrastructure investment*.

Capital wears out and must be replaced periodically. To provide for this, the business makes allowances for depreciation. These are not savings, but nevertheless are another source of funds for new capital expenditures. It should be noted, however, that the expenditure of the cash flow from depreciation does not add to the overall stock of capital. As new capital is coming into being, old capital is being retired. While capital from depreciation allowances is new, it is simply replacing old capital.

2.8 EXTERNALITIES

The basic concepts of microeconomics are predicated on the idea of value accruing to individual agents as a consequence of their exchanges. These values are, however, not the only ones influenced by the agents directly involved in the exchange. Other parties are either benefited or hurt by the economic acts of others. Such value effects are *externalities*. They are external to the agents involved.

A good example of this is the effects of a power company's decision to develop a hydroelectric plant on a stream. The dam that it builds provides a benefit in the form of reduced flood hazards. The economic gain to property holders in the area is real. A local farmer may be able to sell his land for much more after the dam is in place than he could have beforehand. This economic benefit cannot be captured by the power company. It is external to the power company. At the same time as it has created an external benefit in the form of flood-risk reduction, it also causes some pollution to the river. This may require a neighboring town to incur increased water-purification costs. This is a disbenefit. Government can intervene by taxing the power company for the right to pollute and the farmer for the increased valuation of his land. These taxes can then be reallocated to compensate for the externalities.

Ideally no one individual should be either benefited or disbenefited by externalities. In fact, externality effects are inescapable. They constitute a very important aspect of economic activity. Almost all real-estate development, for instance, involves externalities. Whenever a real-estate developer opens up a new area for construction, he causes the value of contiguous property to rise. These effects are outside of market influences.

2.9 RECAPITULATION

This chapter has covered the basic concepts of microeconomics, utility, value, supply and demand, cost, and capital. It has included the basic concepts and principles governing the market as a mechanism for allocation of resources. Specifically, the important concepts are:

1. *Utility.*

   • Utility is a personalized measure of worth.
   • A rational and consistent individual will exhibit a utility function which is rising with a steadily decreasing slope.
   • Utility can be depicted as a tradeoff in preference between any two goods.
   • Individuals may be assumed to make decisions so as to maximize their utilities.
   • When two people make an exchange, each will be increasing his own utility and therefore both benefit from the exchange.
   • Utility may be associated with production as well as with consumption. However, conventional economic theory is based on an implied assumption that work is associated with disutility and that people accordingly trade the disutility of work for the greater utility of consumption. This assumption is only partly valid.

2. *Value.*

   • Value is worth-in-exchange.
   • Value derives from the integrated effects or average of many people's utilities.
   • Price is unit value.

3. *Supply and demand.*

   • The intersection of the supply and demand curves determines the market clearing price under conditions of static equilibrium.
   • Elasticity is the derivative of either the supply or the demand curve at a specific point on that curve. It is, in principle, a measure of sensitivity.

4. *Cost and profit.*

- Unit cost is equivalent to unit value (price).
- Average unit cost is not a suitable decision criterion for pricing.
- Marginal cost is unit cost at the margin, i.e., it is the unit cost for the last increment of supply. Mathematically it is the derivative of the total cost function.
- The optimum price is reached where the marginal-cost curve intersects the demand curve.
- Maximum profit occurs when marginal cost and marginal revenue are equal.
- Opportunity costs are the only costs to consider in an investment evaluation. They derive from optimal use of resources.
- Shadow prices are unit opportunity costs.

5. *Capital.*

- Capital is the produced means of production, i.e., tools.
- Capital is a potential function. Its value is determined by market forces, but those forces are conditioned by the recognition that value derives from its potential for generating a flow of value.
- Capital can come only from savings.
- Capital is measured as the integral of dollars over time and, as such, is dimensioned in dollars. Costs and revenues have the dimensions of dollars per unit time.
- Capital may be viewed as a stock in the static sense of storage, but more importantly it is a dynamic storage, such as the going-concern value of a firm.

2.10 PROBLEMS

1. Contemplate and discuss the philosophical implications of the following ideas:

   a. To what extent does, and should, the desire to create or produce dominate consumption motivations?

   b. How does the average level of personal income affect the production–consumption motivation?

c. How might a pattern of changing life styles in America influence production-driving forces in the economy? Give examples.

2. Compare three functions for representing a utility function:

a. A quadratic.

b. An exponential.

c. A logarithm.

Select appropriate parameters to fit these functions into the interval of zero to unity on the utile scale, and plot the functions.

3. For an iso-utility function for goods X and Y of

$$U = X^2Y$$

and a budget of

$$X + Y = 1000,$$

determine:

a. The optimum budget allocation to maximize utility.

b. Suppose the price of X were to increase 10%, how would the optimum change?

c. Suppose the budget were to increase 10%, how would the optimum change?

4. If the demand for X is

$$P = 125/X$$

and the supply is

$$P = 5X,$$

then:

a. What is the equilibrium price of X?

b. If the supply function were to be increased by 10%, what would the price then become?

c. What is the price elasticity of demand?

5. Suppose that your utility for apples varies inversely with your utility for oranges. Construct a set of iso-utility curves for this condition. If your budget for apples and oranges is $10 and apples are $0.30 per lb and oranges $0.40 per lb, how many of each would you buy?

6. If your budget for the fruit in Problem 5 above were to increase by 50%, how would this affect your purchases?

7. If the price of apples were to rise by 20% and the budget remained the same, how would you adjust your buying?

8. Consider a market for three goods: apples, oranges, and bananas. The supplies are: apples 100 lb, oranges 200 lb, and bananas 300 lb. Choose apples as the *numeraire*, and reference this to an index called dollars by arbitrarily setting the price of apples at $1.00 per lb. What would the prices of the other fruits have to be in order for the market to be cleared?

9. Suppose that the demand for apples varies inversely with price and the supply varies in direct proportion to price. Supply and demand are in balance at a price of a $1.00 per lb. What are the price elasticities for supply and demand?

10. Discuss the question of production in terms of the physical activities involved, and relate the physical process to that of the exchange mechanism.

CHAPTER THREE

Concepts in Economics— Macroeconomics and Money

Macroeconomics is concerned with aggregated effects of economic activity, the mechanism by which all the individual actions of economic agents translate into overall societal welfare. As such, macroeconomics is oriented towards the formulation of national policy. It is concerned with the theoretical basis for the working of the economy as a whole and the means for measuring its performance.

There are two theoretical ideological extremes in economic theory—socialism and capitalism. The first is based on a belief that the market is not an effective mechanism for allocating goods and services and that, accordingly, government must administer prices to meet overall societal goals. Furthermore, and perhaps more significantly, it is contended that the ownership of capital should reside in government. Capitalism, on the other hand, is firmly dedicated to the two principles that the market is the most effective allocation mechanism and that ownership of capital should be private. In practice, no country represents a pure system of either of these polarized views. All economies are mixed economies, with differences in degree distinguishing them from one another.

The United States for example, is dedicated to the efficacy of the market and to private ownership of capital, but there is a large sector of the economy for which administered prices are necessary and government owns or controls a significant share of the capital resources of the society. The question which is always under debate is:

What should be the appropriate allocation of these economic responsibilities between the private and public sectors?

Aside from economic differences between societies, there are also major variations in political philosophy. These political variations may be more significant than are economic differences. People often tend to confuse the two. The United States is firmly committed to a democratic political system and leans toward a capitalistic economic system. By contrast Sweden, also a democratic country, leans toward a socialist economic system. The Soviet system is politically dictatorial and committed almost totally to an administered pricing system, but even here there are some elements of market pricing.

Monetary policy plays an important role influencing the health of the economy—just how important, is a matter of considerable debate. There are those who think that the major control mechanism of the economy should be monetary and that a proper monetary policy is all that is needed to ensure stable economic growth. There are others who think that government fiscal policy is and should be an instrument of economic policy. That government fiscal actions are relevant is hardly debatable. The question is:

What is the appropriate balance between monetary and fiscal policy, and how should each be used for controlling the economy?

The importance of macroeconomics, as background in evaluation of investments, lies in the influence of economic conditions on the outcome of investments. Measurement of the economy is essential for predicting investment results.

3.1 MEASURES OF ECONOMIC ACTIVITY

The measurement of economic performance must start with the economic activity of individuals and must aggregate individual effects to obtain an overall measure. The difficulty is that not all economic activity is recorded. It is virtually impossible to measure aggregate economic activity by recording physical production and consumption. While we may tabulate tons of steel and bushels of wheat produced and consumed, we have no way to relate their relative significance in determining a composite measure of economic activity. It is much easier to record monetary transactions than produc ion or consumption. However, even here, many transactions that are made in money are not recorded and are difficult to estimate. A great deal of economic activity is deliberately hidden from public surveillance in order to avoid payment of income taxes or to conceal other illegal activities. The best we can do in such cases is to make crude estimates of the scale of such exchanges. Various studies have estimated the magnitude of such hidden transactions as varying between $200 billion and $500 billion per year. Fortunately, however, most activity is handled through some form of recorded transaction, such as checks. These are readily aggregated.

There are two ways we might attempt to measure aggregate economic effects: through the purchases people make or through the incomes they receive. We use both but must exercise caution in order to avoid double counting. By such measurements we obtain the output or product of the system.

3.1.1 Measurement of Gross National Product

The *gross national product* (GNP) has become the accepted measure of overall economic activity. This is the sum total of all goods and services produced by the nation per year. The real GNP is the physical flow of labor and material, but the only practical

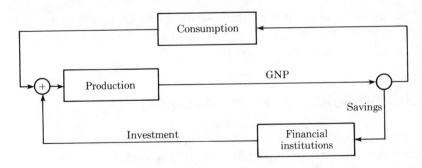

Figure 3.1 The production–consumption cycle.

way to measure it is in dollar terms. This is exemplified in Figure 3.1, which shows, in its most elemental form, the production–consumption cycle as a flow diagram.

It should be noted that the representation of flow is in terms of money and that goods and services actually flow in the opposite direction.

The only split in output shown in this flow diagram is between savings and consumption. Savings feed back into production through investment. Savings are accumulated from individuals and aggregated for investment by financial institutions—insurance companies, banks, stock and bond markets, etc.

The diagram of money flow in Figure 3.1 represents too elemental a model to provide a meaningful measure of the national accounts. It leaves out one of the most important sectors—government. Furthermore, it does not show how productive capacity is maintained or expanded. In order to provide a more complete picture of what is taking place, we need first to distinguish that part of consumption related to the production process itself. This is capital consumption, reasonably approximated by allowances for physical depreciation of capital, plus adjustments for unplanned retirements of plant and equipment. What remains is called *net national product* (NNP).

The system shown in Figure 3.1 is closed. No consideration is made for external inputs or outputs. Thus the flow diagrammed there is more properly called *gross domestic product* (GDP). GDP must include exports minus imports, because what we ship out in excess of what we consume is, clearly, part of our product output.

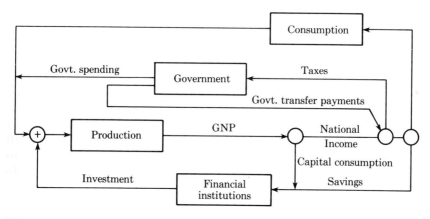

Figure 3.2 GNP including a government sector.

We must also have some means for taking account of growth in output. Savings, the amount fed back for new capital, accounts for this. The GNP composition then appears as shown in Figure 3.2.

Up to this point the flow diagram has remained fairly straightforward. Government complicates it somewhat. In one sense the government is part of the production process, insofar as it provides certain services that are essentially consumer benefits—postal services, for instance. Other services (and/or goods) are in the nature of collective goods which the government may or may not furnish directly. National defense is a good example of this. The services of soldiers are furnished directly, but most military material is purchased from contractors. In one case the government is acting in the role of producer. In the other, it is the consumer.

This same duality, in a sense, applies to the consumer sector, though it appears not to present difficulties there. Each individual is, at the same time, both a producer and a consumer, but the two functions are nicely separated by the boxes in the flow diagram. In the case of the government box, the separation is not evident. The government employee resides in the consumer box, and since he is also a producer, technically he should also be represented in the production box. Nevertheless the connotation of the government box is more one of consumption than it is of production. Most of government expenditure is a flow from the government box to purchases of one kind or another. To the extent that the government is paying its employees, it acts in essentially the same way as any other employer and in this sense is in the production box. We can get around this dilemma by considering all government spending as government purchases, including the payment of wages and salaries for government employees. This keeps the government in the consumer sector. The only difference between the consumption box and the government box is that the consumer box represents individual consumption, and the government box collective consumption.

The purpose of *national-income accounting* is to formulate an overall measure of economic activity. The conventional methods for doing this do not fit conveniently into the pattern of flow diagrams utilized, up to this point, for picturing the basic elements of GNP. Therefore, in Table 3.1 we now provide the structure of the national income accounts in summary form, as they are actually constructed by the Department of Commerce. The data shown are for the year 1980 as reported in the *Statistical Abstract of the United States*.

It should be emphasized that the data in these tables are highly aggregated and summarized. For this reason it is not possible to express all the detail of flows in the form of a flow diagram without unnecessarily complicating the diagram. Therefore, in Figure 3.3, where the data of Table 3.1 are shown in the form of a flow diagram, balancing items are introduced at several points. Because the purpose is to represent product, all financial flows (in particular, interest payments) are left indefinite. However, the diagram shows how the essential money flows take place.

3.1.2 Bar-Chart Representation of GNP

The discussion of GNP was introduced above by means of a flow-chart diagram. The relationships may also be seen by means of bar-chart representation of GNP components. This is shown in Figure 3.4.

While the two diagrams (Figures 3.3 and 3.4) are self-explanatory, some amplification may be desirable. GNP includes the product utilized for (i.e., consumed within) the production process itself. This is appropriately called *capital consumption* and is best approximated by depreciation allowances, with some adjustments

Table 3.1 National income and expenditure (1980)

EXPENDITURE	10^9		%
1. Personal consumption expenditures		1673	64
Durables	212		8
Nondurables	676		26
Services	785		30
2. Gross private investment		395	15
Nonresidential	296		11
Residential	105		4
Change in business inventory	− 6		—
3. Net exports		23	1
Exports	340		13
Imports	317		12
4. Government purchases		535	20
Federal	199		8
State and Local	336		13
Gross national product		**2626**	**100**
INCOME			
1. Compensation of employees		1597	61
2. Proprietors' income		131	5
3. Rental income			
(less capital consumption)		32	1
4. Corporate profits with adjustments		181	7
Before-tax profit	242		9
Capital consumption and			
inventory adjustments	− 20		− 1
Corporation income tax	81		3
Dividends	56		2
Undistributed profits	105		4
5. Net interest		180	7
6. **National income**		**2121**	**81**
7. Business transfer payments		11	—
8. Indirect business tax			
(less subsidies)		207	8
9. **Net national product**		**2339**	**89**
10. Capital consumption		287	11
Gross national product		**2626**	**100**
Breakdown of national income			
6. National income		2121	81
11. Less: Corporate profits	181		7
Social Security taxes	204		8
12. Plus: Government transfers to persons	284		11
Interest income	256		10
Dividend income	54		2
Business transfers	11		—
13. Personal income		2341	89
14. Personal income tax		339	13
15. Disposable personal income		1822	69

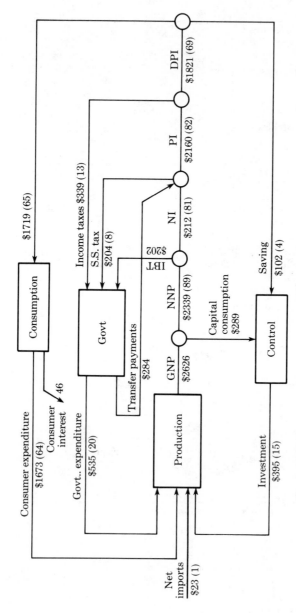

Figure 3.3 Gross national product (1980 data), in billions of dollars; percentages of total given in parentheses.

64

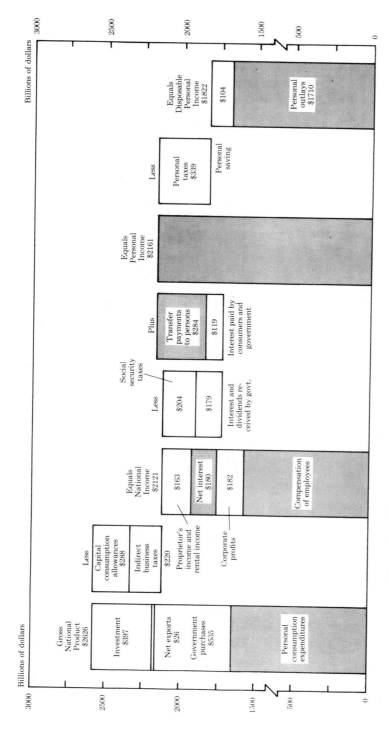

Figure 3.4 Bar-chart Representation of the GNP. Source: Chart prepared by United States Bureau of the Census.

for losses due to nonscheduled retirements of equipment. What remains is defined as net national product (NNP).

Government taps the flow of NNP by taking out *indirect business taxes* (IBT). These are business licenses, excise taxes, and the like. What now remains is the *net national income* (Y). At this point we are interested in determining what is left for individuals, and therefore a number of adjustments are necessary; see Table 3.1. The remaining flow is *personal income* (PI).

An important and special item, identified at this point, is government transfer payments. These are direct payments made to some individuals and are derived from taxes paid by everyone. Transfer payments accomplish a redistribution of the income of society. These kinds of payments, when legislated, are often referred to as entitlement programs. Social Security is the largest of these. Individuals receiving Social Security are no longer in the production stream but are entitled to a pension on the basis of their contribution to production at an earlier stage of their lives. Thus taxes collected from current production workers are transferred to those on a pension, without in any way adding to or subtracting from the GNP.

Government is not the sole source of transfer payments. Any transfer of income from one group to another, without influencing production, is technically a transfer payment. Thus corporate pensions are just as much transfer payments as is Social Security, although these transfers are not identified in the national-income accounting scheme and are recognized as private entitlements. However, they are identical in their effect on overall economic activity.

The government next taps personal income for income taxes, leaving *disposable personal income* (DPI), which is spent or saved as desired. Personal savings is a feedback flow into a control box that, for want of a better term, we might call "financial institutions", corresponding to the box that we depicted in the simplified diagram of Figure 3.1. Together with capital consumption, these savings are available for new investment. In addition there are corporate savings—undistributed profits, which feed back directly into investment. However, in the conventional national accounting system this control box is not shown, and the retained earnings of business, which are unquestionably part of the savings–investment flow, never appear directly.

3.1.3 The Control Function

The flow diagrams of the foregoing discussion will be recognized as the kind of "black box" representation employed in engineering feedback control systems. Financial institutions, together with government, are the control functions. Depending upon the time delays between savings feedback and investment outputs, the flow will produce either a positive or negative feedback into the production box. If it is positive, the output flow is amplified. If it is negative, the system is attenuated and output declines.

John Maynard Keynes, while not stating the concept in this manner because principles of feedback control had yet to be invented in his day, called attention to the fact that investment decisions were not necessarily concomitant with saving decisions. If the investment flow does not approximately coincide with the savings flow (i.e., if there is negative feedback), the economy slips into recession. For this reason, Keynes argued that the government must make up the difference with added spending in order to compensate for the lag in private spending. It was this idea that constituted Keynes's major contribution to economic theory.

3.1.4 Government Deficits

First let us distinguish between debt and deficits. Debt represents an obligation by the government as a result of borrowing funds. The deficit is the difference between cash inflow (revenue) and cash outflow (expenditures). This difference must be financed, either by borrowing or by some other financing mechanism.

Figure 3.3 describes a closed system which, in one way or another, must be in balance. The conventional national accounting system does not show all money flows. Financial flows are left out, because the purpose is to show net dollar values of the actual national product. As a result, government deficits (which in 1980 amounted to $27 billion) do not appear as part of the GNP. Any imbalance of payments due to net exports of goods and services could be represented by an appropriate arrow into or out of the consumption, production, or control boxes. The effect of government deficits, on the other hand, deserves special consideration. See Figure 3.5.

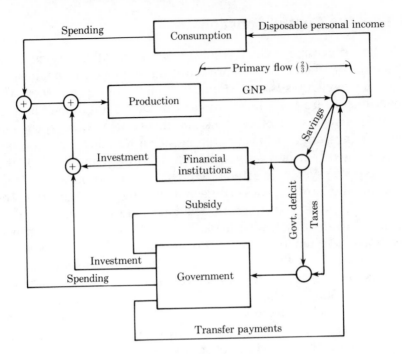

Figure 3.5 GNP with diverted flows.

The system in terms of money flows must balance. If there is insufficient money flow from taxes to meet the government spending stream, there are two ways to bring about a balance.

1. The government can borrow, in effect, by tapping the savings stream. In this case government deficits must offset savings. If savings are not sufficient to accommodate government debt as well as private debt, interest rates will tend to rise in order to bring money markets into balance. Interest may be regarded as the price for borrowed funds in the market.

2. The government can increase money flow by *monetizing debt*, which is popularly called "printing money". What it amounts to is an accommodation of the imbalance of flows into and out of the government box. If the effect of debt monetization is to expand total flow within the system, the effect on inflation will be neutral. Otherwise monetizing debt can be inflationary. These ideas will be further elaborated in Section 3.2.

In the absence of debt monetization, the government must conform to the requirement that the system must balance. If insufficient revenue is derived from taxes, government diverts savings which would otherwise have been available for private-sector investing. This does not necessarily mean that total investment will decline. If government investment makes up for a slack in private investment, net investment will remain unchanged. In any event the government must compete in the market for available savings. It is this debt market that determines interest rates. This kind of diversion of savings flow is shown in Figure 3.5.

It is often argued that the government has more bargaining power in money markets than does the private sector and so will tend to *crowd out* the borrowing needs of the private sector. This so-called "crowding out" is reputed to raise overall interest rates. However the government is only one agent in the market and does not, by itself, establish interest rates.

Interest government must pay on its debt has other important effects on the economy. In the first place, interest is, at least in part, a transfer payment, whether paid by the government or by the private sector. It does not contribute to the product output of the economy. It is an economically justifiable cost inasmuch as the investment of capital creates the potential for increased output. This investment accounts for the growth in GNP, and so it can be shown that the rate of growth of GNP is the real interest rate for society as a whole. If the real interest paid on government debt is at a rate which corresponds to the real rate of growth of the economy, normally about three percent, these government interest payments will remain at a constant ratio to GNP.

It must be stressed that we are referring to real rates—usually defined as the nominal rate less the inflation rate. Under such circumstances government interest payments are neutral, that is, no wealth transfer takes place. However when interest rates are too high, wealth transfers result. The government must collect the interest payments it makes by taxing some of the people in order to pay that interest out to others who lend their savings to the government. Of course, if the lenders are the same individuals who also pay the extra tax, then the effect is again neutral; no wealth transfer will have occurred, although some income transfer may be present.

While government deficits are popularly perceived as undesirable, they are not necessarily so, any more than are private deficits. It is generally recognized that private deficits are undesirable if the resulting debt is used to finance current consumption. However, if debt is for financing an investment having a potential for future return, it may be eminently justifiable. Even when apparently used for financing consumption, debt is often justifiable. For an example, consider the situation of a college student who borrows to finance an education which will eventually enhance his later earnings. This, in one sense, is financing consumption, but in reality it represents an investment in human capital.

The individual debt of the above example serves the function of smoothing the long-term income–expenditure stream of the individual. As another example, when a man purchases a home and finances it by means of a mortgage, he, in effect, runs an enormous deficit (i.e., the amount of the mortgage) in the year of purchase, but a positive balance thereafter (i.e., the part of his monthly payment that increases his equity). He is simply smoothing his income–expenditure stream.

These same characteristics are applicable to government deficits. There is an automatic countercyclical influence of government deficit, in that it smooths year-to-year fluctuations of the economy. Private-sector spending will vary, depending upon other things, such as the mood of the consumer. However, prosperity depends on a steady growth of total spending (i.e., cash outflow), public and private. Spending declines are necessarily recessions. When private spending slackens, there is a contraction of employment, which feeds back into further reduction of spending unless the government compensates with increased spending. However, government revenues are also dependent on maintenance of consumer income, which translates into taxes. As a consequence, government spending can only be compensatory if it runs a deficit.

This is not to argue that government spending is good. Clearly there is much spending by government which is inefficient. The catch is that government spending cuts are not automatically compensated for by increased private-sector spending. In fact, the reverse effect occurs. Government spending cuts tend to induce private-sector cuts.

The other characteristic of good debt—that it be debt used to finance increased productivity—also applies to government. However the nature of such investment, called infrastructure investment, is not always identifiable.

The foregoing discussion is admittedly oversimplified, but it demonstrates one of the basic dilemmas with regard to government deficits. We will treat some of the complexities in a further discussion of this issue after we have laid a foundation in Section 3.2—on money—and explained the technique of monetizing the Federal debt.

3.1.5 Review of Historical Data

The data shown in Figure 3.3 were taken from the *Statistical Abstract of the United States*. Both the values of the GNP and the percentages representing each component are shown. These data are recorded in current dollars. Often statistical data are given in 1972 dollars in order to provide a basis for comparing one year with another. Since the use of 1972 dollars represents an adjustment for inflation subsequent to 1972, amounts after that year are considerably lower than they would be if current dollars were used. It has been standard practice to reference statistical data to a standard year. The year 1958 had been used before 1972 was selected as the reference year.

It is interesting to observe the magnitude of the ratios of GNP components, as well as the way these ratios have changed over the years. Refer to Table 3.2.

The years 1929 and 1933 were included in the table to show two things: the levels that obtained in the boom period after World War I, and the dramatic effect of the Great Depression. From 1929 to 1933 the GNP declined 46% in current dollars. Capital investment virtually dried up, and government, which prior to that time represented a small component of the GNP, expanded dramatically.

Since 1960 government expenditures as a fraction of the GNP had been steadily declining until 1981, when they started to rise again. They are currently about 23% of GNP. It should be noted that the percentages representing government expenditures do not include transfer payments. However, they do include both state and local government, as well as the federal government. The

Table 3.2 Major Components of GNP

	1929	1933	1960	1965	1970	1975	1980	1982	1983 (EST)
GNP (1972 10^9)	—	—	737	929	1086	1234	1481	1485	1536
P.C. (%)[1]	74.8	82.1	61.3	60.1	61.9	63.4	63.1	64.8	65.2
Invest. (%)[2]	15.7	2.5	13.7	15.1	14.3	13.1	13.9	13.5	13.8
Exports (%)[3]	—	—	5.2	5.6	6.6	8.4	10.9		
Govt. (%)[4]	8.5	14.7	23.5	22.6	23.1	21.6	19.6	24.0	25.6

[1] Personal consumption expenditures as a percentage of GNP.
[2] Private fixed investment as a percentage of GNP.
[3] Exports (exports do not always balance imports; either one is an indicator of international trade).
[4] Government purchase of goods and services as a percentage of GNP.

federal component of government spending is about one-third of the total; state and local government accounts for about two-thirds.

One of these statistics that economists have interpreted as unsatisfactory is the proportion of GNP allocated to investment. Since World War II this has been quite steady, around 15%. However, it has been declining steadily since 1979. During the latter part of the 19th century it was generally in excess of 20%. At its peak, it reached 28%. A very large part of investment during that era, following the Civil War, was for infrastructure investment.

While the total investment as a percentage of GNP is of concern, its composition may be even more significant. Investment in housing is important, but it is the investment in industrial plant and equipment that determines the overall productivity of society and enables the economy to grow. The magnitude of investment can be seen in Table 3.3.

The most significant ratio in this table is nonresidential fixed investment. This has been in a precipitous decline since 1980. The dollar amounts have declined at the rate of 6% per year for 1981 and 1982. This ratio is often mentioned as an indicator of the declining competitiveness of the United States economy vis-à-vis Japan and Germany. These countries allocate almost twice as much of their GNP to private fixed capital investment. The percentage of GNP in investment accounted for in the government sector is never identified, but it is likely that most other industrialized countries devote a higher percentage of their government budgets to investment than we do.

Table 3.3 Composition of Net Private Fixed Investment[1]

	1970	1975	1976	1977	1978	1979	1980	1981	1982	1983 (EST)
Total investment	**155**	**162**	**177**	**201**	**216**	**223**	**207**	**226**	**210**	**215**
(% of GNP)	14.3	13.1	13.6	14.7	15.0	15.0	14.0	15.0	13.5	14.0
Nonresidential*	114	119	126	141	153	163	158	166	168	158
(% of GNP)	10.5	9.7	9.7	10.3	10.6	11.0	10.7	11.0	11.3	10.3
structures	44	38	40	41	45	49	48			
(% of GNP)	4.1	3.1	3.1	3.0	3.1	3.3	3.2			
equipment	70	81	86	100	109	115	109			
(% of GNP)	6.4	6.6	6.6	7.3	7.6	7.8	7.4			
Residential*	41	42	51	61	62	59	48	45	44	62
(% of GNP)	3.8	3.4	3.9	4.4	4.3	4.0	3.2	3.0	3.0	4.0

[1] In billions of 1972 dollars and percentages of GNP.

*NOTE: Percentages do not necessarily add to total percentage investment due to inventory investment (disinvestment).

An interesting change in the distribution of GNP, occurring in recent years, is in the amount involved in international trade. Until recently international trade could almost have been regarded as insignificant. The proportion of GNP allocated to this sector has more than doubled within the past 10 years, revealing the growing dependence of the U.S. on foreign markets.

3.1.6 Shortcomings of GNP as a Measure of Economic Activity

The GNP, as a measure of economic activity, measures only aggregated effects of exchanges. If no transaction takes place, nothing is added to the GNP. Thus any activity which is economic (in the sense that production and consumption take place), but does not involve an exchange, will not be taken into account. For example, consider the role of a housewife who accepts employment outside the home. The work that she had been doing as a housewife is a real economic contribution to the welfare of her family. In a sense there is an exchange of services within the family, in the specialization of function of the various members. However, it is informal; no money changes hands. When the housewife works for a firm and thereby gets a wage for her services, she may hire a maid to perform the services that she had been performing previously. A good part of her wages could go to pay for those services. The effect is that the economic consequences of her service are now measured. The converse effect on GNP takes place when a man marries his housekeeper: the GNP declines. This illustration demonstrates that GNP is, in part, a measure of the degree of complexity or specialization and formalized organization of work.

The same kind of loss in measurement occurs within firms. A firm is a collection of individuals who are interacting in a cooperative way to produce salable items. Many exchanges are taking place internally without any external transaction being recorded. Such internal transactions are not entered in the national-income accounts affecting the GNP. Often they will be recorded in the internal records of the firm in dollars, like any other external transaction. However, these are not, in any way, money transactions that influence measurement of GNP. That these dollars represent a different kind of measurement is clear from the fact that people within the firm commonly refer to such transactions as being in "soft" dollars rather than "hard" dollars. They are merely a recognition of internal accounting transfers. They do not affect GNP. Nevertheless, the way firms are organized and the effects of mergers or subdivisions all influence the reported measurements of the economy and its growth.

In spite of these shortcomings, GNP is still the best means for measuring aggregate economic activity. That GNP always tends to grow attests to the fact that, by and large, in making choices to organize their lives in ways they perceive to be preferable, people call for more rather than for less formalized interaction. The housewife, clearly, makes her own choice to work. She and her family see that it represents an improvement in their standard of living. The effect on the GNP will often be incidental to her decision. At the same time, the increase in GNP is not a linear function of satisfaction achieved. The extra benefits to the family are marginal. Offsetting costs may use up a significant part of the extra income.

3.2 MONEY

The exchange process, central to all economic activity, is based on producers offering their products on the market and registering their demands for goods in return. As pointed out in the introduction to money in Chapter 2, the producer brings a single product to market but will desire a menu of goods in exchange. In addition, he will wish to have time to make up his mind what consumer goods he wants. For this reason he will find it desirable to settle for some single good, which he may not want for itself, but which he feels confident can be traded later for goods that he does want. In other words, he trades his product for an intermediate good. The intermediate good has one of the important properties of money, that of allowing time to elapse without risking loss of value. In a sense the intermediate good is a store of value. This system of exchange is one of double trading, but is essentially barter. Because it requires labor and resources to produce, store, transport, and guard an intermediate good, it is a cumbersome and expensive money system.

A better alternative is for the producer to accept promises from consumers to pay him back in goods as he needs them. There must, of course, be general agreement on relative values of the goods he will subsequently claim. If there is universal confidence in the promises held by the seller, then these promises or claims can be repeatedly traded until everyone is satisfied. Goods will have been exchanged for claims, which will in turn have been exchanged for goods. All claims will eventually be exercised and go out of existence. They will have served the same function as the intermediate good, but without any wasted effort in producing and storing the intermediate good. Such claims or promises represent a liquid form of debt and, as such, are money. In other words, **money is debt**. Of course debt always equals credit, and modern money is usually called *credit money*, but it could just as well be called "debt money". The word "credit" originated in the Latin "credere", to believe. Thus the essential element of modern money is a common belief that the debt will be honored. The important thing to keep in mind is that, as a practical fact, **money exists only as debt**.

While money must represent debt in the modern world, the holder of money never perceives it as such. *He* is not in debt. He is a creditor with rights to claim values on demand. Furthermore, he has come to think that, when he receives money for something that he sold, he has been fully paid, whereas, in the true economic sense, payment is only completed when he later surrenders the money for other goods, services, or assets.

The kind of debt that represents money is distinguished from other debt by one important characteristic. In most cases of debt contracts, there is a specific contract between a particular debtor and a particular creditor. The claims that represent money are nonspecific. In effect, all producers have a collective debt, payable on demand. In other words the debt is implicit in the system—it is societal. This universal and ready acceptance of such debt makes it *liquid* (i.e., capable of flowing freely). It is sometimes simply referred to as *liquidity*.

Most money is represented by claims as entries in various kinds of accounts. Transfers between accounts may be made, at will, by direction of the people involved. Such directions are in the form of memoranda, electronic signals, or even by oral communications. Most transactions are made by means of a check, which is a memorandum to the bank to debit one account and credit another. The important concept here is that the claim for value is nothing more than information transmitted by some signaling system. As in any information system, there is a potential for loss of information associated with the means of transmission. This loss results in what is called *money illusion*. This effect occurs when sellers accept more in claims than they can ever deliver. They suffer from an illusion that the value of goods surrendered is higher than is justified by the possibility of delivery of exchange goods. The result is inflation. A claim may retain its magnitude in dollar terms, but the value so represented decays over time.

With this perspective of money, visualization of how the economic system works is relatively straightforward. Everyone contributes the product of his labor, as a more or less steady flow of goods and services, into the exchange process, and in turn demands a more or less steady flow of goods and services out of the process for consumption. This entire flow is facilitated by the signaling system, represented by a counterflow of claims—*money*. The real exchange is the flow of goods and services. It can only continue because of continuing confidence in the information flow. If the transmission is lossy, if the signals are blocked, or if the signals are not transmitted, the economy slows down. These difficulties may occur for a number of reasons, not the least of which are psychological influences that cause people to disturb the flow of signals (i.e., the spending of money). A steady-state flow requires a steady-state liquid-debt level (money supply). Growth of the flow (i.e., the economy), requires growth of debt. In many ways this seems to run counter to the commonly held negative perception of debt. It is true that individual debt can be bad if it becomes overextended, but, in the aggregate, debt is essential for a healthy economy.

3.2.1 Creation of Money

The most important component of money is in the form of demand deposits, i.e., checking accounts. This, together with currency, constitutes the primary measure of money, called M1. Currency, which is issued by the Treasury for the purpose of handling small transactions and for the small change people desire to carry for convenience, is of lesser importance.

How is money created?

We have seen that money is debt, and consequently its creation is innate in the creation of debt. Suppose a businessman, Mr. Green, wishes to borrow $1 million for a worthy project, which the bank agrees to finance. The $1 million is deposited to Mr. Green's account, so that he can immediately write checks against it. However, until he does so, the assets of that bank, or some other bank, are also increased by $1 million, and therefore the bank holding his deposit is immediately in a position to loan the same money all over again. Out of prudence, the bank will not go that far, but will hold a percentage of deposits in reserve. Nevertheless the effect of this practice is a multiplication of the debt by a factor that depends on the level of reserves and the rate at which the infinite series of lending and relending converges. If, for example, the bank loaned 80% of its deposits and held 20% as a prudent reserve in each cycle, the one million dollars of new money loaned would multiply to the sum of the infinite series:

$$\frac{1}{1 - 0.8} = \$5 \text{ million.}$$

3.2.2 The Function of The Federal Reserve System

Prior to 1913, when the Federal Reserve System (colloquially called the Fed) was created by the Congress, each bank set its own reserve policy. Periodically banks would become carried away by excessive optimism and overextend credit, leading to panics when confidence collapsed. Overcontraction of lending would follow. The lack of central control resulted in periodic violent swings in the economy.

The Fed, although created by the Congress, has many characteristics of a private organization. It is managed by the banking industry, even though it is responsive to the Congress of the United States. It consists of a membership of most but not all commercial banks, twelve member reserve banks distributed geographically, and a board of governors. Each of the district reserve banks is managed by a nine-member board of directors, six of whom are elected by the member banks. The other three are appointed by the board of governors of the Fed. The member banks own the capital stock of the Fed.

The seven-member board of governors is appointed by the President of the United States for terms extending far beyond the tenure of the President, in order to ensure its political independence. Since 1935 the terms of the Governors has been fourteen years, with appointments staggered on a two-year cycle.

One of the most powerful arms of the Fed is the Federal Open Market Committee (FOMC). This committee is empowered to set the basic operating policy for buying and selling Government bonds. There are twelve members—the president of the New York reserve bank, four members of the remaining eleven reserve banks on a rotational basis, and the seven governors of the Fed.

When the Fed was created, it was given the primary function of controlling bank reserves and thereby stabilizing money supply and controlling monetary growth. The Fed established the basic principles of reserve banking as one of the methods for discharging its responsibility for stabilizing money. It establishes reserve requirements by prescribing that certain percentages of bank deposits in commercial banks be redeposited with the Fed. The percentage depends on the kind of deposit, varying from 5% for savings accounts to about 12% for checking accounts. However, these percentages will vary from time to time. The amount of debt that may be created in the economy as a whole is limited by this mechanism of fractional reserve banking.

While the Fed can limit debt, it must not be forgotten that the primary decision to create new money rests with individuals desiring to increase their debt.

3.2.3 Monetizing Assets

All money is debt, but not all debt is money.

In the modern world there is no place for an intermediate good to be used as money. Only very liquid debt—that debt which is instantaneously and unconditionally transferable—qualifies as money. However, most debt is not as liquid as money debt.

A great deal of debt is conditionally linked to assets, for example a mortgage on real estate. When a man borrows from a bank, he receives the right to utilize a liquid form of debt, which we have seen is the essence of money. The debt he has incurred is collateralized or secured by assets which he holds. The mortgage may then be sold, but this requires searching for a buyer and satisfying certain formalities connected with the transaction. Furthermore, a mortgage may be exchanged for money, but no new debt is thereby created and no increase in the money supply occurs. On the other hand it is possible to exchange one kind of debt for another and, in so doing, affect the money supply. For example, a savings account (time deposit) is less liquid than a checking account, but can be converted into a checking account with little difficulty. It can thereby readily become money.

Because depositors can so readily change such assets as savings accounts into demand deposits, these savings deposits are called near-money. The ease by which assets are converted from less liquid to more liquid forms is sometimes referred to as the *money-ness* of assets, connoting a property of degree of acceptability in exchange and the vagueness of the concept of money. Because of this indefiniteness of money, the Fed has had to define it in a variety of ways depending on the degree of liquidity. The various classifications are as follows:

1. The most liquid form of money, defined as M1, is currency in circulation plus demand deposits, i.e., checkable deposits.

2. When savings account balances, small time deposits, commercial-bank overnight repurchase agreements, and money-market mutual funds are added to M1, the total is defined as M2.

3. The next level of liquidity, M3, is M2 plus large time deposits and term repurchase agreements.

4. All securities that will mature within 18 months are added to M3, making a total of all more or less liquid assets. Together these are called *L*.

The Fed establishes different reserve requirements for these categories.

There is one other category which must be mentioned to round out the picture of money. This is the monetary base, *B*, which is sometimes called "high-powered money". It comprises currency in circulation plus member banks' deposits with the Fed.

The liquidity of money enables the flow of exchange from goods to money to goods. At any instant in time there is a store of goods (houses for instance) which is not flowing. These assets, held off the market, have the potential of being offered in exchange, thus entering the flow at any time. For example, consider a home investment. The owner, Mr. Y, may have no intention of selling and so the value of his home is not affecting the flow of exchange. However, Mr. Y can elect at any time to monetize part of the value in his home by taking out a mortgage. In effect he would be creating a potential claim against the property in exchange for money. The effect of this action is to increase the money supply without necessarily increasing the flow of goods. (Remember, also, there is the multiplier effect on money creation as described above.)

Mr. Y may, of course, be expected to increase his spending as a result of the money realized from his mortgage, and if the economy is not operating at full supply capacity, it will expand to meet his new demands. However, if the economy is already operating at full production, then the extra money now in the system competes for a fixed supply of goods and thus results in inflation. This inflation would have to be sufficient to reduce the amount of goods demanded by everyone else by enough to offset Mr. Y's added demands for goods. Of course inflation would not have occurred if the mortgage had been negotiated solely for the purpose of paying off some other debt of a similar nature, because then no new money would have been created to compete for the fixed supply of goods. Mr. Y's extra money would have translated into the retirement of another debt. This money finally ends up in the hands of wealthy Mr. Z, who had no mortgage to retire, and decides to increase his consumption immediately. This new consumption exerts an inflationary pressure on the economy.

The same money-creation effect occurs when the federal government decides to monetize the assets of the country. Actually the asset value of the nation is indefinable; there is no way of knowing how large it is, but because of implicit faith that it is vastly greater than any existing debt, the government can borrow to whatever extent it may wish.

Let us examine how this works. If the government borrows, it does so through the Treasury Department, which negotiates a loan from the Fed, acting as the government's bank. It does this by issuing bonds that are bought by the Fed, which, in turn, sells these bonds to the public. This increases money supply in the same way that Mr. Y did when he chose to mortgage his home. He created more spending power for himself. The government, likewise, increases its spending power. Thus government, by increasing debt, stimulates economic activity.

As in Mr. Y's case, if the economy is operating below capacity, the increased debt is monetized and the economy stimulated in exactly the same way as in the home-mortgage example. On the other hand, if the debt is used by the government to increase the demands for goods and services in the public sector, without a corresponding increase in supply developing from either the public or the private sector or both, then the effect is inflationary. If the economy is operating below capacity, the additional government spending is readily accommodated without inflation occurring.

It is noteworthy that this debt and spending sequence has nothing at all to do with the social policy issue of what proportion of total spending should be allocated to the public sector. One may argue that the private sector spends more efficiently than does the public sector and so it is less desirable for the government to create money than for the private sector to do so. The important point is that it really makes little difference, in principle, whether money is privately or publicly created. The effect on the economy is the same except for the question of efficiency.

3.2.4 Control of Money Supply

As seen from the above discussion, inflation is dependent on having the correct growth rate of the money supply to accommodate the increasing volume of transactions. It is the responsibility of the Fed to provide this control. An important characteristic of money, on the macroeconomic level, is its flow. If the flow of goods and services is measured in monetary units (i.e., dollars), then an equal counterflow of money must occur. Otherwise inflation will cause an adjustment to the price index sufficient to make the flow of money coincide with the flow of goods.

The velocity of money is a measure of its rate of turnover, in dollars per year. Since the velocity of money is more or less constant, the variable that makes it possible to control its flow becomes the quantity (money supply). The Fed discharges its responsibility for this function by employing three important devices:

1. Setting reserve requirements for member banks. (This has already been described above.)

2. Setting the interest rate member banks must pay on loans from the Fed. This is known as the discount rate, because it is computed as a discount on the loan, rather than as an add-on to the loan as is typical in private borrowing.

3. Engaging in open-market operations. The FOMC buys or sells bonds on the open market and thereby strongly affects the amount of debt that the public can assume. When the Fed sells bonds, it dries up cash from the market, leaving less money in the banking system available for private lending. Conversely, by buying bonds, the Fed pumps cash into the system, thus expanding bank lending. This increases the money supply, stimulates business, and expands the economy if it is not already operating at capacity.

The last of these three devices is, by far, the most effective tool the Fed utilizes in controlling the money supply. Other mechanisms used include setting margin requirements on security purchases, prescribing bank lending and borrowing rates, etc.

The Fed influences interest rates through its open-market operations. If the Fed is selling bonds, this tends to lower bond prices and, correspondingly, raises interest rates. If it is buying bonds, this tends to raise bond prices, and consequently rates fall. However it must always be remembered that the Fed is competing in a free market and that both business and private borrowing is also part of that market. If there is strong demand for debt from all sources, interest rates tend to rise.

We have defined the various money measures that the Fed monitors. Of these, M1 is the primary money measure, but the indicator of money growth that the Fed controls most closely is the monetary base B, which is very sensitive to the Fed's open-market operations. Banks must respond immediately to changes in deposits resulting from bond purchase or sale, by adjusting their reserves. Sometimes they must borrow overnight from other banks holding excess reserves, in order to meet Fed demands.

Since October 1979 the Fed has, with debatable success, endeavored to control money growth by setting target growth rates for M1. This has meant that it allowed interest rates to be determined by the market. Prior to that time, the Fed would refrain from market intervention if the effect would have been to drive interest rates beyond certain limits. If interest rates threatened to rise above target levels, the Fed tended to let money grow too rapidly. Irrespective of Fed actions, however, the fundamental reason in the past for excessive growth of the money supply had to have been excessive private demand for debt. The ideal situation is for the money supply to grow in phase with the economy, without at the same time creating inflation.

The role of the Treasury in this process must also be understood. The Fed acts as the bank for the Treasury. When Treasury debt expands, the Fed advances funds and then proceeds to sell the corresponding government debt (bonds) to the public. If the new Treasury bonds are not being passed through to the public,

Table 3.4 Composition of the National Debt

| | PERCENTAGE OF NATIONAL DEBT HELD BY | | | |
YEAR	U.S. Agencies	Fed	Private citizens	Foreign-ers
1966	19.3	13.0	66.9	4.8
1967	22.1	13.9	64.1	4.4
1968	21.3	14.7	64.0	4.0
1969	23.2	15.1	61.8	3.3
1970	24.8	15.5	59.6	4.2
1971	25.4	16.3	58.3	8.7
1972	25.7	16.2	58.7	12.1
1973	26.8	16.4	54.8	11.8
1974	28.5	16.7	54.8	11.8
1975	26.2	15.8	58.0	12.3
1976	23.2	14.9	61.9	11.7
1977	21.9	14.4	63.6	13.5
1978	21.3	14.2	64.5	16.3
1979	21.9	13.6	64.4	15.6
1980	20.9	12.9	66.7	14.3
1981	20.0	12.6	67.5	13.7
1982	17.7	11.5	70.9	12.4
*1983	17.1	10.8	72.4	12.1

*To end of second quarter.
Source: Federal Reserve Bank of Saint Louis.

the Fed is *monetizing* government debt, which is equivalent to monetizing societal assets. This is what is really meant when the government is said to be "printing money". Money is only printed in a figurative sense. It is never printed in fact, except for the inconsequential amount represented by currency; money is typed, written, electronically transmitted, or spoken. The word "printed" is misleading.

At any given time the Fed will be holding some percentage of government debt. At the end of 1982 this was about $200 billion. In recent years the proportion of the total debt held by the Fed has been declining, not expanding as most people think. The implication is that, rather than "printing money", the Fed has actually been constraining its growth or, in effect, "unprinting" it (see Table 3.4).

From a peak in 1974 to mid 1983, the proportion of the national debt held by government agencies and trusts (i.e., the government itself) has declined from 28.5% to 17.1%, amounting to a 40.0% decline. That held by the Fed has declined from 16.7% to 10.8% —a 35.3% decline. Perhaps the most dramatic change occurred in the amount of the debt held by foreign investors, rising from a low of 3.3% in 1969 to a high of 16.3% in 1978—almost a 400% increase. However, since 1978 it declined again to 12.17.

If the government, through the Fed, has not been "printing money", who then has been printing it? Where did the excess growth originate? The real culprit in the excessive growth of money, and hence of inflation, may very well have been the degree to which the public has been monetizing private assets, notably real estate.

Real-estate values started to escalate following an inflation spiral that had been triggered by several events. First, during the Vietnam war, the government furnished excessive stimulus by not raising taxes to finance stepped-up military expenditures. Then in the early 1970s the OPEC raised oil prices by a factor of 4, thereby creating an inflationary shock to the economy. A number of things happened in the real-estate market as a consequence. Individuals found that they could capitalize their increased asset values in homes by increasing the level of their mortgages. This, in turn, tended to cause them to scale up their spending, particularly with respect to home purchases, thus creating a speculative boom in real estate. At the same time they were increasing their demands for other outputs, beyond the productive capacity of the economy. In other words, as inflation pushed up asset values, it became very easy for individuals to monetize these increased asset values in order to increase their living standards.

3.2.5 The Demand for Money

In the preceding sections we have dealt with money on the supply side. The discussion of money would not be complete without some consideration for the demand for money. In the first place the demand for money, like the demand for anything else, does not depend simply on people's desires for it. They must have the wherewithal to exercise their demands. This means they must have resources with which they can be in a position to trade. However, money, as we have seen, is nothing more than the right to exercise a claim. The difference between money and any other resource is merely a question of liquidity. Thus the demand for money arises out of the need to have resources in a liquid rather than a nonliquid form. People need this for one primary purpose —to make transactions. In other words, the primary source of money demand is the need to hold transaction balances. Beyond this, holding extra money is uneconomical. Everyone will try to get rid of money beyond this need by trading it for less liquid assets that can earn a return. They are willing to hold money in order only to maintain decision-making flexibility.

We have seen that the supply of money—unlike that of a commodity, which is constrained by the amount of labor and other resources needed to bring it into being—is constrained by policy. Nevertheless, money does have a supply curve (which can be a straight vertical line), and the demand for money will be sensitive to its price (i.e., it will display price elasticity of demand). The price of money is the interest rate.

3.3 INVESTMENT, PRODUCTIVITY, AND ECONOMIC GROWTH

In spite of all the shortcomings of GNP as a measure of economic activity, it is the best measure available and, on a year-to-year comparative scale, is an excellent measure of economic growth.

The growth rate of the economy must first be sufficient to accommodate the growth in population. Growth beyond this point is, then, a measure of an increasing standard of living, in terms of consumption. If the economy is to grow, it can only do so by an increase in productivity. This must be measured by GNP per unit of labor.

There is a common misconception that labor productivity depends upon labor working both harder and more efficiently. This is not necessarily so. Actually, people work fewer days per year, fewer hours per day, and with less intensity of effort than they have ever had to do in the past. Furthermore, the efficiency of their work habits may or may not have increased significantly. Nevertheless, until recently productivity has always grown. The major contributor to labor productivity is capital investment, which is a combined result of improved technology and of more machinery per worker.

The achievable rate of growth is dependent on the percentage of the GNP invested. The economy can grow as fast as the public pleases, but to make it do so, a balance must be struck between rates of saving (reduction of immediate consumption) and expectations of future consumption. In large measure this is a social choice. Everything else being equal, a society oriented toward future consumption, such as Japan, can be expected to grow faster than one oriented toward present consumption, such as the United States.

The growth rate of the United States economy has been remarkably constant over the past 120 years. It has averaged just over 3% per year. While this average has fluctuated with alternating periods of boom and recession, there has been only one significant period of decline. This was during the early years of the Great Depression, 1929–1933. Over that period the real GNP actually declined more than 45% and the index of industrial production declined 53%.

We are now, in 1984, emerging from a second long period of stagnation. Real GNP was slightly lower in the first quarter of 1983 than it was in the last quarter of 1978—a time lapse of four and one-half years.

Because investment is a key element in economic growth, and also because it is the main concern of this treatise, the historical data on it are well worth reviewing.

3.3.1 Historical Perspective

From the close of the Civil War until the beginning of World War I, investment averaged 21% of the GNP and in its peak year was 28%. This was the period in which we built most of the infrastructure, or social overhead capital, that was to underpin subsequent industrial expansion.

World War I interrupted this capital-building era. During any war, a society will operate on its existing capital since it cannot be building for the future when survival is in question. Therefore during the five years from 1914 to 1919, investment declined to an average rate of 13% of the GNP, and dropped for a time to 8%. The investment rate never recovered its former level, but did reach 19.9% in 1929. The depression saw it plummet to 2.9% in 1932, and again in World War II it dropped to 7.4%. These major interruptions meant that the average proportion for the 20 years of the 1930s and 1940s amounted to only 10%. Although it rose again to almost 20% in 1950, it has averaged only 15% since then, falling below 13% for 1982 and even lower in 1983. While it is projected to rise slightly in 1984, this is not expected to be significant.

In some respects these figures mask a great deal of important detail. In the first place, they represent gross private investment, as compiled by the Department of Commerce; they do not include government investment. Before World War II, government was small and did not account for much investment. Ever since that time, its contribution to total investment has been increasing. However, the government does not distinguish, in accounting, between its operating expenditures and its capital expenditures, and therefore there is no way of knowing how much capital investment is due to government. In the 1950s, with highway and other federal and state capital projects, the government component of investment was very large, so that the 15% private sector investment, when combined with the government share, may have been satisfactory. In recent years, however, government investment has also been drying up as the private-sector investment declined. This might indicate that the present 13% of GNP is, in reality, a smaller share than it appears.

In the latter part of the nineteenth century, while investment was largely private, government contributed enormous amounts of real but unidentified capital to the private sector in the form of land grants and indirect subsidies. Many other government expenditures, which are technically capital investment, are also omitted from the record. Much of this has been in the form of investment in people's knowledge—human capital. These investments have also contracted seriously in recent years.

Aggregated statistics manifest one other shortcoming. They fail to classify capital in terms of its potential for increasing productivity. Capital may be classified as consumer capital or producer capital. Approximately one-half of the upsurge in private capital spending immediately after World War II was for residential construction — consumer capital. By 1979 this ratio was about one-third. Residential construction is truly capital, but it does not enhance productivity in the same way that a new factory does. One of the reasons for the poor showing of economic indicators during the recent recession was the serious decline in housing.

3.3.2 The Dilemma of Today

While the present administration clearly saw the crying need for capital expansion and the concomitant need for savings to generate it, two major essential ingredients may have been overlooked. In spite of the widespread and largely justified desire for reduced government spending, it must be recognized that, first and foremost, prosperity depends on steadily increasing total spending. Recession must always accompany a reduction in spending. This is axiomatic. It matters little whether spending is government or private, or whether it is ultimately for desirable things or for undesirable things. The net effect of a reduction in spending is a reduction in aggregate demand, and reduction in aggregate demand is recession. However, if new demands are generated in phase with the elimination of old demands, some types of spending increase as others decline.

The problem, today, is that reduced spending for such things as welfare, a truly undesirable kind of spending, translates into reduced demand for factory output. This means reduced utilization of plant capacity. As a result, corporations can see no need for new investment when existing plants are idle. Inducements to save result in a similar depressing effect. Obviously, what people save they do not spend, and the savings that had been destined for new plant investments are left on the sidelines, as potential future claims.

This may be seen in Figure 3.5. Tampering with the flows on the right side of the control box will not induce changes in investment decisions on the left side. We must find a way to stimulate the investment flow. Many of the tax changes introduced in 1981–1982 were intended for this purpose, but apparently have not worked as envisioned.

The answer to this dilemma seems obvious. New spending should be planned before existing spending is cut. In part, it was envisioned that this new spending would occur as a consequence of increased military budgets. However, a budget is not the same thing as actual spending. There are important lags between appropriation and spending. Thus even a small reduction in government expenditures, even where such spending cuts are desirable as an objective, triggers a much larger reduction in private spending, and sets the stage for disincentives to invest. The result is the exact opposite of what is desired: less rather than more investment.

The administration's objective of stimulating savings was good. Many of the measures introduced for implementing this were sound. The failure in achieving the desired result may lie in not having first devised a mechanism for induced investment in phase with reduced government spending.

In addition, however, too little thought may have been given to the kind of investment needed for revitalizing the economy. The perceived need at present is new capital for reindustrialization. This is not just any kind of capital. It is capital that will restore our national competitiveness and set in place the conditions for growth over the long run. As the economy is recovering from the current recession, there is increasing demand for consumer goods. Only limited capital, directly related to satisfying a resurgence in consumer demand, is needed as an economy emerges from recession. This type of investment might not suffice to bring about the structural change in the economy that is needed to produce sustained secular growth.

At the time this section was written (summer of 1983), the United States economy was giving every indication that a strong recovery was underway. In part, this may be attributable to a burst in the growth of the money supply. Aggregate consumer demand is showing a healthy resurgence. Historically, this phase of a recovery is characterized by considerable inventory rebuilding, but investment spending lags. At present the crucial question remains unresolved: whether there will be sufficient new investment in both the private and public sectors to sustain long-term growth in productivity.

3.3.3 Infrastructure Investment

It is conceivable that the United States economy has been sustained, to a greater extent than was realized, by the infrastructure investment during the last half of the nineteenth century. This infrastructure is now worn out and obsolete. We need urgently to rebuild it. We cannot long avoid making major new investments for energy. Oil must give way to coal or nuclear energy, and the investment needed for that sector alone is enormous. However it will take many years to effect the changeover. At the same time, the limited start already made for production of synthetic fuels has been drastically curtailed as a result of a short-term oil glut. Our resource industry, including our water resources, will require huge infusions of capital. The time has long passed when we could exploit resources with little effort. We have reached the stage where we will have to devise radically new technologies, requiring lower labor intensities, even as the innate difficulties of finding and mining our natural resources increases. Our transportation industry, too, is obsolete. Highways, particularly bridges, if not obsolete, are in need of repair and replacement.

If we are to move ahead and restore sustained and healthy economic growth, we will need to increase capital spending to its former levels—on the order of 20% of GNP per year. In present-day dollars, that would be $600 billion per year, or one-third more each year than we are now spending. If this is too much for the private sector to provide, it must be provided by the public sector.

Our instincts are against expecting government to do this. Therefore some imagination will be needed to devise an institutional framework for accomplishing this capital expansion objective and, at the same time, keeping it largely in private rather than in government hands. But government or private large-scale infrastructure investment must be made.

3.4 RECAPITULATION

1. Macroeconomics deals with the aggregated effects of economic activity and their measurement.

2. The two extreme views on how an economy should be managed are socialism and capitalism. Socialism is predicated on the belief that government should own and control capital in the interests of the people, and that the market is not the best mechanism for the allocation of goods and services. It follows from this that prices are to be determined by administrative fiat. Capitalism is dedicated to the principle of private ownership of capital and the belief that the market is the most efficient mechanism for allocation of resources. No economy exists today that adheres strictly to either of these philosophies. In any society some prices must be administered while others are market-determined.

3. The principal measure of aggregated economic activity is gross national product (GNP), which measures, in money terms, the total output of society. Its main component is personal income, which divides between disposable income and savings after payment of taxes. From the output side, GNP is tapped for capital consumption and indirect business taxes, leaving net national income.

4. Government enters the picture in two ways. It provides goods and services that properly fall into the category of collective goods. Taxes must be imposed for generating the income required to fulfill this function. In addition government makes sizable transfer payments, which represent no increase in product output, but rather a redistribution of income among the members of society.

5. Money is a signaling system for facilitating exchange. While its origin was once that of an intermediate good, today it is a manifestation of liquid debt. All modern money is debt (i.e., credit) money. It can only be created by borrowing.

6. The money supply is controlled by the Fed, whose primary tool is the FOMC, through which it enters the financial markets to buy and sell bonds. By selling, it contracts the money supply, and by buying it expands it.

7. Money is not created by printing it in a literal sense. Money is created by monetizing asset values. If this occurs faster than required for market clearing, the excess is inflationary. One such inflationary effect occurs when the treasury borrows from the Fed and the Fed does not pass the debt on to the public. The pressures for creating money originate in the private sector. The Fed's control is primarily that of a restraint on expansion.

8. Economic growth is a direct result of increasing productivity. Increasing productivity is directly tied to the investment of capital. However, the investment of capital must be properly balanced as to need and effectiveness. Investment is a necessary condition but not a sufficient condition for increasing productivity.

3.5 PROBLEMS

1. Update the breakdown of GNP with the most recent annual data and draw some conclusions as to trends.

2. What are recent money-supply levels, and how have they been growing?

3. Consider various ways for accommodating the rising government debt structure. Show how much it represents of the total debt in the economy as a whole and how it has been changing over the years.

4. Can you form some judgment about the level of transfer payments that is occurring as a consequence of interest paid on the government debt?

5. Capital consumption is deducted from the GNP to allow for the physical depreciation of capital assets in the private sector. The government, both Federal and State, does not identify depreciation, and so the capital-consumption item in GNP includes that of the private sector only. What would the effect be on GNP if the government depreciated its investments and recorded this additional money flow?

○

○

CHAPTER FOUR

Time-Utility and Time-Value Concepts— Discounting

A basic decision confronting everyone is whether to spend or to save income—to consume or to postpone consuming. The choice to save and to invest those savings is made if the utility of the prospect or anticipation of future consumption is greater than that of present consumption. The prospective quantity of the goods and services need not be greater than the goods foregone in the present. Utility is not linearly related to quantity of goods. This means that the number of prospective dollars need not necessarily be greater than the number of present dollars in order to make a decision to invest.

For example, consider a man with a present income sufficiently high that the utility of that portion of it which he may contemplate spending on some added increment of consumption is quite low. As a result he might opt for investing that extra income in his retirement fund, in preference to spending it on a new pleasure boat. The prospective income twenty years hence could have more

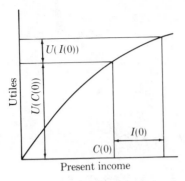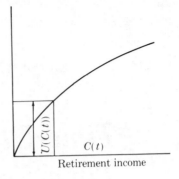

Figure 4.1 Utility function.

utility than does a boat now. This would be true simply because the retirement income will fall into a different range on his utility scale.

His situation is as represented in Figure 4.1. Whatever he saves and invests, $I(0)$, results in $C(t)$. Normally $C(t)$ would be greater than $I(0)$, but for the moment we do not need to place any constraint on its size. As depicted, $C(t) < I(0)$, but clearly $U(C(t)) > U(I(0))$. The point at which he would cut off further consumption and save (i.e., invest), would be where the utility of an incremental amount of future consumption equals the utility of an incremental amount of present consumption, that is,

$$dU(I(0)) = dU(C(t)). \tag{4.1}$$

If the investor were limited to the alternatives depicted, he would choose to save, even if it meant he would have less in the future than in the present. On the other hand, if Figure 4.1 were only one of a number of opportunities, $W(j)$ (Figure 4.2), clearly he would select the best one, $W(3)$. This is the one that would provide the highest income in the future. Because of the increase in productivity arising from capital investment, the average effect of investment is that $C(t)$ is always greater than $I(0)$. However, competition in the market limits the investor's opportunity to some maximum future income at t. To some degree this will depend on the particular markets to which the investor may be limited in his search for opportunities. He will always be expected to select the best opportunity available.

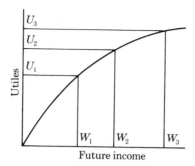

Figure 4.2   Alternative utilities.

4.1   EQUIVALENCE OF VALUE WITH RESPECT TO TIME

The inequality $C(t) > I(0)$ can be changed to an equality simply by multiplying one of the terms by a factor:

$$I(0) = D \times C(t), \qquad (4.2)$$

which establishes an equivalence between a present amount and the *prospect* of a future amount.

Since the future amount is only prospective, there will always be some uncertainty or risk associated with its realizability. However, for the present we will assume that the prospective amount is certain, in order to establish a risk-free concept of equivalence in time. Risk will be taken up in Chapter 9.

We will be interested in examining both the equivalence of utilities and the equivalence of values with respect to time.

4.1.1   The Discount Function

Because $C(t)$ is always greater than $I(0)$, D will always be less than unity, and so we appropriately call it a *discount* factor.

Up to this point we have said nothing about the time dimension. Clearly, the value of D will depend on the futurity of $C(t)$, so D must also be a function of time, $D(t)$. What is this function, and how would we distinguish between the alternative of trading $I(0)$ for $C(t_1)$ and trading $I(0)$ for $C(t_2)$?

Let us start by examining the case where utilities are equal (Figure 4.3). Two utility functions are represented—$U(t_1)$ for

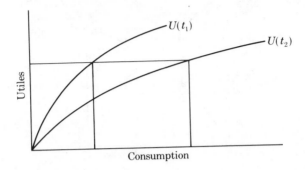

Figure 4.3 Comparison of utilities.

present-time consumption $C(0)$, and $U(t_2)$ for prospective consumption $C(t)$. There is no reason to assume that the shape of the utility function for $C(t_1)$ should be the same as that for $C(t_2)$. However, we obtain an interesting result if it is, i.e., if the ratio $C(t_1)/C(t_2)$ is a constant for all U. We will define this ratio as r for each Δt. Again, there is no reason why this ratio r has to be a constant in time, but for now we will assume that it is. Refer to Figure 4.4. With these idealizations it follows that

$$dC(t) = rC(t)\, dt, \tag{4.3}$$

the solution for which is readily shown to be

$$C(t) = C(0)e^{rt}, \tag{4.4}$$

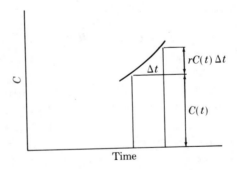

Figure 4.4 Discount ratio.

from which it follows that for this special case

$$D(t) = e^{-rt}. \tag{4.5}$$

Restating this in words, *the discount function is a negative-exponential function of time.*

It will be observed that $D(t)$ is nondimensional, and therefore the dimension of r is the reciprocal of time $(1/t)$. Thus r is a *rate of change*. This rate-of-change parameter will be recognized as an interest rate in continuous form, but the idea of interest on debt has been scrupulously avoided here, in order not to impose it on the reader's mind. Interest is of only incidental concern. The important concept is that value is related to time. It is neither desirable nor necessary to have a mental picture of interest on debt. The emphasis is on the notion of a discounting function rather than a compounding function, and therefore it is more desirable to refer to r as a discount rate than as an interest rate. The reason for this is that we always want to modify a future amount in order to make it commensurate with a present amount, to which we can more readily relate.

4.1.2 The Discrete Discount Function

The discount function, equation 4.5, was developed by assuming that time was continuous and that time value, likewise, varied continuously in time, as depicted in Figure 4.4. If we were to postulate that value changed in discrete steps, we would obtain a somewhat modified functional relationship. In other words, suppose that there could be no value change until the end of a specified period of time and then a sudden jump in value occurred. As for the continuous case, the amount of the jump is proportional to the magnitude at the beginning of the period and to the size of the time interval. In order to distinguish the rate-of-change parameter for the discrete case from the one for the continuous case, we will designate it by i instead of r. Elapsed time must now be represented as a discrete number of periods, n, so that $t = n$. Thus the same relationship, equation 4.4, holds, but with new symbols:

$$\Delta C(T) = iC(n)\,\Delta t. \tag{4.6}$$

However, we take the time unit to be one period, $\Delta t = 1$. (See Appendix C.) Instead of an exponential, we have a geometric progression, which is readily shown to yield the result,

$$C(n) = C(0)(1 + i)^n. \qquad (4.7)$$

The corresponding discount function is

$$D(n) = (1 + i)^{-n}. \qquad (4.8)$$

For any whole number of periods, the results for equations 4.8 and 4.4 will be identical, provided only that the chosen value of r is consistent with that of i. The relationship between i and r is established by setting

$$e^r = 1 + i. \qquad (4.9)$$

From this,

$$r = \ln(1 + i). \qquad (4.10)$$

Provided that r is small, it is approximately equal to i. The magnitude of the difference is seen in Table 4.1.

In recent years, financial institutions have adopted the practice of quoting interest rates as daily rates and showing for comparison the amounts earned in a year. A daily rate is essentially the same

Table 4.1 Difference between Continuous and Discrete Discount Rates

n	10% e^{rt}	10% $(1 + i)^n$	20% e^{rt}	20% $(1 + i)^n$
1	1.1052	1.1000	1.2214	1.2000
2	1.2214	1.1210	1.4918	1.4400
3	1.3499	1.3310	1.8221	1.7280
4	1.4918	1.4641	2.2255	2.0736
5	1.6487	1.6105	2.7183	2.4883
6	1.8221	1.7716	3.3201	2.9860
7	2.0138	1.9487	4.0552	3.5832
8	2.2255	2.1436	4.9530	4.2998
9	2.4596	2.3579	6.0496	5.1598
10	2.7183	2.5937	7.3891	6.1917

as a continuous rate. For example, a 10% continuous rate gives

$$i = e^{0.10} - 1 = 0.105170918, \text{ or } 10.5170918\%.$$

The equivalent daily discrete rate is

$$i = e^{0.10/365} - 1 = 0.00027401,$$

which compounded for 365 days becomes

$$i = (1 + 0.000270401)^{365} - 1 = 0.105170863,$$

which will be observed to be the same as the yield from the continuous rate up to the seventh decimal place.

4.1.3 Ways Of Specifying Interest Rates

The entire emphasis in this chapter is on the concepts of time value. The ideas have been presented without reference to interest on debt contracts. It is important always to keep in mind that the concept of time value is in no way related to debt. At the same time, it will be recognized that the mathematics of the time value relationships is identical, whether one is dealing with profit on money invested, or with interest on a loan, from the point of view of either debtor or creditor.

Interest is specified on loan contracts to establish a legal obligation for a repayment schedule, including a suitable payment to the lender for foregoing the use of his money. A number of different conventions are employed for specifying interest on debt obligations. Any manner of stating interest, without relating it specifically to the length of period over which it is computed, is called *nominal interest*. In other words, it is a convention for naming the interest rate for a particular period when, in reality, interest is to be computed on the basis of a period different from the stated one. For example, revolving charge accounts may state, "The interest rate is to be computed on the basis of 1.5% per month on the unpaid balance, i.e., an annual percentage rate of 18% per year." The 18% was determined simply by multiplying the 1.5% by 12 months. However, the statement that the annual rate is 18% is actually a statement of nominal interest. In fact the interest is never computed at 18%/year; it is computed correctly at 1.5% per month. The 18% rate is a nominal rate.

On the other hand, one might wish to know what an equivalent annualized rate would be if it were a true rate. This would be the same as compounding the interest of 1.5% per month for 12 months in order to see what it would amount to in a year:

$$i(\text{per year}) = (1 + j)^{12} - 1 \qquad (4.11)$$

where j is the monthly rate. For the revolving credit example, the "effective rate", as it is called, is 19.56%—not 18%.

The custom of identifying the interest rate by means of a nominal interest rate is very common. In fact it has been written into a law, called the "Truth in Lending Law", passed by the Congress a number of years ago in order to put a stop to deceptive advertisements of interest charges. The law requires the notification of interest charges by means of the "annual percentage rate". This is abbreviated commonly as APR and is advertised as the basis for comparing interest charges. Unfortunately it is still not a true interest rate, but it is, at least, a standardized notation.

A second common method of stating interest charges is to take the stated nominal rate per year, multiply by the number of years, and divide by the months to determine the monthly payment. This understates the true interest much more than does the so-called "annual percentage rate".

These examples bring out an important caution:

In order to determine values of any money amounts at different points in time, never add them together or subtract them from one another.

This is like adding apples and oranges. You may add apples and oranges as long as you state the answer as a number of pieces of fruit. However, if you want to place a value on the fruit, you must relate the value of an apple to that of an orange. The same applies for money. You may add money amounts at different times just so long as you do not imply value in the total. A dollar today added to a dollar a year from now is no more meaningful than an apple plus an orange. It is easy to avoid making the error of adding apples and oranges because the names for the different fruits are different. Unfortunately we do not assign different names to dollars at different times.

This dictum is constantly violated in everyday life. It is commonplace for politicians to arouse either resentment or support by emphasizing how much some governmental program is going to cost by quoting the sum of the costs over many years. Such numbers are completely misleading and meaningless.

Dollar amounts must always be factored in determining equivalent values in time.

4.1.4 Time-Value Idealizations Reexamined

In order to obtain the negative exponential for the discount function, it was necessary to introduce two very important idealizations.

1. Future money amounts are discounted at a constant ratio r, which is determined by the market. This idealization derives from the assumption that the shapes of the utility functions for different futurities are identical.

2. The incremental change in utility is proportional to time, i.e., equation 4.3.

If we relax these constraints, we may return to the basic equation 4.2 and specify that

$$D = D(C, t). \tag{4.12}$$

However, this does not provide an operationally useful function. We are forced to use simplifying assumptions if we are to compare alternative investments in a rational way.

The market is an averaging device. While everyone has a different utility function, the price in the market reflects the averaged effect of them all. Thus it may be reasonable to postulate an average utility function. Furthermore, it is not implausible to assume, as was done above, that the shape of this averaged function will be constant over time. This latter assumption is plausible on the basis of certain further assumptions. One of these is that the age composition of society remains constant. Young people will have a different perception of the future than will the elderly, and consequently a population with a larger proportion of elderly will be expected to exhibit a somewhat different average utility than a younger population. As the age distribution shifts toward an older population, the average attitude for present versus future consumption will change.

With regard to assumption 2, the utility of prospective consumption will reflect a collective preference for immediate as opposed to future consumption. In addition, the average utility will be influenced by how time itself impinges on people's perceptions. Time is not perceived as a linear phenomenon. Therefore one would expect the shape of the average utility for future income to be different from that for present income. Accordingly, the two assumptions listed above may not be entirely valid.

In spite of these difficulties, the universal practice has been to accept, without further question, the premise that the basic discounting function is, and should be, the negative exponential. An alternative function which is based on how people may actually perceive time on different bases, has been suggested by the author (English 1978).

4.2 DISCOUNTED CASH FLOW

The same discounting principle developed for discounting a discrete future sum applies to discounting a cash flow. Instead of a future amount $C(t)$, we have a flow $y(t)$, with the dimensions of dollars per unit time. Thus

$$p(t) = D(y, t)y(t), \qquad (4.13)$$

where $p(t)$ is the present worth function of $y(t)$. This is represented by the dashed curve in Figure 4.5.

The area under the curve of the present worth of cash flow, $p(t)$, is the total present value of the cash flow. It is called the *present worth, net present value*, or *discounted cash flow*. These terms are used somewhat interchangeably, but the first seems to be more widely used by engineers and the latter two by the business community. The engineer's claim to the term dates back

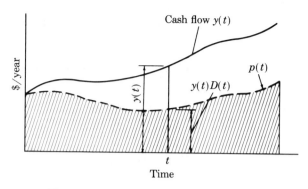

Figure 4.5 Discounted cash-flow function.

at least to J. C. L. Fish (1915). The terms used in the business community evolved much more recently, coming into popular usage only since World War II.

The abbreviation NPV for net present value is also the name of a standard built-in function in many commonly used calculator and software systems, as for example in the Hewlett-Packard HP-12C hand calculator and in VisiCalc, a software package for personal computers. It may be used interchangeably with the term "present worth". In mathematical expressions the symbol P may be used. The generalized function for value of a cash flow is given by

$$P = \int y(t)D(u, t)\, dt, \qquad (4.14)$$

which for the standard exponential discount function becomes

$$P = \int y(t)e^{-rt}\, dt. \qquad (4.15)$$

It is important to restate the admonition of an earlier section, that no value can be attached to the integral of the cash-flow function itself (i.e., the area under the cash-flow curve). The sum of dollars at different times may have significance in an *accounting* sense of counting actual dollars, but never in a *value sense*.

Monies paid at different times must never be added to obtain a measure of value.

4.2.1 Standardized Functions Based on Constant Cash Flow

It is useful to develop formulas for a number of standard cash-flow functions as solutions for equation 4.15. The first one that has widespread application is that of a continuous constant cash flow or annuity. Thus, substituting a constant cash flow A for $y(t)$,

$$P = \int Ae^{-rt}\, dt. \tag{4.16}$$

It will usually be necessary to restrict the cash flow to an arbitrary limit, T. Thus the limits of integration will be from 0 to T. Solving for A,

$$A = \frac{Pr}{1 - e^{-rT}}. \tag{4.17}$$

The ratio A/P—that is, the factor $r/(1 - e^{-rT})$ for finding the annuity from an initial investment—is called the *capital-recovery factor* (CRF). It represents the annual payment stream required to return the original investment of \$1 with a rate of return r. The reciprocal of the CRF is the present worth of the constant cash flow.

It should be noted that, while the concept of debt in establishing equivalence relationships has been deemphasized here, the relationships are valid for debt contracts as well as for all time-related values. Thus the CRF establishes the amount of the payment required to repay a loan by a constant repayment flow, including both principal and interest. Clearly, it is impossible to repay a debt by means of continuous payments. Payments must be made in discrete amounts on a periodic basis. The root of the word "annuity" means "year", and the term came to be used for a scheme of equal annual payments. Nevertheless, the continuous function is theoretically valid for a projected cash-flow return from an investment.

The CRF may be written in at least two other ways as mathematical identities. First, multiply the numerator and denominator by e^{rT}, in order to clear the negative exponent and so obtain

$$\text{CRF} = \frac{r}{1 - e^{-rT}} = \frac{re^{rT}}{e^{rT} - 1}. \tag{4.18}$$

This form is the one most commonly used.

Second, add and subtract r in the numerator and then factor. We obtain

$$\mathrm{CRF} = \frac{r - (r - re^{rT})}{e^{rT} - 1}$$

$$= r + \frac{r}{e^{rT} - 1}. \tag{4.19}$$

Any present worth may be readily converted to a *future worth*, F, by simply multiplying by the compounding factor e^{rT}:

$$F = Pe^{rT}, \tag{4.20}$$

from which we readily obtain the relationship between an annuity and a future worth. Substituting equation 4.20 into 4.17,

$$A = \frac{Fr}{e^{rT} - 1}. \tag{4.21}$$

The factor A/F is called the *sinking-fund factor* (SFF) and again, as related to debt contracts, represents the amount of a constant payment flow into a fund required to reach the amount F in time T. It will be observed that the SFF is simply the CRF minus r. (See equation 4.19.)

4.2.2 Special Limits on *T* and *r*

If the upper limit T goes to infinity, corresponding to an annuity in perpetuity, then equation 4.20 becomes

$$A = P \lim_{T \to \infty} \frac{r}{1 - e^{-rT}} \tag{4.22}$$

$$= P \frac{\dfrac{d}{dT}(re^{rT})}{\dfrac{d}{dT}(e^{rT} - 1)}$$

$$= Pr. \tag{4.23}$$

Equation 4.21 becomes

$$A = F \lim_{T \to \infty} \frac{r}{e^{rT} - 1} = 0. \tag{4.24}$$

These results are intuitively reasonable. If there is never any return of the original investment, the only return will be the interest on the investment.

Let us now change the lower limit from zero to some finite future point in time at which the cash flow starts, say B (Figure 4.6). We need only reevaluate the integral within the upper and lower limits. Let us define the upper limit as $B + T$. The present worth of the cash flow at B (i.e., shifting the origin to B) will be as given in equation 4.17. However, we wish to have the present worth moved back in time, so we merely shift the entire flow by multiplying by e^{-rB}:

$$P(0) = \int_{B}^{T+B} y(t)e^{-rt}\, dt$$

$$= e^{-rB} \int_{0}^{T} y(t)e^{-rt}\, dt. \tag{4.25}$$

We now evaluate the limits of the annuity as r goes to zero. Equation 4.21 becomes

$$A = \lim_{r \to 0} \frac{Fr}{e^{rT} - 1}$$

$$= \frac{\dfrac{d}{dr}(r)}{\dfrac{d}{dr}(e^{rT} - 1)} = \frac{F}{T}. \tag{4.26}$$

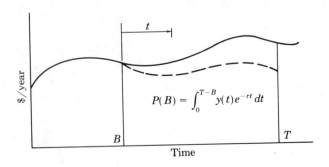

$$P(B) = \int_{0}^{T-B} y(t)e^{-rt}\, dt$$

Figure 4.6 Cash flow starting at B.

Equation 4.17 becomes

$$A = \lim_{r \to 0} \frac{Pre^{rT}}{e^{rT} - 1}$$

$$= P\frac{\frac{d}{dr}(e^{rT})}{\frac{d}{dr}(e^{rT} - 1)} = \frac{P}{T}.$$ (4.27)

4.2.3 Useful Special Functions

The standardized relationships between A, F, and P are very useful for interchanging any of these variables. However, there are many cases for which other functions may be more representative of the cash flows that are of concern than is the highly specialized one of the constant cash-flow case.

It is noteworthy that equation 4.9 is the Laplace transform. A number of writers have developed methodologies that take advantage of this relationship. However, use of the Laplace transform in practice may be of limited value, because of the need to make specific year-to-year cash-flow estimates rather than estimates of entire cash-flow functions.

There are many situation for which a growth function typifies the kind of cash flow that occurs in practice. Growth is typically characterized by an exponential function. For a growth rate g and an initial amount A,

$$y(t) = Ae^{gt}.$$ (4.28)

Substituting this into equation 4.17 and solving results in a function identical to equation 4.19 except that $(r - g)$ is substituted for r:

$$P = \frac{A(r - g)}{1 - e^{(-r+g)T}}.$$ (4.29)

One further useful function is linear growth, or what is sometimes called a gradient cash flow:

$$y(t) = Bt.$$ (4.30)

Substituting in equation 4.19 results in

$$P = \int Bte^{-rt}\,dt, \tag{4.31}$$

and solving, we have

$$P = B\frac{1 - rT}{r^2 e^{-rT}}. \tag{4.32}$$

4.3 TRANSFORMATION OF CASH FLOWS

As shown above, the area under the discounted cash-flow function is the present worth of the entire cash-flow stream from time zero to a defined time limit T. This area represents the equivalent of the value of a point investment I at $t = 0$. Any other area, spread out in any way one might choose, but equal to I, would be an equivalent discounted cash flow. If the discounting process were now reversed by multiplying by e^{rt}, the function so obtained would become a new undiscounted cash flow, representing a value exactly equivalent to the original cash flow. What we would have accomplished is simply a change in shape of the original cash flow. In other words, we would have defined a function $y'(t)$ such that

$$P = \int y(t)D(U, t)\,dt = \int y'(t)D(U, t)\,dt. \tag{4.33}$$

An example will clarify this. Let us start with an easy function for $y'(t)$ by making $y'(t) = A$, a constant cash flow (i.e., an annuity). Using the standard continuous exponential discount function e^{-rt}, we have

$$P = \int y(t)e^{-rt}\,dt = \int Ae^{-rt}\,dt. \tag{4.34}$$

Solving,

$$A = \frac{r}{1 - e^{-rT}}\int y(t)e^{-rt}\,dt. \tag{4.35}$$

An example is shown diagrammatically in Figure 4.7.

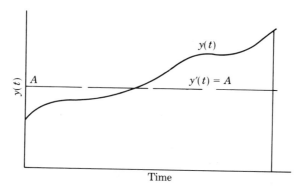

Figure 4.7 Cash-flow transformation.

4.4 CONTINUOUS VERSUS DISCRETE DISCOUNTING

Up to this point, we have assumed a continuous discount function and a continuous cash-flow function. However, the convention in the past has been to use discrete functions for both the discount function and the cash flow. The reason for this is in the origin of discounting practices. The first writers in engineering economics were much more concerned with financial feasibility than with evaluation. Financing often involved debt and contractual arrangements for repayment of it. Therefore early time-value concepts were predicated on debt models which required compound-interest calculations, in which interest was compounded at discrete time intervals. Interest for any part of a compounding period was computed by linear proportionality. It was natural that this practice led to the development of discrete discounting of future cash flows.

Quite apart from questions of tradition, estimations of cash flows are usually more readily made on the basis of discrete year-to-year estimates than by defining a continuous function. This estimating procedure is likely to continue as a practical matter. It may sometimes be easier to define cash flows in continuous rather than discrete form, but normally the discrete form will be more convenient. However, even with discrete estimates of cash flow, continuous discounting can be employed. In practice, cash flow may be estimated discretely and then discounted, using either the continuous function or the discrete function according to preference.

An important question arises with the use of discrete cash-flow estimates: at what point within the time period is the discrete payment made? Usually this point is taken to be the end of the period, and therefore discrete formulas are all based on end-of-period amounts. However it is a simple matter to convert any formula based on end-of-period payments to one based on beginning-of-period payments. For that matter, by proper time-value adjustments, any intermediate time point within the period can be selected. The end-of-period convention reflects the formal manner in which debt contracts are written. Since, in practice, cash flow is likely to be distributed throughout the period, it may be more sensible to use a convention based on lumping all the disbursements into mid-period payments. Before showing how this can be accomplished, it is necessary to consider how the formulas for the continuous case transform into the discrete case. The algebra for doing this is shown in Appendix C.

4.4.1 The Discrete Formulas

In its discrete form, equation 4.15 becomes

$$P = \sum_{j=1}^{n} \frac{y_i}{(1 + i)^j} \qquad (4.36)$$

for discrete discounting and discrete payments, and

$$P = \sum_{j=1}^{n} y_i e^{-rj} \qquad (4.37)$$

for continuous discounting and discrete payments.

Although it is conventional to use integer periods, there is no reason why the discrete times in equations 4.36 and 4.37 should not be fractional values.

EXAMPLE:

With $i = 10\%$ and r set at the equivalent value for i, find the present worth of the following cash flows:

1.

AMOUNT	TIME
$1000	0
250	3
175	7

2. The same as case 1, but using continuous discounting.

3. The same as case 1, but changing the third payment time from 7.0 periods to 7.5 periods.

SOLUTION

All three solutions are now shown together in a tabulation.

- *Step 1: Equivalence of rates.* If $i = 0.10$, then the equivalent r is $\ln(1 + i) = .0953$.
- *Step 2: Tabulation*

j	AMOUNT	e^{-rj}	$1/(1 + i)^j$	$y_j{}^{-rj}$	$y_j/(1 + i)^j$
0	1000	1.0	1.0	1000	1000
3	250	0.751	0.751	188	188
7	175	0.513	0.513	90	90
Sum				1278	1278

- *Step 3:* Replace 7 with the fractional 7.5. The factor for both the discrete and continuous cases is 0.489, showing that the fractional value for j makes no difference in the result.

This is a trivial example, but the arithmetic shows that the results are identical for the discrete and continuous approaches. It is true only because the discount rates for the two cases were equivalent. There would have been some discrepancy if both i and r were taken to have the same value of 10%.

The conventional use of discrete functions requires that payments be made at the end of each time period. The effect of a continuous flow extending over a single time period is slightly different from the same discrete amount occurring at the end of the period. For example, $1.00 per day for one year is not equivalent to $365.00 paid at the end of the year. The equivalent end-of-period amount must be the future worth of the flow over a single period. Thus

$$A(\text{discrete}) = A(\text{cont})\frac{e^r - 1}{r}, \qquad (4.38)$$

but

$$e^r - 1 = i.$$

Therefore

$$A(\text{discrete}) = A(\text{cont})\frac{i}{r}. \tag{4.39}$$

More realistically, estimated yearly revenue or expenditure streams are spread out through the year, and so a mid-period estimate may be a better approximation of a discrete cash flow than would be the end-of-period estimate.

Consider the equivalence in value between the mid-period discrete amount and the continuous constant flow over the period. For $t = 0.5$,

$$A(\text{discrete}) = A(\text{cont})\frac{e^{r/2} - e^{-r/2}}{r}. \tag{4.40}$$

For most values of r, the ratio in equation 4.40 is so close to unity that it may be ignored. For example, for $r = 20\%$,

$$A(\text{discrete}) = 1.00167 \times A(\text{cont}).$$

For lower values of r the ratio is even closer to unity. This means that, for practical purposes, discrete estimates of cash flows can be made and continuous formulas for discounting can be employed. However if it is deemed desirable to retain the end-of-period convention, all the equations should be adjusted in accordance with the ratio of equation 4.39. For example, the capital-recovery factor would be

$$A(\text{discrete}) = P\frac{i}{1 - e^{-rt}}. \tag{4.41}$$

Likewise, for any of the other conventional factors, the end-of-period requirement is satisfied by simply replacing r with i whenever the discount rate in the formula appears outside the exponential. If discrete cash flows are used, it is probably better to depict them as shown in Figure 4.8.

Increasingly, financial institutions are utilizing continuous interest rates in computing interest. Actually they quote their rates as daily rates which, as already demonstrated, are essentially the

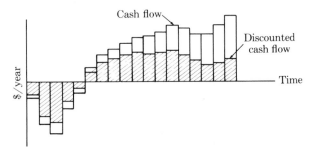

Figure 4.8 Cash-flow diagram.

same as continuous rates. Furthermore, perceptions of changing value with time are continuous. There is a natural continuity to time. For these reasons it may become increasingly desirable to use the continuous discount form.

Perhaps the most persuasive reason for using continuous discounting is the treatment of inflation. Inflation is continuous. In dealing with inflation, inflation rates and interest rates are additive. If continuous rates are used, they can be added together. If the mathematics is discrete, the two rates cannot simply be added, as will be shown in Chapter 8 on Inflation.

4.5 NOTATION FOR FACTORS

The foregoing development established a set of factors for relating three fundamental variables and two parameters. The variables are present worth, future worth, and annuity value. The parameters are the time and the interest or discount rate.

Only two variables may be handled at one time. In the interest of computational ease and in order to provide a scheme that makes it unmistakably clear what transformation is desired, a simple notational scheme has been adopted. One of its major attractions is a mnemonic feature that has resulted in the scheme being universally accepted.

It is conventional simply to list the variables and parameters within a pair of parentheses. The variables are listed first, in the form of a ratio signifying what variable is desired, given the other. This is followed by the discount rate and time, separated by commas. Thus for 12% discrete interest and a time of 15 years, the factor would be designated as

$$(P/A, i, n) = (P/A, 12, 15).$$

This is read "P, given A for i and n".

It is desirable to use this same notation for continuous as well as for the discrete cases. In order to differentiate the continuous from the discrete case, we use braces—e.g., $\{P/A, r, t\}$—instead of parentheses.

EXAMPLE:

A loan is arranged for $10,000 to be repaid in equal monthly payments, comprising principal and interest. The borrower has decided to repay the balance of the loan on the due date of the 20th payment. Interest on the loan is at a nominal 15% per year, and the life of the loan is 42 months.

SOLUTION

The monthly interest rate is $15/12 = 1.25\%$ per month. This is a true rate. It is equivalent to an effective rate of

$$100 \times \{(1 + 0.0125)^{12} - 1\} = 16.075\% \text{ per year.}$$

The monthly payment is

$$A = P(A/P, 1.25, 42) = 10,000 \times 0.18252 = \$182.52.$$

Since the borrower wishes to repay the balance in 20 months, the problem reduces to finding the present worth of the remaining 22 payments. However, a question arises at this point. Has he just made his 20th payment, or is he about to make it? If he has made it, we have

$$P(20 \text{ months}) = A \times (P/A, 1.25, 22).$$

Note that this is the same as shifting to a new zero time 20 months into the future. Thus

$$P = 307.47 \times 19.131 = \$5882.27.$$

If he has not made the 20th payment, he must add another $182.52 to this total.

There is a variety of ways we could have reached the same answer. One way, of course, would be to compute the unpaid balance from year to year, but this would take excessive time. We could also have formulated the solution in one step:

$$P(20) = P(0) \times (A/P, 1.25, 42) \times (P/A, 1.25, 22).$$

As still another alternative, we could have found the future worth of the payments already made and subtracted this from the original principal, moved forward in time to the 20th month:

$$F(20) = P(0) \times (F/P, 1.25, 20) = \$12820.37,$$

$$F(A) = A \times (F/A, 1.25, 20) = 307.47 \times 22.56 = \underline{\quad 6937.38,}$$

$$\text{unpaid balance} = \text{difference} = \$\ 5882.99.$$

The slight difference in the final answer is due to a rounding error.

Note that as long as you bring the dollar amounts to a common reference time point for adding or subtracting amounts, you will never get into trouble.

4.5.1 Techniques for Solving for Time and Rate

Solution for one of the three variables (P, F, and A) is straightforward. The above examples are typical for problems in which both r and t are specified. However, it is often necessary to solve either for the discount (interest) rate, or for time. In many such problems the only possible technique utilizes some form of iterative solution. The techniques for doing this are most readily demonstrated by means of examples.

EXAMPLE:

Find the rate of interest (continuous and discrete) such that money doubles in 10 years.

SOLUTION

$$F/P = 2 = e^{10r} = (1 + i)^{10}$$

for both continuous and discrete forms. Taking logarithms,

$$10r = \ln 2 \quad \text{and} \quad 10\ln(1 + i) = \ln 2,$$
$$r = 0.069315 \quad \text{and} \quad i = \exp(0.1 \ln 2) - 1 = 0.07177,$$

or in percent, $r = 6.9315\%$ and $i = 7.177\%$.

EXAMPLE:

Find the time necessary for money to double at an interest rate of 10%.

SOLUTION

This is similar to the preceding problem:

$$0.1n = \ln 2 \quad \text{and} \quad n\ln(1.10) = \ln 2.$$

Thus $n = 6.9315$ years for continuous discounting, and $n = 7.273$ years for discrete discounting.

It is worth noting that, for continuous interest, r and t are interchangeable. A good rule of thumb for finding either the interest or the time needed for doubling the principal, is simply to divide 70 by one parameter or the other. This is a reasonable approximation. The corresponding number for tripling is 110.

EXAMPLE:

Find the interest rate needed for an investment of $10,000 to buy an annuity of $2000 per year for 12 years.

SOLUTION

For continuous interest

$$\frac{A}{P} = r + \frac{r}{e^{rt} - 1}.$$

The solution requires making a first guess for r, followed by a series of successive approximations. The easiest first guess is $r = 0$. We will use this guess for one part of the equation and solve for r in the other, which we then use as a second guess. We repeat the process until the r from the solution equals the guessed r.

Rearranging,

$$r_1 = \frac{A}{P} - \frac{r_0}{e^{r_0 t} - 1}$$

r_1 in the end must equal r_0. The limit of $r/(e^{rt} - 1)$ as r goes to 0 is $1/t$. Thus $r_0 = 2{,}000/10{,}000 - 1/10 = 0.10$. Using this value for r_0 and substituting again in the second term,

$$r_1 = 0.2 - \frac{0.1}{e^1 - 1} = 0.2 - 0.0368 = 0.1632.$$

Making a second substitution results in

$$r_2 = 0.2 - \frac{0.1632}{e^{1.632} - 1} = 0.1603.$$

Likewise, the third substitution is

$$r_3 = 0.2 - \frac{0.1603}{e^{1.603} - 1} = 0.1596.$$

If we now compare the third approximation with the result of the third substitution we find that the difference is quite small. Convergence is very rapid. The result to four significant figures is $r = 0.1594$, or 15.94%. We may continue the process to obtain any degree of precision desired.

The reader is left the exercise of completing the solution for the discrete rate. The answer is $i = 15.094\%$. However there is a difference in the annuities because, in the case of discrete interest, the annuity calls for end-of-year payments, rather than payments distributed over the year as in the continuous case.

4.6   SUMMARY TABLE OF FACTORS

The factors commonly used are summarized in Table 4.2.

Table 4.2 Time-Value Factors

NAME OF FACTOR	MNEMONIC SYMBOL	FORMULA — DISCRETE	FORMULA — CONTINUOUS
Single payment:			
Present worth	$(P/F, i, n)$	$1/(1+i)^n$	e^{-rt}
Future worth	$(F/P, i, n)$	$(1+i)^n$	e^{rt}
Annuity:			
Capital recovery	$(A/P, i, n)$	$\dfrac{i}{1-(1+i)^{-n}}$	$\dfrac{r}{1-e^{-rt}}$
or	$i+(A/F, i, n)$	$i+\dfrac{i}{(1+i)^n-1}$	$r+\dfrac{r}{e^{rt}-1}$
Present worth	$(P/A, i, n)$	$\dfrac{1-(1+i)^{-n}}{i}$	$\dfrac{1-e^{-rt}}{r}$
Future worth	$(F/A, i, n)$	$\dfrac{(1+i)^n-1}{i}$	$\dfrac{e^{rt}-1}{r}$
Sinking fund	$(A/F, i, n)$	$\dfrac{i}{(1+i)^n-1}$	$\dfrac{r}{e^{rt}-1}$

4.7 RECAPITULATION

This chapter has introduced the basic concepts of time value. Amounts of money at future times are not equivalent in value to a corresponding amount in the present. The future amount must be discounted in order to establish equivalence.

The factor by which a future amount is multiplied is determined by equating the utility of the prospective amount with the utility of the present amount.

1. The basic discount function is

$$D(t) = e^{-rt},$$

and its discrete equivalent is

$$D(t) = (1+i)^{-n}.$$

2. Discounting is extended to cash flows by integrating over time.

3. Money amounts can be transformed at will to any other desired flows or amounts by use of the time-value relationships. Useful functions are provided to relate F, P, and A.

4. Care must be taken to specify whether discrete amounts are being considered at end of period, at some other time within the time period, or over the whole time period.

4.8 PROBLEMS

1. It is instructive to see how the different factors vary. Therefore plot:

   a. P/F for $r = 5\%$, 10%, and 15%, and for $t = 0$ to 20 (continuous).

   b. P/F for $i = 5\%$, 10%, and 15%, and for $t = 0$ to 20 (discrete).

   c. A/P for $r = 5\%$, 10%, and 15%, and for $t = 0$ to 20 (continuous).

   d. A/P for $i = 5\%$, 10%, and 15%, and for $t = 0$ to 20 (discrete).

2. Using the data from Problem 1, plot:

   a. The percentage difference between $\{P/F, r, t\}$ and $(P/F, i, n)$.

   b. The percentage difference between $\{A/P, r, t\}$ and $(A/P, i, n)$.

3. Plot $p(t)$ (the discounted cash flow) for:

   a. A constant cash flow, $A = \$100$, $r = 10\%$, and $t = 0$ to 20.

   b. A growing cash flow, $y(t) = \$100e^{0.05t}$, $r = 10\%$, and $t = 0$ to 20.

4. Plot:

   a. $p(t)$ for $y(t) = Ae^{0.10t}$, for $r = 5\%$, 10%, and 15%.

   b. Discuss the conditions under which $p(t)$ remains finite as t goes to infinity.

5. What cash flow, starting in C years and continuing forever, is equivalent to a cash flow of $1.00 per year from $t = 0$ to $t = C$? Plot this result for a range of values for r and C.

6. Smith borrowed $10,000 for 30 years, to be repaid in equal annual payments of principal and interest. The interest rate is 12% (discrete) per year. On the date that his 10th payment is due, he decided to repay the unpaid balance of the loan. There is no penalty for early repayment. What is the amount of his closing payment?

7. What is the present worth of $1000 to be paid at the end of 7 years plus an annuity for 5 years with the first payment to start in 5 years, and minus a million dollars to be repaid in 100 years? The interest rate is 12%. Before doing this problem state which you think you would prefer to receive, the scheduled payout or the repayment of one million dollars.

8. In recent years of high interest rates it has become common for a man, desiring to sell his house, to accept a mortgage for part of his asking price, with interest at a lower-than-market interest rate. Effectively, he would be taking a reduction in his price, often without recognizing that he was doing so. Frequently such financing arrangements required a balloon (lump sum) payment for the balance of the mortgage in a specified time, which is less than the full amortization time (i.e., the life of the loan). Determine the effective value of such a mortgage at a 12% interest rate when the market rate is 17%. The loan is for 30 years; payments are due at the end of each month. Note that the interest rates on such loans are quoted as nominal annual rates but are computed on a monthly basis.

9. A common practice of financing consumer purchases, such as automobiles, is to compute interest as "simple interest", by taking the stated rate and multiplying by the number of years over which the loan is to be repaid. This full amount of interest is added to the principal of the loan, and the total is divided by the number of months to determine the monthly payment. For example, consider financing the purchase of a car. You wish to finance $8000 of the purchase

price. This is to be repaid in 42 equal monthly payments. The dealer says you will have to pay only 10% interest, and so your payment would be

$$\frac{8000 + (800 \times 3.5)}{42} = \$257.12.$$

He also points out that if you should ever wish to pay the balance early, the interest would be refunded to you on a pro rata basis. That is, you would get back some interest in direct proportion to the time remaining on the contract.

a. What is the true monthly interest rate that the buyer would be paying?

b. What is the nominal annual rate?

c. What is the effective annual rate?

d. Just as a matter of curiosity, what would be the effective rate for a ten-year compounding period?

e. What would the continuous daily rate be?

f. What would your true monthly interest rate have been if you had repaid the loan with a single lump-sum payment when the 20th payment came due?

10. Find a function for a payment S at the end of N years that is equivalent to an annuity A with interest i and life H.

a. Using this function, solve for the case where $A = \$1000$, $i = 10\%$, $S = 10$ years, and $H = 20$ years.

b. Note that for the example chosen, $S = \frac{1}{2}H$. This might lead one to infer that S is the simple sum of A. Compare the answers for parts a and b, and explain the difference.

11. Show that $P/A = Pi$ for $n \to \infty$.

12. Determine the equivalent growth cash-flow function, Ae^{gt}, for T years for an annuity of A that extends for H years.

13. Transform the cash-flow function

$$y(t) = Bt + Ce^{gt}$$

into an annuity A.

14. Transform the cash-flow function

$$y(t) = A \qquad \text{for} \quad t = 10 \text{ to } 30$$

into

$$y(t) = B \qquad \text{for} \quad t = 0 \text{ to } 10.$$

15. Develop a formula for an annuity based on continuous interest, but requiring discrete payments, payable at the end of each m years.

○

○

CHAPTER FIVE

○ # *A Unifying Approach*

○ *to the Evaluation*

○ *of Investments*

○

○

In Chapter 4 we learned how to establish the equivalence of value for different cash flows without any consideration of where the cash flows originate or how the parameters of the discount function are determined. The evaluation methodology requires utilization of the time-value relationships of Chapter 4, and in addition:

- Recognition of the investor's point of view.

- Identification of investment alternatives.

- Prediction of cash flow.

- Determination of the discount rate.

- Consideration of reinvestment.

- Assumptions about termination, abandonment, or replacement.

- Treatment of risk.

In practice, many methods have been employed for comparison of alternative investments or for determination of the suitability of a proposed new project. The principal methods will be discussed at some length later in this chapter, but in order to place them in proper perspective, the general principles on which they are all based will first be developed. Actually, as will be shown, the methods are all essentially the same, provided that the assumptions are carefully and consistently formulated. Different conclusions can be reached by these various methods, but the reasons for these differences can always be traced to the assumptions used. Often assumptions are not explicitly stated and therefore go unrecognized. This can create a false impression of basic differences in the methods.

The principal methods are:

1. Present worth [or discounted cash flow (DCF) or net present value (NPV)].

2. Annualized cash flow (or equivalent annual cost).

3. Internal rate of return (IRR) [or return on investment (ROI)].

4. External rate of return (ERR).

5. Payback period.

6. Benefit/cost ratio (B/C).

An approach that unifies all of these methods is presented here.

5.1 PERSPECTIVE OF THE INVESTMENT — WHOSE VIEWPOINT?

First let us identify the investor and his objectives. It should not be taken for granted that it is understood who the investor is, even though this might seem obvious. When reference is made to "the investor", this means the party in whose interest the investment is to be made. The investor may be an individual, a corporation, or a societal entity such as a municipality, a state, or the entire country.

The individual investor is readily identified. However, his objective may be not simply the highest return on investment, but something more complex. Typically he already has resources invested so that any alternative investments he may be considering represent only a portion of his wealth. This raises a few questions:

1. Is he seeking to derive income from his capital while maintaining his capital intact?
2. Does he wish income that will consume his capital in some specified (or unspecified) time?
3. Does he wish to attain a specific sum of money at some specified future date?
4. Does he merely wish to realize some desired rate of capital growth?
5. What is his attitude toward the acceptance of risk?

These and other questions are pertinent to the decision confronting him.

For the time being, in order to make the problem more manageable, we will exclude risk, which will be covered in Chapter 9. This means that we treat all cash flows deterministically until we reach Chapter 9. But keep in mind that in reality all future cash flows are probabilistic.

As a very simplified case, consider investing available capital in an investment that will generate a constant cash flow for n years and will then be terminated. If the investor desires income that does not erode his capital, he will need to have some plan for reinvesting a part of the cash flow year by year. When the investment is terminated, he must reinvest any remaining capital at that time. The same reinvestment problem arises, in varying degrees, for questions 2, 3, and 4 above. Thus the first investment decision preconditions a chain of subsequent decisions that, in some way, must be taken into account when making the first one. Any alternative that limits the latitude of the investor in making subsequent decisions will be less attractive than one that leaves him greater flexibility. All these things must, in some way, be considered in any evaluation of an investment made in the interest of the investor. His perspective is a key ingredient in the investment decision.

5.1.1 The Corporate Perspective

In theory, the corporation is a legal individual. In practice, the corporation has a utility function representing a complex interaction of all individuals involved in the affairs of the corporation. These include stockholders, bondholders, managers and, finally, employees. Each has an interest, which could influence investment decisions in different ways. Theoretically all decisions are presumed to be made in the interest of the corporation owners (stockholders), but this, of course, is unrealistic. Management decisions are made by a manager, who may be interested mainly in enhancing the investing public's view of the corporation during his tenure in office. Thus short-term reported profits are probably a much stronger motive for the manager than is long-term corporate growth. The bondholder is interested in profit only as an indication that the corporation is healthy enough to ensure maintenance of the interest on the debt he is owed. The employee may have feelings of loyalty and pride in the corporation but, when it comes to either increasing profit or raising wages, he can be expected to opt for higher wages.

Taken as a complex of both conflicting and complementary objectives, the overall objective of the corporation might establish its highest priority as survival, and its secondary priority as steady growth. These two objectives, in themselves, represent a tradeoff between risk and reward. The higher the rate of growth the corporation strives for, the greater must be the acceptance of survival risk.

Return on investments is perceived differently by stockholders and bondholders. The stockholder receives dividends, on which he is immediately confronted with a tax obligation. His net return is what he keeps after taxes. For this reason, if he is in a high tax bracket, he may prefer the company to pay as small a dividend as possible, so that he can realize his return in the form of capital gain from an increased price of his stock. However, if he depends on dividend income for living expenses, he will prefer the income now. Companies that have a long tradition of paying dividends attract investors who are income-oriented, and this, in turn, tends to create a feedback influence on management policy.

Corporations with a high proportion of their capital in the form of debt (i.e., bonds) will likely have a more variable pattern of reported profit from year to year than those with little debt. Investors will perceive stock in a corporation with a large debt as being riskier than stock in which debt financing is absent. A different class of stockholder will be attracted to the riskier than to the less risky stock.

Legally, the distinction between a stockholder and a bondholder is that one is an owner and the other a lender, but in an economic sense, the distinction is between a risk acceptor and a risk avoider. In any event the objectives of the firm, in terms of desired rate of return, are influenced by some integrating mechanism that reflects these diverse interests.

5.1.2 The Public Perspective

While the interests of the constituency in the corporation are, by and large, somewhat diffuse, it is recognized that the underlying objective is profit maximization. However, there are some people today who feel that the corporation has a larger social responsibility than this and that it should accept, at least, a modicum of social cost beyond what is necessary for maximizing its profits. This is not a universal view.

When it comes to government, there is no question about the basic interest that is supposed to be represented. It is the public interest. The question does arise as to what constituency within the general public is the appropriate one for each particular investment. It does not seem reasonable, for example, that the people of Alabama should be taxed to provide a benefit solely for the people of Oregon. This would represent an unacceptable transfer payment. On the other hand, some transfer-payment effect is not only desirable but inevitable.

Apart from this necessary lack of differentiation of public interest, there is still the question of a profit objective. However ill defined the constituency for which a public project may by undertaken, the collection of individuals constituting that constituency is, theoretically, making a choice to invest in the public project rather than in individual private ventures. Collectively, they must weigh that choice in terms of opportunity for profit in exactly the same way as for alternative private ventures.

This principle is neither generally recognized nor generally accepted. As a result public projects have often been justified by using discount rates based on interest rates that the government had to pay for borrowed funds. This use of borrowing rates as an evaluation basis has also been utilized for local agencies, such as municipal utilities. Publicly owned utilities are fundamentally no different from privately owned utilities that usually provide an identical kind of service. People tend to lose sight of the fact that in one case the stockholders are, *de facto*, the rate payers living in the area, and in the other they are private investors who are more widely dispersed.

5.2 IDENTIFICATION OF ALTERNATIVES

The investor is constantly in search of new investment alternatives that will further his objectives. Any money received as income in excess of direct operating cost must be invested immediately, though for a time it may be "parked" in a temporary investment, such as a bank account yielding little or no interest, while the investor searches for and evaluates his alternatives.

In a corporation there are many ways in which existing operations can be improved, in order to either reduce costs or enhance revenues. These range from minor improvements to major projects. All are competing for a limited amount of capital, which must be budgeted in such a way as to maximize the overall return, bearing in mind the points of view described above. One of these alternatives is to keep some, or all, of the capital in liquid form. This capital can be expected to earn the going market rate of return. Such funds are invested in activities that are external to the mainstream investments of the firm. Some funds are allocated to a mix of other investments within the firm, which have been earning a corresponding mix of returns, depending on their various degrees of success. These other investments are likewise external to the project of concern and can be expected to realize an average rate of return consistent with what the firm has earned in the past. This average external rate of return is the opportunity cost of the firm's capital. It is called the *opportunity cost of capital* (OCC). Money invested in a specific capital project should earn at least the OCC rate before the project can be justified at all.

In contrast, the return on the investment in a proposed project is *internal* to the project. Thus it is appropriately called the *internal rate of return* (IRR).

There is an important distinction between liquid capital, external to the project, and capital that is budgeted for a capital project. Once money is committed to a capital project it becomes locked in. If things do not turn out as well as expected, there may be later opportunities for salvaging some of the investment by revising the investment plan, but essentially, these later opportunities represent new investment decisions. On the other hand, the capital in the external opportunity is usually more liquid and can be mobilized for other purposes at will. Therefore some adjustment in the OCC rate is needed to provide for comparability. This adjustment may be made, arbitrarily, by simply specifying a reasonable premium to be added to the OCC. Sometimes the rate so defined is called a *hurdle rate* or *minimum acceptable rate of return*. A more rational way of making an adjustment for lack of liquidity will be discussed in Chapter 9, under Risk.

5.2.1 The Single Project

The single independent project reduces to the decision to undertake an investment or to reject it—"go, or no go". While this does not seem to be a comparison of alternatives, it is actually a choice between investment in the project and in some other unspecified external alternative. Presumably, capital funds are available or can be arranged for, or the project could not be considered at all. Therefore, if the project is rejected, it is rejected in favor of some other investment. This other investment, although not identified, will be expected to yield the OCC. This external opportunity forms the basis for a comparison.

5.2.2 Alternative Projects

Evaluation of alternative projects usually reduces to the conditional decision:

> *Given that, in any event, only one alternative is to be undertaken, which is the best one?*

This means that the investor needs to consider only those features of the various alternatives that differ from one to another. Implicitly, however, there is still the unspecified external opportunity that must be included in the set. The single difference between this external investment and all the other opportunities is its rate of return (OCC). This is taken into account by discounting the cash flows of the various alternatives, using the OCC, or by comparing the IRRs of the alternatives with the OCC.

5.3 PREDICTION

An investment decision is always made in the present, based on prospects in the future. The past is irrelevant, except to the extent that it may have added to our wisdom. All past costs and benefits are **sunk**. They can have no bearing on any investment decision. Unfortunately, this very fundamental principle is often violated in practice. It is so important that it deserves restating:

> *Sunk costs and sunk benefits* **never** *should be considered in making an investment decision.*

Only the future is relevant, and the future must be predicted. We are forced to make estimates of cash flows that will result from an investment decision. Strictly speaking, all that is required is an estimate of the differences that will eventuate as a result of the decision. If the problem is to compare the desirability of several alternative ways of accomplishing some desired result, then the only cash flows to be estimated are those pertaining to specific alternatives. All other cash flows, unaffected by the decision, can be ignored. In deciding whether or not to make an investment at all, an important question is:

> What is the cash flow *with* the project versus what it will be *without* the project?

Many external factors influence cash flow. These can affect comparative alternatives in different ways, and so are relevant considerations in the evaluation. For example, one alternative may seem very attractive if the economy is booming, while another may be markedly better in a recession.

5.3.1 Predicting the Economic Environment

A project considered for investment is embedded in the economy of the individual or firm, which is in turn embedded in the larger economy of an industry, which is part of a region or state, which is part of the country and, finally, of the world. All have some bearing on how well the investment succeeds.

How extensive the evaluation of the external economic environment need be, depends on the size and complexity of the investment being considered. The question may be, simply, which machine to purchase for a particular purpose, given that something must be done to keep a production line going. This hardly justifies a long and involved analysis of where the United States economy is headed. On the other hand, some suppositions about economic factors such as inflation are necessary, even if only the implicit one that prices will remain the same.

5.3.2 Growth

Growth in the economic environment is among the most important factors to consider. Growth establishes the conditions for capacity expansion. When capacity limits are reached, new decisions to replace, modify, or expand capacity come into play. Growth rates to be considered are those of:

- The economy.
- The industry.
- The firm.

To begin with, the growth of the economy may almost be taken as a *given*. In some respects the larger the economic unit under consideration, the easier it is to estimate its direction. Except for one discontinuity of economic growth—the Great Depression of the 1930s—the United States economy has grown at a remarkably steady rate of 3% per year for over a hundred years. In light of this, it really makes little sense to assume that such growth will suddenly stop. On the other hand, there are periodic recessions. These do not affect the basic wisdom of an investment, but they may be very important in the timing of that investment. The many econometric models of the economy, currently in use, are excellent sources for such timing predictions.

Emerging industries, usually associated with new technology, grow at rates in the order of 15% to 20% per year until they reach some maturing level compatible with overall economic growth.

This high-growth phase is always typified by emergence of many new firms and a gradual concentration of the industry, as the less competitive fall by the way. The time perspective for investment evaluation is considerably affected by such factors.

5.4 ESTIMATION OF CASH FLOW

At some point it becomes necessary to make a detailed estimate of the cash-flow stream. It comprises two phases: the capital-investment outflow, followed at the startup of the project by the cash-return flow. The cash-return flow is positive, because in this phase the project is generating revenue. This flow is the difference between revenue and operating expenditures. The capital investment phase is broken into two parts:

- Investigation and design.
- Construction.

At any point in time, a decision may be reached to abandon the project. During design, before large amounts of funding have been committed, there usually are specific predetermined review points for making "go-ahead decisions".

A typical cash-flow pattern is illustrated in Figure 5.1.

Initial cash flow is normally small. Typically, limited funds are allocated for determining the desirability of the project and for the engineering investigation. Following this early study stage, and assuming a positive decision to proceed, the level of

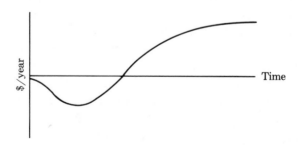

Figure 5.1 Cash flow.

engineering is increased. In many large-scale projects today, considerable time can elapse in obtaining approvals from various regulatory agencies. During this phase a sustaining engineering expense will continue, sometimes at a slightly lower level than during the design phase. Once the final go-ahead is given, expenditure levels increase dramatically during construction.

A period of startup follows the completion of construction or installation. Revenues begin then at a low level and build up more or less gradually to a planned operating level. Operating costs also commence at startup. Normally they will start sooner than revenues and will reach high levels at a faster rate. It is during this phase that operating costs tend to be higher than they will be later, because there is a necessary learning period for working out production problems.

Until revenues commence, cash flow consists of expenditures only. From the startup point on, the net cash flow is the difference between revenues and expenditures. Eventually, capacity output is reached, whereupon decisions must be made to increase capacity, or the project reaches maturity and output decays until the time comes to consider its abandonment. For either of these alternatives, this point of bifurcation of the outcome path is beyond the limit of visibility from the vantage of the initiating decision.

5.4.1 The Horizon or Explicit Planned Life

The horizon concept was introduced in Section 1.3. Traditionally, in economic evaluation, it has been utilized to establish a time limit beyond which all further revenue and expenditure are ignored. It is suggested here that this is unrealistic. We cannot see very far into the future, even under the most favorable circumstances. Optimistically, we might set the time limit for evaluation at the end of the foreseeable life expectancy of the physical system. However, for most successful projects, there is no finite life. Replacement and expansion are the normal order.

In the case of projects in established technologies, the life cycle is replicative. Even here, however, new developments will occur from one life cycle to the next. When new technologies are involved, obsolescence takes place very rapidly and the limit of visibility is correspondingly foreshortened. This indicates that, rather than setting a horizon time in the traditional sense, we arbitrarily set a planned time limit, up to which the estimates of revenues and expenditures are reasonable. Until this time, we can be quite explicit in our estimates. Beyond it, estimating becomes more speculative and subjective.

The life of the investment will normally extend well beyond the horizon time. In fact, the life will, more often than not, be infinite. If the investment is successful, the initial investment will give way to expansions and extensions. However, for practical purposes we must set some time limit for planning. We will call this the *planned life* of the project, with full realization that the use of the word "life" may tend to imply a finiteness that is not justified. In the opinion of the author, this is better than the implications of finiteness associated with the use of the term "horizon time".

5.4.2   The Expanding Variance in Estimates

The estimation of cash flows, up to the limit of visibility, provides us with expected values. However, we arrive at these expected values by extrapolation from past experience. In effect, we make a linear regression on past data. Refer to Figure 5.2.

Past experience can be represented as a set of data points. We may postulate a linear regression function, which can be extrapolated into the future. This will provide an expected-value function, AB, the equation for which is

$$y = \hat{a}t + \hat{b}. \tag{5.1}$$

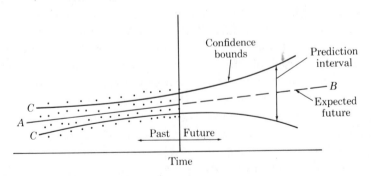

Figure 5.2   Extrapolation into the future.

The parameters $\hat{a}$ and $\hat{b}$ are expected values, with associated variances. Thus confidence bounds, for whatever confidence level one might choose, would be somewhat as represented by curves C. These confidence bounds on the function would extrapolate as divergent functions. The further into the future one extrapolates, the wider will be the variance about the expected value.

Viewed in another way, the smaller the deviation from the expected value, the lower the confidence one would have in the estimate. Furthermore, the more dispersed the data, the shorter will be the future time within which a prescribed level of confidence is reached. It is readily seen that one does not have to extrapolate very far before the confidence in the estimate deteriorates markedly. This limits the futurity of the horizon to no more than 5 to 10 years.

Two ways of circumventing this difficulty have been suggested (English 1972):

1. Beyond-the-horizon decision.

2. The aspiration approach.

We are not limited by the physical horizon in our ability to navigate. Neither need we be limited by the economic horizon in making economic decisions. We must cope with unforeseeable events as they develop.

5.4.3 Beyond the Horizon

When we make the decision to proceed with a project, we do so because we have a strong belief that we will satisfactorily surmount inevitable contingencies which must, by definition, remain unknown. There is always the risk that we will not resolve some unforeseen event and that, as a result, the project will fail. Failure means that the cash flow attributable to the project decays and eventually goes to zero. If such catastrophic events do not occur, then the cash flow will grow. Thus the growth path beyond the horizon will bifurcate at some unpredictable point (Figure 5.3).

If we assign a probability q of eventual success, and assume the worst case (bifurcation occurs at the horizon), then the present

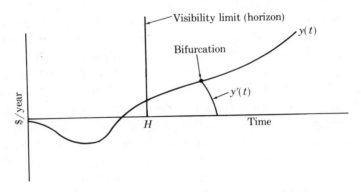

Figure 5.3 Cash flow beyond the horizon.

worth for the project will be

$$P = \int_0^H y(t)e^{-rt}\,dt + q\int_H^\infty y(t)e^{-rt}\,dt$$
$$+ (1 - q)\int_H^\infty y'(t)e^{-rt}\,dt. \tag{5.2}$$

The interesting aspect of this approach is that, given success, the cash flow is likely to be an exponential growth function. There will not be a foreseeable terminal date because, with success, expansion will occur as capacity limits of the initial project are attained. If the rate of growth is equal to or greater than the discount rate, then the value of the second term becomes indefinitely large. Correspondingly, for the third term of equation 5.2, the value becomes small. Because of the necessarily subjective nature of all values beyond the horizon, the third term may be ignored.

5.4.4 The Aspiration Approach

The aspiration approach is a means of avoiding the basic predictability problem. Rather than predicting the future, an exercise often claimed to be impossible, we simply aspire toward ultimate success and postulate those conditions that ensure success. This will mean assuming a suitable economic environment, compatible with normal economic growth. Having done this, the conditions necessary for project success must be examined, the feasibility of attainment analyzed, and specific goals identified. This establishes the aspiration level.

In a sense, such an approach has the characteristics of self-fulfilling predictions. The aspiration determines what needs to be done. The actions taken raise the probability that what was predicted will eventually be realized.

The decision to proceed with a project is seldom unanimous. There will usually be some who oppose the proposed project from the outset and predict its ultimate failure. Such a situation is typical of many long-range programs involving new technologies. Inevitably, as time passes, problems arise, which strengthen the position of the opponents of the project. At the same time, the proponents are stimulated to harden their defensive arguments. One or the other faction will eventually prove successful, and either the project aspiration is achieved or the project fails. It is probably just such a phenomenon as this that explains the bifurcation described above.

5.5 EVALUATION OF THE SINGLE PROJECT

We have been establishing the preconditions for evaluation. The decision to proceed with a project sets in motion a chain of events, resulting in a cash flow (a stream of expenditures, followed by a return stream) which theoretically extends to infinity. The present decision to accept the project may be expected to lead to a series of follow-on decisions, which in principle extend its life indefinitely. However, for practical reasons we must arbitrarily specify a conclusion to the project. This conclusion to the project requires a *terminal time*, or *planned life*, at the end of which we must specify a *terminal value* for the project. The terminal value must be estimated on the basis of consideration of what may follow the planned life. Most text books use the term "salvage value" in place of "terminal value". However, this connotes abandonment which should be considered only as one possible option. Whatever the terminal value is, the cash flow beyond the terminal time will be zero. Thus the use of a terminal value establishes a finite limit or planned life for the project.

We now transform the cash flow into a discounted cash-flow stream and find its equivalent present worth, using the OCC as the discount rate. In Chapter 4, we demonstrated how this is done. Equation 4.15 is

$$P = \int y(t)e^{-rt}\,dt.$$

This present worth is compared with that for the external reference opportunity, and if it is larger, the project is chosen over the external investment, regardless of the shape of the return from investment in it. As will be shown, the present worth of the external investment opportunity is always zero. Therefore, if the present worth for the project is greater than zero, the project is acceptable.

This conclusion follows from the fact that the present worth of the external opportunity is always zero, but we must show that this is so, even if it may seem intuitively obvious. If instead of investing in the proposed project, we invest that money in the unspecified external opportunity, it will generate a return cash flow $y(t)$. This will be exactly that which, when discounted at the OCC, will equal the investment. Thus

$$P = -I + \int y(t)e^{-rt}\,dt = 0. \tag{5.3}$$

EXAMPLE: Present worth

If an investment is $10,000, the OCC is 12%, and the return flow is a point return of $31,058 in 10 years, then

$$P = -10,000 + 31,058(P/F, 12, 10) = 0$$

for the external opportunity. Therefore, the condition for acceptance of the project is

$$P(\text{project}) > P(\text{external investment}) = 0.$$

Since the projected cash flow, from $t = 0$ to the terminus of the project at $t = H$, always follows a cycle with an initial negative area succeeded by a positive area, the question is one of whether the net area under the discounted cash flow is at least equal to zero. Because the comparison of all other external opportunities has been fully considered in the choice of the discount rate, the condition $P = 0$ determines the point of indifference between acceptance and rejection of the project.

If $P > 0$, the project should be accepted. This is correct regardless of how large P is. Any P larger than zero signifies the present worth of the extra profit, beyond what was required by the OCC. It sometimes is referred to as the "premium worth". The larger P is, the more attractive the project, but the relative scale of the premium worth is not, in itself, open to interpretation as a degree of acceptability.

While the condition that $P > 0$ in equation 4.15 establishes acceptance of the project, we can transform equation 4.15 in several different ways to represent the same result. It cannot be emphasized too strongly that representing equation 4.15 in different ways does not constitute establishing different evaluation methods, nor can this change the conclusion. It can only change the appearance of the result. In spite of this seemingly obvious observation, it has become commonplace to regard such mathematical transformations as constituting separate and distinct methods.

5.5.1 The Internal Rate of Return

Very often there will be some uncertainty as to the proper discount rate to use. Therefore it may be desirable to leave the OCC unspecified, set P equal to 0, and solve equation 4.15 for r. This value for r will be the IRR for the project. It is commonly referred to as the *return on investment* (ROI). In spite of the widespread use of ROI, the term IRR is preferable, because it emphasizes the *internal* nature of the return.

The criterion for acceptance of the project now becomes one of comparing the IRR with the OCC. If the value of the internal rate of return is above the OCC, the project is worth undertaking. It is clear that this criterion is exactly equivalent to making $P > 0$. The point of indifference occurs when IRR = OCC.

5.5.2 A Technique for Solving for the IRR

In Chapter 4, iterative solutions for finding r were shown for the case of a constant cash flow. It is always necessary to resort to an iterative technique when finding r (or i). Where the cash flow is not readily expressed as a simple function, the problem, while the same in principle, is computationally more difficult. More skill may be required in making the first guess for r (or i).

A computer program in BASIC for the Apple II for solving such problems is provided in Appendix E. The solution to this problem is also a standard built-in function for the Hewlett-Packard HP-12C and other programmable hand calculators. It is desirable, however, to know how to solve the problem without such computational aids. This procedure is best described by following an example.

EXAMPLE: Iterative solution for the IRR

A cash flow is shown in Table 5.1. Find the IRR.

Column A shows the capital cash outflow or investment flow; B shows the cash return flow. The total dollar outlay amounts to $15,000, and the return is $24,000. Therefore we can be assured that there is at least a positive IRR. The next step is to make an educated guess as to what i is, assuming that the estimates are end-of-year amounts and we are using discrete discounting.

The total dollar profit amounts to $9200 over 6 years or, as a rough approximation, $1500 per year on an investment of $15,000. This would indicate a first guess for i of 10%. We will try this. Column C lists the factors, $(1 + i)^{-n}$, for a discount rate of 10%. Column D is the corresponding present worth. Summing, we see that the total present worth is

Table 5.1

| | A | B | C | D | E | F |
| | INVEST- | CASH | | | | |
n	MENT	FLOW	FACTOR	$P(n)$	FACTOR	$P(n)$
0	1,000	—	1.000	−1000	1.000	−1000
1	10,000	—	0.909	−9090	0.893	−8930
2	4,000	—	0.826	−3306	0.797	−3188
3	—	200	0.751	150	0.712	142
4	—	2,000	0.689	1366	0.636	1272
5	—	6,000	0.621	3726	0.567	3456
6	—	8,000	0.564	4516	0.507	4056
7	—	7,000	0.513	3592	0.452	3164
8	—	1,000	0.467	476	0.404	404
Sum	15,000	24,200		421		−626

$421. This is too high. Since we are trying to make the present worth equal to zero, we must guess again, using a higher value for i. The next two columns show values for a 12% guess. This second guess is seen to yield a negative present worth. By interpolation we find

$$i = \frac{421}{624 + 421} \times (12 - 10) + 10 = 10.806\%.$$

This answer must be recognized as another approximation, because by interpolating we were assuming the relation is linear when in fact it is not. The validity of this new approximation is dependent on making two guesses that are reasonably close to a final correct answer. The process may be repeated to obtain whatever degree of precision is desired. The correct solution to 6 significant figures is $i = 10.731454\%$. The interpolated solution is less than 1% in error.

If the OCC is 10%, the present worth is $421 (greater than zero) and therefore the project is justified. Or, viewed from the perspective of the IRR, the IRR is greater than 10%, and therefore the project is justified.

5.5.3 Levelized or Annualized Cash Flow

We will start with the basic relationship of equation 4.15, and equate it to an annuity or, in other words, a levelized cash flow:

$$P = \int_0^H y(t)e^{-rt}\,dt = \int_0^H Ae^{-rt}\,dt. \qquad (5.4)$$

Solving,

$$A = \frac{(1-e)^{-rH}}{r} \int_0^H y(t)e^{-rt}\,dt, \qquad (5.5)$$

or in terms of conventional symbolism,

$$A = \{A/P, r, H\} \int_0^H y(t)e^{-rt}\,dt. \qquad (5.6)$$

However, A is merely P multiplied by a constant, providing us with a mathematical identity. Thus the criterion $P > 0$ is equivalent to $A > 0$.

5.6 COMPARING PROJECTS

The foregoing section focused on the single project. In principle, this is a comparison of investment in the proposed project with investment in some external opportunity, which is unspecified but which is always available. In short, if the project is not accepted, the capital will still earn its OCC somewhere else. In a sense, then, even the single project is a case of comparison of alternatives.

We will normally have more than one way of accomplishing a given objective. Each of these alternatives can be considered as a separate project. The one with the highest present worth will be selected.

Basically, the essential problem in comparing alternatives is to establish the correct standard for comparability. While the cash flows for all alternatives, in principle, are for infinite time, as a matter of practicality we have to settle for an arbitrary planned life. The first requirement for establishing comparability is to make the planned life the same for all alternatives. This might seem obvious, but what do we do when the expected physical lives of the alternatives are not the same?

Another question concerns the comparability of scale of the alternatives. One alternative might require a larger initial investment and have lower operating costs than another. Even if revenue streams are identical, the project with the larger investment would be considered the larger project. However, is this necessarily the criterion on which we would have to establish comparability of scale?

5.6.1 Scale Comparability

For purposes of showing how scale effects influence the decision, only two alternatives, A and B, will be considered. The principles will apply for more than two. Let us assume project A to be the larger of the two, as measured by investment. In order for A to be a valid alternative, there must be sufficient capital for financing it. Consequently there will be unutilized capital if B, the smaller project, is selected. The extra capital, over and above what is needed for funding B, may be visualized as being invested in some other available opportunity which will just return the OCC. In making the comparative evaluation, each separate present worth must utilize all available capital—not just the capital needed for each project.

If we agree that the present worth of total capital is the criterion for selection, we reach the apparently trivial conclusion that the present worth of the cash-flow return on the extra investment in A over B is equal to the extra investment (i.e., $P = 0$). This is true simply because all we are specifying is that the only income we expect from the investment of the extra capital will be exactly what is required to yield the OCC.

The conclusion is clear. Regardless of the scale of initial investment, the only criterion is: select the alternative with the larger P.

EXAMPLE: Present-worth comparison

Consider two alternatives with point investments and point returns. The planned life is 10 years, and the OCC is 12%:

	INVESTMENT	RETURN	P
A	$2000	$7000	$254
B	$800	$4000	$488
$D = A - B$	$1200	$3727	0

By comparing the present worths of A and B without giving any consideration to the extra investment of $1200 in A above that of B, it is indicated that B, with the larger P ($488), should be selected. The difference between the two investments, $D = A - B$, would be invested at the OCC, 12%, which, if it returned a lump sum in 12 years, would amount to $3727. The resulting net present worth of the investment in D is 0. Therefore even if the second alternative is a portfolio of investments, comprising B coupled with D, it has the same P as B by itself has (i.e., $488).

This may seem to be belaboring the obvious, but it is essential to keep in mind that the important criterion is the return on total capital. This principle is not so obvious when we consider the IRR as a criterion.

The IRR is found by solving

$$\frac{F}{A} = (1 + i)^n = \frac{7000}{2000} = (1 + i)^{10}.$$

From this, the IRR for A is 13.35%, and likewise we find the IRR for B is 17.46%.

However, this latter IRR is not the return on all the capital. It represents only the return on that portion, $800, invested in B. To obtain the rate of return on the portfolio of investments, comprising both B and D, we must combine the return for B with that for D. This is

$$\$4000 + \$3727 = \$7727,$$

which is returned on the original investment of $2000. The IRR for this total return is 14.47%.

In this example, the conclusion that B should be selected, based on selecting the higher IRR, is the same conclusion as that based on the present-worth calculation. Let us see what the conclusion might have been if the amounts were slightly altered. Suppose that instead of $7000 return on A, it were $8000. The IRR for A would then be 14.87%. This is less than 17.46%, the IRR realized on B alone. The conclusion, based only on comparison of the IRRs, would still be: choose B. However as we have seen, the return on total capital for B is only 14.47%, and therefore A would be the better choice. You may verify this by finding the new present worth of A ($576 > $488). By failure to take account of total capital, a wrong conclusion would have been reached.

As exemplified by the above example, the point that must be made is:

Consideration of the IRR on each alternative, taken separately, results in a distorted measure of return. Consideration of the present worth is valid by itself because total investment is implicitly included. Total investment must be considered explicitly when using the IRR in order for there to be comparability of scale.

There are other difficulties associated with using the IRR as a criterion for evaluating or comparing projects. In the example, we assumed that the difference in the initial investments between A and B would be so invested as to return the same shape of cash flow (i.e., point return) as for the other investments. Suppose, instead, we were to assume a constant cash flow. In place of the return of the lump sum $3727 in alternative D, an equivalent constant cash flow is considered to be

$$A = 1200(A/P, 12, 10)$$
$$= \$228 \text{ per year for 10 years.}$$

This is exactly equivalent to $3727 in 10 years.

The IRR for this investment, coupled with the investment in B, is 15.42%. (You may wish to verify this answer for yourself as an exercise.) This is not the same answer as before (14.47%), demonstrating that the IRR is sensitive to the shape of the cash flow.

The problem with the IRR as a criterion lies in the lack of realism in its underlying assumptions. In effect, it is valid on the basis of withholding all the return cash-flow from reinvestment. It would be valid, for example, for the case of a man who buys an annuity to provide retirement income for the sole purpose of covering living expenses, and who has no intention of ever reinvesting any of that money. Actually, in the business world all cash flow, except for dividends, is reinvested. The rate of return on such reinvestment is properly considered to be the OCC.

The IRR (or ROI as it is more popularly called) is used extensively and probably will continue to be utilized in spite of its inherent flaw. It should always be utilized with full awareness of the distortions incorporated in it.

5.6.2 Cancellation of Common Cash Flows

We have established that we should rank-order the acceptability of projects in terms of their present worths. With respect to two projects, A and B, if

$$P(A) > P(B), \tag{5.7}$$

select A. Recall that

$$P = \int y(t)e^{-rt}\, dt.$$

The cash-flow function $y(t)$ comprises a number of elements. These include revenues and various kinds of costs. If we take only revenues and costs for illustration, then

$$y(t) = \mathrm{rev}(t) - C(t), \tag{5.8}$$

and therefore, if

$$\int [\mathrm{rev}(A(t)) - C(A(t))]\, dt > \int [\mathrm{rev}(B(t)) - C(B(t))]\, dt, \tag{5.9}$$

then we should select A.

If there are identical terms on each side of the inequality, they may be canceled. If the cash-flow component for costs of *A* are exactly equal to those of *B*, then the comparison reduces to that of revenues only. Likewise, if the revenues are identical in all respects, the comparison reduces to that of costs only.

The same principle applies for any other elements of the cash flow. The ability to cancel terms is particularly useful when considering intangibles—elements of either cost or benefit that are not readily quantified. All that is required is to estimate the differences between alternatives. An example will help to show how this works in practice.

EXAMPLE: Comparison of two alternatives

A company is considering installing a special-purpose machine for enhancing the production of its widget shop. The output of the shop will remain the same, but a reduction of costs is expected. The decision has been narrowed to a choice between two machines, the characteristics of which are as follows:

- For machine A the first cost is $10,000, its operating and maintenance cost is $2000 per year, and it is expected to have a terminal value in ten years of $2,000.

- For machine B the first cost is $6000, its operating and maintenance cost is $3000 per year, and it will have no terminal value in ten years. The OCC is 12%.

SOLUTION

The revenue from the operation is indeterminate, but is irrelevant as long as we can assume that it will be the same regardless of the choice of machine. It may well be that the operation is losing money, but that does not matter. Given that one or the other machine is to be chosen in any event, then all such common cash flows may be canceled from each side of the inequality. All we need to do is compare costs:

	MACHINE A	MACHINE B
Initial investment	$10,000	$6,000
P of operating cost	11,300	16,951
P of terminal value	− 644	0
Total cost	$20,656	$22,951

The answer is clear: A is less expensive than B, and therefore A should be chosen.

5.6.3 Comparability in Time

By cutting off cash flows for all alternatives at the same planning time, we have dodged the issue of dealing with differences in life expectancies. Nevertheless we must, in one way or another, adhere to the principle of using a common planned life in order to ensure that the alternatives are truly comparable. What then do we do when there are recognizable differences in life expectancies associated with the different alternatives? The best example of this is in dealing with replacement alternatives. This subject will be treated in Chapter 10; the question at issue is this: should one replace an old piece of equipment, which can be expected to last for only one more year, or invest in a new one, which may have a life of many years? In most situations the difference in time is not as dramatic as one more year versus many years, but the essence of the problem is the same:

How do we deal with different life cycles?

Two extreme and unrealistic assumptions may be made:

1. There is no replacement at the end of either life cycle. The cash flow for the shorter-lived investment is simply foreshortened, and there is no cash flow from the end of its life to the end of the longer-lived alternative. Clearly this would penalize the shorter-lived alternative.

2. The shorter-lived alternative is taken for the planning period, and any value that may be ascribed to remaining cash flow for the longer-lived alternative is simply ignored. In this case we penalize the longer-lived alternative. See Figure 5.4.

We can narrow these extremes somewhat by taking the planned life to be that of A, with the shorter life H_A, and then estimating a terminal value for the longer-lived alternative at H_B. The question then is: How do we arrive at a reasonable terminal value for project B at H_A? We might be inclined to obtain this terminal value by finding the discounted cash flow, at H_A, of the remaining cash flow of B. However, this is also unrealistic. It is identical to assuming condition 1 above. What must be realized is that there is some advantage associated with the flexibility to make a new decision at H_A, instead of having to wait until H_B. Therefore we would need to make some adjustment in estimates of the remaining cash flow due to this flexibility and the opportunities for taking advantage of any technological improvements that might have become available at H_A. This would imply a need for a reduction in the terminal value from the discounted cash flow for the remaining life of B. The result would be a terminal value falling somewhere in between the extreme positions of zero (i.e., extreme 2) and the full discounted value of the continuing cash flow (i.e., extreme 1).

EXAMPLE: Comparing different-lived alternatives

Consider two alternatives, A and B. These will be the same as chosen for the previous example, except that the life of A will be extended to fifteen years instead of the ten years used before. The terminal value will also be eliminated.

SOLUTION

The solution for the earlier example applied to the case where we ignore the extra life of A. The previous terminal value would correspond to a judgmental assessment of $2000 for a terminal value, in order to make the planned life identical for the two alternatives. If we were to

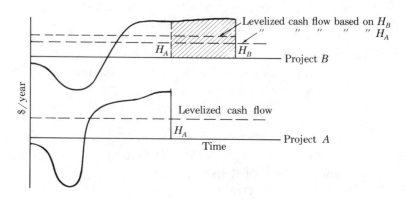

Figure 5.4 Different lives.

ignore this terminal value, the present worth of A would be

$$\$10,000 + \$11,300 = \$21,300$$

compared with the value of $22,951 for B.

If we now ignore what the options are at the end of the life of A, we obtain for A a value of

$$\$10,000 + 2000(P/A, 12, 15) = 10,000 + 13,987 = \$23,982.$$

This would weight the choice in favor of B.

Clearly the difference between the two lives may be significant. We should have the same planned life for both alternatives in order to make them comparable. For this reason let us assume that we establish the terminal value for A, as the present worth of extra benefit associated with the longer life. Recall that we do not have any measure of revenues; we assumed them to be identical for both alternatives. However, the benefit derived from A is the cost foregone for the period from the tenth to the fifteenth year. Thus, if we were to take the terminal value to be the discounted cash flow of A, we would obtain a terminal value of

$$F = 2000(P/A, 12, 5) = \$7210.$$

Using this terminal value, we would now find the net present value of A to be

$$P = 21,300 - 7210(P/F, 12, 10) = \$18,979.$$

As was pointed out above, neither of these values for the present worth for A is realistic. The choice will swing from one to the other alternative, depending on the assumption used for the terminal value. An arbitrarily assigned value for the terminal value is a reasonable compromise. It forces the explicit assessment of the value of flexibility. We are also in a position to assess this with respect to the extreme assumptions that constitute bounds on the solution. A technique for doing this will be covered in Chapter 10.

5.7 CONVENTIONAL APPROACHES

Various methods in common use were listed at the beginning of this chapter. Provided that assumptions are specified consistently, it will be shown that they are mathematical transformations of the basic concept of present worth. Actually the reason that present worth is suggested as the basic method is because decisions are always made in the present. There is no reason why we could not just as well transform the present worth to a future worth at any point in time we choose, and use that future worth as a reference for comparison. However, people find it difficult to relate to future dollar amounts; the magnitude of the numbers tends to be misleading in a psychological sense.

There are other transformations that do provide measures to which people can more easily relate. Many of these are useful. However, difficulties can arise whenever we depart from the use of the OCC for discounting cash flow and attempt to evaluate a rate of return. Unless special precautions are taken, it is possible to overlook principles of comparability.

Most textbooks treat all of the various approaches to evaluation as separate and distinct methods. It is one of the purposes of this text to demonstrate a unified approach. Therefore, all of the so-called methods will be discussed below and related to the basic present-worth evaluation technique, shown above.

5.7.1 Annualized Cash Flow

We have shown how the cash flow for a single project can be transformed into a levelized or annualized cash flow. The latter is probably the most widely used approach for comparing projects when the only consideration in the comparison is cost. Thus it is usually called an *annual-cost method* or *uniform annual-cost method*.

Quite often an annualized cost comparison is utilized for investments in equipment and machinery, where the life of the asset is taken, without further reflection, as the physical life expectancy of the asset. Since the lives of the different alternatives may not be the same, the question arises as to how to establish comparability in time.

When the levelized cash flow for each project is determined, the usual procedure is simply to rank by levelized costs, accepting the one with the lowest such cost. In doing this, there is an implied assumption that this levelized cost continues indefinitely into the future. In other words, the original investment will be replicated repeatedly at the end of successive life cycles. In effect, without explicitly stating it, or for that matter thinking about it at all, the planning period is assumed to be infinite.

Refer to the discussion of Figure 5.4 in Section 5.6.3. The procedure is to levelize the cash flow for project A to H_A and for project B to H_B. These levelized values are simply compared. Replication is implicitly assumed in each case. Thus each time A reaches the end of its life, the continuing cash flow is essentially replicated, and likewise for B. This means that the planning period is implicitly infinite.

If we levelize the cash flow for A to H_A, and take that as the planning period, we obtain

$$A = \{A/P, r, H\} \int_0^A y(t)e^{-rt}\,dt. \qquad (5.10)$$

This solution for A, of course, leaves us with the same dilemma we had before in the discussion of Section 5.6.3. We are ignoring the value of the continuing cash flow associated with B beyond H_A. On the other hand, by levelizing the cash flow of project A to H_B, as is usually done, we are overweighting the importance of the continuing cash flow beyond H_A.

If we use H_B for the planning period, we revert to the other dilemma, that of overweighting the continuing value of the extra cash flow for project B.

With this caveat in mind, we find that the annualized cash flow provides the identical criterion we utilized by ranking the project alternatives by P. The annuity A is merely P multiplied by a constant, determined by a mathematical identity. Consequently, we obtain the same conclusion whether we compare investment alternatives by their present worths or by their annualized cash flows.

As stated above, the advantage in using the annualized cash flow in preference to present worth lies in cost comparison. Clearly, if we postulate that for the alternatives being considered the revenue streams are identical, then the comparison reduces to that of annual costs. Here the magnitude of the numbers being compared seems to have greater intuitive appeal than do present worths.

5.7.2 The Internal Rate of Return

The determination of the IRR was shown in Section 5.5. It is widely used for ranking projects, under the more popular name of *return on investment.* However, its validity depends on the unrealistic assumption that no reinvestment of the return cash flow is made. Furthermore, the difference in investment levels of alternative projects is ignored. As was demonstrated in the present-worth comparisons, we do not need to consider, explicitly, the difference in investment levels, because this is automatically taken into account. Such is not the case if we attempt to rank by IRR.

The difficulty in interpretation of the IRR can be appreciated by examining how the present worth varies as a function of r, in Figure 5.5. Consider two alternatives, A and B. Typically the present worths for these may cross at some point C. The IRR for each is, by definition, the intersection of the present worth function with the rate-of-return axis. Thus on the basis of the IRR selection criterion, A would presumably be preferred to B. However, if the OCC should happen to fall to the left of the intersection C, then, based on present worth, B is preferred to A. The intersection C represents the point of indifference.

This apparently anomalous situation may be explained by considering what is implied by a reinvestment. Although no reinvestment is assumed for either alternative, as a practical matter reinvestment must take place. Ranking by IRR is equivalent to arguing that if A is chosen and reinvestment is made, the return on the second investment would again be the IRR realized on A, but if B had been selected originally, the return on the reinvestment would then have been the IRR for B. This is obviously

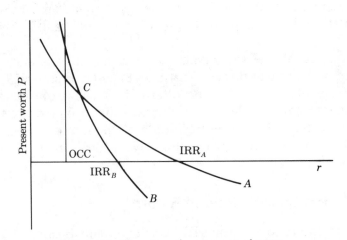

Figure 5.5   Present worth versus rate of return.

absurd. There can be no rational argument for assuming that the same opportunities will exist for reinvestment as are being considered in the first instance. By the definition of OCC, the only justified return on any subsequent reinvestment is the OCC.

The way to get around this difficulty is to use what is usually referred to as the "external rate of return method".

5.7.3 The External Rate of Return

The only way we can resolve the inconsistency arising from the use of the IRR is to consider the issue of comparability between the alternatives. The shapes of the alternative cash flows are different. This means that in one project the cash available for doing something else will be different from that in other cases. Consider, for example, the case where one project locks in the funds until the end of the planning period and the alternative project repays an annuity. In the first there is no cash flow until the end of the life span, and in the second it is returned as a steady stream.

The OCC not only determines the opportunity for a return on capital, given that the investment is made, but also represents the point of indifference between consumption now and consumption postponed. Therefore we do not need to consider this choice further. It is the equivalent of keeping all the capital invested all of the time. Thus as the cash-flow stream is returned, it must be assumed to be reinvested at the OCC rate.

Consider the case of a point investment, I, and a return cash flow, $y(t)$, deriving from the project. We will reinvest $y(t)$ at r_0 (the OCC) until H. This changes the cash flow withdrawn by shifting it all to the end of the planning period (i.e., zero for $0 < t < H$, and a point return at H). The point return at H will be

$$
\begin{aligned}
F &= \int_0^H y(t) e^{(H-t)r_0} \, dt \\
&= e^{Hr_0} \int_0^H y(t) e^{-r_0 t} \, dt.
\end{aligned} \tag{5.11}
$$

The IRR for this revised cash flow is obtained by solving

$$
\begin{aligned}
P &= -I + F e^{-rH} \\
&= -I + e^{(r-r_0)H} \int_0^H y(t) e^{-r_0 t} \, dt = 0.
\end{aligned} \tag{5.12}
$$

The value of the integral is the present worth, P_0, of the return cash flow discounted at the OCC. Thus

$$P = -I + P_0 e^{(r - r_0)H},$$ (5.13)

from which

$$r = r_0 + \frac{\ln(I/P_0)}{H}$$ (5.14)

The ranking of alternative projects would now be accomplished by comparing r's.

The rate of return determined by equation 5.14 is not the IRR for the cash flow as it originates but for a modified cash flow. For this reason it is inappropriate to refer to this rate of return as the IRR. Canada and White (1980) refer to this solution as the "external rate of return method". However, it must be observed that the value for r, strictly speaking, is not a true external rate of return. We have already defined the rate of return on an external investment as the OCC. Perhaps it is better called a *modified internal* rate of return.

The above discussion addresses the question of comparability in terms of reinvestment, but we must still consider comparability of scale. In the present-worth analysis, the present worth of the difference in investments for comparable projects was shown to be zero as long as we discounted all cash flows at the OCC. However, in using the IRR as a decision criterion, the extra investment in the larger alternative will be earning a return that is higher than the OCC, and so the present worth on the increment will be greater than zero.

Consider two projects A and B for which we specify that the investment in A is larger than for B. Equations 5.13 and 5.14 will apply for both, but in order for the comparability principle to be maintained, we must make I_A equal to I_B. It follows that P is also larger by the difference in the investments. Thus for B, equation 5.14 becomes

$$r = r_0 + \frac{1}{H} \ln \frac{I_A}{P + I_A - I_B}.$$ (5.15)

With these modifications, ranking by the modified IRR is consistent with ranking by P or by A. The anomaly posed by the intersection of the functions $P(r)$ does not arise, because the curves, as can be demonstrated, are parallel. They cannot intersect (see Figure 5.6). If the value of the IRR from equation 5.14 is larger for project A than the IRR from equation 5.15 for project B, then the present worths will also be larger for A, regardless of the values of the modified IRRs.

EXAMPLE: Comparison of methods

Compare two projects by means of the conventional methods and show the kinds of discrepancies that may arise. The two projects are specified to give a wide variation in the shape of the cash flow. Project A is a point investment of $800 and has a point return in 10 years of $3000. Project B is a point investment of $700 and provides an annuity of $200 per year for 10 years. The OCC is 12% (discrete). The planning period will be taken as 10 years, corresponding with the cash flows.

SOLUTION

1. *Present worth.*

		A	B
(for A)	$P = -800 + 3000(F/A, 12, 10)$	166	
(for B)	$P = -700 + 200(P/A, 12, 10)$		430

On the basis of present worth B is better than A.

2. *Annualized cash flow.*

		A	B
(for A)	$A_A = 166(A/P, 12, 10)$	29	
(for B)	$A_B = 430(A/P, 12, 10)$		76

The same factor applies for each P, and so the conclusion is unchanged. The numbers compared are different, but the rank order is not altered.

3. *Internal rate of return.* Setting $P = 0$ in solution 1 above for both alternatives, we find the IRR for A to be 16.14% and for B to be

25.16%. These, along with the break-even rate of return, are shown in Figure 5.5. The conclusion would be the same if the selection were to be made in terms of the IRR as for the present worth or levelized cash flow. However, what would the choice have been if instead of 12% for the OCC, it had been 5%? Now A would appear to be better. It will be left to the reader to determine the point at which the choice will cross over (i.e., the break-even rate).

4. *External rate of return.* For A there is no reinvestment, because the cash flow is a lump sum at the end of the planning period. Therefore the same curve that represents P as a function of i will apply for alternative A. However, the situation for B is markedly altered. As the $200 per year comes in, it is immediately reinvested at the OCC until the end of the planning period in 10 years. Thus there is no actual cash flow in the interval. From equation 5.13 we obtain the value of $P(i)$, which is plotted in Figure 5.6. This does not intersect the present-worth curve for A, and so it is seen that the conclusion that A is the better option is valid for any value of OCC.

5.7.4 Multiple Values for the IRR

The foregoing discussion has demonstrated the serious limitations on the use of the IRR criterion. Nevertheless, it is likely to maintain its widespread popularity. It has some value for ranking projects as long as its limitations are recognized. One other anomaly occurs with the IRR, which is more a curiosity than a

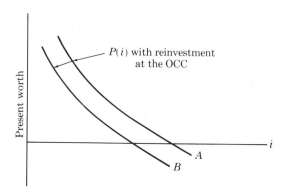

Figure 5.6 $P(i)$ for example problem.

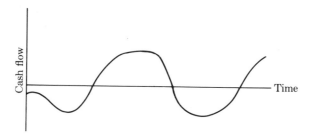

Figure 5.7 Multiple solutions for the IRR.

matter of concern. It is possible to find multiple solutions for the IRR. This will occur when the cash flow cycles from positive to negative more than once (Figure 5.7).

The way in which this dilemma of multiple solutions is readily resolved is to cut off the planning time at the end of the first cycle. Clearly, if the return on the second cycle were inadequate, the project would be abandoned at that point in any event. Thus the multiple-solution problem is mostly of academic interest.

5.7.5 Benefit / Cost Ratio

The benefit/cost ratio (often referred to as the cost/benefit ratio) is another transformation of the same basic present-worth formula, with the cash-flow stream explicitly divided into its components of costs and revenues:

$$y(t) = \text{rev}(t) - \text{cost}(t). \tag{5.16}$$

Thus

$$P = \int [\text{rev}(t) - \text{cost}(t)] e^{-rt} dt$$
$$= B - C, \tag{5.17}$$

where B is the integrated discounted revenue, and C the integrated discounted cost. The fundamental condition for acceptance of the project, namely that $P > 0$, becomes $B - C > 0$. Dividing by C leads to the conclusion that the condition for acceptance is that

$$B/C > 1. \tag{5.18}$$

The benefit/cost ratio approach came into use for evaluation of government projects, largely because many of the benefits in the public sector cannot readily be determined as dollar revenues.

5.7.6 Payback

The simplest and most common payback criterion is:

> If the investment in the project is paid back within N years, where N is a specified time, (usually on the order of 3 or 4 years), the project is accepted.

This approach to project evaluation has widespread acceptance, in spite of almost universal rejection by theoreticians.

The theoretical defect is that no value is accorded to any cash flow beyond N and no time value is assessed for the cash flow up to N. Clearly, this is unreasonable. It is equivalent to using an OCC of zero for $t = 0$ to N and using an infinite OCC for $t > N$.

Occasionally the payback criterion is modified to include a specification that it must yield a rate of return as well as full payback of the investment within the specified time. This does not alter its inherent theoretical defect of according no value to any expenditure or revenue beyond N.

The payback approach cannot be justified on the basis of any rational argument, either for the evaluation of a single project or for the comparison of alternative projects. Nevertheless its widespread use is not without some justification. If it is viewed as an averaging approach to the selection of many projects, an interesting result is obtained. It amounts to defining a turnover rate of capital with a specified rate of return, which is determined implicitly by specifying the payback period N.

Normally firms make more or less uniform annual investments. Thus their investments constitute investment flows $I(t)$. Assume that a point investment $I(t)$ results in a point return $R(t + N)$. The point return is paid back in N years, at a rate r, such that

$$I(t) = R(t + N)e^{-rN}. \qquad (5.19)$$

Instead of a point return R, the return could just as well be a cash-flow equivalent stretching out over time, from t to some time beyond N. Then the payback criterion becomes the equivalent of a rate of return r for a return cash flow $R(t)$ that is in phase with an investment stream $I(t)$ and is lagged by N.

This is not an argument in favor of payback, but rather an argument that, over a large number of investment decisions, it averages out to be valid.

5.8 REVENUE REQUIREMENTS

The determination of the suitability of a project depends on $P > 0$. In many cases the product price will be determined by cost. The assumption here is that the market is insensitive to price. A good illustration is the way in which utility companies evaluate proposed new projects. These companies are natural monopolies, and the price for the product is determined by Public Utilities Commissions.

Often it will be easier to estimate a schedule for the physical output of a project than it is to estimate dollar revenues. First, the final planned capacity is estimated. Normally full capacity will not be reached until some time has elapsed. An estimation of the buildup to planned capacity is necessary. The price of the product can be left as an unknown. If no rising price trend is anticipated, there will simply be a single price. If the price is expected to rise or fall in the future, the unknown price can be entered as a price function. Thus the basic present-worth equation 4.15 becomes

$$P = \int s(t)x(t)e^{-rt}\,dt, \qquad (5.20)$$

where $s(t)$ is the price function and $x(t)$ is the physical-output function:

$$y(t) = s(t)x(t). \qquad (5.21)$$

EXAMPLE: Revenue requirements for synfuel plant

Consider a synfuel manufacturing facility with a planned final output capacity of 10,000 barrels of synthetic gasoline per day. It is expected to start production at 20% capacity and add another 20% each year until capacity is reached. Annual operating costs are expected to be $28 million per year. The operating life of the project is 30 years. It is expected that it will require 6 years to reach startup. The total investment at that time, allowing for capitalizing interest, is $1,400 million. The company OCC is 10%. No taxes are considered.

Determine the price that must be charged per barrel if the price over the 30-year period rises at 3% per year.

SOLUTION

In many ways this is a highly artificial situation. It would be most unlikely for operating costs to remain constant while prices were rising. On the other hand, it may be realistic to assume that the price of fuel will rise faster by 3% than the general inflation rate, and we can therefore use the conventional approach of assuming constant dollars (i.e., no inflation) in the analysis. If this were a public utility company, current practices for regulating prices would be incompatible with the solution that follows. This example reveals the methodology of the revenue-requirements approach.

The planned capacity of the plant is 3,650,000 barrels per year. The calculations are shown in Table 5.2. In order to avoid carrying an excessive number of zeros, we make all calculations in thousands of barrels and thousands of dollars, and we assume all rates are discrete.

Taking the present worth of the cash flow will result in

$$P = 0 = 43,999s - 263,947 - 1,400,000,$$

from which

$$s = \$38.82.$$

This means that six years from now (at the zero-time point for the calculation) the price would have to be initially established as at least

Table 5.2 Cash-Flow Table

YEAR	PRICE	QUANTITY	REVENUE	COST	CASH FLOW
1	$1.030s$	730	$751.9s$	28,000	$751.9s - 28,000$
2	$1.061s$	1460	$1549.0s$	28,000	$1549.0s - 28,000$
3	$1.093s$	2190	$2393.7s$	28,000	$2393.7s - 28,000$
4	$1.126s$	2920	$3287.9s$	28,000	$3287.9s - 28,000$
5	$1.159s$	3650	$4230.4s$	28,000	$4230.4s - 28,000$
⋮	⋮	⋮	⋮	⋮	⋮
30	$2.427s$	3650	$8858.6s$	28,000	$8858.6s - 28,000$

$38.82 in order to justify the project. In addition, this price would then have to be escalated at the rate of 3% per year for the next 30 years.

It should not be inferred that we have considered inflation in this problem because of the escalation of the synfuel price. Such an escalation of price could be independent of inflation. The treatment of inflation will be covered in Chapter 8.

5.9 SENSITIVITY ANALYSIS

The criteria for evaluation and selection of a project have been demonstrated. It is, however, also desirable to develop a feel for the sensitivity of those values, on which the choice depends, to changes in the several variables that determine them. It must always be kept in mind that the results depend on estimates of future cash flow, the OCC, the length of the planning period, and the terminal value. Of necessity these are subject to considerable variability. For this reason it is well to make a sensitivity analysis.

It was shown in Chapter 2 that elasticity, as defined by economists, is in reality a sensitivity in the change of one variable to a change in another. The same principle applies for any pair of variables. Thus the sensitivity of X to Y may be more broadly defined as

$$s = \frac{Y}{X} \frac{dX}{dY}, \tag{5.22}$$

where X and Y are any two variables.

We can apply this definition to the sensitivity of the present worth to the variables that determine it and hence the choice we make.

Let us consider a variety of cash flows with a planning period H and no terminal value.

5.9.1 Point Investment and Point Return

The present worth is

$$P = Fe^{-rH}. \tag{5.23}$$

The sensitivity of P with respect to changes in r will be

$$s = \frac{r}{P}\frac{dP}{dr} = -\frac{HFr}{P}e^{-rH}. \tag{5.24}$$

But $Fe^{-rH} = P$. Therefore

$$s = -Hr. \tag{5.25}$$

It will be noted that the same sensitivity of P with respect to H will occur as in the example above.

A value of $s = -1$ corresponds to the condition that a positive change in the value of either H or r will produce exactly the same percentage change in the value of P. It is interesting that, for example, we have the same sensitivity to change for an OCC of 10% coupled with a ten-year planned life as we would have for an OCC of 20% coupled with a five-year planned life. In both cases the present worth would be reduced 10% for a 10% increase in either H or r. The sensitivity is linear in the product of the two variables. It should also be noted that this result would not be quite the same for discrete discounting.

5.9.2 Point Investment and Exponential Cash-Flow Return

The special case of an exponential cash flow is the annuity where the growth parameter goes to zero. Therefore the sensitivity for exponential-growth cash flow reduces to the sensitivity for the annuity. Using the same procedure as before,

$$P = A\frac{1 - e^{(g-r)H}}{r - g}. \tag{5.26}$$

Differentiating,

$$\frac{dP}{dr} = -A\frac{1 - e^{(g-r)H} - He^{(g-r)H}}{r^2}. \tag{5.27}$$

Solving for s (equation 5.22) and substituting equation 5.26,

$$s = -1 + \frac{H(r - g)}{e^{H(r-g)} - 1}. \tag{5.28}$$

This function is plotted in Figure 5.8 to show the sensitivity as a function of r for several growth rates and a value of 20 years for H.

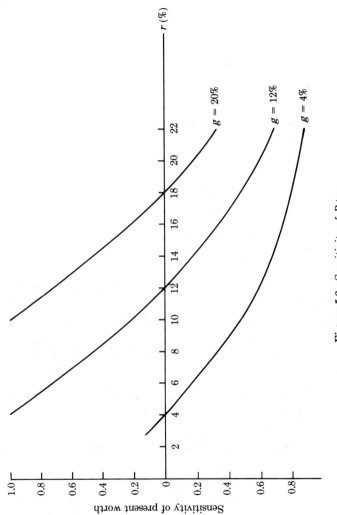

Figure 5.8 Sensitivity of *P* to *r*.

It is of interest that the sensitivity of P converges to a minimum value of -1 when $H(r - g)$ goes to infinity, provided that $H(r - g)$ is positive. For negative values of $H(r - g)$, the present worth goes to infinity as H goes to infinity, and correspondingly the sensitivity also becomes indefinitely large. It is also interesting that as long as the discount rate is larger than the growth rate, the sensitivity is negative (i.e., as the parameter gets larger, P gets smaller) but when the growth rate exceeds the discount rate, the sensitivity is positive.

5.10 RECAPITULATION

1. The evaluation of any project should start with a specific identification of whose viewpoint is to be of concern. The answer can be an individual, a corporation, or the public. If it is a corporation, then is it really the stockholder's interest that is of primary concern, or is it some joint interest?

2. The identification of alternatives requires consideration of a universe of choices. It is not practical to consider more than a limited number in detail, and therefore some unspecified opportunity must be established as a standard external opportunity against which all the detailed alternatives are compared. This external opportunity is taken into account explicitly by choosing the opportunity cost of capital. The single project evaluation is a limiting case of comparison of alternatives, in that there is an implicit comparison with the external opportunity.

3. • Only the future is relevant in an evaluation. Sunk costs are past costs and as such should be ignored.
   • Prediction of the future is an inescapable necessity. However, the future cannot be predicted very successfully, and so, in reality, the prediction is more in the nature of an aspiration or self-fulfilling prediction.
   • The horizon concept, while useful, should not limit the planned life of the project. Posthorizon actions must be planned.

4. Evaluation, by whatever method, is fundamentally a question of determining a go-ahead decision on the criterion that the present worth of the projected cash-flow stream is greater

than, or at least equal to, zero. The internal rate of return, the most widely accepted criterion, is predicated on hidden assumptions of reinvestment. Often such assumptions are invalid, and so the criterion can result in incorrect choice.

5. Care must be exercised to ensure comparability of alternatives. In particular, either the planned life for all alternatives must be the same, or some adjustment must be made to ensure the equivalence of a common planned life. Secondly, there must be comparability of scale.

6. Any cost stream or benefit (i.e., revenue) stream that is identical for all alternatives can be deleted from the comparison.

7. The evaluation is not complete without an evaluation of sensitivity of the decision to changes in the important parameters and variables.

5.11 PROBLEMS

1. Find the P for the following investments (using discrete discounting).

   a. A point investment of $10,000 and a cash return flow of $3000 per year for 10 years. The opportunity cost of capital is 12%.

   b. A sum of $1000 is invested every year for 5 years, followed by a cash return flow of $1000 per year for the succeeding 25 years. The opportunity cost of capital is 10%.

   c. The following cash-flow stream, with an opportunity cost of capital of 10%:

n	CASH FLOW
1	$-\$1000$
2	$-\$2000$
3	$-\$2500$
4	0
5	$500
6	$1000
7	$1200
8	$1500
9–15	$1600/year

2. Determine the internal rate of return for the examples in Problem 1.

3. Consider the continuous idealized case of a constant investment flow of $1000 for T years, followed by a constant cash return flow of $$A$ to the time, F years. (See Figure 5.9.)

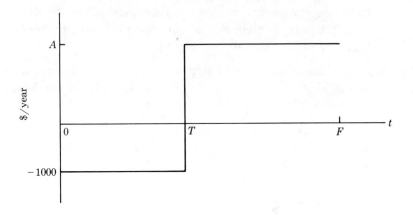

a. Plot A as a function of r, assuming that $T = 8$ and $F = \infty$.

b. Plot A as a function of T, assuming that $r = 10\%$ and $F = \infty$.

c. Repeat part b assuming that $F = 30$.

d. Plot T as a function of r, assuming that $F = \infty$, $A = 2000$.

○

○

CHAPTER SIX

○ *Accounting and Taxes*

○

Accounting is retrospective. Its purpose is measurement of costs and revenues and their interpretation in order to provide an estimate of how well a firm has been doing. Cost accounting, a subdivision of accounting, has a specialized function, that of providing an allocation scheme for assigning appropriate current and historical costs to various departments, projects, product lines, etc.

Accounting is concerned only with keeping track of, and properly allocating, expenditures that have been made or obligated in the *past*. The expenditure stream is modified by making arbitrary allocations of costs over time in order to represent a better picture of the expense stream. *Expenditures* are defined as actual dollar outlays or disbursements; *expenses* are adjusted costs. Expenses are then subtracted from the revenue stream to determine a profit stream. Expenses may be expenditures, but by definition they are adjusted or modified expenditures. This is an important distinction, which will become more apparent later when we discuss depreciation.

Accounting, in contrast to economic evaluation, is not concerned with opportunity costs or opportunity benefits, or with future or projected costs or revenues. In sharp distinction to economic evaluation, accounting *is* concerned with sunk costs. Furthermore, although concerned primarily with the past, accounting takes the future into consideration to the extent that a past expenditure must be allocated against future revenue. Such allocations require decisions as to how far into the future they should be made.

Accounting can be a useful source of information for making cost estimates. However, the way in which various accounting allocations are made may provide distorted measurements in estimating cash flows. Therefore, accounting data must always be utilized with a degree of caution when employed for evaluating the economic justification of a proposed project.

One main purpose of accounting is the allocation of capital costs over time. This is commonly called *depreciation* and is essential in measuring the current status of a project or firm. It is this function of accounting that is of greatest concern to us here.

6.1 ACCOUNTING PRACTICE

No attempt is made in this book to provide a comprehensive coverage of accounting. Rather, the elements of accounting, germane to investment analysis, will be touched on in sufficient detail to provide a rudimentary understanding of accounting objectives. The purpose in doing this is to place accounting in proper perspective, relative to finance on one hand and to economic evaluation on the other. To a great extent the main points will be developed in relation to the fundamentals of the financial report of the firm.

6.1.1 Cash and Accrual Accounting

Cash accounting requires keeping track of expenditures or receipts as they are paid or received. Accrual accounting requires keeping track of expenditures and receipts as they are obligated. For the latter, therefore, sales are reported when orders are shipped although payment must still be made, in contrast to cash accounting, which requires reporting only as the money is received or spent.

The books (accounts) of any enterprise may be kept on either the cash or the accrual system of accounting. Small businesses sometimes elect to use the cash system, but all large firms and most small ones find that the only practical system is the accrual system.

6.1.2 The Double-Entry Principle

As the name implies, the double-entry system requires that all transactions be recorded twice, once on the right-hand side of a book and once on the left. This practice originated to provide an automatic partial check of the arithmetic involved. This is of minor concern today, with almost all accounting done on computing equipment. However, there is a more important reason for using the double-entry system than that of simple arithmetical checking. All left-hand entries are based on how they affect assets in the firm. All right-hand entries are based on how they affect a vested interest in those assets. The vested interest is divided between the ownership, or *equity*, and those to whom money is owed, or *liabilities*.

Increases in left-hand entries are called *debits*. Those in right-hand entries are *credits*. This convention was derived from the fundamental concepts of debt and credit. Thus an increase in an asset value is a debit entry, but it represents a credit to the owner or to one who may have loaned money. While this explains the terms, it is simpler to think of them as mere conventional names for the left and right sides of the ledger.

The accounts of the firm are of importance in evaluating its status and, when summarized and organized, result in the development of three important reports—the balance sheet, the income statement, and the statement of reinvested earnings. The explanation that follows will be easier to grasp if while reading it one follows the example financial report, Figure 6.1.

6.2 THE BALANCE SHEET

When all accounts are collected and integrated into a condensed or summary set of items, the result is a *balance sheet*. Basically a balance sheet is an equation of state of the firm:

$$\text{assets} = \text{liabilities} + \text{ownership},$$

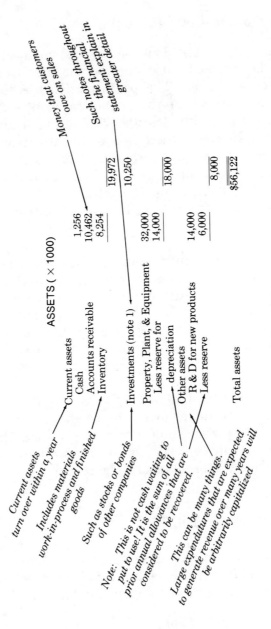

ASSETS (× 1000)

Current assets		
Cash	1,256	
Accounts receivable	10,462	
Inventory	8,254	19,972
Investments (note 1)		10,250
Property, Plant, & Equipment	32,000	
Less reserve for depreciation	14,000	18,000
Other assets		
R & D for new products	14,000	
Less reserve	6,000	8,000
Total assets		$56,122

Current assets turn over within a year

Includes materials work-in-process and finished goods

Such as stocks or bonds of other companies

Note: This is not cash waiting to put to use! It is the sum of all prior annual allowances that are considered to be recovered.

This can be many things: Large expenditures that are expected to generate revenue over many years will be arbitrarily capitalized

Money that customers owe on sales

Such notes throughout the financial statement explain in greater detail

Figure 6.1A

172

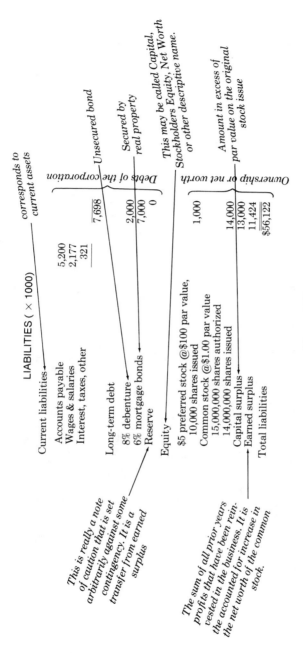

Figure 6.1B

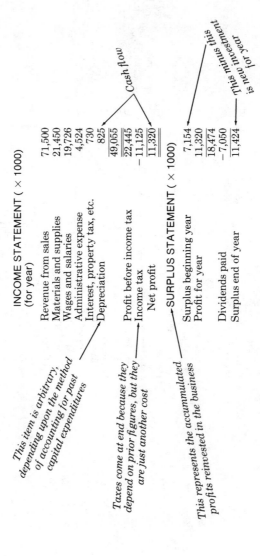

INCOME STATEMENT (× 1000)
(for year)

Revenue from sales	71,500
Materials and supplies	21,450
Wages and salaries	19,726
Administrative expense	4,524
Interest, property tax, etc.	730
Depreciation	825
	49,055
Profit before income tax	22,445
Income tax	− 11,125
Net profit	11,320

Cash flow

This item is arbitrary, depending upon the method of accounting for past capital expenditures

Taxes come at end because they depend on prior figures, but they are just another cost

SURPLUS STATEMENT (× 1000)

Surplus beginning year	7,154
Profit for year	11,320
	18,474
Dividends paid	−7,050
Surplus end of year	11,424

This represents the accumulated profits reinvested in the business

This minus this is new investment for year

Figure 6.1C

or, worded alternatively,

$$\text{assets} = \text{debt} + \text{equity}.$$

The balance-sheet statement amounts to a snapshot of the accounts at a specific point in time. The balance sheet contains no clues as to how the firm reached that state. Current practice is for companies to publish financial statements showing two consecutive years. In this way it is possible to see the change from one year to the next.

6.2.1 Assets

The asset side (left) of the statement is divided into three major parts:

1. *Current assets*, as a matter of convention, represent all those assets which, in the normal course of business, can be expected to *turn over* in a period of less than one year. These include cash, inventory, and accounts receivable.

2. *Other assets* are investments, usually financial, which are not in the main stream of the firm's normal business. They represent assets available for financing other projects; in the meantime, they are held in separate accounts.

3. *Fixed assets, or capital assets*, representing the main operating plant and equipment investments, constitute the principal capital investment of the firm. Capital assets are listed at their original installed cost. In addition, the accumulated costs, already accounted for as depreciation or amortization, are listed. Deducting these allocated costs from the original cost furnishes the net book value of capital assets.

This deduction has been historically called *reserve for depreciation*, or *reserve for amortization*. The latter term is used for investments that are made for intangible developments, such as research and development, and that are carried in the capital accounts of the firm. The term depreciation is used when referring to physical assets that are subject to wear and tear and hence depreciate physically.

This so-called reserve is the sum of prior allocations of capital up to and including the current year. It is more appropriately called *accumulated depreciation allowances*. Modern practice is to designate items in financial reports in descriptive terminology. The older term *reserve* conjured up a mental image of money, sitting off to the side, with nothing to do but wait for something to happen. This is misleading. The reserve, or sum of past depreciation allowances, is nothing more than a recognition of the amount of the original expenditure that has been accounted for in the books up to the report date. The net fixed assets—that is, the difference between original expenditure and the accumulated depreciation—is properly referred to as *book value*. In no way may it be construed as having any tangible value.

The sum of the three asset categories described above constitutes total assets.

6.2.2 Current Assets

Current assets are cash, accounts receivable, and inventory. Cash is self-explanatory. It is the money held in the bank for handling day-to-day transactions. Clearly, since it is not earning interest, it is to the advantage of the firm to keep this item as small as possible, consistent with efficient operating procedures.

Receivables also are straightforward. These represent billings for goods or services delivered and not yet paid for. Again it is in the best interest of the firm to manage its receivables so as to keep customers up to date in their payments.

The third item, inventory, is probably the most complex of the three, because accounts have to be recorded in money terms rather than in terms of physical quantities. There are two methods employed by firms for keeping track of inventory:

1. *First in first out, or FIFO.* The FIFO method is to charge for materials, no matter when they are taken out of inventory, at the prices paid as they came into inventory. It is not necessary that materials be physically withdrawn from inventory on that basis; it is only that charges are made that way.

2. *Last in first out, or LIFO.* In this method, items are charged out of inventory at the price of the most recently purchased

items. As for FIFO, this does not mean that the physical quantities need be put in or taken out in that sequence.

Inventory includes everything from raw materials recently purchased to finished goods awaiting shipment to the customer. The general classification is:

- Raw materials.
- Work in process.
- Finished goods.

During production, labor is being expended to add value to the product. These labor costs, together with the *burden* (fixed costs that must be allocated) are charged against the product as part of the cost and therefore are reflected in the value of inventory carried on the books. Note however that these values are strictly *book* values. They reflect accumulated accounting allocations and bear no relationship to market values. If a firm were forced to liquidate inventory, it would be highly unlikely that it could realize anything like the book value. Work in process might be worthless on the market, and finished goods might be worth much more than the value recorded on the books.

6.2.3 Liabilities

The liability side of the statement—the right-hand side—is, like the left side, divided into several classifications. The first, matching that of the left, is current liabilities. The second is long-term debt. A third category (which, strictly speaking, is not debt at all) is called *reserves* or *reserves for contingencies*, and is always explained in footnotes contained in the report. In effect this represents a way of saying that, should the situation for which the reserve has been established eventuate, then that amount would be available. In order to create this reserve some other item has had to have been reduced. The other item is ownership. In a sense, reserve is a precautionary item to indicate that ownership would have to be reduced if the contingency should materialize.

Long-term debt, defined as obligations coming due in more than one year, may take many forms—mortgages, notes to the bank, or bonds in various forms. Bonds will be discussed in detail in Chapter 7 on Finance.

6.2.4 Current Liabilities and Working Capital

In parallel with the conventions for defining current assets, current liabilities are defined as those obligations which, in the normal course of business, will be turned over within a one-year period. The first current liability item is wages and salaries currently owed to employees. The employees of a firm work before being paid, so that at any point in time the company will owe them wages. The second item is current bills awaiting payment, or *accounts payable*. There may be other items, such as interest obligations due on a note.

Current assets and current liabilities together represent the normal flow of day-to-day transactions. Capital must be set aside for these day-to-day operations of the firm. This is *working capital*, defined as the difference between current assets and current liabilities. An important measure of the liquidity of the firm and of its ability to cope with business fluctuations is the ratio of current assets to current liabilities, and is called the current ratio. An even more stringent measuring technique is to remove receivables and inventory from the current assets and use this adjusted ratio, called the *acid-test ratio*, as a measure of liquidity.

6.2.5 Equity or Ownership

The remaining items on the right side of the balance sheet statement must balance the accounting equation. In its simplest form, this could be the total balancing term, *equity*. It breaks down in more detail into the original investment of the owners, usually in the form of common stock, plus all profits reinvested since the firm was organized. Formerly this latter contribution was called *surplus*, and to some extent this term is still used. The term *surplus* is connotationally misleading, however, and modern practice is to use a more descriptive term, such as *reinvested earnings*.

In the original capitalization of the firm, the state, in issuing the charter to do business, authorizes the issuance of a specified number of shares at a *stated price* or *par value* per share. These items represent legal niceties and for our purposes need not be elaborated upon, except to note that the par value has no meaning whatever in terms of value. However, its formal existence does require that the money committed to the original capitalization of the firm be broken into two parts:

1. The amount received for each share, issued at the specified price (par or stated price), times the number of shares.
2. The amount subscribed in excess of that price.

The latter is called *capital surplus*.

The company may issue various kinds of stock. The most significant, by far, is common stock. This is the voting stock, which retains residual ownership of the firm. All other stock is in the form of some category of *preferred stock*. It is preferred because it receives a specified dividend before any dividend is paid on the common stock, and in the event of dissolution it has a higher priority claim on assets of the company than common stock does. There are countless variations and special provisions attached to preferred stocks.

6.3 THE INCOME STATEMENT

While the balance sheet represents the equation of state of the firm, the income statement represents the money flow. The unit of all balance-sheet items is dollars. The unit of the income-statement items is dollars per year. The balance sheet is a report on the condition of the firm, as of a particular date. The income statement is for a particular time period, usually for one quarter or one year. It is always for a period immediately preceding the date of the balance sheet.

In its simplest form, the income statement is merely a statement of revenues minus all expenses, in order to show the profit for the period—the "bottom line". However, such a simplified income statement would be too condensed. More detail is desirable, and therefore the more important components of revenues and costs are provided. These are evident from the illustrative example (Figure 6.1).

For the most part, this illustration requires no further elaboration. It should be noted that inventory is the flow or consumption of materials and supplies for the period. It will therefore show up in the income statement as the difference between the amount at the beginning and end of the period, plus additions to inventory made during the period.

6.3.1 Depreciation and Income Tax

Two items deserve special mention: depreciation and income taxes. All the expense items on the statement, with one exception—depreciation—are also expenditures. They are cash-flow items. Depreciation is, properly, an expense, but it is *not* an expenditure. It is an allocated cost and is arbitrary. The amount of the allocation depends on the length of time over which the cost of the asset being depreciated is to be recovered, and on the particular method employed for making this allocation.

Income taxes are computed on the basis of profit before provision has been made for these taxes. Therefore, while taxes are costs, they cannot be computed until after everything else has been taken into account. Furthermore taxes depend on the difference between revenues and all other expenses, all of which are cash flows, with the one notable exception of depreciation. Therefore, the tax obligation incorporates the same arbitrariness as does the depreciation allowance. The Internal Revenue Service allows considerable latitude in the choice of depreciation method. This translates into a corresponding latitude in stating what the tax obligation will be. The higher the depreciation allowance, the lower will be the tax.

It must be recognized, however, that the sum of all depreciation allowances over the life of the asset can never exceed the original expenditure. In the end, and barring a change in tax rates, the same total tax must be paid. The important thing is that the effect of stating high early depreciation allowances, is to shift the incidence of the tax obligation to a later date. This introduces a time value for the postponed tax and, consequently, a great deal of effort is devoted to finding ways for shifting the time when taxes become payable. It also means that depreciation is primarily a parameter in the tax computation formula—even more than it is a measure of a wasting away of asset value. This tax use for depreciation is a subversion of its original purpose, that of providing an appropriate mechanism for time allocation of expenditures in order to measure current profitability.

6.4 THE RETAINED-EARNINGS STATEMENT

The retained-earnings statement (or surplus statement, as it was called until recently) is straightforward. It is needed to round out the financial statements by forming a bridge between the income statement and the balance sheet. Thus the change from one year to the next is:

retained earnings (surplus) as of the prior statement period

+ profits for the period

− dividends (i.e., distributions to owners)

= retained earnings (surplus) for the new statement year.

6.5 FINANCIAL-REPORT ANALYSIS

The financial report provides a summary of all data pertinent for measuring how well the firm has been doing. The final measure of interest is profitability. This has come to be called colloquially the "bottom line". It is a statement of reported profit and is not necessarily a measure of true earnings. As a result, financial analysts often qualify such profit measures by subjective comment on what they refer to as "quality of earnings".

The data of the various reports cannot always be interpreted solely on the basis of the data contained in the reports themselves. For this reason the financial report contains extensive explanation in the form of footnotes. These footnotes provide information which must be evaluated by judging its long-term possible effects on the firm's viability and profitability.

An important means for interpreting the significance of financial statements is by means of ratios. Ratios of balance-sheet items to one another and of income-statement items to balance-sheet items provide appropriate indicators of corporate performance. Comparison of a number of such ratios for one firm with ratios that apply to successful and to unsuccessful firms in comparable industries provides useful assessments.

The magnitude of some ratios is quite specific to the particular industry, while others have a general applicability. For example the ratio of inventory to sales for a fresh-food merchandiser will be entirely different from that of an aircraft manufacturer. Their profit on book value, on the other hand, could be the same.

Some of the important ratios are:

1. *Current ratio.* This is the ratio of current assets to current liabilities. It provides a measure of the adequacy of the working capital (i.e., current assets minus current liabilities).

2. *Inventory turnover.* This is the ratio of sales (revenues) to inventory. The reciprocal of this ratio times 365 is the average number of days in process. Clearly, in the case of a fruit stand, very few days should elapse for an inventory turnover, but for airplane manufacturing, it could well be a year.

3. *Turnover of receivables.* This is the ratio of sales (revenues) to accounts receivable. As above, the reciprocal times 365 results in the average time it takes the firm to collect its bills. If this stretches into weeks, it may be a sign that the company is not managing its working capital very well, and something may be seriously wrong.

4. *Ratio of depreciation allowance to net fixed assets.* A high value can be a sign of obsolescence of existing plant. On the other hand, it may mean that the firm is writing off assets too rapidly and, accordingly, understating profit to some degree.

5. *Ratio of net profit to sales.* The appropriate level of this ratio depends on the kind of business. Capital-intensive businesses will show higher profit ratios than will labor-intensive ones.

6. *Profit on book value.* This ratio is meaningful only to the extent that book value itself is meaningful. Since book value reflects only the historical capital expenditure, it can often be a gross understatement of value in terms of potential earnings.

7. *Ratio of common-stock equity to the sum of preferred stock and long-term debt.* This ratio is a measure of leverage on the common stock. Its reciprocal is a measure of safety or conservatism in the company.

6.6 DEPRECIATION FUNCTIONS

All the items of the income statement, with one notable exception, are cash receipts or expenditures. The exception is depreciation or amortization. Furthermore, there are no listings of capital expenditures. There are two important reasons for structuring the financial statements this way—smoothing of the expense stream and phasing of expenses with revenues.

The main purpose of the accountant is to prepare a report to management and to the owners, which will reflect how well the firm did for the immediate past reporting period. If the accountant simply subtracted expenditures from revenues, the picture would be badly distorted. Operating expenditures are almost synchronous with revenues, but leading them by a few weeks. Thus the cash-flow stream, which is represented by the difference between revenue and expenditure streams, is reasonably smooth. This is not so for capital expenditures. Capital expenditures are "lumpy". Some years they may be large, and other years almost nonexistent. In addition, by the very definition of a capital expenditure, the revenue attributable to it is delayed and spread out over time. For this reason, the accountant allocates the capital cost against future revenue to determine a *depreciation expense.*

If he takes the time over which the allocation is made to be the physical life of the asset, then when it is worn out and must be replaced, he can repeat the process with its replacement. Thus there is a rationale for calling such an allocation cost a depreciation expense. Nevertheless it is just an accounting convenience. There need not be any relationship between physical depreciation and depreciation expense. Some equipment, an automobile for instance, will actually depreciate in market value along a declining exponential. Other equipment may lose value all at once, and still others will appreciate in value, all of which is irrelevant in the accounting context.

Another important aspect of depreciation is that it is involved in the rules by which income-tax obligations are computed. This is unfortunate, because it tends to obscure the essential reasons for time-allocated expenses; therefore, we will postpone treatment of taxes to Section 6.8.

It will be noted that the depreciation allowance is *not* a cash flow. The accountant does not identify capital expenditures as cash flows, simply because there is no place to report it in the income statement. His definition of cash flow, then, is simply profit plus depreciation.

There are a number of conventional ways for making such time allocations of capital costs. All of them have certain advantages and disadvantages, mostly with respect to the effect on taxes.

The various methods described in the next few sections are all incorporated in the computer programs of Appendix E.

6.6.1 Straight-Line Depreciation

Straight-line depreciation is the simplest and most widely used depreciation method. The asset value is divided by the number of years over which it is to be depreciated, in order to obtain the depreciation allowance for each year—the depreciation expense that is chargeable to the expenses for that year.

For example, if the asset originally cost $10,000 and its depreciable life is 10 years, the depreciation allowance would be $1000 per year. The original expenditure for the asset would never appear in the financial statement. Each year $1000 would be charged, until the entire original amount is finally accounted for. The book value of the asset each year would be the book value for the previous year less the allowance made for the year.

6.6.2 Declining-Balance Depreciation

Declining-balance depreciation is computed as a negative exponential, but the calculation is done in discrete increments. For instance it could be stated as a 20% declining balance. This would mean that the first year's depreciation allowance would be 20% of the original asset cost. For the above example, that is $2000. Accordingly, the book value at the end of the first year is $8000, the first cost less the depreciation of $2000.

The second year's depreciation would now be 20% of the book value, or $1600, and so the new book value would be $6400. The procedure is repeated for subsequent years. Clearly, declining balance never reaches a zero book value. To overcome this difficulty, the accountant switches to straight line at some point.

The percentage rate of decline is usually based on taking the same life as for straight-line depreciation and establishing what percentage of the asset is represented by the straight-line depreciation. Thus for the example chosen, it is 10%. This causes the depreciation to stretch out over too many years, and therefore the percentage rate is arbitrarily multiplied by a factor. When the factor used is two, the resulting method is called *double declining balance*. Precedence for its use as well as for the one and one-half declining balance, has been established in the income-tax rules.

6.6.3 Sum-of-the-Digits Depreciation

The sum-of-the-digits method has one distinct advantage over the declining-balance method. The latter never reaches a zero value. Theoretically, it represents an infinite life. The sum-of-the-digits provides a declining allowance schedule that brings the value to zero at the end of the depreciable life.

The sum-of-the-digits allowance is found by summing the years of depreciable life:

$$S = 1 + 2 + 3 + 4 + \cdots + n. \tag{6.1}$$

The jth year's allowance is then the ratio

$$\frac{n - j + 1}{S} \tag{6.2}$$

times the original asset cost.

For example, if the depreciable life is 5 years, then $S = 15$ and the first year's depreciation will be $\frac{1}{3}$ of the asset value.

6.6.4 Sinking-Fund Depreciation

Sinking-fund depreciation is no longer in current use. Nevertheless it has important theoretical significance. It is a special case of the generalized depreciation function, which will be discussed next, and so is covered in more detail in Section 6.7.

The basis of the sinking-fund depreciation method is a hypothetical deposit into a sinking fund which, accumulated at a specified interest rate, will amount to the original asset value at the depreciable asset life. Thus the initial allowance will be

$$\text{depr. allowance} = (\text{asset value}) \times (F/A, i, n). \qquad (6.3)$$

The book value is

$$BV(1) = (\text{asset value}) - \text{depr}(1). \qquad (6.4)$$

In the second year, the allowance is

$$\text{depr}(2) = BV(1) \times (F/A, i, n - 1), \qquad (6.5)$$

and in general, for the mth year it is

$$\text{depr}(m) = BV(m - 1) \times (F/A, i, n - m + 1) \qquad (6.6)$$

and the book value is

$$BV(m) = BV(m - 1) - \text{depr}(m). \qquad (6.7)$$

It will be noted that sinking-fund depreciation is the same as the proportion of an annuity payment that is allocated to the retirement of the principal.

6.6.5 Comparison of Methods

The various methods can be compared by examination of Figure 6.2, showing the way in which book value declines with time. Straight-line depreciation is constant, and the book value is linear. Sinking-fund depreciation has the effect of producing a slow decline of book value in early years and a faster decline in later years. The declining-balance and sum-of-digits methods both have the reverse effect.

Declining-balance and sum-of-digits depreciation often tend to approximate the trend of resale values of assets. For this reason, it is often contended that they are more realistic than straight line or sinking fund depreciation. However, this contention is *not* valid, because we are not concerned with salvage value in account-

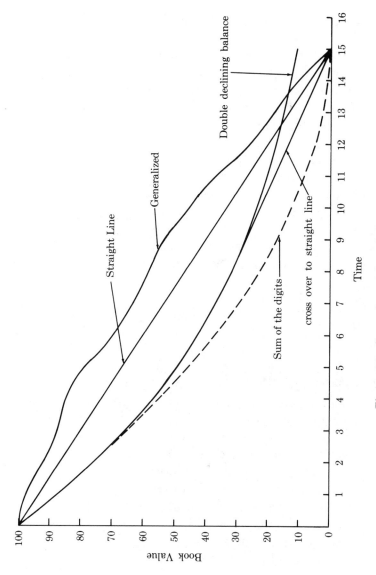

Figure 6.2 Comparison of depreciation methods.

ing. Realism depends on the appropriate way to allocate the cost of the asset value over the life of the asset in order to report each year's profit.

6.7 A GENERALIZED DEPRECIATION FUNCTION*

Depreciation, in an accounting sense, may bear only an incidental relationship to physical wear or obsolescence. Its primary function is the arbitrary allocation of a prior expenditure over time. There are two distinctly different reasons why this allocation might be desired, namely, determination of income tax and measurement of the firm's performance. Different functions are appropriate for each. Here we consider only the need to develop a suitable function for measuring year-to-year performance.

In order to determine a suitable measure of profitability, we will examine a single project that is independent of any other activities of the firm. The decision to invest in this project is presumed to have been made on the basis of the usual estimates of expenditures and revenue streams. The discounted cash flow establishes an acceptable internal rate of return, r, and so the project is undertaken. At some time t after startup, it is desirable to know how well the project is performing, relative to what had been forecast. In other words, is the expected rate of return materializing?

If the stated profit (i.e., the cash flow less the depreciation allowance) is divided by the book value (BV), we obtain a rate of return on book value. If we have been using conventional depreciation accounting, such as straight line, sum of digits, or declining balance, the rate of return on book value will vary widely from year to year. It will be of little use as a current measure of how well the project is doing. Its deviation from the appropriate measure r will stem from two causes. In the first place, the depreciation allowance was not selected so as to provide a valid measure for an individual project. In the second place, it would be sheer coincidence if the projected cash-flow stream materialized exactly as projected. Let us examine these two issues separately.

---

*To the best of the author's knowledge, the material of this section is completely new. It has never been published before.

For the time being we will ignore the difference between forecast and realized cash flows, by first supposing the unusual situation where they match exactly. In this way we can develop a depreciation function (DF) that will yield precisely a stated rate of return, at all times, identically equal to r. Let us designate time as t, and make T the time at which we wish to determine current performance (present time). The time H is the life of the project, and x is time measured into the future from T. The discount function is taken in continuous form, e^{-rt}. Let the depreciation function be $D(t)$, and the cash flow be $y(t)$ (Figure 6.3). Therefore the profit $\mathrm{pr}(t)$ is

$$\mathrm{pr}(t) = y(t) - D(t). \tag{6.8}$$

The rate of return is

$$r = \mathrm{pr}(t)/\mathrm{BV}(t). \tag{6.9}$$

From this,

$$D(t) = y(t) - r\,\mathrm{BV}(t). \tag{6.10}$$

We can make r a constant by determining $\mathrm{BV}(T)$ to be the present worth of the remaining cash flow from T to the finite life H. Thus

$$\mathrm{BV}(T) = \int_0^{H-T} y(t)e^{-rx}\,dx. \tag{6.11}$$

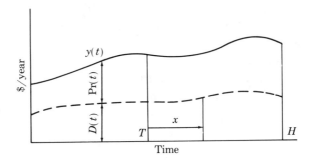

Figure 6.3   Depreciation function.

6.7.1 The Special Case of a Constant Cash-Flow Function

Equation 6.10 coupled with equation 6.11 provides a generalized function for depreciation, which meets the performance measurement criteria described above. This applies for any cash-flow function. An interesting special case is that of a constant cash flow. Let $y(t) = A$, a constant cash flow or annuity. Then equation 6.11 can be shown to reduce to

$$BV(T) = \frac{Ar}{e^{r(H-T)} - 1},$$
(6.12)

and equation 6.10 reduces to

$$D(T) = A\left(1 - \frac{1}{e^{H-T} - 1}\right).$$
(6.13)

This is sinking-fund depreciation in continuous form.

6.7.2 Reconciliation of Actual with Projected Cash Flow

The actual cash flow will always be different from what has been projected. Since the depreciation function must be established *a priori*, the stated profit or return on book value [which we may distinguish as ROI(T)] will vary accordingly. However, the generalized depreciation function will provide a more realistic measure than that now used in common practice. The resulting performance measure can also be interpreted by comparison of ROI(T) with the r used for development of the depreciation function. If ROI(T) is larger (smaller) than r, then project performance is better (worse) than projected.

A further indicator of performance may be used to assess the accumulated extra cash flow from the project. This can be seen in Figure 6.4. Let the extra cash flow be

$$XCF(T) = BV(T) \times [ROI(T) - r].$$
(6.14)

These extra cash flows may be accumulated by compounding at

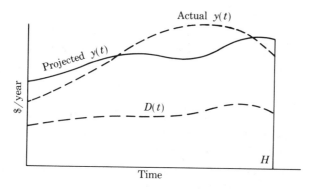

Figure 6.4 ROI with actual cash flow.

rate r:

$$\text{acc}\,\text{XCF}(T) = \int \text{XCF}(t)\,e^{-rt}\,dt, \tag{6.15}$$

where acc XCF designates the present worth of this accumulation.

If it develops that the project yields an overall rate of return r, as expected, but the shape of the cash flow is different from the projected cash flow, then the value of acc XCF(t) will vary over time from positive to negative. However, in the end, acc XCF(H) will be zero. As time unfolds, it provides a measure of how well the project is doing.

6.7.3 The Project as an Item in the Corporate Portfolio

Each project is embedded in the framework of the overall corporate investment portfolio and is not readily separable from it. It may be difficult to establish any specific rate of return for each separate project. In effect, once a project is installed, it can be assigned only that return which is realized by the enterprise itself. Thus it may be reasonable to select r on the basis of a target rate of return for the corporation. Under these circumstances the same r would apply for all depreciation allocations.

Prior to the 1930s, sinking-fund depreciation was used routinely by the public utilities. It should be noted that, for a constant cash flow, sinking-fund depreciation is the only theoretically correct method for providing an ongoing measure of profitability. However, it also presupposes that the lives of assets are precisely known. At the same time, an averaging effect comes into play to make all depreciation methods approximately equivalent to the more generalized function described above. This averaging arises from the fact that there are many investments made each year, and as new investments are made, others are retired.

The simplest way to depreciate assets is to take a single one-time allocation, equal to the total investment, but displaced in time by one-half the average asset life. This can be shown to be approximately equivalent, on average, to any other method, provided that the investments made are more or less homogeneous from year to year and are made uniformly over time.

Finally it should be reemphasized that the generalized depreciation function is not advantageous for determining income-tax obligations. It is also worth restating: **a depreciation allocation function need not be representative of physical depreciation.** Physical depreciation can be reflected in a decline in salvage value, according to a negative-exponential function. This is only relevant in considering a possible sale of the asset. As long as the objective is measurement of profit for the latest time interval, the generalized depreciation function is a theoretically correct method for allocating past costs to meet the objective of a constant return on investment.

6.8 INCOME-TAX CONSIDERATIONS

Taxes are costs, no different in principle from any other costs. Like all costs, it is in the interest of the individual investor or firm to minimize them. Property taxes, excise taxes, and the like are levied directly and present no problem of strategy for reducing them. They are accounted for in essentially the same manner as expenditures for labor or materials. Income taxes must be treated differently. Income tax is based on stated profit, before provision is made for the income tax itself. Because of the arbitrariness in stating profit, there is also arbitrariness associated with the tax obligation. With the single exception of depreciation expense, all costs and revenues are objectively determined. Thus the way in which depreciation is handled determines the tax cost.

Although the tax laws change from year to year, there are certain basic principles that are invariant. To the extent that the tax can be shifted forward in time, the individual or firm realizes the time-value derived from the postponed payment. This is why it is advantageous to accelerate depreciation allocations. It has the effect of reducing the stated before-tax profit. It also reduces stated after-tax profit. Thus finding ways for reducing taxes is equivalent to finding ways for reporting lower profits. It should be emphasized that this time-shifting strategy does not lower taxes in dollar amounts. The same tax will be paid eventually, but in early years tax levies will be lower than in later years.

Aside from the time value gained from postponing taxes, there is the possibility of changing the tax classification of the income on which the tax is levied, from income to capital gains. Capital gains are taxed at 40% of the income-tax rate. Until recently the double-declining-balance method of depreciation accounting was used extensively for this purpose. The very high allowances in the first few years of an asset life, resulting from this depreciation method, had a significant tax-reducing effect. If the asset could be sold early to generate a capital gain, then this gain would be taxed at 40% of the rate of income taxes. The tax basis on which the capital gain is calculated is, of course, the depreciated book value at the time of sale. This is lower than if straight-line depreciation had been used, but the reduction in the income tax due to accelerating the depreciation is not nearly offset by the small additional capital gains tax.

The IRS looks upon this device as a loophole. As a result, it now recaptures such lost taxes by taxing the difference between straight-line depreciation and any accelerated method, at the income-tax rate.

EXAMPLE:

Consider the tax implications of double-declining-balance depreciation versus straight-line depreciation for an asset originally costing $100,000. It is depreciated over a 15-year life. The income-tax rate is 40%. The asset is sold in 4 years for a price of $80,000. Assume that the OCC is 20%.

SOLUTION

1. *Straight-line depreciation.* At the end of four years the book value and, hence, the tax basis of the property will be

$$\$100,000 - (4 \times 100,000/15) = \$73,333.$$

The annual tax bill will have been reduced, as a result of owning the asset, by 40% of the depreciation allowance, that is, $2667. The capital gains at sale will be $80,000 − $73,333 = $6667, on which a tax of $2667 would now be paid. The present value of the tax savings is

$$P = 2667(P/A, 20, 4) - 1067(P/F, 20, 4) = \$6390.$$

This represents the gain in real value.

2. *Double-declining-balance depreciation.* The depreciation parameter will be $2/15 = 0.1333$. At the end of four years the book value and, hence, the tax basis of the property will be

$$\$100,000 \times \left[(1.1333)^4 - 1\right] = \$64,980.$$

The capital gain is $80,000 − $64,960 = $15,020. The income tax saving is shown in the following table:

YEAR	AMOUNT	$(P/F, 20, j)$	PRESENT WORTH
1	5,333	0.833	4,442
2	4,622	0.694	3,208
3	4,006	0.579	2,319
4	3,472	0.482	1,674
Total			$11,643

The present worth of the capital-gains tax is

$$\$15,020 \times 0.16 \times 0.482 = \$1158,$$

making a net gain in terms of a present worth of

$$\$11,643 - \$1158 = \$10,485,$$

amounting to $10,485 − $6390 = $4095 better than the straight-line case. However, if recapture is made by the IRS, the difference between straight-line and declining-balance capital gains is $15,020 − $6667 = $8353, taxable at the full 40% rate. Thus the capital-gains tax is

$$\$8353 \times 0.4 + 6667 \times 0.16 = \$4408,$$

for which the present worth is $2125. Contrast this with the $1158 payable before recapture. It is $967 less favorable as a result of recapture, but using the declining-balance method is still considerably better than using straight-line depreciation.

6.8.1 Tax Shelters

A tax shelter is a device for structuring investments in such a way that taxable income from one source can be offset by stated losses from another. Typically, a person whose primary income derives from his profession finds that a sizable proportion of his income is in excess of his living expenses. Ideally he would pay income taxes only on the living-expense part of his income and invest the remainder in such a way as to make it tax-exempt. In one way or another this involves paying out that extra income as qualified business expenses.

It should be apparent that it is not sufficient to pay that extra income to someone other than the IRS, unless the result of so doing is a later return. The later return must be sufficient to offset the tax payment that is avoided and, at the same time, earn the OCC.

The most common method for accomplishing this objective is through financing some investment by means of debt. Interest on this debt is tax-exempt expense. In addition the investment can show a year-to-year reported operating loss, which is also tax-exempt. The success or failure of such a tax-shelter scheme depends on the eventual sale of the investment at a capital gain. The essential ingredients of all tax shelter plans are (1) this shifting of tax to some time in the future when the marginal tax rate is lower and (2) a change in the classification of ordinary income to capital gain.

6.9 RECAPITULATION

1. Project evaluation is prospective. Accounting is retrospective. The engineer's or investor evaluator's function is to predict the overall profitability of a project from beginning to end. The accountant's function is to measure and report on the results of investments as time passes.

2. Accounting practice is based on an accrual system and double entries of all transactions—one in the debit column and one in the credit column.

3. The fundamental accounting equation of state is

$$\text{assets} = \text{liabilities} + \text{ownership}.$$

This is reflected in the firm's balance sheet.

4. The balance sheet is a report on the status of the firm at a specific time point. The income statement is a measure of flow of revenue minus expense and so is expressed in dollars per period.

5. Depreciation is the one item in the income statement that is not cash flow, but rather an arbitrary time-allocated cost.

6. The three common depreciation methods are straight line, declining balance, and sum of digits. There is a generalized depreciation function that would result in a constant reported rate of return on book value, provided that the cash flow eventuates as predicted. This function reduces to the special case of sinking-fund depreciation when the cash flow is constant.

7. The theoretical justification for depreciation is to produce valid reports of the current operating performance of the firm. The use of depreciation for determining taxes subverts its primary purpose. The most efficacious method of depreciation accounting for minimizing taxes is incompatible with depreciation accounting for valid performance reporting.

8. Tax minimizing or the construction of tax shelters involves techniques for shifting reporting times for taxable income to later times and for changing income classification from ordinary income to capital gains.

6.10 PROBLEMS

1. Prepare a financial report (balance sheet and income statement) for the data listed below. The values are in millions of dollars. Wherever there is a question mark, the value can be calculated from the other data.

1. Labor expense	$85
2. Interest on debt	$10
3. Cash in the bank	$100
4. Long-term debt	$120
5. Accumulated depreciation	$600
6. Cost of materials	$125
7. Income tax at 20%	?

8. Common stock, 10 million shares issued	$100
9. Accounts receivable	$120
10. Administrative expense	$40
11. Accounts payable	$40
12. Property taxes paid	$5
13. Profit	?
14. Dividends paid	$20
15. Plant and equipment at cost	$1000
16. Inventory	$80
17. Cost of goods sold	?
18. Reserve for contingencies	$40
19. Profit before income taxes	?
20. Capital surplus	$100
21. Wages and salaries payable	$50
22. Other investments	$150
23. Accumulated reinvested earnings	?
24. Sales revenue	$350
25. Depreciation allowances	$15

In addition to making up the financial statement, answer the following questions:

a. What is the dividend per share?

b. What is the net worth of the company?

c. If the stock is selling for $32, what is the price/earnings ratio?

d. What is the net working capital?

e. What is the inventory turnover rate?

f. What were the accumulated reinvested earnings for the previous year?

2. For (a) straight-line depreciation and (b) double-declining-balance depreciation, for a life of 10 years and an investment of $10,000, show the year-to-year rate of return on the investment. Assume that the cash flow it produces is $1770 per year. After doing this, use a 12% sinking-fund depreciation and find the year-to-year rate of return. What conclusions do you draw from the answer you get?

3. Draw up a table for a generalized depreciation schedule where the cash flow is expected to grow, on a discrete basis,

at 5% per year. The life of the asset is 10 years, and the historical rate of return the company has maintained is 9%. Assume that the asset value was originally $10,000.

4. If it develops that the investment, in the preceding problem, generated a cash flow of $1200 per year for the first 4 years and then jumped to $2000 per year for the next 6 years, what would the reported year-to-year rate of return be, assuming you had used the generalized depreciation schedule?

5. An up-and-coming professional engineer has reached a stage in his career where income from his profession places him in a 40% income-tax bracket. In order to shelter this income from excessive taxes he has decided to invest in an apartment complex through a limited partnership. The general partner, who has suggested the investment, will make all the arrangements and manage the property. The engineer's share of the investment is $20,000. The general partner projects that there will be a positive cash flow to the engineer of $1000 per year. This takes into account the fact that the engineer's share of the mortgage payment will be $10,710 per year. Of this, on average, $9500 per year will be interest. The depreciation allowance will be $5000 per year, using straight-line depreciation. This makes a reportable loss of $4000 per year. Assume that these estimates are reasonable and conservative and answer the following questions:

a. What will be the reduction in the engineer's reportable taxable income?

b. In terms of cash flow, how much will the engineer be ahead each year, assuming that the tax shelter does not change the tax rate on his taxable income?

c. If, in five years, the property is sold on terms that result in no net capital gain or loss, what rate of return will the engineer have realized on his investment? (Include his tax savings as gain.)

d. What rate of return would he have realized if none of his income were taxable?

A project evaluation is made to determine which of several alternatives is likely to prove the best investment. The financial analysis, which should follow the evaluation, is for the purpose of determining the best means of implementing that choice. In other words: given the choice of alternatives, how should the necessary flow of funds for implementing the investment be managed? This analysis must include consideration of the source of funding.

7.1 SOURCES OF CORPORATE CAPITAL

There are two sources of corporate capital: internally generated funds and externally generated funds. Internally generated capital is essentially cash flow—profits plus depreciation. However, some cash flow is reserved for dividends, which is the part of profit distributed to shareholders. Therefore internally generated capital consists of profits plus depreciation, minus dividends.

Recall that depreciation is not a cash item but is the allocation of previously incurred expenditures for investments in physical assets that will some day wear out or become obsolete. Thus some of the cash flow must, normally, be allocated to replacement of worn-out equipment. Nevertheless, depreciation allowances are available for new capital, and whether these allowances are spent on a proposed new project or on replacement of a worn-out asset is immaterial.

Internally generated capital is limited by cash flow, and therefore year-to-year availability of these funds depends on the profitability of the enterprise. However, cash flow in any one year may exceed capital needs for that year. Under such circumstances, the excess must be temporarily invested in securities. These constitute reserves for new investments to be made in subsequent years.

External financing is funding contributed by the public through various kinds of financial instruments, specifically in the form of securities (stocks and bonds) or loans from financial institutions.

7.2 CLASSIFICATION OF SECURITIES

Securities can be divided into two basic types, equity and debt. Equity represents shares in the ownership of an enterprise. Debt is represented by the bonds and other loans made to the firm. Debt may be negotiated as a single loan contract between the lender, such as a bank, and the borrower. However, if the loan is large, it is often desirable to divide it into a large number of individual units. Such shared debt is represented by bonds. A bond is simply a loan made by a number of lenders to a single borrower. Because of the multiplicity of lenders, it is necessary for these collective lenders to be represented by a trustee. The trustee, usually a major bank, looks out for the interests of the bondholder, negotiates the loan terms, ensures regular compliance with the terms of the contract, and finally acts for the bondholder in the event of default. In all other respects various kinds of bonds are identical, in principle, to any other debt negotiated between one individual and another.

7.3 BONDS

There are many variations in bond provisions, corresponding to countless contract arrangements involving lending and the repayment of debt. Typically, however, bonds are issued for a specified amount to be repaid according to a set schedule, with interest at a stipulated rate. Bonds are usually issued in denominations of

$1000 per bond, and interest is paid semiannually, but is specified as a nominal annual rate.

The denomination of a bond, that amount which is repayable, is called the *face value*. The interest rate, payable under the terms of the contract, is called the *coupon rate*. Bonds are issued as either registered or bearer bonds. Bearer bonds are not recorded in the name of the holder and therefore no record is maintained of their holders. At one time bonds were commonly issued to bearer. The claim to interest due on them was recognized by means of printed coupons attached to the bond. The holder had only to clip the appropriate coupon off the bond and surrender it to receive the interest to which he was entitled. Because the coupon established a legal obligation to pay interest, the stipulated interest rate came to be known as the *coupon rate*. Today it is more common to have the bond registered to the bondholder and interest payments made by check as they come due.

In 1982 the Congress legislated discontinuance of bearer bonds, as a means for controlling cheating on income taxes. As long as bonds were issued to bearer, it was virtually impossible to trace taxable interest income from them. However, many states still have bearer bonds specified in their constitutions and the constitutionality of prohibiting them remains unresolved.

7.3.1 Types of Bonds

The common categories of bonds are:

- *Mortgage bond.* Secured by real property. In principle, no different from a mortgage on a home.

- *Debentures.* Unsecured notes. Value depends on continued earning power of the borrowing firm or agency. In principle, this is the same as an unsecured personal note at the bank.

- *Equipment trust certificates.* Lease–purchase contracts, in which the security is assured by the lender's retention of legal title to equipment, until the note has been paid off. These certificates are like the personal financing of an automobile for which the bank holds the pink slip.

- *Tax-exempt bonds.* The interest on bonds issued by states or local government agencies is not taxable by the IRS.

Therefore such bonds can be sold to the public at considerably lower interest rates than can taxable bonds. The individual in a high tax bracket finds them particularly attractive as a means of reducing his taxes. This gives to these bonds a competitive edge over other bonds and results in their lower coupon rates.

- •*Revenue Bonds.* These are debentures issued by local government agencies, and cannot be foreclosed. The payment of interest on these bonds is dependent on the generation of income. One widely used form of revenue bonds is the local industrial development bond. In effect, the municipality is willing to share its tax-exempt interest-rate advantage with firms willing to select business sites within the municipality issuing the bond. Such bonds represent hidden subsidies.

7.3.2 Call Provisions and Repayment of Principal

Individual debt obligations usually require repayment of principal by means of some form of annuity—equal regular payments including both principal and interest. Most bonds, however, require only regular interest payments with no regular payment on principal. Repayment of principal is made in a lump sum at the end of the bond life (the maturity date). Serial payment of principal, if and when provided for, is normally made in constant payments. Since the bond is held by a large number of individuals, the serial repayment is often determined by lottery.

When a bond comes due for repayment at its maturity date, funds for repayment are usually not available, and so the debt must be refinanced or "refunded". However, if the firm wishes to retire the debt at maturity it can set up a sinking fund for that purpose. This fund is provided for at the time of issuance of the bond. The company pays into it, as into a savings account, in accordance with a prearranged schedule.

An alternative method for retiring debt is to buy back the bonds on the open market. However, this method is limited, because the activity thus induced in the market will have a tendency to raise the market price of the bonds.

A company sometimes provides for early retirement of a bond issue by insertion of a *call* provision in the bond contract. A call is simply an option retained by the company to repay the debt at its election, usually after some specified minimum holding period.

A call provision is not always in the best interests of the bondholder. Therefore, in order to sell a new issue of bonds, it is necessary to provide a premium to the bondholder for incorporating in the bond provisions a right to call. In general, this premium takes the form of a higher price the company will be required to pay in the event that it exercises its call. Premiums are typically 10% to 15% of face value of the bond.

7.3.3 Convertibility Features

Some bonds are issued with provisions for conversion into common stock, at the election of the bondholder. Usually a price slightly above the market price of the stock at time of issuance of the bond is selected as the conversion value. This establishes an equivalent value for the bond in terms of the stock.

Consider a stock currently selling at $48 per share. A price of $50 per share might be chosen as the conversion price. Thus a $1000 bond would be convertible into 20 shares of stock. Clearly an investor in the bonds of the company would not be tempted to exercise his conversion option if the price of the stock remained below the conversion price of $50 per share. On the other hand, if the company prospers, the stock price may be expected to rise and the bondholder will accordingly benefit from the convertibility option.

Normally the bondholder will never take advantage of the conversion option, because his bond price will rise along with the stock price and will continue to sell at a premium above the conversion value. Thus it is seen that a conversion provision adds to the attractiveness of a bond. This in turn makes it easier for a company to issue a convertible bond than a regular bond. At the same time, the interest rate will be less than for a bond without the convertibility feature.

The convertibility provision, an option in favor of the bondholder, may be detachable from the bond, so that it can be sold by the bondholder as a separate security called a warrant. Warrants will be discussed in more detail in Section 7.4.2.

While the idea of financing by means of convertible bonds seems very attractive, there are disadvantages to the existing stockholders when a company decides to issue such securities. If a conversion option is exercised, the original common-stock interest will be *diluted*. The very fact that a convertible bond may be selling at a significant premium above its face value means that, in effect, the bondholder can elect to share in the ownership with the original stockholder by buying shares at a considerable discount from market prices.

Dilution of ownership occurs whenever an original stockholder ends up with a smaller proportion of ownership than he held originally. If for example he owned 50% of the firm before the exercising of a convertibility option, he could finally own considerably less than 50% after the holder of the convertible bond exercised his option.

7.4 STOCKS

Stocks are certificates of ownership, or equity. When a firm is incorporated, the state authority issuing its charter authorizes the issuance of a specific number of shares, into which the total ownership is divided. The firm usually will issue only a portion of the authorized shares and reserve the remainder for various purposes, such as stock-option bonuses for executives. If there is only one category of ownership, each share represents its proportionate value of the total assets of the firm. Such stock is called common stock and carries one vote for each officer to be elected to the board of directors of the firm.

Not all stock in a firm necessarily carries proportionate rights to equity. Some shares may have certain circumscribed rights. Some classes of stock have no voting rights, but in a legal sense are, nevertheless, classified as ownership.

7.4.1 Preferred Stock

Preferred stock is one of the limited classifications of stock mentioned above. It is called *preferred* because it has first claim on dividends. In general a preferred stock will be specified in terms of the dollar amount of the dividend it earns regularly, usually quarterly. There is no default if the dividend is not paid on time—unlike the case of a bond, which is in default if interest payments are missed. In addition to preference in payment of dividends, preferred stock has a higher claim on the assets of the firm, in the event of liquidation, than does the common stock. However, this claim has a lower priority than debts the firm may have incurred. In many respects preferred stock is like a bond with a fixed return, but without a maturity date. Legally, preferred stock is ownership, and any dividend, unlike bond interest, must come from after-tax earnings.

Preferred stock sometimes has the same convertibility feature a bond has. Furthermore, it can be issued with participating and/or cumulative provisions. Participating preferred stock will participate or share with the common stock in any dividend distribution, beyond some prescribed limit and in accordance with some prearranged formula.

The cumulative provision requires that any dividend payment that is missed will accumulate at a set interest rate and become an obligation of the firm, for payment in subsequent years. Accumulated dividends together with accrued interest must be fully paid before any dividend distribution can be made to the common stockholder.

7.4.2 Warrants

A warrant is not stock, but rather a claim on stock as an option to purchase a share of common stock directly from the firm at a stipulated price, called the exercise price. The firm will issue warrants as a sweetener to make the initial sale of a security more attractive to potential investors. Warrants are often issued in conjunction with bonds, as described above, but may be issued for a variety of other reasons. Frequently they are issued in conjunction with a financial reorganization of the firm. Warrants always have a limited time to expiration and a specified exercise price.

7.5 OPERATION OF FINANCIAL MARKETS

When it becomes necessary for a firm to raise further capital from external sources, the usual procedure is to arrange a new issue of either bonds or stocks through an investment banking firm. The investment banker, typically a large brokerage firm such as E. F.

Hutton or Merrill Lynch, agrees to *underwrite* the issue. That is, the investment bank contracts to dispose of the shares or bonds by distributing them to the investing public. A price, called the underwriting price, is agreed upon in advance, and this is what the firm will receive for the issue. The investment banker makes his profit by selling securities at a slight premium above the underwriting price. In the case of bonds the issuing firm will be obligated to repay the face value of the issue. The underwriting price will be in the order of a fraction of a percent below face value. Therefore the firm does not realize full face value of the issue, but in the case of a bond, is obligated to repay the full amount.

In the case of bonds, face value is always set at a round number, typically $1000. The interest rate on the bond must be compatible with current market interest rates for bonds of that risk category.

In the case of a stock issue, the price agreed upon as the underwriting price is slightly below current market price. The underwriter counts on being able to maintain that price until the issue has been fully distributed. However, he takes some risk of not being able to sell the full amount of the issue at a favorable price. Nevertheless, the firm is assured of receiving the total capital arranged for under the terms of the underwriting agreement, even if the underwriter must finally hold some of the issue himself.

In the case of a new company, or an existing company whose shares had heretofore not been traded publicly, there is no market price as a guide for establishing an initial underwriting price for that issue. Therefore the underwriter must agree with management and existing owners on what is deemed to be fair. Often, the market price after the market has had time to stabilize, will be quite far off the issuing price. This can result in either very large profits or losses for the early buyers of the new shares.

7.5.1 Security Markets

Once securities are issued and become widely held by the public, their prices are subject to market forces of supply and demand. The markets on which shares are exchanged have, over the years, become highly organized and efficient mechanisms for evaluating company prospects. Widespread dissemination of information, coupled with the large number of buyers and sellers of securities, has resulted in stocks being traded very efficiently. This has meant that securities markets play an important role in allocating capital to the most promising private investment opportunities in society.

When a firm's securities are selling at high prices on the market, it is easy and attractive to existing owners to issue new securities. Contrariwise, low prices inhibit new capital offerings. Thus the market will determine the flow of new capital into the more promising opportunities.

In the United States, today, there are a number of organized auction exchanges. They include the New York, American, Pacific, Midwest, and Philadelphia. These have recently been unified into a single integrated network by means of telecommunications, so that they effectively act as a single unit. By far the largest of them is the New York Stock Exchange. In addition, there is a second large network called the *over-the-counter market* (OTC). This operates through an information net known as the National Association of Security Dealers Automated Quotation or NASDAQ. Both systems are auction markets, but they operate on somewhat different principles. The historical development of these exchange systems is of interest in explaining these differences.

7.5.2 The Historical Perspective of the Stock Exchange

Very early, New York City became the center of financial transactions in the United States. Owners of businesses and investors seeking business opportunities went to New York, to the district in the vicinity of Wall and Broad streets, to find an agent who engaged in arranging loans and exchanges of ownership of businesses, much as real-estate agents operate today. Often such agents conducted their business from local coffee houses and sidewalk cafes, in a highly informal manner. In 1792 a group of some of the more influential agents formed a club, which they named the New York Stock and Exchange Board, later to be renamed the New York Stock Exchange. The club moved into a building and established a set of operating rules for auctioning securities of the larger firms. Their rules ensured that the club would remain exclusive by predetermining a fixed number of members. The membership grew to 1100 by 1881 and remained fixed at that number until 1928, when it increased to its present level of 1375. A new member can join only if some existing member is willing to sell his membership and the club membership so agrees.

As a result of this exclusivity provision, there has always been a market for memberships. Depending on business conditions, the value of a membership (called a *seat* on the exchange), has varied widely over the years. At one point after World War II the price of a seat dropped to as low as $8000, and at other times it has approached a million dollars. Currently a seat sells for about $480,000.

The rules of the exchange are primarily concerned with conditions for trading securities. The stocks of only a selected list of companies can be traded on the "floor" of the exchange. These stocks, which must meet prescribed conditions, are called *listed stocks*. In general, the select list is composed of the larger and stronger firms, currently on the order of two thousand companies. All others are traded by separate negotiation, as they were before the advent of the club.

After the New York Stock Exchange was formed, those agents and rokers who were not members decided to form their own club. During the interim they had to do business outside on the street or curb. For this reason they decided to call their less elite club the Curb Exchange, a name held until the late 1950s, when it was decided to give it a more dignified title: the American Stock Exchange. However even today one will hear old timers fondly referring to the American Exchange as "the Curb".

The stocks traded on the American Exchange must also meet certain criteria of soundness, reporting, and size, but the companies tend to be smaller than those traded on the New York Exchange. Many more stocks are listed on the New York Exchange than on the American Exchange.

While these two exchanges, along with many other regional exchanges, take care of the trading needs of a great many companies, by far the largest number of companies are too small to be listed on any formal exchange. Other companies, some quite large, choose not to be listed. For example, American Express, until recently, was traded on the OTC. Since listing on the New York, just a short time ago, it was included in the Dow Thirty Industrials.

These unlisted companies may be held by a fairly wide distribution of ownership. Thus an additional mechanism is needed for exchanging their shares. Brokerage firms, including members of the organized exchanges, deal in such stocks outside the exchanges or "off the floor". They used to accomplish this by direct negotiation. However, they now handle the transactions in their offices. They also execute this kind of business over the counter with clients who, so to speak, walk in off the street. Hence stocks, traded in this manner, are called *over-the-counter* stocks, whence the name of the market itself.

7.5.3 Operation of the Exchange

The exchange mechanism is an auction in which all members are both auctioneer and bidder. Listed stocks are divided into groups and assigned to one of eleven different trading posts on the floor of a large auction room. Trades are made in lots, where a lot is defined as one hundred shares. The auction is effected by calling out prices, as either bids or offers. On the market, the offer is termed an *ask*. Each floor broker acts for his client to secure the best possible price in the auction. When the price is deemed suitable, the trade is closed by a sign or word and the exchange is recorded by the clerk at that particular trading post. The news of the trade is immediately transmitted by wire service or ticker tape as a quotation specifying the number of shares and the price of the transaction.

Because of the oral nature of the transaction, prices are always quoted in eighths of a share. Decimals offer too much chance for error of interpretation and take too long to say. The exchange remains open for six hours each trading day. In that time as many as 150 millions shares may change hands. This constitutes upwards of 100,000 separate transactions, amounting to as much as $9 billion, all executed by word of mouth, with minimal exchange of paper. The legal documentation follows later. On a record-breaking day, such as just described, the ticker tape may run late by as much as an hour. Normally, however, the transmission of information of a sale will be accomplished within a minute of the execution of the transaction.

That transactions are made in lots of one hundred shares does not mean that smaller trades cannot be accommodated. Some brokers act as *odd-lot dealers*. They stand ready to buy or sell blocks of less than one hundred shares. They enter the auction to buy or sell round lots, out of which they resell the required odd lot. A fraction of a point is charged for this service.

7.5.4 Published Information

The transactions on the exchanges and OTC are reported daily in the *Wall Street Journal* and the financial sections of other daily newspapers. These data include:

1. *Summary statistics on the market.* The number of shares traded (volume), number and volume of stocks advancing and declining in price, odd-lot data, stocks making either new highs or new lows within the past 12 months, etc.

2. *Statistics on individual stocks.* The highest price, the lowest price, and the closing price (i.e., the last trade made) for all stocks traded during the day, price change from the previous day's closing price, the volume, and current dividend yield.

3. *Stock indices.* The Dow Jones averages, Standard and Poor's averages, the New York Stock Exchange index, and others.

Much other useful information is available periodically as well as daily. Knowledge of such things as big-block activity, insider transactions, specialists' short sales, and many other data are useful to the active trader in the market.

Perhaps the most widely followed data are indices of overall market performance. In this regard the Dow Jones Industrial (DJI) average is the most popular measure of market performance. The other two Dow Jones indices, the transportation and utility averages, should not be overlooked. These Dow indices were developed and put into use in 1898. At that time all computation was manual, and so the indices were based on what was felt to be a representative sample of stocks. Thirty of the largest and most significant companies were chosen to represent the industrial sector of the United States economy. The prices of their stocks were simply added and divided by thirty to provide an average price. As time elapsed, various companies split their stocks from time to time. In order to maintain the same weighting, the average had to be maintained in terms of prices prior to splits. Thus as the years rolled on, the divisor was revised from 30 to an adjusted value, reflecting the effects of splits. Currently (January 1984) the divisor is 1.194. This means that the value of the index, in the neighborhood of 1250, is nothing more than an index number. The dollar prices of the stocks included in the average are no longer reflected directly. It should be recognized that the DJI is much too selective to be representative of the market as a whole.

The Standard and Poor's index is an average of a far larger and more representative group of stocks (500 companies). Each company is weighted by the number of its shares and, correspondingly, like the DJI, the Standard and Poor's average tends to weight the larger companies more heavily than the smaller ones. However, the Standard and Poor's average is still only a sample.

The advent of the computer has eliminated the necessity for relying on a sample average for measuring the market. There is no longer any reason not to use all available data. In response, the New York Stock index has been instituted. This index is also weighted for scale in terms of the number of shares for each company. It should ultimately replace the older indices, but long tradition and emotional attachment to the older indices perpetuate adherence to them.

Other indices which are not as commonly quoted are:

- *The Value Line.* An unweighted price average of a mix of approximately 1700 stocks traded on a number of exchanges and OTC. These 1700 are stocks reviewed by the Value Line investment service.

- *The Wilshire index.* An unweighted average of 5000 stocks, including all the New York Stock Exchange stocks, the American Exchange stocks, and a large number of OTC stocks.

7.5.5 Mechanics of Trading

An investor, wishing either to buy or to sell, enters his order with his broker as a market order, as a limit order, or as a stop order:

- *Market order.* This simply directs the broker to enter the auction to obtain the best price available but not to wait until the price bid changes. In other words, if he is buying the asked price will be accepted, and if selling, the bid price will be accepted.

- *Limit order.* A price is specified with the order, and the broker is directed to withhold accepting a bid or an ask until the specified price is reached in the auction. The broker must buy for that price or less or must sell for that price or more.

- *Stop order.* This is often called a *stop-loss* order. Again a price is specified, but in this case the broker must take no action until a transaction has occurred at that price. When that happens the order automatically becomes a market order. Thus if a sell-stop order is placed below the market price, the stock will not be sold until that price is reached, but will be sold before the price can deteriorate much further.

At any instant in time, it is unlikely that those wishing to buy will want the same amount of stock as those wishing to sell. This could result in wild swings in price. For this reason a number of members of the exchange act as specialists in certain stocks. Each specialist is assigned a particular list of stocks. These members do not trade as brokers; they trade only for their own interest, but are expected to maintain an orderly market for their assigned stocks, by standing ready to balance buy and sell orders. If there is an excess of sell orders, they buy and wait for the time when the trend of orders switches to buying, at which time they reverse their position to dispose of the stock that they accumulated earlier.

7.5.6 Margin and Short Selling

When a transaction has been completed on the exchange, the seller has 5 days in which to deliver the stock certificates to the broker. The change in the registration of ownership takes longer. If the transaction is for cash, the broker makes arrangements for registration and transfer of the stock certificates to the new owner. As a rule, this will take some weeks to complete. If the new owner so desires, he need not have the stock registered in his own name, but can leave it registered with the broker or, in market jargon, in "street name". Normally an investor will leave the stock in street name if he intends to resell it again soon, or if he is buying on margin.

In the case of a margin purchase, the buyer does not fully pay for his stock. He pays a percentage of the purchase price and owes the balance. The amount he pays down is called margin. The permissible margin levels are prescribed by the Federal Reserve Bank, currently a maximum of 50%. One must pay the going broker loan rate of interest on any unpaid balance. The loan is secured by the stock, which is held by the broker in street name.

An investor purchasing a stock anticipates that he will realize a return on his investment. Often, if not usually, his interest in the company itself is incidental. Whether the company makes a profit or not may not concern him as long as his personal investment is successful. He stands to gain from dividends and from selling his stock for a higher price than he paid for it. In short, he aims to buy low and sell high. He may even sell first and buy later—in which case he is selling a stock he does not already own. This is known as *selling short*. In this case the broker lends the seller the stock certificates for him to deliver, as required by the 5-day delivery rule. The broker holds the money realized from the sale together with additional margin the seller is required to deposit. Eventually the seller buys the stock and returns the borrowed shares to cover his short position. When margin on a purchase is 50%, the margin on a short sale is 150% (i.e., the amount realized from the sale plus an additional 50% to cover the possibility of a price rise).

Margin has the effect of *leveraging* an investment. For a limited sum available for investing, the number of shares bought can be increased in inverse proportion to the amount of margin. Correspondingly the return on the investment is amplified or *levered*. Neglecting interest on the debt, margin of 50% will permit the number of shares purchased to be doubled and the return will then be leveraged by a factor of two. Of course, whatever applies for a gain applies equally for a loss.

EXAMPLE: Leverage effect

Consider purchasing a stock for $20 per share and using 40% margin. The margin interest rate is 12%. You have $10,000 available to invest.

You expect that in 6 months the price of the stock will have increased 30%. What will be your return if you invest all your funds:

1. If you do not use margin?

2. If you use the 40% margin?

3. If the stock price does not rise as expected and instead declines 10%?

SOLUTION

	WITHOUT MARGIN	WITH MARGIN
Number of shares	500	1,200
Amount of debt	0	$15,000
Interest cost	0	$1,800
Sale with gain	$13,000	$32,500
Net profit	$3,000	$15,700
Return (%)	30.0	157
Sale with loss	$9,000	$21,600
Net loss	$1,000	$5,200
Return (%)	− 10	− 52

Leverage multiplies the return by a factor of 5.23 on the upside and 5.2 on the downside.

7.6 EVALUATION OF SECURITIES

Fundamentally the evaluation of a security is no different from the evaluation of any other prospective cash flow. In the first place it should be remembered that the return on a particular investment really should be considered as part of the return on the investor's total capital, as was demonstrated in Chapters 4 and 5. However, it is conventional to consider the prospective return in terms of the internal rate of return. In other words, we look at each investment as if it were entirely independent of anything else.

Under these circumstances, the problem is to find the present worth of the future cash flow resulting from the investment. This principle applies equally well to both bonds and stocks. The difference between them is largely a matter of risk, which we will postpone considering until Chapter 9.

7.6.1 Evaluation of Bonds

The typical bond is a contract to repay the principal of a loan as a lump sum on a specific date. In addition, interest is to be paid at a specified nominal rate (usually semiannually) on a predetermined schedule. The face value of the bond should therefore be the present worth of this cash flow. Let us consider an example to verify that this is true.

EXAMPLE: Value of a bond when it yields its coupon rate

Consider a bond with interest at 6% s. The interest rate on a bond is written with a small s to indicate that it is paid semiannually, (i.e., a coupon rate of 3% per period of six months), due in the year 2004, twenty years from now. The face value of the bond is $1000. This means a semiannual interest payment of $30 for each of 40 periods. If interest on the bond is representative of market interest rates, then its value should be as follows:

present worth of repayment of $1000 is

$$P = 1000 \times (P/F, 3, 40) = \quad \$306.56$$

present worth of the interest payments is

$$P = 30 \times (P/A, 3, 40) = \quad \underline{\$693.44}$$

as expected, present worth of bond = $1000.00

It is noteworthy that the interest contributes significantly more to the present worth than does the original amount of the loan to be repaid.

Six-percent interest is not a usual rate in this day and age, but it was representative of market interest rates a number of years ago. For example, such a bond might well have been issued 10 years ago. Today the contract is still fixed by its original terms. However, an investor is not likely to be interested in buying it now from the original lender, unless he can get today's market interest rate which is, let us say, 12% s. If the new owner elects now to keep the bond to maturity, he would realize a yield on the bond of 12% s. In other words, his internal rate of return would be 12% s. For this reason the bond will not sell for its face value, but at a considerable discount. To find the current market value consistent with a 12% s market rate, we must find the present worth using 12% s (i.e., 6% per period). That is,

$$P = 1000 \times (P/F, 6, 40) + 30 \times (P/A, 6, 40)$$

$$= 97.22 + 548.61 = \$645.83.$$

An alternative solution for P may be utilized as follows: As was shown above, if the bond has a coupon rate and a yield rate that are identical, the face value and the present worth are also equal. Therefore if the coupon rate were 12% s instead of the actual 6% s, the interest payment would be the difference $(60 - 30)$. In other words, the present worth of $1000 in the year 2003 would be excessive by the present worth of the difference between what *should be* and what actually *is* the interest payment:

$$P = 1000 - (60 - 30) \times (P/A, 6, 40) = \$645.83.$$

Thus we see that we obtain the same answer as before.

The yield to maturity on a bond will be recognized as an internal rate of return. The same shortcomings of the IRR apply in evaluating a bond as in evaluating a project. The opportunity for reinvestment at the OCC is ignored. Nevertheless the yield to maturity is universally utilized as a basis for comparing bonds. This is valid as an index for bond values, but it should be recognized that each investor must consider his bond investment in the context of his portfolio of investments and in relation to his own OCC.

7.6.2 Determining the Yield on a Bond

The *yield to maturity* is defined as the internal rate of return on the bond. In general the present value of a bond is established by the bond market. The newspaper listing of bond values indicates what people are paying currently. For any particular bond, an investor can obtain a quotation from his broker. What the investor needs to know is: what is the yield corresponding to the quoted price, assuming that the bond is held to maturity?

The solution to this problem cannot be reached directly. It is only possible through some form of iteration, requiring a first guess and successive approximations.

If the bond market price is less than the face value, the yield will be more than the coupon rate. The reason for this extra yield is twofold. First, the coupon rate, based on the face value, will be returning the interest payment on less than the full value of the bond. Secondly, the bond appreciates in value from the purchase price to the face value at maturity. The first part of the return is the *current yield*. In order to determine current yield, suppose the bond does not appreciate for the first year after purchase. In other words, consider what an investor might have realized as a return if he purchased the bond one year and sold it the next at exactly the same price. His return or current yield is the coupon rate divided by the decimal value of the price. The yield to maturity will comprise both parts, the current yield plus the appreciation. The solution of this is best explained by means of an example.

EXAMPLE: Iterative solution for bond evaluation

Consider the same bond as in the previous example, selling on the market for $530. The coupon rate is 6% s, and maturity date is 2004. It will, of necessity, rise eventually to its face value of $1,000 at maturity, assuming no default. This means that in 40 periods it will appreciate $1000 - 530$, or $470. An approximation of the yield is obtained simply by proportioning the appreciation linearly.

If the bond did not appreciate at all, an investor would realize only the interest payments on his investment of $530. Thus the current yield is $6/0.53 = 11.32\% \, s$.

Now we must add something to this average interest to take care of appreciation. If we divide the $470 appreciation by 40 to obtain the average value, we get 1.175% more per period, or a nominal additional return of 2.35% s, which we must add to the current yield.

This gives us an approximation of 13.67% s. The current-yield portion is correct, but the linear portion is only an approximation, because, as you are well aware, no linear money allocation over time is correct. The correct solution can only be obtained by successive approximations.

We can start with the above approximate yield of 13.67s as a first guess, since it is clearly quite close to the correct solution. However, as you will see, we get a rapid convergence toward the correct solution. Therefore we can show this by taking the current yield as a first guess.

Use $11.32/2 = 5.66\%$ as the yield per period. Find P:

$$P = 1000 - (56.6 - 30) \times (P/A, 5.66, 40) = 581.99.$$

This value for P is clearly too high; remember we are attempting to reach a value of 530 for P. Try a slightly higher i, say about 10% higher, or $i = 6.25\%$:

$$P = 1000 - (62.50 - 30) \times (P/A, 6.25, 40) = 526.01.$$

This is closer to 530, but now is too low; we may now interpolate:

$$i = 5.66 + \frac{(6.25 - 5.66)(581.99 - 530)}{581.99 - 526.01}$$

$$= 6.208\%.$$

Checking this value,

$$P = 1000 - (62.08 - 30) \times (P/A, 6.208, 40) = \$529.70,$$

almost exactly the target value of $530. This value is clearly within practical limits, but further iteration could be made for refinement if one so desired. The correct nominal yield is 2×6.208 or $12.416\% s$.

Compare this correct value with what we first obtained as an approximated value: 13.67%—a little high.

A similar method for determining yield is applicable when considering the sale of a bond at some expected price on some given target date. Such would be the case if a call provision on the bond were to be exercised on some prescribed date. Often the call provision cannot be exercised prior to a specified date.

EXAMPLE: Yield to call

Find the yield to call for a $12\% s$ bond, maturing in February 2004 and selling currently (February 1984) for 92% of face value. The call premium is 15% but is not exercisable until February 1987.

SOLUTION

Appreciation in 3 years will be from $920 to $1150 if the call is exercised. This averages $(1150 - 920)/6 = 38.33$ per period. The coupon rate of 6% plus this appreciation of almost 4% might indicate a first guess of 10% as reasonable:

$$P = 1150 \times (P/F, 10, 6) + 60 \times (P/A, 10, 6)$$

$$= \quad 649.15 \quad + \quad 261.32 \quad = 910.46.$$

The 10% rate is too high, but only by a small amount; therefore let us try 9.5%:

$$P = 1150 \times (P/F, 9.5, 6) + 60 \times (P/A, 9.5, 6)$$

$$= \quad 667.13 \quad + \quad 265.19 \quad = 932.32.$$

By interpolation, the yield is found to be 9.72% or a nominal $2 \times 9.72 = 19.44\% \, s$ per year.

Checking:

$$P = 1150 \times (P/F, 9.72, 6) + 60 \times (P/A, 9.72, 6)$$

$$= \quad 659.14 \quad + \quad 263.47 \quad = 922.62.$$

This may be as close as one would wish to come, but let us make a further refinement to illustrate the approach. Making a second interpolation between 9.72% and 10.0% results in 9.78%. Again, checking by means of the same procedure gives a revised P of 920.00. This is correct to two places of decimals.

Therefore the yield to call is 19.56% s.

The foregoing illustrations do not make any allowance for the fact that the date at which the evaluation is being made is not the same as the interest and maturity dates. Interest on a bond between interest payment dates is calculated by linear proportion. Thus if the date when the evaluation is made falls at $\frac{1}{3}$ of the time between payment dates, the price is adjusted accordingly. The investor selling the bond at the quoted price receives the pro rata interest for a two-month period, and the buyer is charged for this interest, raising his price by that amount. Furthermore, the time to maturity is no longer an integer. However this is of no consequence. The discrete interest formulas apply for noninteger values as well.

Bond problems are readily solved on the HP-12C calculator. It is not very difficult to solve them using any programmable calculator or microcomputer. A program for the Apple II is included in Appendix E. The reader is urged to experiment with this program.

7.6.3 Value of Stock

Theoretically, the price that a stock should sell for may be solved by using the basic principle of discounted cash flow in exactly the same way as for a bond. The only difference is that the cash flow on a stock is not explicitly determined by contract as it is for a bond. The investor must make a judgment or speculation as to what the price of the stock will be at some future time of interest to him.

Dividends are not guaranteed, but are nevertheless more predictable than is the future price of the stock. Companies usually establish a consistent dividend policy. If earnings are such that the dividend must be reduced or omitted, the stock price can plummet. For this reason dividends are, as a matter of course, not cut except under very adverse conditions. On the other hand, strong, thriving companies frequently have a policy of regular dividend increases with a direct relationship to rising earnings.

Some approaches to stock evaluation are based on company earnings, on the contention that earnings belong to the stockholder and should be the primary factor in determining the stock price. While the first part of this statement is certainly true, the stockholder does not have discretionary use of this money until it is distributed as dividends. On the other hand, the value of the stock will ultimately reflect its earnings trend.

Regardless of the effect of earnings on stock price over a long period of time, short-term prices will fluctuate rather widely. From a fundamental point of view, such fluctuations must be ignored in evaluating stock, and the long-term perspective must be taken. To the extent that earnings are not paid out in the form of dividends, they are reinvested in the business and may be expected to earn a return commensurate with earlier investments the firm has made. Thus earnings will grow indefinitely and future dividends will keep pace with the earnings growth.

Conversely, the payment of dividends reduces the value of stock. This is recognized as a basic principle in the market. When the directors of the firm announce a dividend is to be paid, they specify that on a prescribed date, holders of record on the roster of stockholders as of that date will receive the dividend at some other designated date. The latter date is referred to as the *ex-dividend* date. On the particular day that a stock is traded ex-dividend, the price for the previous day is reduced by the amount of the dividend in order to compute the change for today.

For example, suppose the ABC Company closed yesterday at $24\frac{1}{2}$ and the dividend paid today is $1.00 per share. If today's closing price is $24\frac{1}{4}$, the wire service reports the change for the day as plus $\frac{3}{4}$. The stock actually advanced to $25\frac{1}{4}$, after which a dollar was paid out in cash, making its adjusted value $24\frac{1}{4}$.

As emphasized in Chapter 5, the validity of evaluating a single investment by means of the internal rate of return makes sense only if the investor eventually closes out his investment. There-fore, the present value of a stock which has never paid any dividends and is never sold would be zero even though its price may have grown consistently (i.e., there is no cash flow). Clearly this would be absurd, but it is the inevitable conclusion reached if we use the criterion of internal rate of return.

To overcome this difficulty, the investor might define for him-self a target price and also a time for reaching it, as a hypothetical close-out of the investment. In this way he will be able to obtain a meaningful value for the IRR.

EXAMPLE: Stock evaluation (1)

Suppose the ABC Company has had a consistent record of paying dividends and has, in fact, shown a steady dividend growth of 5% per year for at least 10 years. The current market price is $72 immediately after the stock has gone ex-dividend—$0.40 quarterly. On the basis of your assessment of the company, you expect that the stock should be worth $120 in three years, assuming no splits. What is the indicated IRR?

SOLUTION

The appreciation factor is $120/72 = 1.667 = (P/F, i, 3)$. Solving for i, on the basis of appreciation alone, indicates a yield of 13.85%. This makes no provision for the dividend, so we must add a little more than the 5% dividend in order to allow for its growth. This might indicate a first guess of a 20% nominal rate, or 5% per period. Thus,

$$P = 120 \times (P/F, 5, 12) + 0.40 \times (P/A, 5, 12) = 70.37.$$

This value for P is a little low, and so a more refined estimate of the return is now made, by choosing a slightly lower value for i, and repeating the above calculation. Let us do this for practice—though, given the highly speculative nature of the projected price, this refinement will be gilding the lily. Try a second guess of 4.75% for i:

$$P = 120 \times (P/F, 4.75, 12) + 0.40 \times (P/A, 4.75, 12)$$
$$= 72.35.$$

By interpolation the quarterly yield is 4.79%.

The foregoing example is somewhat unrealistic because the investor would not normally have occasion to make this kind of judgment about a prospective stock price. It is more likely that he will have some idea about a target price within a set period of time. His assessment of the price will then be determined, in his own mind, by formulating a judgment about expected growth rates. His decision to invest will be predicated, not on an internal rate of return, but on a comparison with his perceived opportunity rate of return. In this respect the dividend, along with its rate of growth, must be coordinated with the return realized from the expected growth in stock price.

EXAMPLE: Stock evaluation (2)

The ABC Company has had a consistent 10% growth rate in earnings for the past 10 years and is expected to continue that pattern into the future. Its price/earnings ratio is 12. Earnings last year were $2.50 per share and dividends were $1.00. Dividends are expected to grow at a rate of 5% per year. What is the rate of return?

SOLUTION

In this case the selling price is not predetermined. It is assumed that the price will always be determined by growth conditions. As long as the investor continues to believe that this growth represents a return in excess of his other opportunities (considering such things as risk, which will be discussed in Chapter 9) he will have no reason for selling.

The current price per share is $25. The dividend represents a return of 4%, based on current price. Since the dividend itself is growing at a rate of only 5%, that rate of return represented by the dividend will decline as time passes. In 3 years, the stock will be expected to reach a price of

$$F = 25 \times (F/P, 10, 3) = 33.28.$$

The dividend in 3 years will be

$$\text{Div} = 1.0 \times (F/P, 5, 3) = 1.16,$$

or a rate of 3.5%.

Clearly the true rate of return, assuming a sale in 3 years, must be the growth rate plus the average dividend rate. The exact value for the rate of return would have to be determined by the same procedure used in the previous example. However, a reasonable approximation is reached by taking the arithmetic mean of the dividend, thus making the return

$$i = 10\% + \frac{5\% + 3.5\%}{2} = 14.25\%.$$

One might well ask if it is realistic to assume that the rate of growth of dividends would differ from that of earnings. However it is not uncommon for the price/earnings ratio to grow over long periods during bull markets and to decline in bear markets. This reflects the difference in dividend growth patterns exemplified above.

The foregoing discussion offers a very elementary treatment of some basic long-term principles for evaluating stocks. obviously the price of stocks fluctuates rather widely, due to general economic conditions as well as sentiment in the market. The decision to invest is very much a question of timing. Many short-term traders may jump in and out of the market simply to take advantage of short-term swings. The judgment required for evaluating stocks under these conditions is an entirely separate art.

7.7   RECAPITULATION

1. Corporate capital available for investment derives from two sources:

   • Internally generated funds—profit plus depreciation less dividends.
   • Externally generated capital from the sale of new securities —stocks and bonds.

2. Bonds are generally classified as mortgage bonds (which are secured by property) or debentures (which are unsecured). A bond is a debt contract providing for a repayment schedule and a stipulated rate of interest. The interest is specified on the face value of the bond (usually $1000) as a nominal rate, normally payable semiannually. This interest rate is called the coupon rate.

3. Bonds may have call provisions, a specified penalty for early repayment, or convertibility features. A convertible bond is one that can be converted into common stock at the election of the bondholder.

4. Stocks represent ownership of the firm. The principal form of ownership is common stock, which retains the voting rights for election of directors. Preferred stock, also ownership, is more like a bond. It is preferred as to dividends and claims on assets in event of dissolution of the company. A preferred stock may be convertible into common stock under certain conditions.

5. Warrants are options to purchase stock. They often come into being as part of the convertibility of a bond or as a sweetener in a new financing plan.

6. Financial markets are auction markets for trading in securities. The New York Stock Exchange, the American Exchange, and the OTC are the three principle exchanges. The last of these operates in a different way from the other two.

7. Securities are valued on the basis of the present worth of expected cash flow. The internal rate of return is readily found for a bond, but not for a stock. The internal rate of return on a bond is called its yield to maturity and is the standard means of comparing the attractiveness of bonds.

7.8 PROBLEMS

1. Find a stock quoted ex-dividend in the newspaper. Note that it is shown with the letter x following its listing. Find what its closing price was on the previous day. Record all pertinent data.

2. Comment on reported dividends in the newspaper for a firm of your selection. What is meant by "Paid to holders of record 12/3/1982 on 1/30/1983"?

3. What should a bond sell for in order to yield 9%s if its coupon rate is 4%s, and it matures in 2001?

4. What is the yield to maturity of a 6%s bond, maturing in 1998, and selling for 66% of face value?

5. Select a bond from the newspaper and determine its yield to maturity.

6. Look up data on a company in which you might be interested and determine what price it should reach in 4 years, assuming that the price earnings ratio of the Dow Industrials rises to 16 and the company shows a corresponding change in its P/E. What would be a good price for this stock now?

7. The Congress, in order to encourage the development of low-cost housing for the poor, authorized the issuance of tax-exempt municipal bonds for the purpose of building low-rent apartment units. A builder can borrow funds for a project provided that he reserves at least 20% of the apartment units for low-income renters. The way this works in practice is that the city or municipality arranges the bond issue through an underwriting firm. Builders bid on the funds derived from the sale of these bonds by surrendering points and agreeing to pay the city a premium interest rate. Points represent a discount from the face value of the loan. This might be 9.5%. Thus the builder technically borrows $100 but receives only $90.50. He might also agree to pay a premium interest rate, such as 10.5% on the face value of a bond bearing a coupon rate of 9.5%. The investment banker (i.e., the underwriter) then splits the points with the city in some agreed ratio such as 50% for each. Typically the bonds mature in 15 years and have a call provision in 5 years at a premium of 15%. The builder benefits by virtue of the lower interest he pays, due to the tax exemption which the bondholder receives on the interest. The city receives the premium on the interest as well as the points paid by the

builder or developer. What is the effective interest rate the builder pays? Supposing the builder wished to pay off the loan to the city in 5 years and was charged the call premium, what would his effective rate have been in that case?

Until a few years ago, inflation was largely ignored in project evaluation. In the first place, inflationary rates did not seem to be excessive until the early 1970s, when the sudden rise in oil prices triggered the upward inflationary spiral that has since been so persistent. Largely because inflation had been nominal, it was contended that evaluation could be made by using constant dollars (i.e., inflation removed) without introducing error. The argument was that all prices would be affected in much the same way and so inflation effects would tend to wash out.

Even in the absence of high rates of inflation, these assumptions are worth reexamining for the following reasons:

1. Not only has inflation been high, but it has fluctuated widely.

2. Relative prices tend to change more when inflation is high. (Inflation is measured by a change in the general price level in terms of an index. Relative prices can change even under conditions of zero inflation if some prices are rising enough to offset others that are falling.)

3. Inflation induces important wealth-transfer effects, particularly between debtors and creditors.

4. While inflation is ostensibly removed by use of constant dollars, it often remains hidden, when implicitly incorporated in the discount rate.

5. Inflation impinges seriously on the ultimate profitability of investments.

For these reasons it is important to have a consistent and practical way of taking account of inflation in project evaluation. Furthermore it is essential to make some prediction of future inflation rates and to have some insight into the basic causes of inflation.

8.1 CAUSES OF INFLATION

Unfortunately, the causes of inflation are imperfectly understood. If a sound and generally accepted theory had been available, it is not likely that the solution of the recent inflation problem would have proven to be so intractable. The diversity of explanation and multiplicity of theory clearly indicate the lack of a valid theory. Under such circumstances it is only natural that a number of false and popular notions should gain widespread currency.

First, what is inflation?

Inflation may be defined as a rise in the index of all prices. Its measurement depends on how well the price index, however defined, represents the weighted average of the prices for all transactions within the economy as a whole. The two most widely used price indices are:

- The consumer price index (CPI), based on a representative sample of goods and services in the typical family budget.

- The GNP deflator, based on the ratio of nominal to real (constant-dollar) GNP.

Rising prices of some goods are not, in themselves, an indication of inflation. Prices of other goods might, at the same time, be falling sufficiently to compensate for these. Relative prices may always be expected to change without either inflation or deflation occurring. In fact, without a money exchange system there could not be inflation, because the adjustment of relative prices would be automatic.

8.1.1 Inflation Is a Monetary Phenomenon

Money serves as an index of value, but it is not a constant index. The total amount of money utilized to facilitate exchange of all goods over an average turnover period represents the value of those goods. If the total amount of money is increased for the same volume of turnover, prices in terms of money must rise in proportion. The real values of the goods remains the same regardless of the amount of money used for facilitating the exchanges. A simple example will illustrate this point.

EXAMPLE:

We will postulate a highly idealized economy, comprising only two individuals, Smith and Jones. Within a given time interval, Smith has only one good to sell, apples. Jones has only oranges. Smith has 100 apples, and Jones 200 oranges, making the relative price of an apple, in terms of oranges, two oranges. At this point we will introduce a bank to provide a mechanism for Smith and Jones to trade their goods with one another. The bank also makes it possible for Jones and Smith to avoid the fundamental idea that, for the present, an apple is worth two oranges. They can now start thinking of apples as worth some arbitrary sum of money.

Jones first negotiates with Smith to buy his apples and suggests a reasonable price of $0.50 each. They agree. Jones arranges with the bank for a loan of $50, which he then uses to pay Smith for the apples. Note that this money was created for the one purpose of buying apples. Smith and Jones could just as well have set any price for the apples. The amount of the loan would have reflected this fact.

Now that Smith has sold his apples and feels $50 richer, he immediately looks around for something on which to spend his newly acquired wealth and decides on Jones's oranges. Suppose they agree on what, in this overly simple case, is the obvious price of $0.25 per orange. Jones gets back the $50 for the oranges and repays the original loan to the bank. We will not complicate the problem at this point with such mundane matters as interest. The money goes out of existence with the completion of the transaction cycle, and the *real* things, apples and oranges, which had to be exchanged, have been traded utilizing money as a medium.

Clearly, in our illustration, each man would know how many pieces of fruit the other held and would set the price of his own fruit accordingly. However, suppose that Jones, who was somewhat careful with his money, suffered from the illusion that oranges were worth $0.30 each and held out for that price. One of two things could happen. Smith, also careful with money, could say he would not borrow additional money but would remain content to spend his $50.00 and buy only 167 oranges. Alternatively, he could go to the bank and borrow more money. In either event, he would be wiser the next time around. He would not only raise his price for apples by the 20% extra he had to pay for the oranges, but might be tempted to add a further increment to make up for his first mistake. In the first case there would be 33 unused oranges that could spoil. This constitutes an *unemployed resource*. In the second case there would be no unemployment of resources, but prices would have risen by 20% with a built-in "inflationary expectation" of more price rises to come.

If the bank were in a control position and could prohibit the creation of more money, Smith would be out of luck. He would have had to settle for too few oranges, but, at the same time, inflation would have been stopped. However, next time he might attempt to get even by forcing Jones also to suffer the effects of the unemployment of resources.

The real problem stemmed from Jones's original illusion that money had greater value than could be justified by the necessity for market clearing. This is called *money illusion*. In one way or another money illusion is the essential cause of inflation. It cannot be too strongly emphasized that money has value only to the extent that it provides for the exchanges needed for market clearing.* Sufficient money can always be created to facilitate complete exchange, but if this is done it may exacerbate inflationary expectations, though at the same time ameliorating effects of unemployment.

8.1.2 Institutional Pressures on Inflation

In the presence of inflation, each individual feels entitled to higher wages (or prices) in order to maintain his relative position on the income scale. Thus each person or group tries, through legal

---

*Money also has value as a reserve or "store of value". In this sense it has, in essentially the same way, the potential for exchange.

means, to lock in adjustments. For example, labor-union contracts have built-in escalation clauses for adjustments, based on the change in the CPI. Social Security encompasses similar clauses enacted by the Congress. When prices rise, wages rise, which then makes prices rise again—there is a positive feedback effect ratcheting prices upward. This is a manifestation of the money illusion. The fact that any one group is aware of this principle does not prevent that group from fighting to maintain a position already attained.

As unpalatable as this fact is, it could be that the only way for inflation to be modulated is for the central bank to restrict money growth sufficiently to create unemployment. We have been speaking of unemployment here in the generic sense of unemployed resources. It may show up initially as excess inventory, but in the end tends to shake down to unemployed labor.

The usual definition of unemployment is too narrow. It represents only those people looking for employment. The broader meaning of unemployment used here would have to include all those working below their skill levels and desired levels of effort. This is usually called *underemployment*.

8.1.3 Cost-Push and Demand-Pull Theories of Inflation

Many economists have theorized that inflation can be explained either by a "cost-push" or a "wage-pull" concept. Manufacturers are inclined to establish prices for their products on the basis of their costs, plus a reasonable addition for profit. They are not immediately responsive to market forces. Thus they tend to pass costs through to the consumer. If consumers don't respond, producers will withhold their products from the market. Of course they can do this for only a limited time, but in the process, this policy creates a "push" on prices, hence inducing inflation.

On the other hand, labor, chronically feeling underpaid for its services, tends to hold out for a higher wage than can be justified by productivity. Employers, suffering under illusions of being able to pass the higher wage costs through to the consumer, do not offer sufficient resistance to wage raises. Wage adjustments translate into increased consumer demands. This increased demand exerts a pull on prices. Fundamentally these two effects must, to some extent, operate in concert. They are not, however, working in phase. Together they really are a manifestation of the money illusion.

8.1.4 An Uncertainty Explanation of Inflation

In the highly idealized example above, both Smith and Jones would know what each had to offer. They could be expected to talk things over and exchange information. Let us constrain our example to establish a rule that no information could be exchanged and that each, on the basis of past experience, could only *judge* the probable quantities available for exchange. Under these circumstances, the only illusion might be related to the innate uncertainty associated with the probability distribution functions of crop sizes. This situation is typical of the real world. Even where all participants in the game are willing to exchange information, there can never be perfect information. It is impossible to eliminate uncertainty.

In the face of such uncertainty, Jones and Smith might agree to set their respective prices at the expected prices needed for market clearing. However, the probability is zero that the expected price would result in market clearing. Either Jones or Smith will end up with some fruit left over as an unemployed resource. It can be readily seen that the expected level of unemployed resources would be a function of the probability distributions of expected clearing prices. In a generalized model of the economy (rather than the idealized two-person economy), this would depend on many factors. Two obvious factors are:

1. Nature, affecting natural outputs, such as crops.

2. Variability of individually desired consumption choices.

The first factor is determined by nature but results in a distribution pattern that is fairly well understood. Even if there were no variability in the second factor, we would still have to deal with the variability in nature—storms, bumper crops, droughts, etc.

In the absence of inflation, the conclusion drawn from the foregoing discussion is that there will be a minimum level of unemployment arising from statistical uncertainty. Remember, however, that the central bank can reduce unemployed resources simply by allowing the quantity of money to grow and, thereby, accepting a corresponding increase in inflation. This trade-off between unemployment and inflation was observed by A. W. Phillips (1958), who demonstrated the inverse relationship between these two undesirable phenomena. Phillips, a British electrical engineer, did not develop a theory of inflation. Rather, from a study of the British economy over a hundred-year period, he drew attention to this inverse relationship, called the Phillips Curve. During the 1970s, when a new trend of rising inflation was accompanied by rising unemployment, the so-called Phillips theory, or curve effect, seemed to have been discredited.

This apparent conflict of trends, which seems still to hold true, does not necessarily contradict the Phillips curve effect. From approximately 1965, some major structural changes began to develop within the U.S. economy. The illusion that the Vietnam War could be financed without curtailing current consumption was the first such factor. This was followed by rapidly changing life styles that altered relative values for goods and services. Finally there was a series of oil price shocks in the 1970s. These effects were bound to change the distribution functions for market-clearing prices. In turn, this was automatically manifested in an increase in the variances of market-clearing prices. These increased price variances indicated that the inflation-free employment level would rise and also that the level of inflation for a reasonably low unemployment level would rise. If this speculation (English, 1974) is correct, it may explain not only the apparent deviation from the Phillips curve but also why the inflation–unemployment tradeoff tends to be higher in developing countries, where greater uncertainties already exist.

8.2 WEALTH-TRANSFER EFFECTS OF INFLATION

Project evaluation depends on how inflation affects both revenue and cost streams. Any influence that impinges on the end user's ability to purchase the product will have an impact on revenues and hence on the ultimate success of the project. Therefore it is important to assess the transfer effects of inflation.

It should be kept in mind that inflation is not all bad. As was indicated above, inflation that ensures a more fully employed economy may be desirable. However if it becomes excessive, efficiency is impaired and total output diminished. Nevertheless, in the absence of destructive inflation, while there will be many losers, there will be many gainers.

Important wealth-transfer effects occur with a steady-state inflation rate. Still other effects come into play with changes in inflation rate, particularly when an accelerating rate gives way to a decelerating rate. Under conditions of steady-state inflation, people learn to adjust and make their decisions in terms of the expectation that whatever rate is attained will tend to continue. Under a steady-state positive inflation rate the transfer effects are:

1. Those on fixed incomes, such as pensioners, tend to lose to those on variable incomes, such as salesmen on commission.

2. Borrowers gain at the expense of lenders, such as those who put their savings into bonds. In effect, debt is repudiated by inflation. The size of a debt diminishes relative to the income available for paying it.

3. Capital-intensive projects tend to be favored over labor-intensive projects. As labor costs escalate, the total cost per unit produced will not rise as rapidly for the capital-intensive firm as for its labor-intensive competitor. Capital costs are fixed and labor costs are variable.

4. Speculators are favored over conservative investors. The speculator will benefit from buying highly leveraged assets to sell at ever rising market prices. This has been amply demonstrated in the real-estate markets, in rapidly developing regions of the Sunbelt.

5. The government sector tends to grow at the expense of the private sector. This has been true in the past, largely due to income-tax bracket creep, which has effectively raised tax rates.

These effects are not necessarily bad. Some are and some are not. However, inflation effects induce people to devote excessive time to protecting their economic position, thus detracting from their primary productive activities. To the extent that this occurs, inflation has the effect of decreasing overall economic efficiency.

Debtors, as well as those who invest in capital-intensive projects, are still further favored during an acceleration of inflationary rates. In recent years, interest rates adjusted slowly to increasing rates of inflation. The result was that for a very long time, real interest rates remained much too low. The real interest rate is usually defined as the nominal rate, as dictated by market forces, less the steady-state inflation rate. On this basis, from 1978 through 1983, real rates have been very high by comparison with historic norms. During the prior decade, real interest rates were actually negative at times.

8.3 RELATIVE PRICES AND INFLATION

Relative price changes are, at the same time, both cause and effect of inflation. When the price of a commodity is suddenly raised due to some unexpected and external cause, this induces inflation. For the reasons outlined above in Section 8.1, as well as because of a built-in inertia in the market, prices of other goods do not adjust downward to compensate. If the commodity in question, such as oil, is a major component of the economy, the inflationary shock to the economy can be quite pronounced.

When such an event occurs, people search for substitutes for the suddenly more expensive items and this causes a realignment of other prices. Therefore a relative price change for one item induces a relative price change in other goods. For example, the oil price jumps of the 1970s induced a restructuring of transportation prices. People searched for ways to reduce travel. One alternative they found was to substitute telephoning for traveling.

Because of inflation-induced relative price changes, it is necessary in project evaluation to estimate both inflation and relative price changes induced by inflation.

8.4 INFLATION IN PROJECT EVALUATION

There are three ways in which we may take account of inflation in project evaluation. These are:

1. Constant-dollar estimates.
2. Nominal (i.e., current) dollar estimates.

3. Constant-dollar estimates with escalation adjustments for relative price changes.

8.4.1 The Constant-Dollar Approach

The most widely used and, by far, the simplest method for treating inflation in project evaluation is to assume constant dollars. This would be satisfactory and a valid approach if all prices responded proportionately to inflation. As was brought out in the above discussion, prices are likely to adjust at different rates, and so the constant-dollar method is subject to error, to the extent of the differences in relative price changes.

In effect, the assumption of constant dollars takes all inflation out of the analysis. However, to be consistent, it is necessary to remove all inflation effects. In particular and most importantly, inflation must also be removed from the discount rate that is utilized for time-value analyses. Failure to do this is a serious and all too common error. Often a discount rate that is in keeping with perceived currently acceptable rates of return is used. This is incorrect. Psychologically it seems difficult for investors to think in terms of rates of return of 3% or 4% as reasonable for evaluation when nominal returns are in the order of 15% or 16%. However, the latter include inflationary expectations.

The relationship between real and nominal rates should be taken into account. Consider the discounted value of a prospective amount at time T. With inflation,

$$F = Se^{gT}. \tag{8.1}$$

If we take the present value in nominal dollars,

$$P = Fe^{-rT}. \tag{8.2}$$

Substituting from equation 8.1,

$$P = Se^{(g-r)T}. \tag{8.3}$$

However the real discount rate is $r_r = r - g$. Therefore

$$P = Se^{-r_r T}. \tag{8.4}$$

The time-value equivalence is established between the discounted constant-dollar amount S and the discounted nominal amount F by using the real rate for discounting S and the nominal rate when discounting F.

8.4.2 Discrete Rates versus Continuous Rates

It will be noted that in the previous section, when continuous discounting is employed, the discount and inflation rates are simply added or subtracted as desired. This is approximately valid for discrete rates, as long as both interest rates and inflation rates are low. Error can be introduced when they are high. In the case of multiplication of two exponential compounding factors, the exponents are additive. However the multiplication of equivalent discrete factors is

$$(1 + i) = (1 + i_r)(1 + g) = 1 + i_r + g + gi_r. \qquad (8.5)$$

Thus the nominal rate is the sum of the inflation rate, the real rate, and a small additional amount consisting of the product of these two rates:

$$i = i_r + g + gi_r, \qquad (8.6)$$

or, rearranging,

$$i_r = \frac{i - g}{1 + gi_r}. \qquad (8.7)$$

EXAMPLE: Comparison of continuous and discrete inflation rates

Suppose the rate of inflation is 5% and the discount rate is 6%. If these were continuous, the nominal rate of discount would be 11%, the sum of the two. However, if they were discrete, we might be tempted to simply take the sum of two as before. The correct nominal rate, however, is

$$0.05 + 0.06 + (0.06)(0.05) = 0.113, \text{ or } 11.3\%.$$

This is quite close to the approximate value of 11%.

In contrast if we start with a high nominal rate and a high inflation rate, the error becomes significant. Consider the case of a nominal rate of 18% and an inflation rate of 15%. If we were using continuous rates, the real discount rate in this case would be the difference between the nominal rate and the inflation rate, or 3%. For the discrete case, the real rate is

$$\frac{0.18 - 0.15}{1 + (0.18)(0.15)} = 0.026, \quad \text{or} \quad 2.62.$$

8.4.3 Nominal-Dollar Approach

The principal danger in using constant dollars is in the choice of the OCC, which must be specified in terms of the inflation-free or real interest rate. However people have come to relate to current interest rates and find it difficult to use the much lower rates for discounting future cash flows even when these are in constant-dollar estimates. The second difficulty arises in the need to make relative-price adjustments.

Both of these difficulties are avoided if all estimates are made in current or nominal dollars. This means that the project evaluation must include estimates of how price changes will occur in the future for all the separate components of revenue and cost. In addition, the course of interest-rate changes must also be estimated and the OCC adjusted accordingly.

When inflation rates change from year to year, the discount rate used for discounting the projected cash flow will also have to change. Recall that the discount rate is the sum of the inflation rate and the real interest rate. The advantage of using inflating-dollar estimates is that the evaluator is forced to consider inflation effects explicitly. Secondly, the effect of debt financing is taken into account automatically. Debt repayment including interest payments is unaffected by inflation, with the result that the significance of the debt-related part of the cash-flow stream tends to decline in importance as time elapses. This does not show up in the constant-dollar approach unless the debt is artificially reduced as time elapses. Such a procedure would be difficult to explain in the analysis.

The disadvantage of the nominal-dollar approach lies in the fact that the estimates of dollar amounts in a very few years become so large that people have difficulty in relating to the magnitudes of the numbers.

8.4.4 Constant Dollars with Special Escalations

A compromise method that overcomes most of the objections to either the constant-dollar approach or the current-dollar approach is to use the constant-dollar approach and to make specific adjustments for special items, the prices of which are expected to rise faster than the general inflation rate.

This method overcomes the difficulty of using numbers to which people cannot relate. On the other hand, the problem of taking inflation out of the discount rate must still be recognized. In addition, where debt financing is involved, the transfer-payment effect of inflation can easily be overlooked. The method suffers the same deficiencies as the constant-dollar approach.

8.5 EXAMPLE OF AN INVESTMENT IN A HOME

The evaluation of an investment in real estate is ideally suited for demonstrating the effects of both inflation and financing on the overall profitability of an investment. Typically, a potential home buyer's investment is a down payment of 20% of the purchase price. The viewpoint of the investor or purchaser of a home is certainly not the same as the joint-venture viewpoint of the mortgage company and the homeowner together. The purchaser has no interest at all in the mortgage company's profit from the venture. His viewpoint is exclusive. Therefore his primary cash flow is the fixed monthly payment on the mortgage.

The opportunity cost of living in one's own home will depend on:

1. The fixed cash flow determined by the mortgage contract.

2. The final selling price (terminal value) at the end of a planned holding period. This selling price will be dependent on inflation rates.

3. Tax advantages (i.e., subsidies).

4. The buyer's OCC.

We will consider a typical home price of $200,000. Assume a fixed-rate mortgage for thirty years at an interest rate of 12% APR. Selling a house will always involve a transaction cost: salesman's commission, escrow charges, removal expense, etc. We will assume all of these together will amount to 7% of selling price.

In addition to capital costs, there will be an annual maintenance cost as well as property taxes. Let us ignore maintenance, because it is a simple matter to add it on later. Property taxes are a different matter. These are deductible from current income in computing income-tax obligations. We will assume that property taxes amount to $2000 per year. Property taxes are limited by state laws. In California, for instance, the rate is limited to 1% of assessed valuation, which at the outset is the purchase price. Thereafter the assessed valuation can only be changed by 2% per year. This 2% applies as reassessments are made on a three-year cycle. Thus the tax will rise by 6% every three years. We will assume this is the pattern for the example.

A buyer will have some idea as to his housing requirements for a short time into the future. A young man, just establishing his family, might be looking ahead to the time when his children reach their teens. Thus an eight-year planned holding period would be reasonable. In no way does this dictate that, if he chooses to consider changing houses again in eight years, he necessarily will do so. Clearly, at any time during the eight-year planned holding period, he may change his mind; his prospects will be different; things may have altered considerably from what he predicted.

We will assume an income-tax rate of 40% and a capital-gains tax of 20%. However if the capital gain on a home is completely reinvested in a new home within a reasonable time, the capital-gains tax can be postponed indefinitely. For this reason, we will ignore capital-gains taxes.

PROBLEM:

Determine the opportunity cost of home ownership. This is the equivalent of finding a rent that one might pay oneself for living in one's own home. Determine the sensitivity of this home-owner-ship cost to inflation and to the OCC.

SOLUTION

First we will consider all the fixed components (i.e., those costs which are unaffected by the inflation rate and the OCC).

The interest on the mortgage is 1% per month. The monthly payment is

$$A = 160{,}000 \times (A/P, 1.0, 360) = \$1645.78.$$

Annualizing this, the equivalent annual payment is

$$A = 1{,}645.78 \times (F/A, 1.0, 12) = \$20{,}878.61.$$

Alternatively, we could have obtained the same result by using the effective annual interest rate. Recall that the term APR is a convention for stating nominal interest rates. Thus the effective annual interest rate is

$$i = (1 + 0.01)^{12} - 1 = 12.68\%,$$

and the annualized yearly payment is, effectively,

$$A = 160{,}000 \times (A/P, 12.68, 30) = \$20{,}878.61.$$

The unpaid balance of the loan in 8 years is the present value of the remaining payments, or

$$\text{balance} = 20{,}878.61 \times (P/A, 12.68, 22) = \$152{,}678.50.$$

This is after all payments for the 8th year have been made. The interest portion of each payment is deductible from taxable income, thus reducing the actual annual cash flow by the amount of the tax savings. This varies from year to year as the interest component declines. See Table 8.1.

It should be noted that the payment on the principal in any one year is the sinking-fund depreciation on the balance at that time.

The cash flow including property tax will be as shown in Table 8.2. The property tax is deductible from taxable income, and so

Table 8.1 Cash Flow for Annual Costs

YEAR	BALANCE	AMOUNT PAID ON PRINCIPAL	INTEREST	TAX SAVING	CASH FLOW
1	159,419.39	580.61	20,259.00	8103.60	12,775.01
2	158,765.15	654.24	20,218.37	8087.35	12,791.26
3	158,027.93	737.22	20,135.40	8054.16	12,824.45
4	157,320.05	830.71	20,041.90	8016.76	12,861.85
5	157,197.22	936.07	19,936.54	7974.62	12,903.99
6	155,206.36	1,054.79	19,817.83	7927.13	12,951.48
7	154,017.80	1,188.56	19,684.05	7873.62	13,004.99
8	152,678.50	1,339.30	19,533.31	7813.33	13,065.28

the net tax to be paid is 60% of the original tax obligation. In other words, the Federal Government subsidizes the high-bracket taxpayer. The initial tax payment of $2000 effectively amounts to $1200.

These figures will be sensitive to the OCC but not to the inflation rate. Therefore the present worth of the cash flow is shown in Table 8.3 for a range of values for the OCC. It is noteworthy that the cash flows do not change a great deal over time. We are being too refined in taking such precise figures, when all we really want is to obtain a reasonable estimate. If we take the average value of the total cash flow we will not be far off the mark. The average value of the cash flow is $14,161.35 per year. Using an OCC of 12%, the present worth of the average is

$$P = 15,004 \times (P/A, 12, 8) = \$70,348.46.$$

Table 8.2 Addition of Property Tax

YEAR	CASH FLOW (TABLE 8.1)	PROPERTY TAX	TOTAL CASH FLOW
1	12,775.01	1,200.00	13,975.01
2	12,791.26	1,200.00	13,991.26
3	12,824.45	1,200.00	14,024.26
4	12,861.85	1,272.00	14,133.85
5	12,903.99	1,272.00	14,175.99
6	12,951.48	1,272.00	14,223.48
7	13,004.99	1,348.32	14,353.31
8	13,065.28	1,348.32	14,413.60

Table 8.3 Present Worth of Cash Flow

OCC (%)	PRESENT WORTH
8.0	$81,230.15
10.0	$75,378.33
12.0	$70,159.94
14.0	$66,490.47
16.0	$61,298.38
18.0	$57,522.92
20.0	$54,112.29

By contrast the value of P for the actual cash flow is

$$P = \$70,159.94,$$

which represents an annualized cash flow of $14,123.40, a difference of only 0.3% from the average.

Now we will consider inflation effects. The only thing that inflation affects is the resale value. Discrete rates will be used for inflation.

Although it is desirable to consider a range of values for inflation, the calculations for only one rate, 10%, will be shown. If the inflation rate is 10%, the selling price F will be

$$F = 200,000 \times (F/P, 10, 8) = \$428,717.76.$$

The net, after transaction costs, will be

$$0.93 \times 428,717.76 = \$398,707.52.$$

After paying off the mortgage, assuming no prepayment penalty, the owner will realize

$$\$398,707.52 - \$152,678.50 = \$246,029.02.$$

The present worth of this amount at an OCC of 12% is

$$P = 246,029.02 \times (P/F, 12, 8) = \$99,366.99.$$

The total present worth is the sum of the two fixed components—the down payment of $40,000 and the annual cash

Table 8.4 Monthly Opportunity Cost of Home Ownership

INFLATION RATE (%)	OPPORTUNITY COST OF CAPITAL (%)					
	8	10	12	14	16	18
0	1497	1559	1622	1703	1748	1812
4	960	1075	1158	1271	1494	1639
6	632	755	874	1008	1347	1539
8	257	406	547	706	822	951
10	−170	9	181	364	504	655
12	−654	−441	−238	−26	142	319
14	−1203	−952	−712	−467	−268	−62

flow of $70,159.99, less the return of $99,366.99. This amounts to $10,792.95. If we now annualize this amount, the annual opportunity cost of ownership is

$$A = 10{,}792.95 \times (A/P, 12, 8) = \$2{,}172.65 \text{ per year,}$$

a nominal $181.05 per month.

The opportunity cost or rental-equivalent cost of home ownership of $181.05 per month seems very reasonable, as indeed it is. However, this low cost came about almost entirely as a result of inflation.

The opportunity cost of home ownership is sensitive to both inflation and the OCC, as can be seen by examination of Table 8.4. This table is represented diagrammatically in Figure 8.1.

It is noteworthy that the sensitivity of the cost of home ownership to inflation is such that higher inflation rates reduce the costs considerably. The opportunity cost of capital, on the other hand, raises costs. Approximately, a 4% increase in OCC offsets a 2% increase in the inflation rate.

It will be recognized that the current OCC is inflation-inclusive. If the real OCC is 4% and we add the inflation rate, then the function for the levelized monthly opportunity cost of home ownership will be as depicted by the dashed line in Figure 8.1.

8.5.1 Extension of the Real-Estate Example

This same problem takes on quite a different aspect if we examine the desirability of investing in the property for the purpose of

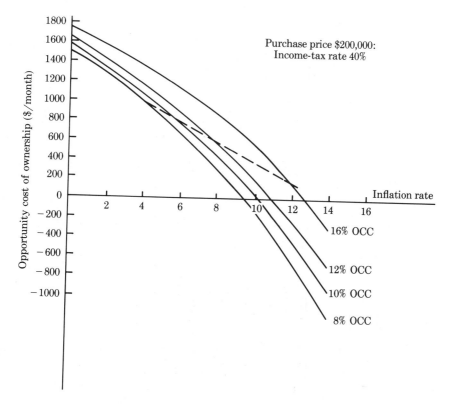

Figure 8.1 Cost of home ownership in $/month.

renting it to others. The major change is that depreciation now becomes a tax-deductible cost.

We will assume that the property can be rented for $1750 nominal per month, or $21,000 per year. This is fixed by a long-term lease. The cash-flow analysis is shown in Table 8.5.

The capital gains on the property will be the difference between the realized proceeds of the sale and the cost basis of the investment (i.e., the book value):

$$\text{capital gains} = \$398,707 - \$118,197 = \$280,510$$

(assuming 10% appreciation rate);

$$\text{capital-gains tax} = 0.20 \times \$280,510 = \$56,102.$$

Table 8.5 Cash Flow for Rental Property

n	INTEREST	PROPERTY TAX	DEPRECIATION ALLOWANCE	BOOK VALUE	TOTAL COST	PROFIT	INCOME TAX[1]	NET PROFIT	CASH FLOW[2]
1	20,259	2000	16,000	184,000	38,259	−17,259	−6904	−10,355	5645
2	20,218	2000	13,867	170,133	36,085	−15,085	−6034	−9,051	4816
3	20,135	2000	12,018	158,115	34,153	−13,153	−5261	−7,892	4126
4	20,042	2400	10,415	147,700	32,857	−11,857	−4743	−7,114	3301
5	19,937	2400	9,027	138,673	31,364	−10,364	−4146	−6,218	2809
6	19,818	2400	7,823	130,853	30,041	−9,041	−3616	−5,425	2398
7	19,684	2544	6,780	124,073	29,008	−8,008	−3203	−4,805	1975
8	19,533	2544	5,876	118,197	27,953	−6,953	−2781	−4,172	1704

[1] Income tax is negative because the investor has other income against which a loss on the property investment is offset.
[2] Cash flow = depreciation + profit.

The investor realized $246,029 before a capital-gains tax. This is now reduced by the tax to $189,927.

We can now determine the IRR, which is based on this final cash from the sale, the cash flow for the 8 years, and the initial down payment of $40,000. The IRR is 31.02%, a very sizable rate of return.

On the other hand, if inflation had not occurred, the story would be decidedly different. If the home owner were to sell the property at exactly what he paid for it, there would still be a capital gains tax, because the tax is computed on the sale price in excess of book value. The book value is the *tax basis* (i.e., the value used by the IRS) because income taxes have already been reduced because of the depreciation allowances. Net after closing costs would be $186,000, and the capital gains would therefore be $67,803, on which there would be a tax of $13,561. Thus the cash out would be:

$$\$186,000 - \$152,078 - \$13,561 = \$20,361.$$

The IRR is now 3.09%.

Alternatively, we can now find what rent to charge in order to justify a particular value for the OCC.

It is noteworthy that the cash flow for the project is positive, but only because of the income tax saved. If this had not been so (as for a man who makes a living from rental income), the cash flow would have been negative. This means that, indirectly, there is a hidden subsidy to renters, as well as to home owners, in the interest exemption on Federal income taxes.

It should be further noted that no allowance was made for maintenance. This is clearly an added expense, which must be included in the rent.

8.6 RECAPITULATION

1. Inflation is defined as the rise in the general level of prices as measured by means of a representative index. The two most representative indices are the consumer price index (CPI) and the GNP deflator.

2. Inflation is a monetary phenomenon. It is related to the illusion that prices can be justified at higher levels than

those needed for market clearing. This is known as the *money illusion*.

3. Inflation is exacerbated by institutional forces that produce ratchet effects on prices.

4. Inflation can be explained in part by cost-push and demand-pull effects. It is also related to the uncertainty of prices.

5. There is a tradeoff between unemployment and inflation. The historical relationship has changed in recent years, but the underlying phenomenon remains. This relationship, expressed as a function of the two rates (inflation and unemployment), might possibly be explained by price uncertainties.

6. There is an important wealth-transfer effect caused by inflation, which has particular significance in project evaluation. Since inflation favors the borrower over the lender, debt-financing decisions shift returns from one class of investor to another.

7. In project evaluation, consideration must be given not only to general price changes resulting from inflation, but also to relative price changes.

8. The three methods for considering inflation in project evaluation are based on the use of:

   a. Constant dollars.

   b. Current dollars.

   c. Constant dollars with escalations of some prices.

9. The discount rate, when using current dollars, should be the real rate plus the inflation rate. In continuous form these are simply additive; in discrete form an adjustment is needed. When a constant-dollar approach is used, the inflation rate must be subtracted from the nominal discount rate in order to ensure that the correct rate is being used.

10. In using constant-dollar approaches, care must be exercised to adjust for the transfer effect of debt financing.

8.7 PROBLEMS

1. Using continuous rates, find the IRR for a cash flow that runs for 20 years. The investment is $10,000, and the initial cash flow is $1200 per year. The inflation rate is 5%.

   a. What are the real and nominal values of the IRR?

   b. If the OCC is 10%, find the present worth that should be used for comparing this investment with some other alternative.

   c. Suppose that the investment is partially financed by a debt of $8000 at 9% interest. What should be the present worth on which the evaluation is based? Let the point of view be that of the equity investor. Consider both current-dollar and constant-dollar approaches.

2. Reevaluate the home-investment example, using no debt financing. Assume the prospective buyer pays all cash.

○

○

CHAPTER NINE

○ *Risk*

○

Risk can be defined as the probability of an unfavorable outcome. What is deemed unfavorable is, of course, relative to what is expected. Investments are made in anticipation of gainful outcomes in uncertain futures. Therefore all investments are risky. The question is never how to avoid risk. Rather it is how to live with it and manage it.

How do we measure risk in order to make investment decisions, with the correct balance between risk and expected gain?

A risk taker justifies his preference for a risky investment over a conservative investment by his expectation of a greater gain from the more risky alternative. At the same time, his acceptance of risk represents the possibility of a high degree of variability in the outcome. Therefore the measure of risk is normally taken to be a measure of the expected deviation in the outcome: the variance V, which in mathematical terms is defined as

$$V = \frac{\sum_{i}^{n}(x_i - \bar{x})^2}{n}, \tag{9.1}$$

where $\bar{x}$ is the mean. The square root of variance is the standard deviation.

9.1 THE RISK – REWARD MAP

In principle, there is a tradeoff between risk and expected gain or reward. Given a choice between investments promising the same return, all rational investors will prefer the investment promising the lower risk. Alternatively, for the same level of risk, they will choose the higher expected return. A tradeoff between risk and reward must be made whenever the alternative is between higher risk coupled with higher return and lower risk coupled with lower reward. This is exemplified as a risk–reward map in Figure 9.1.

Consider projects A, B, C, and D. Depending on the degree of risk acceptance, the projects toward the lower right-hand corner of the map will be preferred. The most conservative investor will select the lowest risk, C. The most aggressive (i.e., least risk-averse) will select the project with the highest expected gain, A. It should be noted that project D would not be selected under any circumstance—any of the three other alternatives is further to the right and lower down on the map than D. Therefore the convex boundary ABC determines an admissible set of investments. All points within the convex set are said to be *dominated*.

A question remains as to possible preference of B over the other two admissible investments, A and C. Clearly this choice must be determined by consideration of the investor's attitude toward risk. To examine this, it is necessary to review the characteristics of the investor's utility function. The investor may be expected to choose the alternative that will maximize his utility.

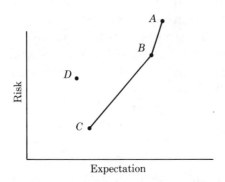

Figure 9.1   Risk–reward map.

A generalized utility function of wealth W may be represented by a polynomial

$$U(W) = a + bW + cW^2 + dW^3 + \cdots . \qquad (9.2)$$

Define the utility function to make $a = 0$, corresponding to a zero utility when W equals zero. Taking expectations, we have

$$E(U(W)) = bE(W) + cE(W^2) + dE(W^3) + \cdots . \qquad (9.3)$$

Because of its highly subjective nature, it is not practical to define a utility function very precisely. Also, even if we choose a third-degree polynomial, the expectation for the cubic term is zero for a symmetrical probability density function. Therefore it is reasonable to approximate a generalized utility function as a quadratic, within the region of concern. The constants must, of course, be chosen to satisfy the condition that the utility function is monotonic with decreasing slope.* This leads to a simplified form for the function of equation 9.3:

$$E(U) = E(W) - CV(W), \qquad (9.4)$$

where K is a parameter for the investor's risk attitude and $V(W)$ is the variance of the resulting wealth W, invested (i.e., risked).

For purposes of evaluating a proposed risky investment, it is necessary to establish a risk standard. While there is no such thing as a truly riskless investment, one may be hypothesized in order to establish a standard as a reference for measuring risk. Equating the utilities for the expectation of the riskless and the risky investments will determine for us a point of indifference between the two.

An investment in the riskless opportunity will be expected to increase wealth to $W_0 + \Delta W_0$, within some given time period. Alternatively the same investment in the risky opportunity will become $W_0 + \Delta W$. The equivalent rates of return for the period

---

*You may wish to reread Chapter 2 on Utility.

will be i and i_0. The final riskless equivalent wealth, W_0, will be

$$W_0 + \Delta W_0 = E(W + \Delta W) - CV(W + \Delta W). \qquad (9.5)$$

By dividing through by W_0, the equivalent riskless rate of return becomes

$$\frac{W_0 + \Delta W_0}{W_0} = i_0 + 1 = E(i) + 1 - CWV\frac{W_0 + \Delta W}{W_0},$$

or, simplified,

$$i_0 = E(i) - CWV(i). \qquad (9.6)$$

The value of C will depend on how much of the investor's capital is at risk. It must be emphasized that the return i is for a single unspecified time period. Thus i is dimensionless. The risk parameter C, therefore, has the dimensions of $1/W$. The significance of this is intuitively appealing. Clearly an investor will be much less concerned about risking one dollar on an even-money bet than about risking all his wealth on a gamble that might be expected to pay off with a very high return. Since we wish to consider the enterprise as a whole, we might sidestep the question of how C varies with W and determine the value of a new parameter, $K = CW$, pragmatically and independently of W. This is the equivalent of using a nondimensional K and dropping W from equation 9.6, which then becomes

$$i_0 = E(i) - KV(i). \qquad (9.7)$$

This function is shown on the risk–reward map in Figure 9.2. It is a straight line with slope $1/K$, which we will call the *risk-preference line*.

This almost totally risk-averse investor will exhibit a K sufficiently large to make i at least equal to the equivalent riskless rate of return i_0, which might be available on the market. The risk-insensitive gambler type, on the other hand, will have a K approaching zero. Most people exhibit values for K falling between $\frac{1}{4}$ and $\frac{2}{3}$.

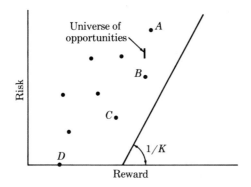

Figure 9.2 Risk-preference function.

Admittedly it is difficult, if not impossible, to specify a meaningful value for K. At best, it is highly subjective. Nevertheless we can examine a range of values that K must assume in order to make any one investment more attractive than others. In Figure 9.2, B would be the choice in preference to either A or C, for a range of values of K. Note that the choice must be specified as follows:

> Given that you must choose one of the four alternatives, which one would you choose?

If we also include the alternative of keeping our money in the riskless investment, we will select B in preference to the riskless alternative only if the risk-preference line intersects the reward axis to the right of the risk-free rate i_0 available on the market.

9.2 RISK-REDUCTION STRATEGY

So far, we have examined only the case where we must choose among a set of alternative investments when we are constrained to pick one and only one. What happens if we remove this constraint and can divide our capital continuously between a number of investment alternatives? Such a situation is approximated in the purchase of stocks, for instance, where one may buy as small an amount as one share.

Allocation of the total capital among a set of investment alternatives (called a universe) represents *diversification*. The set of chosen investments is called a *portfolio*. The question is:

> Does a diversification strategy reduce risk, and if so, how?

To answer this question, we must examine the concepts of what has come to be known as *modern portfolio theory*, originally developed by Harry Markowitz (1952). Markowitz developed his theory for the selection of securities on the stock market. However, the concepts of portfolio theory have broader applicability, and we will later examine them in the context of project evaluation.

The Markowitz model requires that all capital be invested in some subset of a universe of investment opportunities. This could include a portion that we can choose to leave in a risk-free asset—perhaps cash or a cash equivalent, earning moderate interest.

Consider separately the two terms of equation 9.7, expectation and risk.

9.2.1 The Expectation Term

Let

$$\sum x_j = 1 \qquad \text{for opportunities } j = 1 \text{ to } n, \qquad (9.8)$$

where x_j is the proportion of capital in the jth opportunity. The expected return on the portfolio will be

$$E(i) = \sum x_j i_j. \qquad (9.9)$$

If we were insensitive to risk, we would merely wish to maximize $E(i)$. Clearly we would select the opportunity having the largest i_j and would allocate all of our capital to it (i.e., $x_j = 1$). In other words, we would put all our eggs in one basket.

9.2.2 The Risk Term

Since we are concerned with risk, we must consider the risk term in equation 9.7. It can readily be shown that

$$V(i) = \sum_{j}^{n} \sum_{k}^{n} V_{jk} x_j x_k, \qquad (9.10)$$

where V_{jk} designates the covariance of the jth and kth opportunities. When $j = k$ the covariance becomes the variance.

Covariance is a measure of correlation of returns between investments. The actual return on the jth investment will not correlate with the kth if they are statistically independent. In other words, whatever return eventuates from the jth investment can have no bearing on what happens to the kth investment. Conversely, if there is correlation, they will be deterministically linked together. A change in the jth investment automatically induces a deterministic change in the kth. Most investments lie somewhere between the two extremes. For example, common stocks will tend to rise and fall with some degree of correlation with overall market conditions. At the same time, they will exhibit independent price movements of their own.

Investments within any firm tend to be highly correlated with one another. They are coupled into the production system with a high degree of interdependence. For example, the production of one shop depends on the output of another. The separate investments in the two shops are complementary and integral components of the total production system. They cannot be separated. In this case the correlation coefficients of investments within a production entity are unity. However, the investments within the set are complementary; there is no option available for selecting only one of them. At the same time, the firm may have a diversified set of product lines not tightly coupled within the firm, but perhaps correlated to some degree with the local or national economy.

In the case of *perfect correlation*, the least risky investment is the one with the lowest variance; it does not pay to diversify. This is the same situation as in the case of maximum expectation. The only question is the appropriate tradeoff between risk and reward.

In the case of *statistical independence* (covariances = 0), equation 9.10 reduces to

$$V(i) = \sum_{j=1}^{n} x_j V(i_j), \qquad (9.11)$$

which is the average variance of the n investments. As an example, consider the special case of n investments, each using a fraction $1/n$ of the capital and each having the same variance. Then

$$V(i) = V(i_j)/n. \qquad (9.12)$$

It will be observed that the variance of such a portfolio may be made as small as one pleases, simply by choosing a sufficiently large n. The best investment strategy, then, is to diversify. The interesting conclusion in this case is that a portfolio of a single conservative investment is less conservative than a portfolio comprising, for instance, ten risky investments.

EXAMPLE: Risk–reward tradeoff

Given that:

- A is a single conservative investment.
- B is a typical risky investment and there are 10 of these, which are statistically independent.
- C is a riskless investment.
- $K = 0.5$.
- i_0(riskless) = 0.09.
- i_A(conservative) = 0.15.
- i_B(risky) = 0.25.
- V_A(conservative) = 0.20.
- V_B(risky) = 0.50.
- $n = 10$.

For a portfolio of 10 different investments in the B category,

$$V_{PB} = 0.50 \times \tfrac{1}{10} = 0.05$$

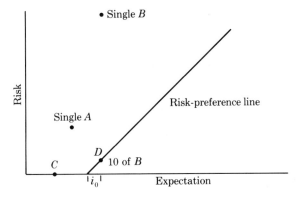

Figure 9.3 Risk–reward map for example case.

which is less than the value $V = 0.2$ for the single conservative investment. The equivalent riskless return on the B portfolio is

$$i_0 = 0.25 - (0.5 \times 0.05) = 0.225.$$

For a single investment in A,

$$i_0 = 0.15 - (0.5 \times 0.2) = 0.05,$$

and for C, $i_0 = 0.09$.

This example is shown on the risk–reward map of Figure 9.3. Clearly, the effect of a diversification strategy is to create an effective new alternative investment, point D in Figure 9.3, superior to any of the other three nondiversified alternatives.

The most general case of the portfolio problem is one in which there is neither full dependence nor full independence between investments but some intermediate degree of correlation. If K is specified, a theoretical optimum capital allocation can be determined. However as we shall see later, from a practical point of view such an optimum may not be very meaningful. Nevertheless, the solution of the theoretical optimum is of value in contributing towards understanding of the concepts underlying the principles of portfolio theory.

The solution for the optimum portfolio requires finding the values of $\{x\}$ to maximize i_0. We impose the constraints that

$$x_j \leq 1 \quad \text{for all } j$$

and

$$\sum_{j=1}^{n} x_j = 1.$$

The requirement that total capital equals unity corresponds to a requirement that there be no borrowing. This constraint can be relaxed if it is desired to allow some borrowing. Under such circumstances, there will be interest paid on that part of the portfolio representing borrowed funds. The value of x in borrowing will be constrained to

$$-L \leq x_B \leq 0,$$

where L is the borrowing limit. This refinement is not necessary for the ensuing discussion.

Thus the problem is formulated as follows:

$$\text{maximize} \quad i = x_j E(i_j) - K \sum_{j}^{n} \sum_{k}^{n} V_{jk} x_j x_k \qquad (9.15)$$

subject to

$$\sum x_j = 1$$

and

$$0 \leq x_j \leq 1 \qquad \text{for all } j.$$

The solution for this problem can be obtained by means of linear programming, utilizing the device of the Lagrange multiplier. Except for cases of a very few securities, a computer will be needed.

We will illustrate the use of the Lagrangian and ignore the second constraint. This yields a solution that indicates values of $\{x\}$ outside of the range we have specified for $\{x\}$. Simply stated, the partial derivatives of the objective function plus the Lagrange multiplier times the partial of the constraint equation, are equated to zero:

$$\frac{\partial i_0}{\partial x_j} = 0 = i_j - K \left\{ 2 x_j V_j + \sum_k x_k V_{jk} \right\} + \Lambda. \qquad (9.16)$$

The n such equations plus the constraint equation constitute a set of simultaneous equations which can be solved for the x values.

An example will illustrate the procedure, and at the same time point out the innate difficulties in the use of portfolio theory as a practical operating procedure.

EXAMPLE: Portfolio problem

Consider a universe of five investments, including one riskless investment, with pertinent data as shown in Table 9.1. It will be observed that covariances permute, so that the covariance of the portfolio is double the values found on one side of the diagonal values plus the diagonal values. The diagonal values are the variance terms: by definition, the covariance of one investment with itself is its variance. E is the riskless investment and thus has no covariance.

We will first consider the optimum portfolio comprising the four risky investments, and then will examine the effect of adding the riskless investment. By plotting these investments on a risk–reward map, Figure 9.4, it will be observed that B is dominated, because it is well within the convex boundary $ACDE$. Therefore we might be inclined to eliminate it from further consideration. However, it could still be a factor in a diversified portfolio.

Suppose we now choose an arbitrary value of $\frac{1}{2}$ for K and solve equation 9.15 for the optimal $\{x\}$ values. Using the values of the covariance matrix in equation 9.16 yields the solution

$$x_A = 0.52,$$

$$x_B = 0.07,$$

$$x_C = 0.28,$$

$$x_D = 0.13.$$

Table 9.1 Covariance Matrix

INVESTMENT	$E(i)$	A	B	C	D	E
A	0.12	0.08	0.04	0.02	0.025	0
B	0.10	0.04	0.12	0.04	0.03	0
C	0.15	0.02	0.04	0.15	0.09	0
D	0.18	0.025	0.03	0.09	0.30	0
E	0.10	0	0	0	0	0

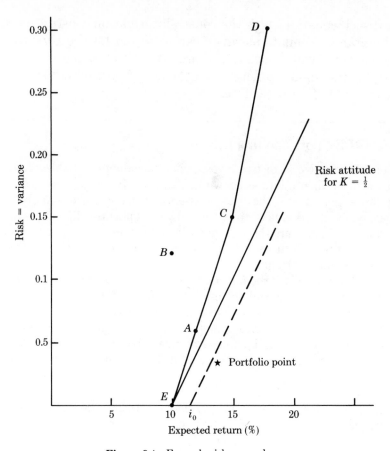

Figure 9.4 Example risk–reward map.

Substituting these values into equation 9.15 results in

$$E(i) = 0.1348, \text{ or } 13.48\% \text{ expected return},$$
$$V(i) = 0.0381,$$

and we also get an equivalent risk-free return of 11.58%.

If we plot the portfolio point in Figure 9.4, the effect of a diversification strategy becomes evident. We have found a way to move both down and to the right on our map.

It can be shown that a riskless investment can be combined with a portfolio separately, without disturbing the optimum ratios of the risky investments in the portfolio. Therefore we can now see the effect of such a combination.

Let y be the proportion of capital in the risky subportfolio; $1 - y$ is then the capital in the riskless investment. Then

$$i_0 = 0.1348y + 0.1(1 - y) - (0.5)(0.03841)y. \qquad (9.17)$$

Differentiating, equating to zero, and solving for the optimum y yields

$$y(\text{opt}) = 0.906,$$
$$E(i) = 0.1315, \text{ or } 13.15\%,$$
$$V(i) = 0.0315,$$
$$i_0 = 11.57\%.$$

If we add a riskless investment into which we put 9.06% of our capital, the new portfolio point is moved a very small distance toward the lower right-hand corner. This reduces both expected return and risk and, at the same time, increases the equivalent risk-free return so slightly that it is barely perceptible.

Suppose we do not attempt to determine the optimum allocation, but simply decide to place one-fifth of our capital in each investment, including the riskless one. Taking the values directly from Table 9.1, the expected return will be the arithmetic average:

$$i_0 = \frac{0.10 + 0.12 + 0.10 + 0.15 + 0.18}{5} = 0.13.$$

The average variance will be

$$V = \frac{0.08 + 0.04 + 0.12 + 0.15}{25}$$
$$+ (0.02 + 0.04 + 0.025 + 0.04 + 0.03) \times \tfrac{2}{5}$$
$$= 0.0776.$$

Thus $i_0 = 0.13 - 0.0776/2 = 0.0912$, or 9.12%. This is almost 2% less than the optimal value.

The values obtained for the optimal allocation are quite sensitive to slight changes in parameters. At best, the estimates of expectations and variances are crude—little more than guesses. Covariance estimates must be made for all possible pairs, and this, as well as being less accurate than estimates of other parameters,

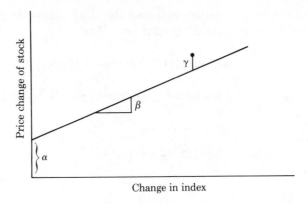

Figure 9.5 Stock movement relative to an index.

becomes impractical. There are just too many investment pairs to be considered.

The *diagonal model*, a method for circumventing the difficulty of excessive dimensionality of the general portfolio problem, was suggested by William Sharpe (1963). Sharpe modified the Markowitz model by introducing an additional pseudo security that was essentially an index of the market as a whole.

Rather than attempting to assess the covariances of all individual stocks, it is relatively simple to assess how each stock may be expected to perform relative to the market as a whole, as gauged by some recognized index of the market, such as the DJI or the Standard and Poor's index (Figure 9.5). Each stock can be expected to realize a return, α, if the market does not move at all. Furthermore its price will increase by some fraction β of the market change. In addition there will be a random change γ, which is independent of the market movement. Thus the expected return on the portfolio will be

$$E(i) = \sum_{j=1}^{n+1} x_j(\alpha + \beta I + \gamma), \qquad (9.16)$$

where I is the return on the index (i.e., the rate of change). Now

$$\sum_{j=1}^{n+1} \gamma x_j = 0 \qquad (9.17)$$

by definition, and

$$\sum_{j=1}^{n+1} \beta_j x_j$$

is the weighted average of the β's. We can regard the $(n + 1)$th investment as an investment in the index, for which the x value is this weighted average. Then the value of equation 9.16 becomes

$$E(i) = \sum_{j=1}^{n} x_j \alpha_j. \tag{9.18}$$

Using similar reasoning, the expected values of the squares of the α's with respect to the mean is the variance. Thus

$$V = \sum E\{x_j(\alpha + \beta I + \gamma_j)\}$$
$$= \sum \left[E(x_j \alpha_j) + E(x_j \beta I) \right]. \tag{9.19}$$

The second term is the variance in the index, and so equation 9.19 becomes

$$V = \sum x_j^2 V_j + V(I)P. \tag{9.20}$$

All the terms in γ have dropped out because they are zero. However, the second term of equation 9.19 has been shown to be the equivalent of an investment in the index, and therefore equation 9.19 becomes

$$V = E(x_j \beta_j). \tag{9.21}$$

It is seen that the $n \times n$ covariance matrix has been reduced in size to a diagonal matrix of $n + 1$ terms. This considerably simplifies the computational problem and also places the evaluation of correlations in a new perspective. We relate each investment to the movement of the market as a whole.

The tremendous advantage introduced by the Sharpe modification to the Markowitz model brought the use of portfolio theory into widespread acceptance by portfolio managers. As a result, the

Beta coefficient is now regularly evaluated by investment advisory services, such as Value Line. The historical value of a Beta is probably more predictive of a future Beta than the past rate of price appreciation is for future price appreciation.

An important conclusion can be drawn from further examination of equation 9.20. The first term can be made as small as desired, simply by increasing the number of securities. For equal allocations, for example, we have $x = 1/n$. Therefore, for n securities all with the same variance, the first term of equation 9.20 becomes

$$V = x_j V_j / n. \qquad (9.22)$$

On the other hand, the second term reduces to the variance of the index, times the square of the average Beta.

This illustrates the possibility of diversifying away the risk from individual stocks by selecting a portfolio comprised of a sufficient number of securities. The market risk is unchanged by a diversification strategy. The optimal allocation can be determined from equations 9.15 and 9.16 as before.

EXAMPLE: The diagonal model for portfolio evaluation

Consider a portfolio in which the market conditions are such that, in the next year, the index (adjusted for dividend distributions) is expected to rise 10%. The variance of the index is 5%. The data for five stocks considered as candidates for a portfolio are given in Table 9.2.

The solution of this problem is only practicable by means of the computer program. (See Appendix E.) An additional constraint was imposed that no stock have a negative amount invested. The answer is

Table 9.2

STOCK	$E(i)$ (%)	β	VARIANCE (%)
A	7	0.8	5
B	9	0.9	10
C	11	0.95	15
D	13	1.1	18
E	12	1.0	17

that there should be 15.1% in *B*, 35.4% in *C*, and 49.5% in *D*. Stocks *A* and *E* are eliminated.

While the Sharpe contribution made portfolio theory tractable, it did not make it more than a conceptual tool. Portfolio theory is not, in itself, a practical operational method for determining an optimum portfolio. The percentage allocations are sensitive to slight changes in the parameters. It is not reasonable to estimate variances and expected returns with the precision that is needed for anything more than classifying securities into groups by average risk and average expected return. Then equal amounts of capital can be allocated to each stock in the group. A portfolio can then be constructed from sets of such stocks, considered as if each set were an individual security.

It should not be inferred that the shortcomings of portfolio theory render it useless, but rather that so refined a mathematical procedure is hardly justified by the fuzziness of the data.

9.3 THE TIME PERIOD

Validity of the solution of the portfolio problem is predicated on the assumption of a single time period. The length of this period can be a day, a month, a year, or many years. The parameters must be consistent with the chosen time period, and the return is based on that period. Correspondingly, the variance is a measure of the values at beginning and end of the period. Any deviation of portfolio value during the interval is ignored.

When we are dealing with a portfolio of securities, this single-period constraint on the solution may not be serious. As a matter of course, an investor would want to reevaluate and revise his portfolio of stocks on a regular basis. However, there are transaction costs associated with making changes. In addition to commissions, there are losses in execution of sales and purchases. There has been a great deal of research done, and much literature published, to develop a satisfactory theory of portfolio revision. However, such extension of the theory is beyond the scope of this book.

Our interest lies in seeing how the concepts of portfolio theory might apply to the case of a project investment. While the rates of return are for the single period over which the portfolio exists as an unrevised entity, they can always be referenced to annualized rates of return. Thus if the period for the portfolio corresponds to the life cycle of the project, the rate of return that is significant in the context of a portfolio is the return for the period from inception to termination. This might, for example, be for 20 years with a return of 2000% per 20-year period. Most people would not relate to a number of this magnitude. However 2000% per 20 years is the equivalent of 16.2% per year, a number that is readily related to an investor's sense of proportion.

Actually the end of any project is unforeseeable. A successful outcome leads to subsequent expansion decisions. Thus each project is, in effect, an incident in a continuum. Profitability of the expanded operation must be partially attributable to earlier decisions that led to the initiation of the project. On the other hand, if a project is not successful, it will most likely be prematurely abandoned. In either case, the year-to-year variance in performance of the project is not the measure of variance that is meaningful for portfolio analysis.

Even though the variance of year-to-year return does not apply in a project evaluation, there is nevertheless risk that is related to the variance of cash flows. The stockholder will recognize this to be so because the variance of cash flow will reflect the yearly variance in the price of his stock. He is not as concerned with return on the project from beginning to end, as he is in the perceived profitability of his personal short-term investment in the company's stock. Furthermore, management will tend to be evaluated on the basis of its year-to-year performance and not on how well any one project does over the long run. Thus the perception of risk will translate into short-term variances in cash flow. On the other hand, the owner–manager need not be sensitive to short-term variability as long as he is confident that he will not go bankrupt in the short run. However, even he will be influenced by the year-to-year cash-flow fluctuation.

The real risk in any project, of course, will depend on the variance in the overall shape of the entire cash-flow stream. As a rule, if the cost or the revenue stream starts to deviate from that projected, this trend will continue, because one year's revenue or expenditure is not independent of that of the previous year. With these caveats in mind we can examine the characteristics of the cash flow for a single project.

9.4 CASH FLOW FOR A SINGLE PROJECT

The cash flow may be estimated in accordance with procedures in Chapter 5. Our concern here is the variance in this cash-flow stream. During the investment phase, the cash flow consists only of expenditures. The uncertainty associated with these will increase with futurity, and therefore the variance in the estimates will tend to expand exponentially into the future. The transition from a positive to a negative cash flow commences with startup, when construction is ended and the project goes into operation. A whole new set of uncertainties develops at this stage. Unexpected delays are encountered; unforeseen disruptions occur; design errors tend to come to light. All these things create increased variance in the cost streams. Once revenues commence, the cash flow then becomes the difference between revenue and expenditure streams. Both of these come under close management scrutiny, so that, coupled with the learning-curve effect, the variance will tend to diminish. This presupposes, of course, that the project will prove viable. This pattern of variance as a function of time is depicted in Figure 9.6.

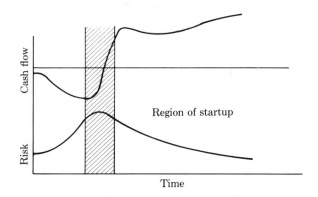

Figure 9.6 Variance in cash flow with time.

9.4.1 An Equivalent Discount Rate, Allowing for Risk

It has been a long-standing practice to attempt to compensate for risk by choosing a discount rate that is adjusted upwards from the risk-free rate in order to take account of risk. The major difficulties in this method of allowing for risk are twofold:

1. There are no established guidelines by which a meaningful assessment of risk can be made in relation to the rate of return.

2. The incremental rate of return for risk is often erroneously added when it should be subtracted. During the investment phase the concern is that costs might run higher than estimated. If one uses a discount rate higher than the riskless rate, the result is exactly opposite to that desired.

As will be demonstrated by examples in Section 9.4.2, this practice of factoring the discount rate for risk should be categorically rejected. *It is an incorrect method for taking account of risk.* The expected rate of return for a given level of admissible risk, as shown on the risk–reward map, may be utilized for evaluating a risky investment. However, in doing so, it would be necessary to determine what this rate should be for a project in which the variance of cash flow is a function of time. This could not be easily done, because it is difficult, if not impossible, to develop a sense of risk for the project as a whole. It is possible to make an assessment of the cash-flow variance as described above and, from this, transform the rate of return into a risk-factored rate of return. Working back from this risk-factored rate, we can find a measure of overall risk in the project. While this roundabout approach is interesting and a helpful aid to understanding, it is not a practical method of risk evaluation.

One recommended procedure for evaluating risk is to add an increment for risk to the cash-flow stream. This could be done by adding a fraction of a standard deviation (standard deviation is the square root of variance) to the expected value of the cash flow. This would now produce a higher internal rate of return. This higher IRR is the OCC necessary to allow for risk.

The interesting fact that this procedure reveals is the magnitude of adjustment required for different cash-flow shapes. Not only does this risk-factored rate of return change nonlinearly with variance of cash flow, but it is also very sensitive to the shape of the cash flow.

9.4.2 Example of Equivalent Risk-Factored Discount Rate

Three examples will demonstrate the sensitivity of the risk-factored OCC.

EXAMPLES: Two cases of risk-factored rates

1. A point investment and point return.

2. A point investment and a constant-cash-flow return.

In both examples, the risk-free OCC will be specified as 10%.

Example 1: Assume a standard deviation of 10%, a return period of 10 years, and $F = 1$. Let the risk factor be 1 standard deviation. Then

$$P = (1 + 0.10)^{-10} = 0.386.$$

Now add the standard deviation of 10% to F (i.e., $F = 1.1$); P must remain the same:

$$P = 0.386 = (1 + i)^{-10}.$$

Solving, we have $i = 11.04\%$, or a 10.4% increase in i for a 10% risk factor in the cash flow.

If we were to repeat this example for a 5-year life, we would find it necessary to increase i by 12.12%. This means that the risk factor in the rate of return must be higher for shorter-lived projects.

Example 2: For the constant-cash-flow case, we will again assume 10% increase in cash flow and a 10-year life. The cash flow is $A = 1$, so

$$P = (P/A, 10, 10) = 6.145.$$

Again add the standard deviation of 10%, this time to A. The investment P is fixed. Then

$$P = 6.145 = 1.1(P/A, i, 10).$$

Solving, we have $i = 12.28\%$, a 22.8% increase over the riskless rate.

Table 9.3 Comparison of Risk-Factored Discount Rates

	RISKLESS RATE 10%		RISKLESS RATE 5%	
	Risk-factored	Increase	Risk-factored	Increase
n	i	(%)	i	(%)
2	17.38	73.8	11.99	139.8
5	13.84	38.4	8.55	71.0
10	12.28	22.8	7.01	40.2
15	11.78	17.8	6.45	29.0
20	11.44	14.4	6.15	23.0
25	11.28	12.8	5.98	19.6

If we repeat this procedure for different lives and with a new riskless rate of return of 5%, we find some interesting results as shown in Table 9.3. The wide disparity in these rates of return clearly shows how difficult it is to judge what factor should be used for adjusting the discount rate for risk. It is also noteworthy that the shorter the life of the project, the higher will be the level of indicated adjustment for risk.

9.4.3 A Better Procedure for Considering Risk

The foregoing exercise clearly demonstrates the difficulty of employing a risk-factored discount rate for project evaluation. The procedure which should be followed is to adjust the cash flow by subtracting an arbitrary fraction of cash flow. Note that this is just the opposite of what we did to find a risk-factored rate of return. There we added the risk component. Since by doing this we have taken risk into account, the discount rate should be the risk-free rate. Sensitivity of the decision to accept or reject the project, is determined by evaluating its present worth, using a range of factors for the risk function.

9.4.4 The Net Present Worth with Risk Included

As emphasized in Chapter 5, the IRR approach to evaluation is valid only for the special case of no reinvestment of the return cash flow. The present-worth approach is preferred. This means that we should reduce the cash flow by the increment-risk adjustment as we did in the previous section. However we should now use the riskless OCC for discounting cash flows.

EXAMPLE:

Consider the case of an investment that will generate an expected cash flow of $1100 per year for 10 years. We will use the same discount rate and planning period as in the previous example, in order to illustrate the principle. Therefore we will assume that the risk in the cash flow is $100 per year. If we possessed the wisdom to have made the analysis of the previous example, we would have been able to see that the risk-factored OCC would be 12.28%. Thus the present worth of the cash flow would be

$$P = \$1100 \times (P/A, 12.28, 10) = \$6145.$$

We should use the riskless rate of 10% and make the adjustment in the cash flow, by subtracting $100 per year from the expected cash flow of $1100. Thus the present worth is

$$P = (1100 - 100) \times (P/A, 10, 10) = \$6145.$$

This is a somewhat trivial example, but it illustrates why the adjustment in cash flow should be made by subtracting the risk component.

9.5 RISK ASSOCIATED WITH PROJECT SLIPPAGE

While the risk, as measured by variance of cash flow, increases during the period of transition from construction to startup, the magnitude of the cash-flow stream is relatively small. During this stage the risk is more likely to be related to *stretchout*, or delay in startup, than it is to the variance of the cash flow. Delays can have a significant effect on long-run profitability.

In order to see this, we can idealize the cash-flow stream into a constant negative cash flow during construction followed by a constant positive cash flow at startup. Ideally, the positive cash flow follows immediately after the negative cash flow (Figure 9.7). We will introduce slippage at startup. The typical project cash flow is shown as the dashed line, and the approximation of this is represented by the two rectangles. The investment phase is as-

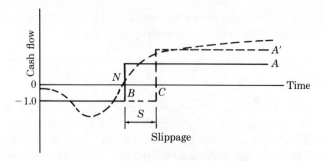

Figure 9.7 Effect of slippage on cash flow.

sumed to take N years, at a level of expenditure of unity, which would require an annuity in perpetuity at a level A if the transition to positive cash flow occurs at point B, and at level A' if it occurs at point C. Slippage is represented as the difference S between B and C.

The difference between the annuities, $A' - A$, is the additional cash flow needed to compensate for the slippage, and hence is a measure of the cash-flow adjustment needed to allow for risk of slippage:

$$P = 0 = (P/A, i, N) = \frac{A(P/F, i, N)}{i} = \frac{A'(P/F, i, N + S)}{i},$$

$$(9.23)$$

from which

$$A' = i(P/A, i, N)(F/P, i, N + S) \qquad (9.24)$$

and

$$A = i(P/A, i, N)(F/P, i, N), \qquad (9.25)$$

$$A' - A = i(P/A, i, N)\{(F/P, i, N + S) - (F/P, i, N)\}$$

$$= i(P/A, i, N)(F/P, i, N)\{(F/P, i, S) - 1\}. \quad (9.26)$$

From this we can obtain the percentage increase needed in the cash flow in order to compensate for the risk of slippage. The percentage change $A_\%$ in A is:

$$A_\% = \frac{A' - A}{A} \times 100 = \{(F/P, i, S) - 1\} \times 100. \quad (9.27)$$

This will be recognized as the effective discount for the time period of the slippage. In other words, the cash flow must be adjusted by a percentage corresponding with the OCC. If we use the riskless rate for discounting, we will subtract this percentage from the projected expected cash flow. For example, if we compensate for a possible slippage of 4 years in the project startup, and the OCC is 10%, we will reduce the projected cash flow by

$$\{\text{reduction of } (F/P, 10, 4) - 1\} \times 100 = 46.4\%.$$

This demonstrates the seriousness of the effect of slippage in startup.

9.6 TREATMENT OF RISK IN COMPARING ALTERNATIVES

The problem of coping with risk, when choosing between alternatives for accomplishing some specified objective within the firm, involves a conditional decision. The question is:

Given that, in any event, at least one alternative will be accepted, which is the best choice?

As was shown in Chapter 5, on comparison of alternatives, all cash flows that are identical in all respects for all alternatives may be canceled from both sides of the present-worth inequalities. For this reason the revenue stream, which is usually independent of the choice of alternatives, may be omitted and the comparison be based on costs only.

The same argument applies to the treatment of the risk-factored cash-flow function. All risks associated with revenue become irrelevant. The only risks that need be considered are those which differ from one alternative to another.

What then should the discount rate be?

To answer this we must recognize the inherent risks in the business in which the firm is engaged. These characteristic risks are revealed by the actual rate of return that has been realized for the stockholders over the long run. Individual investors demand a higher return on what they perceive as a risky investment than they do on a conservative investment. This higher rate of return represents an integration of risk effects and, as such, is the OCC for the business. Furthermore, since all component investments are complementary, they must be assumed to justify this same OCC. It is this rate of return that should be used in the project comparisons. While it does not represent a riskless rate, it is a rate from which all but the risk innate in that business has been squeezed out.

9.7 RISK ASSOCIATED WITH PREMATURE ABANDONMENT

One might well question why variance, as a measure of risk, is of concern as long as the project proves viable—i.e., does not go broke (Oakford 1982). It can be argued persuasively that, as long as the firm grows, yearly profitability fluctuations do not matter in the long run. However, as pointed out above, divergences from predicted trends are worrisome to investors holding securities in the firm. These stockholder worries transform into management worries and, if they become acute, lead to questions of abandonment of projects, change of management, and restructuring of the organization. Furthermore, the stockholders' perspective is short. Deviation from projected results can have devastating consequences on stock prices. It is the price of the stock to which the ordinary stockholder reacts.

Unplanned abandonment of a project usually results in a significant loss. The occurrence of such an abandonment is unpredictable; it is over the horizon at the time of project initiation. However as a matter of prudence, some subjective probability q may be assigned to this occurrence. The course of the cash-flow stream bifurcates in the post-horizon period, as depicted in Figure 9.8. This situation is typical of long-term large-scale systems, where the positive cash-flow stream has not yet started to grow significantly. If the project turns out to be successful, the growth phase that results will lead to expanded growth, including capacity expansions and other subsequent investments, all of which

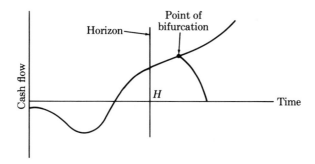

Figure 9.8 Bifurcated cash flow beyond the horizon.

must be attributed to the investment under consideration. Conversely, if the project turns out to be unsuccessful, the cash flow will peak early and will subsequently decay until an abandonment decision is reached. The probability of success is, correspondingly, $1 - q$. We may now multiply the entire post-horizon cash flow by this probability and obtain a risk-factored P for this kind of risk.

It is not possible to estimate when such a bifurcation point will occur, except that we know it must be over the horizon. Therefore the most conservative policy will be to assume it is on the horizon and that the cash flow for the unsuccessful outcome goes to zero immediately. Thus the discounted post-horizon cash flow would automatically be zero.

The present worth for the project would then be

$$P = \int_0^H y(t)e^{-rt}\,dt + \int_H^\infty (1 - q)y(t)e^{-rt}\,dt. \qquad (9.28)$$

Now the function $y(t)$, beyond the horizon, is typically an exponential with a growth rate g. Since this function represents the conditionality of success, it can be expected to continue into the indefinite future. If we assume that time is infinite, we see that the condition for acceptance of the project reduces to an assessment of the growth rate g. If g is equal to or greater than r, the value of the integral goes to infinity and acceptance of the project is indicated as long as there is even a miniscule probability q of success.

Clearly, time is not infinite, and some finite time must be introduced. This can be stretched far into the future and still will provide a meaningful answer.

EXAMPLE: Evaluation of a risky project

Suppose the project planning period is 100 years, the horizon is 10 years, and the riskless OCC is 4%. The consensus of all connected with the program is that the probability of the project not proving viable is 0.4, quite a high chance of failure.

There is a two-year study and engineering phase at a level of expenditure of $1 million, after which construction starts and will run at a level of $75 million per year for the next 6 years, when startup is planned. This places startup at the end of the 8th year. Given that eventually the project is a success, the initial cash flow will be $12 million per year and will grow for 100 years, at a rate of 3.5% per year.

The initial cash flow has already been adjusted downwards by 30% to allow for slippages. There are differences of opinion as to the sustainability of the long-term growth. Some believe it is 10% too high.

Is the project economically justified?

SOLUTION

- *Present worth of capital investment.*

$$P = 10(P/A, 4, 2) + 75(P/A, 4, 6)(P/F, 4, 2)$$
$$= \$381.82 \text{ million.}$$

- *Present worth of net cash-flow return.*

$$P = y(8) \times (P/A, i - g, 100)(P/F, i, 8) \times (1 - q)$$
$$= 12 \times (P/A, 0.5, 100)(P/F, 4, 8) \times 0.6$$
$$= \$413.21 \text{ million.}$$

Since the estimate of the full cash flow must be considered valid up to the horizon, there is a slight adjustment needed to add back $q \times$ (the cash flow from the 8th to the 10th year). This is

$$\Delta P = 12 \times (P/A, i - g, 2)(P/A, i, 8) \times 0.4$$
$$= \$6.96 \text{ million.}$$

Therefore the net present worth is

$$P = 413.21 + 6.96 - 381.82 = \$38.35 \text{ million.}$$

The project is worth undertaking.

- *Effect of a changed growth rate.* Consider the effect of a 10% reduction in revenue growth. The present worth of the return cash flow is

$$P = 12 \times (P/A, 0.85, 100)(P/F, 4, 8) \times 0.6$$
$$= \$353.44 \text{ million}$$

plus the adjustment

$$\Delta P = 12 \times (P/A, 0.85, 2)(P/A, 4, 8) \times 0.4$$
$$= \$6.93 \text{ million.}$$

The new net present worth is

$$P = 353.44 + 6.93 - 381.82 = -\$21.45 \text{ million,}$$

indicating that the project is unattractive. On the other hand, if the growth rate had been 10% higher, the outcome would have been considerably different. Repeating the calculation will reveal that the net present worth would then be $113.38 million.

The sensitivity of the solution to the difference between the growth rates and the discount rates is very high. It turns out that the sensitivity to futurity is not nearly as significant as one might expect if the difference between the discount and growth rates is more than 5%, but it is very significant if the difference, as in this case, is small.

9.8 RECAPITULATION

1. Risk is an important consideration in project evaluation. It is measured by expected deviation of the outcome of the decision, or the variance of the expected outcome. This leads to the concept of a *risk–reward map*. The objective is always to move down and to the right—to maximize return given an objective level of risk, or to minimize risk given an objective level of return.

2. A risk-preference function is represented by a straight line, the slope of which is the degree of risk the decision maker is willing to accept. The preferred investment corresponds to the point on the convex boundary of the universe of investment opportunities that becomes the point of tangency to the risk-preference line as it is moved in from the right. All interior points in the set are dominated by the convex boundary.

3. Provided that investments are not correlated, a strategy of diversification will reduce risk. Risk can never be reduced below the weighted-average covariance of the set of investments in the portfolio, but it may approach that level with a sufficiently large number of investments. In short, market risk cannot be diversified away, but individual-stock risk can be. Since the blue-chip investments are highly correlated with the market, and speculative issues are less so, the most conservative strategy is a portfolio of risky stocks.

4. The principles of portfolio theory are applicable for a single time period. However, to some degree, the concepts may be extended to project investment decisions. While the variance in cash flows is theoretically of no concern as long as it does not induce bankruptcy, such variance does have an impact on the stockholder. As such, it does provide a surrogate for risk in the project.

5. The traditional way of allowing for risk in a project, by adjusting the discount rate upward, is not a valid approach. There is no consistent way in which judgment can be brought to bear on how large this factored discount rate should be. It is too sensitive to the shape of the cash-flow function.

6. The variance of the cash flow in a project is a function of the futurity of that cash flow. It rises during construction to a peak at startup, and declines with the learning-curve effect as the operating life is extended.

7. The preferred method of risk assessment is to use the riskless discount rate for the OCC and a reduced cash flow (increased cash flow for the investment phase) adjusted for risk.

8. The transition period at startup is related to slippage, a problem that seriously influences the required return cash

flow. This risk effect can be translated into an adjustment of the cash flow to allow for this.

9.9 PROBLEMS

1. On the basis of a 15% standard deviation adjusted for risk, in a ten-year cash flow return on an investment of $1000 on which the return is 12%, determine a risk-adjusted rate of return. (Follow the example problem in the text.)

2. Refer to the portfolio problem example in the text. Examine the sensitivity of the portfolio proportions to a change in parameters of stock A. Consider how the expected return will be affected by a change of plus or minus 10% of the values given, and by an increase in the variance from 0.06 to 0.07.

3. A short sale is one in which stock is borrowed in order to satisfy a delivery requirement. A cash deposit must be made to secure the loan of the certificates. This deposit, as regulated by the Federal Reserve Bank, is 50% of the proceeds of the sale in addition to the proceeds from the sale (i.e., 150% margin). Later the stock will be purchased and the borrowed stock delivered, thus producing a profit if the stock price declines.

• Construct a portfolio of stocks along with cash, either borrowed or loaned. For a set of 10 speculative stocks, assume that you cannot differentiate between risks and returns but assess them to be all the same, with a Beta of 1.7 and a variance of 30%. The variance of the market index is 10%.
• You have identified a second set of 10 stocks, which you expect will go down or, at least, not rise as fast as the first 10 if the market rises. Let us say their Betas are -1.6.
• For both sets you expect that the returns will average 12% if the market index does not move. This presupposes that you will sell short on the negative-Beta stocks.
• You will realize 8% on the cash you lend (e.g., put in a money market fund), and you will pay 10% on the cash you borrow. You cannot borrow more than 50% of your capital, but may lend all of it.

- Evaluate the proportions of your capital you would allocate to these four options (the first stock list, the second stock list, borrowing and lending). Note: you will not lend and borrow simultaneously.

4. Determine a risk-adjusted discount rate for comparing two alternatives with different cash-flow shapes:

   a. Point investment and point return in 15 years.

   b. Point investment and a negative-exponential return for which the rate of decline is 8%.

   Solve, assuming that the riskless rate is 5%, and then repeat using 12%. Try guessing what the adjusted rates should be before you start.

5. Determine the percentage adjustment for the cash return flow you would need to allow for a startup slippage of S years, where the cash flow is:

   a. A finite time of 20 years, instead of infinity as in the text example.

   b. An exponential, where the growth rate is 10% per year for 20 years.

   Assume that the riskless rate for the OCC is 5%.

○

○

CHAPTER TEN

○ *Change:*

○ *Capacity, Replacement,*

○

○ *and Abandonment*

○

Anticipation of change must be part of the evaluation process. It would be a most unusual project in which, after initiation, something did not happen that required change. Usually regular reviews are scheduled during the design phase in the development of a project. What is learned during this phase can trigger questions of the ultimate viability of the project and, in any event, may require modifications of the original plan.

The question of possible abandonment can always arise. Some projects are dependent on a long period of investigation and development, where the final outcome could be in considerable doubt. A good historical example of such is the supersonic transport aircraft (SST). The British–French Concord development program was started in the early 1950s. An American SST project was started a few years later. While the Concord was finally introduced into service in 1977, by then the decision had already been made to abandon the program. The American SST program, on the other hand, had been scrapped during the engineering phase after many millions of dollars had been spent on development. There had been considerable controversy over both of these programs, right from the start. Questions had been raised from the outset concerning the economic viability of any SST program, but the greatest issue was environmental (Grobecker et al. 1975). Finally the oil-price escalation killed both the American and European SST programs. Most of the final issues were not, or could not, have been foreseen at the outset.

Other programs, less dramatic than the SST, can well be modified or canceled for a variety of reasons at any time during construction. After startup further changes will be needed, often requiring retrofit but sometimes dictating model changes almost immediately after introduction into service. Again, drawing an example from the air-transport industry, it has been common practice, almost as soon as a new model airplane has been introduced into service, to change the design by stretching the airplane fuselage to increase its capacity.

Finally the project may reach the limit of useful life where either further capacity expansion or abandonment is indicated. These possible changes must be considered at the outset and included in the project-evaluation methodology.

A needed modification can result in either escalation of costs or decline in projected revenue, thus resulting in a reassessment of the wisdom of the initial decision. However, all expenditures incurred up to the point of potential abandonment become *sunk costs*, and as such are completely irrelevant in considering any program change. The inclusion of sunk costs in an evaluation is one of the most common errors made. The billions of dollars spent in developing the Concord have nothing to do with whether or not it is a good idea to continue operating existing Concord aircraft. It is probably a very profitable operation from the standpoint of current operating costs, but from the accounting standpoint, it will continue to show losses as long as it is operated. The important point is that the loss was sustained as a consequence of the original decision, not from the current decision to continue flight operations.

In addition to obsolescence and wear, program changes may be necessitated by prematurely reaching the capacity limit of the project. This raises the question of whether simply to add more units (i.e., replicate the project) or to abandon the first project and replace it with a single new unit that can take advantage of economies of scale. Finally there is the decision as to when to abandon a project altogether.

10.1 CAPACITY PLANNING

It is almost always necessary, in order to accommodate growth, to provide more capacity than is required to satisfy the level of demand existing at startup. Excess capacity requires extra capital investment as well as increased operating expense. These extra costs are justified to the extent of the savings potential associated with what it would otherwise cost to make the change later on, when such extra capacity can finally be utilized. Clearly, if it is possible to add new capacity when and if needed, at no greater expense at that time than it would have cost initially, it will not pay to incur the added initial expense.

It will pay to incur added initial expenditure when that added expenditure is much less costly than it would be later. A good example is a freeway overpass that is built to accommodate an eventual six-lane highway when all that is needed in the first project is a four-lane highway. The span for the six-lane overpass is not a great deal more expensive than it is for a four-lane overcrossing, but it would cost a great deal to have to replace the narrower overpass fifteen years from now. If the discounted value of the six-lane overpass is not less than the incremental cost of increasing the size at the outset, it will pay to accept that extra cost for the added capacity now.

10.1.1 The Functional Relationship for Added Capacity

How much added capacity should be provided?

We can examine this question by means of a number of idealizations, which represent reality reasonably well (English 1967). First we will assume that demand grows exponentially at a rate a. A capacity limit will be reached when the growth in demand intersects the capacity limit at time L (Figure 10.1). If the net cash flow is exactly proportional to capacity—an idealization—then

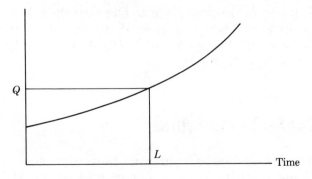

Figure 10.1 Plant capacity.

demand Q is

$$Q = Q_0 e^{at} \tag{10.1}$$

and the cash flow is

$$AQ = AQ_0 e^{at}, \tag{10.2}$$

where A is the cash flow per unit of Q.

The difference between the capacity limit and the initial demand is the excess capacity to be provided—if, indeed, any is warranted. If the investment cost is also exactly proportional to the demand (i.e., there is no economy of scale), no extra capacity can be justified. Therefore we must assume a function to represent economy of scale.

The effect of economies of scale is that the investment cost, while growing with increasing capacity, will grow at a slower rate than will the demand. Let this slower rate be $a - b$, where b is a parameter of scale effects. In other words, capacity would have to grow at rate a in the absence of scale effects, but because of scale economies, the capital growth rate will be less than a, by the rate adjustment b.

Because the increase in capacity must still have a cost, $a - b$ must be positive—i.e., $a > b$. If I is the investment required per unit of Q, then total investment is

$$IQ = IQ_0 e^{(a-b)L}. \tag{10.3}$$

The present worth of a project that initially has sufficient excess capacity to reach its capacity limit in L years will now be

$$P = -IQ_0 e^{(a-b)L} + AQ_0 \int_0^L e^{(a-r)t} \, dt. \tag{10.4}$$

Integrating, this becomes

$$P = -IQ_0 e^{(a-b)L} + AQ_0 \frac{e^{(a-r)L} - 1}{a - r}. \tag{10.5}$$

Differentiating and equating to zero in order to find the L that maximizes P, we obtain

$$\frac{I}{A} = \frac{e^{(b-r)L}}{a - b}. \tag{10.6}$$

The L that maximizes P is the theoretical optimum life for the project. The value for P in equation 10.5, as a minimum requirement to justify the project, is zero. Consequently, when we maximize P, that maximum must be zero. Therefore, setting P in equation 10.4 equal to 0, we get

$$\frac{I}{A} = \frac{e^{(a-r)L} - 1}{(a - r)e^{(a-b)L}}. \tag{10.7}$$

Combining equations 10.6 and 10.7, we obtain

$$L = \frac{\ln\{(a - b)/(r - b)\}}{a - r}. \tag{10.8}$$

The solution for equation 10.8 may be negative, depending on the relative values of the three parameters, a, b, and r. A negative value for L indicates that no excess capacity is justified. Therefore we must examine the conditions for which L is positive.

If $a > r$ and $(a - b)/(r - b) > 0$, then the logarithm must be positive. However if $a > b > r$, the logarithm will be negative, giving a negative value for L when $a > r$, but positive when $a < r$.

Two interesting results occur when b tends to zero and when a tends to r. In the first case, there are no economies of scale and

$$L = \frac{\ln(a/r)}{a - r}. \tag{10.9}$$

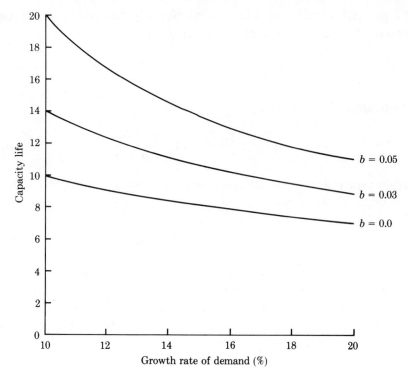

Figure 10.2 Capacity life for various rates. The OCC for all curves is 10%.

The greater the spread between the growth rate and the discount rate, the shorter will be the capacity life. The limiting condition can be found by taking the limits as $a \to r$:

$$\lim_{a \to r} L = \lim_{a \to r} \frac{\ln(a/r)}{a - r} = \frac{1}{r}. \tag{10.10}$$

For the case where $b > 0$ this limit is

$$\lim_{a \to r} L = \frac{1}{r - b}. \tag{10.11}$$

If the difference between a and r is greater than zero, the capacity life will be shorter than that derived from equation 10.11.

We now consider a range of growth rates, scale parameters, and discount rates. The solution for equation 10.8 is shown in Figure 10.2. These curves show clearly the sensitivity of the capacity life to the discount rate. Scale effects and rate of growth are less significant.

10.1.2 Practical Considerations

The idealized analysis for determining the capacity life of an asset is instructive for showing why a theoretical life exists for the project. However, as a practical matter, the swing from a zero life to a very long life is extremely sensitive to the differences between the growth and discount parameters. For this reason, the theoretical capacity life is more of a guide than an operationally useful methodology. In many cases a zero capacity life is indicated.

A zero capacity life means that capacity expansion should take place continuously. However, this is not possible. There is a minimum capacity life, below which it does not pay to go. It takes time to place each new increment of capacity into use. The capacity life becomes the minimum time required for installation of each new addition.

10.1.3 Replacement or Expansion

When the capacity limit is reached, a decision must be made either to expand the existing facility by addition of an incremental unit of capacity, or to abandon the existing facility and replace it with a new one that is large enough to take care of the increased demand. An economic advantage will accrue to the latter alternative if the economies of scale for the expanded size exceed those of the incremental addition.

As an example consider the options facing an airline when the capacity limit of a Boeing 727 is reached for a particular route. The airline can buy a second B727 or replace the existing B727 with a B747 or a DC10.

The evaluation is made by comparing the cost of a new large-scale replacement unit with the combined costs of the existing unit plus the added unit.

Care must be exercised here to evaluate the existing unit at its terminal value or salable salvage value. If it is not salable, its value can only be properly determined as the difference between the present worth of the cash flow for the new replacement and the present worth of the cash flow to be derived from the added unit.

EXAMPLE: Expansion or replacement

A new plant unit, A, was installed 5 years ago and was expected to be adequate to meet demand for the next 15 years. Its original cost was $2.12 million. It is being depreciated over 20 years on a straight-line basis, so that now its book value is $1.767 million. Its current cash-flow generation is $580,000; it is growing at a rate of 10% per year and is expected to continue indefinitely at this rate. A new addition, B, to the existing plant, which will accommodate this growth for another 15 years, will cost $5.0 million.

New developments render the present plant much less efficient. As a consequence, it might pay to scrap it and build a single new plant, C, at a cost of $6.0 million. It is estimated that the terminal value of the new larger plant will be $3 million in 15 years and that of the add-on unit, will be $2.0 million. The existing installation will be worthless by then and will have been fully depreciated in the accounts.

The firm's OCC is 5% (exclusive of inflation). Which is the better choice, the add-on B or the new installation C? What is the value of the existing plant A now?

SOLUTION

We will use discrete compounding.
Fifteen years from now, the cash flow should be

$$F = 580,000 \times (F/P, 10, 15) = \$2,422,800.$$

The added capacity provided by plant B must provide for

$$\$2,422,800 - \$580,000, \text{ or } \$1,842,800$$

in increased cash flow in that fifteen-year time. The present worth of this cash flow is

$$P = 580,000\{(P/A, 5 - 10, 15) - (P/A, 5, 15)\}$$
$$= \$7,418,000.$$

This problem has been formulated in an oversimplified way. For one thing, tax considerations have been excluded in order to keep the focus on the replacement issue. In a real-world situation, the cash flow will probably be different for each of the alternatives. However, in this problem we have specified the same cash flow for both alternatives, and therefore the present worth of the revenue of $7,418,000 is common to both, and can be ignored. On the other hand the terminal values are different.

The present worth for the single plant C will be the initial cost less the present worth of the terminal value, or

$$P = \$6,000,000 - 3,000,000 \times (P/F, 5, 15)$$
$$= \$4,556,900.$$

For the combined plants A and B, the present worth will be only the cost of the addition, as there is no salvage from plant A:

$$P = \$5,000,000 - 2,000,000 \times (P/A, 5, 15)$$
$$= \$4,038,000.$$

This present worth of A and B is less than that of the single enlarged-capacity plant, C, and so the add-on is the preferred alternative.

The undepreciated book value, $1,767,000, of the existing system is totally irrelevant. The value of the existing system can only be assessed as the difference between the present worth of the enlarged-capacity plant, C ($4,556,900) and the present worth of the add-on alternative ($4,038,000). This difference, $418,900, is the comparative value at the present time for A.

10.2   THE OPPORTUNITY COST OF CHANGE

The decision to accept one alternative project in preference to others implies a commitment to keep that project in place for a period of time corresponding to its economic life. The basis for determining what that economic life should be will be postponed until Section 10.3. Whatever that life is, immediately the system is installed and costs thereby sunk, a question can be raised about a replacement. A new alternative can arise to challenge it. We will name this new alternative the *challenger* and the existing system the *defender*.

This is a convention, originally introduced by George Terborgh (1958) of the Machinery and Allied Products Institute (MAPI).

Terborgh was a pioneer in developing basic principles governing equipment replacement. As a result of his work, the MAPI techniques have become standardized. The approaches developed herein are consistent with the MAPI formulas but are somewhat more general.

Assume the challenger is clearly superior to the defender, but was not available at the time the original decision was made. Therefore, if it had been available at that time, and if its advantages had been known, it would have been chosen in preference to the defender. On the other hand, the fact that there are now sunk costs associated with the defender gives it a distinct advantage. For the challenger to be accepted as a replacement, capital investments must be made, but no new capital cost will be incurred for the defender. The only costs applicable to the defender will be those which might be realized by salvaging it. Therefore the fact that an earlier decision was made to accept a particular option, tends to preclude its replacement. The acceptance of an investment tends to lock in that investment.

This tendency represents an opportunity cost, chargeable against any new challenger. The acceptance of an investment alternative means that the investor to some extent foregoes the option to take advantage of the (as yet unknown) new alternatives when they arise. We will call this *the opportunity cost of change* or the opportunity cost of prospective improvements.

For example, consider the decision you face in buying a new automobile. If you buy the automobile for the current model year, you are not likely to find it desirable to trade it in again for another four or five years. Therefore by buying the current model, you are, in effect, foregoing the option of taking advantage of whatever improvements will occur in the models coming out over the next few years. If you could have those next-year improvements in this year's model you would be willing to pay extra for them right now. Because you do not have that opportunity, you are paying an opportunity cost in buying the present model.

There are two basic ways in which the opportunity cost of future change develops. These are:

1. Steady year-to-year technological improvements.

2. Sudden obsolescence due to new developments.

10.2.1 Technological Improvement

Most technological change takes place at a reasonably steady rate. This depends, to a large degree, on the dynamics of the particular industry. The rate of change is more or less related to the growth rate of the industry. The computer industry, for example, currently is growing very rapidly, and the developments of one year are being virtually obsoleted by those of the next. Because of this, the economic life of new equipment tends to be quite short.

Let us suppose we have established this economic life to be L years. We are considering early replacement with a challenger of life L. If we could have one future year's improvement now, it would be worth its present capital value enhanced by the growth of improvements. We will assume that the improvements are growing at rate a. Thus the capital value of the model that will be available in L years would be

$$I = I_0 e^{aL} \tag{10.12}$$

where I_0 is the capital cost at present. Thus the equivalent capital cost of obsolescence (Cap obs) is

$$\text{Cap obs} = I_0 e^{aL} - I. \tag{10.13}$$

The modified capital cost, I, includes a premium to allow for the opportunity cost of the steady year-to-year improvements.

10.2.2 Sudden Obsolescence

By its very nature, the obsolescence of an existing system as a consequence of a new development or invention is unforeseeable. The value of an existing system will drop instantly when a new development is introduced. The amount of the drop will be equal to the difference between its pre-new-development value and the value it would assume in comparison with the new development. This represents an opportunity cost of expected obsolescence, which we will designate as OC.

We cannot know when such obsolescence will occur, but we can assign a probability q that it will occur within a year. Thus q OC is the annual cost of obsolescence arising from this source. The equivalent capital cost of obsolescence, Cap obs, will be

$$\text{Cap obs} = q \sum_0^L OC(t)e^{-rt} dt. \qquad (10.14)$$

The cost of obsoleting an existing system will decline as that system gets older. This requires making an assumption as to how the terminal value will decline with time. Typically the market value of used equipment in the absence of sudden obsolescence will exhibit an exponential decay.

We can now combine these two sources of opportunity costs of obsolescence. The total capital cost of obsolescence will be

$$\text{Cap obs} = I_0 e^{aL} - I + q \sum_0^L V(t)e^{-rt} dt. \qquad (10.15)$$

This equation can be expressed in discrete form if desired. It will be noted that the integral term of equation 10.14 is the equivalent of a present worth of the opportunity cost function. Thus

$$\text{Cap obs} = I(F/P, a, n) - I + q \sum_{j=1}^n OC(1+i)^{-j}. \qquad (10.16)$$

EXAMPLE: Cost of obsolescence

The probability of a new invention completely obsoleting an existing plant is 0.02 per year. If the invention materializes, the value of the existing facility will drop to its salvage value of $10,000. The cost of a proposed new operating system is $100,000. The pattern of developments in the technology of such machines has shown a 5% improvement each year, and this rate of change is expected to continue.

The life of such machines is 10 years. The OCC is 12%. What is the cost that should be considered for this machine in comparing it as a challenger to an existing operating machine?

SOLUTION

1. *Sudden obsolescence.* If, at any time, the obsolescence should occur, the loss sustained would be the difference between the value

of the asset just prior to the obsoleting event and its value following that event. Clearly, the going-concern value will decline as the machine gets older. This requires that some assumption be made as to how such decay in value develops. Let us make the simplified assumption of a negative exponential at a decay rate of 20% per year. (This is typical of how the market value of used equipment declines in price.) Thus OC will be a function of time:

$$OC(t) = 100,000e^{-0.2t} - 10,000,$$

from which, using equation 10.13, the capital cost of sudden obsolescence would be

$$\text{Cap obs} = 0.02 \int_0^{10} \{100,000e^{-0.2t} - 10,000\} e^{-0.12t} \, dt.$$

Solving this shows the capital cost of obsolescence to be $18,536.

2. *Continuous technological change.* From equation 10.12, the capital cost of obsolescence is

$$\text{Cap obs} = 100,000e^{0.5} - 100,000 = \$64,872.$$

10.3 ECONOMIC LIFE

In the preceding section we left the question of the economic life L unresolved. The end of the life of a project occurs when the incremental cost for continuing it in service becomes greater than the annualized cost of its replacement alternative. The problem is to determine *a priori* when this will be.

It should be observed that there are several components of annualized cost for any system. These are:

1. Capital costs.

2. Annual operating costs.

3. Opportunity costs (i.e., obsolescence, lost revenue, etc.).

The longer the life, the lower will be the annualized capital cost A in Figure 10.3. This cost is a declining function of project life.

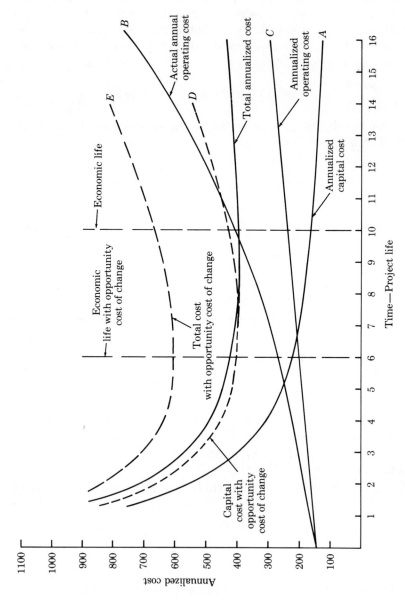

Figure 10.3 Cost functions.

On the other hand, operating costs tend to rise with time. Maintenance and repair costs rise, breakdown frequency increases, and the quality of output will decline. Likewise, opportunity costs rise with time.

One such opportunity cost, discussed above, relates to change. Another, which is even more subtle, is that of declining competitive position in the industry. A firm usually bases its pricing policies on cost rather than on direct market assessment. This can mean that without realizing what is happening, its competitive position in the market is eroding. This affords a competitor an opportunity to enter the market in which the firm in question has been enjoying a favored position. An illustration of this might be the way in which the United States steel industry lost its competitive position in the world market. It should have been modernizing even before it realized that it had a problem.

We will lump all the rising costs into a single rising cost function of time, B, in Figure 10.3.

The rising cost function for annual operations will increase with time. However to make this comparable with capital costs, we must annualize it as a function of the life L of the project. In order to do this we must take the present worth and then transform that into an annualized cost function of L, which is an unknown. We will let A_0 be the initial value of the rising cost function, $A_R(L)$ be the annualized rising cost function, and $A_C(L)$ be the annualized capital cost function. Then

$$A_R(L) = A_0 e^{at} \int_0^L e^{-rt} \, dt \times (A/P, r, L). \qquad (10.17)$$

The annualized capital cost will be

$$A_C(L) = I \times (A/P, r, L). \qquad (10.18)$$

It should be noted that the investment I must incorporate the equivalent capital cost of obsolescence. If we were to consider only the capital cost of continuous technological improvement, then I in equation 10.18 would be the value of I obtained from equation 10.12. The total annualized cost is the sum of equations 10.17 and 10.18:

$$A(L) = A_R(L) + A_C(L). \qquad (10.19)$$

The minimum value for $A(L)$ establishes the economic life of the project. Clearly it will not pay to keep the asset in service beyond the point where annualized costs are expected to rise. This economic or optimum life can be found by differentiating equation 10.19 and equating to zero. However, the computer program of Appendix E does this simply by finding where the minimum point, to the nearest year, occurs.

It will be noted by examination of Figure 10.3 that the sensitive component is the capital cost, which falls off very rapidly at first. The sensitive parameter here is the discount rate. There is a long period of relatively little change in the total-cost curve.

The purpose for establishing the economic life is primarily to find the minimum annualized cost. There is no significance to the economic life in itself. Certainly it must never be used, *a priori*, to determine when an asset should be replaced. It is a means only for determining the cost of a challenger. If the cost of the defender for the next period exceeds the annualized cost of the challenger, the defender should be replaced.

For this reason it is essential to introduce the concept of the opportunity cost of change as discussed above. When we do this, we adjust the capital cost of the challenger. In Section 10.2 this was done by taking L as a given. We can now take it as a variable, changing equation 10.16 to

$$A_C(L) = I(L) \times (A/P, r, L), \tag{10.18}$$

where $I(L)$ is the investment function, allowing for the opportunity cost of change. When we do this, we obtain a modified function for annualized capital costs, curve D in Figure 10.3. The total annualized cost (curve E) is now increased somewhat, and the economic life is reduced. Clearly the effect of introducing the opportunity cost of change penalizes the challenger and inhibits the making of premature replacement.

An interesting conclusion is that a sufficiently rapid rate of technological change may be the only rising-cost effect necessary to obtain a minimum point in the annualized cost curve. This does not include the effect of sudden obsolescence, which tends to be in the opposite direction to that of gradual technological change. If the obsoleting event has the effect of producing a loss that is independent of when that event occurs, the annualized cost of such event is constant and therefore has no effect on determining the economic life. (Recall that the derivative of a constant is zero.) Where the loss declines as time unfolds (the case in which the terminal value decays with time), the effect of such obsolescence is to extend the economic life.

The effect of changing the various parameters and variables may be studied by running the computer program for economic life, given in Appendix E. The curves shown in Figure 10.3 were based on a rate of technological improvement of 10% per year accompanied by a discount rate of 10%. A rate of technological change of 20%, coupled with only a 5% rate of increase in operating cost, forces the economic life to 6 years.

10.4 THE ECONOMIC LIFE OF THE DEFENDER

The economic life of the existing system (the defender) can be determined in exactly the same way as for the challenger. Remember, the economic life of the challenger is defined as the life for which the annualized cost is a minimum. This is also true for the defender. However, in the case of the defender, under normal circumstances, only one cost function exists, namely the increasing cost function. There is no offsetting declining annualized-capital-cost curve.

The declining cost function is due to the capital expenditure, which must be recovered over the life of the asset. This capital expenditure includes the cost of the asset, installed, and the opportunity cost of technological advancements that may occur subsequently. Normally, given that the asset is already in place, there is no capital cost. The investment is largely, and in most cases wholly, a sunk cost. The exception depends on its terminal value, as will be discussed in Section 10.5. The opportunity for technological change is also sunk, in the sense that the opportunity to take advantage of such change by waiting has already been foregone.

Thus the economic life of the defender is, theoretically, zero. Any life beyond the present time will result in a higher annualized cost. This does not indicate replacement. If the annualized cost of the challenger is higher than the annualized cost of the defender, taken over the next single period, it will pay to keep the defender in service.

10.4.1 The Capital Cost of the Defender

The fact that the capital cost of the defender is sunk does not imply that its capital value is zero. It does have value to the extent of any terminal or salvage value realizable from its disposal. This terminal value will change from year to year, normally declining at an exponential rate. Thus the economic life of the defender can be determined, as before, by finding the point of minimum cost but, at the same time, excluding the opportunity cost of change.

If the drop in terminal value for the next time period is less than the increase in operating cost for that period, then the economic life is zero. In other words, the total-cost function will be rising from time zero. Under these circumstances, the capital cost is simply the OCC on the terminal value, plus the difference in terminal value at the beginning and end of that single period.

10.4.2 Economic Lives and a Common Planned Life

In Chapter 5 it was emphasized that alternatives must be compared on the basis of a common planned life. However, the economic lives of defender and challenger are distinctly different. When we compare annualized costs, the difference in time is implicitly assumed to be taken into account by replication of the annual cost of the shorter-lived asset to match the life of the longer-lived asset. This is valid provided that the opportunity cost associated with the time difference is correctly estimated. When we adjust the annualized cost of the challenger to account for the opportunity cost of change, we have satisfied this requirement. Therefore the comparison of annualized costs automatically takes account of the requirement for a common planned life.

10.4.3 The Trade-In Value Error

A common error in replacement-economy analysis is to consider the trade-in value of the defender by taking it as a deduction off the investment cost of the challenger. This is rationalized by the implicit assumption that the terminal value of the defender, i.e., the trade-in value, is a capital cost common to both alternatives and so can be canceled. This is incorrect.

As brought out in Chapter 5, any cash-flow item that is identical in a comparison of two alternatives may be canceled. However, it is essential that they be identical in all respects. While the trade-in value is an equivalent investment in dollar amount, chargeable either to the defender or to the challenger, the period over which it is recovered is different for the defender than for the challenger. If we are making the comparison on the basis of annualized costs, the annual cost of the defender is for a one-year interval, while that for the challenger is for its economic life of many years.

10.5 THE SUNK-COST DILEMMA

It cannot be emphasized too strongly that sunk costs are irrelevant. Nevertheless, accounting practice requires some method for recognizing all *historical* costs. Depreciation allocations are predetermined by extending capital recovery over the expected life of the asset. Premature replacement will result in a need for the accountant to do something about the remaining book value. It is this that commonly leads to the statement, "We cannot replace this asset because it will cost us its unrecovered book value." The converse statement is "Now we can replace an asset because it is fully depreciated." Both statements are patently nonsense.

The obvious and necessary accounting action is to write off the displaced asset as a capital loss. This leads to the interesting situation that, if replacement is not made, stated profits will be unaffected. On the other hand, if replacement is made, there is a reported loss. This can result in misinterpretation of accounting reports.

10.5.1 Tax Consequences of Early Replacement

While sunk costs are irrelevant, the tax consequences in dealing with undepreciated or unamortized book values must be considered. Any dollar cash flows that are influenced by a decision are future values, and tax costs or tax benefits change in the future as a result of a replacement.

Keeping the defender will not change the depreciation schedule, and hence the tax bill will be unchanged. Retirement, on the other hand, will mean that the undepreciated book value will be written off, resulting in a capital loss. This will mean a reduction in taxes and thus influences the choice in favor of the challenger.

10.6 RECAPITULATION

1. After the decision has been made to proceed with a project, changes may become necessary because of:

   a. Problems encountered in any stage of the program.

   b. Growth in demand reaching the designed capacity earlier than expected.

   c. Costs exceeding those of some newly discovered alternative.

   d. Revenues not materializing as projected.

   e. New inventions making the project suddenly obsolete and so dictating abandonment.

2. The initial scale of the project must allow for growth. There is a theoretical optimum extra capacity, which is sensitive to the rate of growth and the discount rate. Fundamentally, the extra capacity that is justified depends on the comparison of the extra investment required with the discounted value of the additional investment that will be needed when the time arrives for expansion. If that extra initial investment is not justified, the added capacity should be as small as practicable.

3. By proceeding with a project in the present, future improvements from advancing technology will be foregone. The opportunity cost of these foregone improvements must be assessed against the challenger. This favors retention of the defender.

4. Replacement can only be justified if one of the component cost functions rises as time passes. Such a rising cost function is part of the normal pattern of operating costs, but it can also include the opportunity cost of technological change, either gradual or sudden.

5. The comparison of challenger with defender is based on annualized costs. The annualized cost of the challenger is based on its economic life; that of the defender is based on the next year's cost. The economic life is that time for which the annualized cost is a minimum.

6. The requirement for comparability of time periods is satisfied by using annualized cost, with due allowance for opportunity costs of technological change.

7. Tax consequences should be considered. Only to the extent that future taxes may be affected by sunk cost does sunk cost become a consideration.

10.7 PROBLEMS

1. Demand is expected to grow at a rate of 10% per year for the foreseeable future. Economies of scale are such that the plant-capacity cost increases at a rate of 80% of a base value C per increment of additional expansion. In other words, if the plant were to be doubled in size from the minimum practical level of added expansion, it would only cost 80% more. How much added capacity should be provided now to accommodate the projected growth in demand? Assume two OCCs, 10% and 20%.

2. What is the capacity life for Problem 1?

3. A new plant was constructed 3 years ago at a cost of $1.5 million. It was expected then to be adequate for the next 20 years and was being depreciated on a sum-of-digits method over 20 years. If it is replaced now, it will be written off, and a capital-gains tax may be applicable at 40% of ordinary income tax rates of 25%. It is assumed that a capital loss can be recovered by offsetting it against other gains. The possibilities are as follows: A new addition can be put in place to supplement the existing facility. This will cost $500,000. Alternatively a completely new facility can be constructed to completely replace the existing facility. It will cost $2 million. The cash flow from these alternatives will be the same. In either case the life will be another 20 years with no

terminal value. If the OCC is 10%, which is the better alternative?

4. A proposed investment in a special-purpose machine is being considered for the replacement of an existing unit. The value of the existing equipment (defender) is carried on the company books at $3000, but if it is replaced, it will be worthless. Its operating cost is $2000 per year. The new equipment will require an investment of $10,000. Its operating costs are expected to be $1000 per year, but are expected to increase at 3% per year. Its estimated life is 10 years with no salvage value at the end of that time. Experience has indicated that this kind of equipment will undergo steady model improvements from year to year, which would enhance its value by 8% per year. On the other hand, the product it is used for manufacturing may be made obsolete by some unexpected event. If this were to occur, the resale value of the equipment would be very small: only $1000, regardless of when the event occurred. The probability of this occurring is estimated to be 0.05. If OCC is 12%, what would you recommend?

5. In Problem 4 the life was given as 10 years. On the basis of the data given, what is the economic life?

6. Check your answer to Problem 5 by means of the computer program ECONOMIC LIFE in Appendix E. Evaluate the sensitivity of the economic life to changes in the parameters.

○
○
○ *A Comprehensive*
○
○ *Example Project*
○

In all the preceding chapters, the examples employed were designed for the purpose of illustrating particular points, pertinent to the topic being discussed. This was best done by keeping the example simple and somewhat unrealistic. In this chapter we will endeavor to integrate most of the material covered in the book by means of one overall comprehensive example.

This example is a synfuels project. The project is constructed to bring out the difficulties associated with long-term and large-scale projects.

The example will not be representative of any actual program in existence or even in a planning stage. All the numbers used will be hypothetical. This is done to avoid any direct criticism of evaluations that may already have been made of existing projects. Many present-day engineering systems have been undertaken, are in place, and are proving to be successful economic ventures, although originally justified by completely erroneous evaluation techniques. It is also quite likely that many others have been rejected and have never seen the light of day because of erroneous evaluations.

The example chosen will be as realistic as possible, but detailed cost elements will be omitted. In practice, a great deal of work must go into the gathering of very specific and detailed information. However, in the end, this is all summarized in a cash-flow projection, comprising revenue and expenditure streams. The only subdivisions of these streams that we will consider are interest expense and income tax. The latter requires consideration of depreciation. In practice it would be desirable to examine many other components of both costs and revenue.

The solution of the project example for a variety of conditions is to be made by means of the computer program PROJECT EVALUATION in Appendix E. For this reason all detailed calculations will be omitted. The reader may satisfy himself that the calculations are correct by following the procedures outlined in previous chapters.

11.1 SYNFUEL FACILITY

The synfuels project example is based on a number of conditions of paramount importance to society today. We have experienced a decade of disturbances in the world economy that have been related to dislocations of petroleum supply. A tenfold increase in oil prices during the 1970s was instrumental in producing inflation but, at the same time, stimulated a search for oil substitutes. Shortages have been followed by apparent glut. It is evident that whatever the current conditions are, there will be further problems confronting the energy industry in the future. It is inconceivable that by the turn of the century we will avoid the necessity of being well along with some transition from an oil-based energy economy to an other-than-oil-based energy economy. Sooner or later the world's oil supplies will run out and we will have to take action. Whatever is done will, of necessity, require a very long lead-time to make the transition. Even with a developed technology, the scale of the program will dictate that considerable time will be required to effect the change.

In light of this economic prospect a major company, the ABC Energy Company, is contemplating investing in a synthetic-liquid-fuel plant. The synfuel is to be manufactured from coal. Preliminary studies and discussions with the Department of Energy indicate that, to be at all economical as a commercial venture, the plant should process 50,000 tons of coal per day. The coal will be of a quality that on average will yield 8000 BTUs per pound. If we assume that the plant will operate at 75% efficiency, the output will be approximately 50 million barrels (bls) per year of fuel, yielding 18,000 BTU/lb.

In 1973, when oil prices were still relatively low, it seemed possible to produce a synfuel for $10/bl. As oil prices rose, the estimates of synfuel costs rose even faster, with the result that the prospective cost of synfuel always seemed to stay ahead of petroleum fuels. It is like a dog chasing its tail. Ultimately, a major effort will be needed to establish a viable synfuels industry. For this reason, in the interest of a national energy policy, various subsidy plans have been considered for financing commercial-scale synfuels projects in order to have plant capacity in place at the time when such fuel can become competitive with petroleum.

We will consider the economic evaluation of such a hypothetical project, but will devote little space to the more esoteric aspects of the problem. Clearly, projections of future markets, prices, supplies, and the like are essential ingredients of the evaluation. These would need detailed and sophisticated analysis. We cannot pretend to cover these in the necessary detail.

11.1.1 The Point of View

The point of view from which such a study is made, should encompass not a single special interest but several. We will assume that the investment decision is primarily the responsibility of the ABC Company. The company acts in the interests of its stockholders, and so theirs is the primary viewpoint. However, the federal government will be providing funding, as either direct or indirect subsidies, and must make its decision to participate in the venture from the point of view of the public.

The scale of such a project is so great that considerable debt financing will be needed. This means that prospective bondholders must be considered, and therefore their viewpoint must be taken into account.

We will cover these three viewpoints eventually, but will start out with the usual approach utilized in project evaluations and will ignore the question of whose interest is really being represented. To do this we will make the arbitrary assumption that the OCC of the company is the only one considered, and its OCC is 15% per year before allowing for inflation.

11.1.2 Capital Expenditure and Cash-Flow Projections

The feasibility study for the project will extend over 2 years at a budgeted level of $300,000 per year. Assuming a go-ahead decision is made, the engineering design, including environmental-impact studies, public hearings, and the obtaining of permits and approvals, will extend over the following 3 years at a level of expenditure of $10 million per year.

Construction could start within five years and be completed in another five. Preliminary planning indicates that this will require $500 million the first year, $650 million the second, $850 million the third, $950 million the fourth, and $1,000 million the fifth.

The eleventh year will be devoted to getting the plant into operation. An additional $100-million expenditure for startup costs will be required during that year. In addition, normal operating costs will amount to $50 million exclusive of the coal supply. Also, for getting started an inventory accumulation of 20,000 tons of coal per day will need to be purchased at a price of $30 per ton (present-day prices), but synfuel production in the first year will only amount to 5% of capacity.

Following the startup year, the plant operating costs are expected to increase to $70 million in the second year and $80 million in the third, which will be the peak year. With experience these costs will decline to $60 million by the eighth year of operation. The plant output will reach 25% of capacity in the second year and add a further 25% each year until 100% of planned capacity is reached.

Additional data on risk, tax obligations and interest on debt financing will be given in subsequent sections.

11.1.3 First Economic Evaluation of the Project

At this stage, we will make a preliminary evaluation, ignoring many important factors that must ultimately be taken into account. We will arbitrarily take a planned life of thirty years of operation and assume no terminal value at that time. Thirty years' operating experience must be added to the ten-year capital-investment phase, making a total of forty years. It is customary for large-scale long-term projects, to take the startup time as the reference zero time. Thirty years of operation is the time commonly taken for the planned life, for the simple reason that it is the usual time over which debt is financed.

The data provided above are organized in Table 11.1. The capital-expenditure phase is shown as negative time from startup. This means that future worths of capital must be computed to transform the capital-expenditure stream into an equivalent future worth rather than a present worth. This is just a matter of preference; our choice follows the accepted practice.

The computer program is organized to take account of the cash-flow stream by separately handling operating cost, revenue, taxes, depreciation, and interest on debt. No breakdown of various components of these items is included. For this reason we will have to calculate such detail outside the program. In the synfuels example, the only two special items are (1) the cost of coal as a purchased material and (2) all other operating expenses.

The revenues of Table 11.1 are based on an assumed price of $40.00 per barrel for the product. The present-worth solution is given in the computer printout in Figure 11.1. In this first trial solution we have not considered the effects of debt, taxes, or inflation.

Investors have come to look upon rates of return on the order of 15% or 20% as quite normal, even while contending that the analysis should be based on constant dollars. For this reason, the first trial solution will be based on a discount rate of 15%. However, because inflation is, in effect, assumed to be zero, the OCC should be taken as an inflation-free rate. The 15% to 20% rates are reflections of inflationary expectations. The real rates of return must be the current nominal rate, less the expected rate of inflation. Historically, real risk-free rates are on the order of 3% to 4%. In 1983, the nominal rate of interest less the current inflation rate indicated a real rate of 7% to 8%. This really implies that expectations of inflation were still considerably higher than was the actual inflation. What then should the OCC be for a project of such scale? The historical rates of return that the ABC Company

Table 11.1 Present-Worth Analysis of Synfuel Plant

YEAR	CAPITAL EXPENDITURE	COST OF COAL	DIRECT OPERATING EXPENSE	OPERATING COST	REVENUE @$40/bl	CASH FLOW
-9	300					-300
-8	300					-300
-7	10,000					-10,000
-6	10,000					-10,000
-5	10,000					-10,000
-4	500,000					-500,000
-3	650,000					-650,000
-2	850,000					-850,000
-1	950,000					-950,000
0	1,000,000					-1,000,000
Total capital						-3,980,600
1	100,000	54,750	50,000	204,750	100,000	-104,750
2		68,437	70,000	138,437	500,000	361,563
3		126,875	80,000	216,875	1,000,000	783,125
4		204,562	76,000	280,562	1,500,000	1,219,438
5		273,750	72,000	345,750	2,000,000	1,654,250
6		273,750	68,000	341,750	2,000,000	1,658,250
7		273,750	64,000	337,750	2,000,000	1,662,250
8		273,750	60,000	333,750	2,000,000	1,666,250
...30		273,750	60,000	333,750	2,000,000	1,666,250

SYNFUELS PROJECT

DATE: 10/10/1983

THE MAGNITUDES ARE IN THOUSANDS OF DOLLARS

THE ECONOMIC EVALUATION IS BASED ON THE NET PRESENT WORTH APPROACH WITH THE CONDITIONS OF THE PROJECT AS FOLLOWS:

1. THE RATE OF RETURN IS 15% PER YEAR. (THIS IS OCC OR IRR.)
2. THERE IS NO DEBT FINANCING.
3. THE INCOME TAX RATE IS 0% AND THE CAPITAL GAINS RATE IS 0%.
4. THE METHOD OF DEPRECIATION IS STRAIGHT LINE
5. THE TERMINAL VALUE OF THE PROJECT IS $0 AND THE FINAL BOOK VALUE IS $0.
6. THE CAPITAL GAIN IS $0.
7. THE RATES OF PRICE ESCALATION FOR CAPITAL COST, OPERATING COST, AND REVENUES ARE 0%, 0% & 0% RESPECTIVELY.
8. OTHER DATA ARE PROVIDED IN THE TABLES BELOW:

TABLE I

CASH FLOW EVALUATION

YEAR	CAPITAL INVESTMENT	REVENUE	OPERATING COSTS	INTEREST	DEPR.	BEFORE-TAX PROFIT	INCOME TAXES **	NET PROFIT	CASH FLOW	DCF
-9	300								-300	-1,055
-8	300								-300	-918
-7	10,000								-10,000	-26,600
-6	10,000								-10,000	-23,131
-5	10,000								-10,000	-20,114
-4	500,000								-500,000	-874,503
-3	650,000								-650,000	-988,569
-2	850,000								-850,000	-1,124,125
-1	950,000								-950,000	-1,092,500
0	1,000,000								-1,000,000	-1,000,000
0	....FUTURE WORTH OF CAPITAL IS -5,151,514 *									
1		100,000	204,750		171,717	-276,467	0	-276,467	-104,750	-91,087
2		500,000	138,437		171,717	189,846	0	189,846	361,563	273,394
3		1,000,000	216,875		171,717	611,408	0	611,408	783,125	514,917
4		1,500,000	280,562		171,717	1,047,721	0	1,047,721	1,219,438	697,218
5		2,000,000	345,750		171,717	1,482,533	0	1,482,533	1,654,250	822,455
6		2,000,000	341,750		171,717	1,486,533	0	1,486,533	1,658,250	716,907
7		2,000,000	337,750		171,717	1,490,533	0	1,490,533	1,662,250	624,901
8		2,000,000	337,750		171,717	1,490,533	0	1,490,533	1,662,250	543,392
9		2,000,000	337,750		171,717	1,490,533	0	1,490,533	1,662,250	472,515
10		2,000,000	337,750		171,717	1,490,533	0	1,490,533	1,662,250	410,883
11		2,000,000	337,750		171,717	1,490,533	0	1,490,533	1,662,250	357,289
12		2,000,000	337,750		171,717	1,490,533	0	1,490,533	1,662,250	310,686
13		2,000,000	337,750		171,717	1,490,533	0	1,490,533	1,662,250	270,162
14		2,000,000	337,750		171,717	1,490,533	0	1,490,533	1,662,250	234,924
15		2,000,000	337,750		171,717	1,490,533	0	1,490,533	1,662,250	204,281
16		2,000,000	337,750		171,717	1,490,533	0	1,490,533	1,662,250	177,636
17		2,000,000	337,750		171,717	1,490,533	0	1,490,533	1,662,250	154,466
18		2,000,000	337,750		171,717	1,490,533	0	1,490,533	1,662,250	134,318
19		2,000,000	337,750		171,717	1,490,533	0	1,490,533	1,662,250	116,799
20		2,000,000	337,750		171,717	1,490,533	0	1,490,533	1,662,250	101,564
21		2,000,000	337,750		171,717	1,490,533	0	1,490,533	1,662,250	88,316

Figure 11.1 Printout of present-worth solution for data in Table 11.1.

22	2,000,000	337,750	171,717	1,490,533	0	1,490,533	1,662,250	76,797
23	2,000,000	337,750	171,717	1,490,533	0	1,490,533	1,662,250	66,780
24	2,000,000	337,750	171,717	1,490,533	0	1,490,533	1,662,250	58,070
25	2,000,000	337,750	171,717	1,490,533	0	1,490,533	1,662,250	50,495
26	2,000,000	337,750	171,717	1,490,533	0	1,490,533	1,662,250	43,909
27	2,000,000	337,750	171,717	1,490,533	0	1,490,533	1,662,250	38,182
28	2,000,000	337,750	171,717	1,490,533	0	1,490,533	1,662,250	33,201
29	2,000,000	337,750	171,717	1,490,533	0	1,490,533	1,662,250	28,871
30	2,000,000	337,750	171,717	1,490,533	0	1,490,533	1,662,250	25,105

```
                    AFTER-TAX CAPITAL GAIN IS $0
                    PRESENT WORTH OF CASH REALIZED ON SALE

                                                        ------------
                                    NET PRESENT WORTH IS    2,405,832
```

* NOTE: THE REFERENCE ZERO TIME IS 9 YEARS FROM START OF CAPITAL INVESTMENT PHASE.
   THE VALUES SHOWN ARE END OF YEAR AMOUNTS IF DISCRETE DISCOUNTING IS USED,
   BUT DISTRIBUTED OVER THE YEAR FOR CONTINUOUS DISCOUNTING.

** NOTE: THE TAX MAY BE NEGATIVE ON THE ASSUMPTION THAT THERE IS OFFSETTING REVENUE FROM OTHER SOURCES.

TABLE II

RETURN ON EQUITY

YEAR	BOOK VALUE	NET PROFIT	RETURN ON INVESTMENT
1	4,979,797	-276,467	-5.55
2	4,808,080	189,846	3.95
3	4,636,363	611,408	13.19
4	4,464,646	1,047,721	23.47
5	4,292,929	1,482,533	34.53
6	4,121,211	1,486,533	36.07
7	3,949,494	1,490,533	37.74
8	3,777,777	1,490,533	39.46
9	3,606,060	1,490,533	41.33
10	3,434,343	1,490,533	43.4
11	3,262,626	1,490,533	45.69
12	3,090,909	1,490,533	48.22
13	2,919,191	1,490,533	51.06
14	2,747,474	1,490,533	54.25
15	2,575,757	1,490,533	57.87
16	2,404,040	1,490,533	62
17	2,232,323	1,490,533	66.77
18	2,060,606	1,490,533	72.33
19	1,888,889	1,490,533	78.91
20	1,717,171	1,490,533	86.8
21	1,545,454	1,490,533	96.45
22	1,373,737	1,490,533	108.5
23	1,202,020	1,490,533	124
24	1,030,303	1,490,533	144.67
25	858,586	1,490,533	173.6
26	686,869	1,490,533	217
27	515,151	1,490,533	289.34
28	343,434	1,490,533	434.01
29	171,717	1,490,533	868.02
30	0	1,490,533	-4.69632506E+10

Figure 11.1   (*Continued*).

has earned in the past provide little guidance here. The project must be considered too different from all previous experience for such criteria to be helpful.

Risk is another issue that will need to be addressed; but, as we have seen, risk is not something that can be taken care of by factoring the discount rate. We must assume that risk is properly accounted for in the estimates of cash flows. Therefore the appropriate OCC might well be taken as a nominal premium over the long-term riskless rate of return to society at large. Let us say this premium is 2% above the long-term real rate of 3% (i.e., 5%).

One solution might be to use a 15% discount rate. The present worth then is $2,415,455,000. This would indicate acceptance. Using a 5% OCC, the present worth is $17,259,625,000. However, both solutions have omitted too many important considerations.

11.1.4 Explanation of the Computer Solution

The program for project evaluation has been designed to handle a wide range of parameters, but there are some it cannot encompass. The program is menu-driven. It asks the operator to choose one of four approaches:

1. Present worth.

2. Internal rate of return.

3. Revenue requirements.

4. External rate of return.

The data inputs include particulars of the debt financing, tax rates, depreciation method, and terminal value of the project. The capital schedule can extend up to 10 years, and the cost and revenue cash flows up to 30 years.

Some explanation of the output of the computer program is in order. An introductory statement and eight items are printed out to summarize the basic parameters of the project. These are standardized to encompass a wide range of options, and some may seem unnecessary, being irrelevant for the project specified. The lead-in statement calls attention to the fact that the units are thousands of dollars if the project is very large. If the units are dollars, no such statement appears. The next line indicates the approach chosen for the solution. The eight specific items cover the details of the problem as follows:

1. The rate of return used as a discount rate is shown. If the solution requires finding the IRR, then this is shown instead of the OCC. Otherwise the OCC appears here.

2. This statement describes the debt financing for the project.

3. The income tax and capital gains tax rates used are shown. If taxes are ignored, the values are simply recorded as zeros.

4. The depreciation method requires no explanation. The options are straight line, declining balance, sum of digits, or a combination of the first two. This combination option utilizes a crossover from declining balance to straight line at the point where the annual allowance from straight line exceeds that of declining balance.

5. The terminal value specified as a data input is shown, together with the final book value of the project at the terminal date.

6. The capital-gains item is only relevant when the project is sold at the terminal date. However, if no sale is contemplated, the capital gain is shown as if a sale had been made at the terminal value. No tax consequence of this gain is included.

7. This item deals with inflation by explicitly considering the separate rates of price increase for capital expenditures, operating costs, and revenues. Whatever rates are specified, they are programmed to remain constant for the life of the project.

8. Table I in the printout is the cash-flow analysis. The last column is the discounted cash flow. The reference zero time is taken to be startup. Thus the DCF column is actually a future-worth column for the capital-outflow phase. This is totaled for the capital at the zero-time point.

At the end of the table, the after-tax capital gain is shown along with the present worth of the cash realized from the sale. This is computed by first calculating the difference between the terminal value and the balance of debt outstanding at the terminal time. If no sale is made, this item in the statement will be blank.

The final figure is the net present value of all cash flows. Obviously, if the operator has elected to find the internal rate of return or the price for the revenue requirements, the net present value will be zero.

The two footnotes are more or less self-explanatory. One of the prompts incorporated within the program asks whether continuous or discrete discounting is desired. If discrete discounting is elected, all payments are end-of-year amounts. If continuous interest is elected, the debt payments are computed as discrete, but all discounting is based on a continuous rate. In this case the estimates should be considered as being distributed over the year rather than occurring at the end of the year.

Taxes are assumed to be negative if there is a reported loss for any year. Usually ways can be found to offset other income with reported losses associated with the project. This amounts to a negative tax. Of course, if such tax-offsetting is not possible, then the tax would have to be reported as zero and the operating loss carried forward. The program does not provide for this refinement.

Table II of the printout shows the reported rate of return based on each year's profits on the book value for that year. This is an accounting figure and has no significance, in itself, as a factor in the overall evaluation. The very large number shown for the last year comes from the fact that theoretically this quantity tends to infinity as book value goes to zero.

11.1.5 Economic Evaluation of the Project with Consideration of Taxes and Debt

Even though it may be in the national interest to subsidize such a synfuels project, such subsidies should be explicitly related to the national purpose. This does not mean that income taxes should not be paid. Our ABC Company should pay income taxes on the same basis as any other firm. We will assume an income-tax rate of 30%. Capital gains, on the other hand, need not be considered, because it would hardly make sense to contemplate the resale of such an enterprise. This does not mean we should ignore the question of terminal value. We will discuss its ramifications later.

The very long capital-investment phase will necessitate financing a sizable part of the investment by means of debt. The initial engineering and exploratory phase will be funded from existing corporate capital but, by the time construction started, funding commitments from financial (banking) establishments will have to have been made. This does not mean that all the required capital will be available at the outset. Bond issues will be floated at prescribed times in order to have the funding on hand to meet contractual obligations as they arise. This means that funds in excess of immediate needs will be temporarily invested in financial instruments. With careful money management, the interest earned on such excess funds will almost balance the debt interest on each funding.

On the other hand, as soon as money is committed to the project, interest expense will start to accumulate. The interest on bonds must be paid long before the project starts to generate a return cash flow. From an accounting standpoint such interest expense can be *capitalized*, that is, it can be carried in the accounts as a capital expenditure and accumulated year by year until the year of startup. Let us assume that such capitalized interest expense is included in the capital-expenditure budgets each year, as shown in Table 11.1.

Normally, the principal on a bond is not repaid serially, but is paid at the maturity date when the entire debt comes due and payable. In the interim, regular interest payments are made as prescribed by the loan contract. The interest negotiated at the time of bond issuance is determined by market conditions at that time. This means that inflationary expectations as they are at the time of bond issuance are factored into the contractual interest rate. Thus the interest expense remains fixed throughout the life of the bond. When market interest rates decline, which will be the case in the absence of inflation, the bond value will decline. However, the company will not be in a position to take advantage of such a price decline of its bonds. Thus the debt interest will be fixed at a high rate even while the OCC is low. Let us assume that money-market conditions are such that debt financing must be made at an interest rate of 10%.

The computer program (Appendix E) is not designed to provide for several debt fundings, but only for that debt which exists at startup. Under most circumstances it would not be considered prudent for a firm to finance by utilizing more than 40% debt and 60% equity. One of the ways in which government can effectively induce private investment decisions is to guarantee the loan against default. This does not affect the government budgeting process. It amounts to an acceptance by society of the risk inherent in the enterprise. It represents a true opportunity cost but not an accounting cost, and so is politically more acceptable. Let us assume that this provision makes it possible to finance with bonds up to 75% of the total capital, not including capitalized interest or $2,985 million.

In the second solution we will use the revenue-requirements approach. The present worth is automatically zero, and revenue is adjusted by price to ensure that this is so. The printout for the solution is shown in Figure 11.2. Figure 11.3 includes considerations for inflation that will be discussed in Section 11.1.6.

11.1.6 Inflationary Effects

The next consideration is that of inflation. We have considered the effects of inflation, in part, as it affects debt financing. The possibility of raising funds from debt issues determines the long-term interest-rate commitment on that debt. This is predicated on present-time perceptions of future inflation rates. However, if inflation remains low for the entire capital-construction phase, bond rates will likely be low at the time of funding the capital investment. We have assumed that these rates will not be materially different from present bond rates.

To be consistent with this view, we would have to make some assumption about future inflation rates. In particular, we would have to consider relative-price effects. There are two major cost components that could be affected by general inflation in different ways. These are the direct plant operating costs and the price of coal.

Direct operating costs derive principally from labor needed to maintain the plant. Such labor would represent a wide diversity of skills, ranging from high-level technical and managerial to unskilled maintenance personnel. As a consequence, it might be reasonable to assume that direct operating costs will keep pace with general levels of inflation.

REPORT ON THE ECONOMIC EVALUATION OF:

SYNFUELS PROJECT

DATE: 10/10/1093

THE MAGNITUDES ARE IN THOUSANDS OF DOLLARS

THE ECONOMIC EVALUATION IS BASED ON THE REVENUE REQUIREMENTS APPROACH WITH THE CONDITIONS OF THE PROJECT AS FOLLOWS:

1. THE RATE OF RETURN IS 10% PER YEAR. (THIS IS OCC OR IRR.)
2. THE DEBT FINANCING AMOUNTS TO $2,985,000 AT 10%, REQUIRING AN ANNUAL PAYMENT OF $298,500 AND THE LIFE OF THE LOAN IS 30 YEARS.
3. THE INCOME TAX RATE IS 30% AND THE CAPITAL GAINS RATE IS 0%.
4. THE METHOD OF DEPRECIATION IS STRAIGHT LINE
5. THE TERMINAL VALUE OF THE PROJECT IS $0 AND THE FINAL BOOK VALUE IS $0.
6. THE CAPITAL GAIN IS $0.
7. THE RATES OF PRICE ESCALATION FOR CAPITAL COST, OPERATING COST, AND REVENUES ARE 5%, 2% & 2% RESPECTIVELY.
8. OTHER DATA ARE PROVIDED IN THE TABLES BELOW:

TABLE I

CASH FLOW EVALUATION

YEAR	CAPITAL INVESTMENT	REVENUE	OPERATING COSTS	INTEREST	DEPR.	BEFORE-TAX PROFIT	INCOME TAXES **	NET PROFIT	CASH FLOW	DCF
-9	300								-300	-707
-8	315								-315	-675
-7	11,025								-11,025	-21,485
-6	11,576								-11,576	-20,508
-5	12,155								-12,155	-19,576
-4	638,141								-638,141	-934,302
-3	871,062								-871,062	-1,159,384
-2	1,196,035								-1,196,035	-1,447,203
-1	1,403,583								-1,403,583	-1,543,941
0	1,551,328								-1,551,328	-1,551,328
0	....FUTURE WORTH OF CAPITAL IS -6,699,109 *									
1		87,100	254,581	298,500	223,304	-689,285	-206,785	-482,499	-259,196	-235,632
2		444,209	175,572	298,500	223,304	-253,166	-75,950	-177,217	46,087	38,089
3		906,186	280,551	298,500	223,304	103,831	31,149	72,682	295,986	222,378
4		1,386,464	370,196	298,500	223,304	494,465	148,340	346,126	569,429	388,928
5		1,885,592	465,334	298,500	223,304	898,454	269,536	628,918	852,221	529,162
6		1,923,303	469,150	298,500	223,304	932,350	279,705	652,645	875,949	494,450
7		1,961,770	472,932	298,500	223,304	967,034	290,110	676,924	900,228	461,959
8		2,001,005	482,390	298,500	223,304	996,811	299,043	697,768	921,071	429,687
9		2,041,025	492,038	298,500	223,304	1,027,183	308,155	719,028	942,332	399,641
10		2,081,846	501,879	298,500	223,304	1,058,163	317,449	740,714	964,018	371,671
11		2,123,482	511,916	298,500	223,304	1,089,762	326,929	762,834	986,137	345,635
12		2,165,952	522,155	298,500	223,304	1,121,994	336,598	785,396	1,008,699	321,403
13		2,209,271	532,598	298,500	223,304	1,154,870	346,461	808,409	1,031,712	298,850
14		2,253,457	543,250	298,500	223,304	1,189,403	356,521	831,882	1,055,186	277,863
15		2,298,526	554,115	298,500	223,304	1,222,607	366,782	855,825	1,079,129	258,335
16		2,344,496	565,197	298,500	223,304	1,257,496	377,249	880,247	1,103,551	240,165
17		2,391,386	576,501	298,500	223,304	1,293,082	387,924	905,157	1,128,461	223,260
18		2,439,214	588,031	298,500	223,304	1,329,379	398,814	930,565	1,153,869	207,533
19		2,487,998	599,792	298,500	223,304	1,366,403	409,921	956,482	1,179,786	192,904
20		2,537,758	611,787	298,500	223,304	1,404,167	421,250	982,917	1,206,221	179,297
21		2,588,513	624,023	298,500	223,304	1,442,686	432,906	1,009,881	1,233,184	166,641

Figure 11.2 Printout of solution for revenue requirements.

22	2,640,283	636,504	298,500	223,304	1,481,976	444,593	1,037,383	1,260,687	154,870
23	2,693,089	649,234	298,500	223,304	1,522,052	456,616	1,065,436	1,288,740	143,924
24	2,746,951	662,218	298,500	223,304	1,562,929	468,879	1,094,050	1,317,354	133,745
25	2,801,890	675,463	298,500	223,304	1,604,624	481,387	1,123,237	1,346,540	124,280
26	2,857,928	688,972	298,500	223,304	1,647,152	494,146	1,153,007	1,376,310	115,480
27	2,915,086	702,751	298,500	223,304	1,690,531	507,159	1,183,372	1,406,676	107,298
28	2,973,388	716,806	298,500	223,304	1,734,778	520,433	1,214,345	1,437,648	99,691
29	3,032,856	731,143	298,500	223,304	1,779,910	533,973	1,245,937	1,469,240	92,620
30	3,093,513	745,765	298,500	223,304	1,825,944	547,793	1,278,161	1,501,464	86,047

```
                        AFTER-TAX CAPITAL GAIN IS $0
                        PRESENT WORTH OF CASH REALIZED ON SALE

                                                    ------------
                                          NET PRESENT WORTH IS        0
THE PRICE OF THE PRODUCT TO GENERATE THE REQUIRED REVENUE IS
  << .701 >> TIMES THE PRICE USED ORIGINALLY
IF THE ORIGINAL INPUT WAS QUANTITY, THEN THIS NUMBER IS THE PRICE.

    * NOTE: THE REFERENCE ZERO TIME IS 9 YEARS FROM START OF CAPITAL INVESTMENT PHASE.
            THE VALUES SHOWN ARE END OF YEAR AMOUNTS IF DISCRETE DISCOUNTING IS USED,
            BUT DISTRIBUTED OVER THE YEAR FOR CONTINUOUS DISCOUNTING.

   ** NOTE: THE TAX MAY BE NEGATIVE ON THE ASSUMPTION THAT THERE IS OFFSETTING REVENUE FROM OTHER SOURCES.
```

TABLE II

RETURN ON EQUITY

YEAR	BOOK VALUE	NET PROFIT	RETURN ON INVESTMENT
1	6,475,805	-482,499	-7.45
2	6,252,501	-177,217	-2.83
3	6,029,198	72,682	1.21
4	5,805,894	346,126	5.96
5	5,582,591	628,918	11.27
6	5,359,287	652,645	12.18
7	5,135,983	676,924	13.18
8	4,912,680	697,768	14.2
9	4,689,376	719,028	15.33
10	4,466,072	740,714	16.59
11	4,242,769	762,834	17.98
12	4,019,465	785,396	19.54
13	3,796,162	808,409	21.3
14	3,572,858	831,882	23.28
15	3,349,554	855,825	25.55
16	3,126,251	880,247	28.16
17	2,902,947	905,157	31.18
18	2,679,643	930,565	34.73
19	2,456,340	956,482	38.94
20	2,233,036	982,917	44.02
21	2,009,733	1,009,881	50.25
22	1,786,429	1,037,383	58.07
23	1,563,125	1,065,436	68.16
24	1,339,822	1,094,050	81.66
25	1,116,518	1,123,237	100.6
26	893,214	1,153,007	129.09
27	669,911	1,183,372	176.65
28	446,607	1,214,345	271.9
29	223,304	1,245,937	557.96
30	0	1,278,161	3.61058369E+10

Figure 11.2 (*Continued*).

319

REPORT ON THE ECONOMIC EVALUATION OF:

SYNFUELS PROJECT

DATE: 10/10/1983

THE MAGNITUDES ARE IN THOUSANDS OF DOLLARS

THE ECONOMIC EVALUATION IS BASED ON THE REVENUE REQUIREMENTS APPROACH WITH THE CONDITIONS OF THE PROJECT AS FOLLOWS:

1. THE RATE OF RETURN IS 10% PER YEAR. (THIS IS OCC OR IRR.)
2. THE DEBT FINANCING AMOUNTS TO $2,985,000 AT 10%, REQUIRING AN ANNUAL PAYMENT OF $298,500 AND
   THE LIFE OF THE LOAN IS 30 YEARS.
3. THE INCOME TAX RATE IS 30% AND THE CAPITAL GAINS RATE IS 0%.
4. THE METHOD OF DEPRECIATION IS STRAIGHT LINE
5. THE TERMINAL VALUE OF THE PROJECT IS $0 AND THE FINAL BOOK VALUE IS $0.
6. THE CAPITAL GAIN IS $0.
7. THE RATES OF PRICE ESCALATION FOR CAPITAL COST, OPERATING COST, AND REVENUES ARE 5%, 3% & 2.25% RESPECTIVELY.
8. OTHER DATA ARE PROVIDED IN THE TABLES BELOW:

TABLE I

CASH FLOW EVALUATION

YEAR	CAPITAL INVESTMENT	REVENUE	OPERATING COSTS	INTEREST	DEPR.	BEFORE-TAX PROFIT	INCOME TAXES **	NET PROFIT	CASH FLOW	DCF
-9	300								-300	-707
-8	315								-315	-675
-7	11,025								-11,025	-21,485
-6	11,576								-11,576	-20,508
-5	12,155								-12,155	-19,576
-4	638,141								-638,141	-934,302
-3	871,062								-871,062	-1,159,384
-2	1,196,035								-1,196,035	-1,447,203
-1	1,403,583								-1,403,583	-1,543,941
0	1,551,328								-1,551,328	-1,551,328
0	....FUTURE WORTH OF CAPITAL IS -6,699,109 *									
1		89,961	283,422	298,500	223,304	-715,265	-214,579	-500,685	-277,382	-252,165
2		459,925	197,378	298,500	223,304	-259,257	-77,777	-181,480	41,824	34,565
3		940,546	318,488	298,500	223,304	100,255	30,076	70,178	293,482	220,497
4		1,442,563	424,375	298,500	223,304	496,384	148,915	347,469	570,773	389,845
5		1,966,694	538,667	298,500	223,304	906,224	271,867	634,357	857,660	532,539
6		2,010,945	548,408	298,500	223,304	940,733	282,220	658,513	881,817	497,763
7		2,056,191	558,249	298,500	223,304	976,138	292,842	683,297	906,601	465,229
8		2,102,456	574,997	298,500	223,304	1,005,655	301,697	703,959	927,262	432,575
9		2,149,761	592,247	298,500	223,304	1,035,711	310,713	724,997	948,301	402,172
10		2,198,131	610,014	298,500	223,304	1,066,313	319,894	746,419	969,723	373,870
11		2,247,588	628,314	298,500	223,304	1,097,470	329,241	768,229	991,533	347,526
12		2,298,159	647,164	298,500	223,304	1,129,192	338,757	790,434	1,013,738	323,008
13		2,349,868	666,579	298,500	223,304	1,161,485	348,446	813,040	1,036,343	300,192
14		2,402,740	686,576	298,500	223,304	1,194,360	358,308	836,052	1,059,356	278,961
15		2,456,801	707,173	298,500	223,304	1,227,824	368,347	859,477	1,082,781	259,209
16		2,512,079	728,389	298,500	223,304	1,261,887	378,566	883,321	1,106,625	240,834
17		2,568,601	750,240	298,500	223,304	1,296,557	388,967	907,590	1,130,894	223,741
18		2,626,395	772,748	298,500	223,304	1,331,844	399,553	932,291	1,155,594	207,844
19		2,685,489	795,930	298,500	223,304	1,367,755	410,327	957,429	1,180,732	193,059
20		2,745,912	819,808	298,500	223,304	1,404,301	421,290	983,010	1,206,314	179,311
21		2,807,695	844,402	298,500	223,304	1,441,489	432,447	1,009,043	1,232,346	166,528

Figure 11.3 Revenue-requirements solution with inflation and showing sensitivity.

320

22	2,870,868	869,734	298,500	223,304	1,479,330	443,799	1,035,531	1,258,835	154,643
23	2,935,463	895,826	298,500	223,304	1,517,833	455,350	1,062,483	1,285,787	143,594
24	3,001,511	922,701	298,500	223,304	1,557,006	467,102	1,089,904	1,313,208	133,324
25	3,069,045	950,382	298,500	223,304	1,596,859	479,058	1,117,801	1,341,105	123,779
26	3,138,098	978,894	298,500	223,304	1,637,401	491,220	1,146,181	1,369,484	114,907
27	3,208,705	1,008,260	298,500	223,304	1,678,642	503,592	1,175,049	1,398,353	106,663
28	3,280,901	1,038,508	298,500	223,304	1,720,590	516,177	1,204,413	1,427,716	99,003
29	3,354,722	1,069,663	298,500	223,304	1,763,255	528,976	1,234,278	1,457,582	91,885
30	3,430,203	1,101,753	298,500	223,304	1,806,646	541,994	1,264,652	1,487,956	85,273

AFTER-TAX CAPITAL GAIN IS $0
PRESENT WORTH OF CASH REALIZED ON SALE

NET PRESENT WORTH IS   0

THE PRICE OF THE PRODUCT TO GENERATE THE REQUIRED REVENUE IS

<< $.704 >>

* NOTE: THE REFERENCE ZERO TIME IS 9 YEARS FROM START OF CAPITAL INVESTMENT PHASE.
        THE VALUES SHOWN ARE END OF YEAR AMOUNTS IF DISCRETE DISCOUNTING IS USED,
        BUT DISTRIBUTED OVER THE YEAR FOR CONTINUOUS DISCOUNTING.

** NOTE: THE TAX MAY BE NEGATIVE ON THE ASSUMPTION THAT THERE IS OFFSETTING REVENUE FROM OTHER SOURCES.

TABLE II

RETURN ON EQUITY

YEAR	BOOK VALUE	NET PROFIT	RETURN ON INVESTMENT
1	6,475,805	-500,685	-7.73
2	6,252,501	-181,480	-2.9
3	6,029,198	70,178	1.16
4	5,805,894	347,469	5.98
5	5,582,591	634,357	11.36
6	5,359,287	658,513	12.29
7	5,135,983	683,297	13.3
8	4,912,680	703,959	14.33
9	4,689,376	724,997	15.46
10	4,466,072	746,419	16.71
11	4,242,769	768,229	18.11
12	4,019,465	790,434	19.67
13	3,796,162	813,040	21.42
14	3,572,858	836,052	23.4
15	3,349,554	859,477	25.66
16	3,126,251	883,321	28.25
17	2,902,947	907,590	31.26
18	2,679,643	932,291	34.79
19	2,456,340	957,429	38.98
20	2,233,036	983,010	44.02
21	2,009,733	1,009,043	50.21
22	1,786,429	1,035,531	57.97
23	1,563,125	1,062,483	67.97
24	1,339,822	1,089,904	81.35
25	1,116,518	1,117,801	100.11
26	893,214	1,146,181	128.32
27	669,911	1,175,049	175.4
28	446,607	1,204,413	269.68
29	223,304	1,234,278	552.74
30	0	1,264,652	3.57242436E+10

Figure 11.3 (*Continued*).

```
                        TABLE IIIA
                        SENSITIVITY

THE TABLE SHOWS THE VARIATION DUE TO A CHANGE IN OCC IN INCREMENTS OF 20%+/-   FROM  THE BASIC VALUE OF 10%.

   OCC     PRESENT WORTH
----------- --------------
    4       8,569,942
    6       4,770,863
    8       2,033,200
   10              0  BASIC VALUE
   12      -1,557,136
   14      -2,786,991
   16      -3,788,244
   18      -4,627,525
```

```
                        TABLE IIIB

                        SENSITIVITY

     TABLE SHOWS INFLATION EFFECT ON PW.
        INFLATION RATES (%)
     CAPITAL  COST  PRICE  PRESENT WORTH
     -------  ----  -----  ------- -----
        5      3      0     -4,531,392
        5      3      2       -626,181
        5      3      4      5,573,682
        5      3      6     15,549,645
        5      3      8     31,810,448
        5      3     10     58,633,535
        5      3     12    103,348,190
        5      3     14    178,553,346
```

```
                        TABLE IIIC

                        SENSITIVITY

THE TABLE SHOWS THE VARIATION IN        DEBT INTEREST IN INCREMENTS OF 20%+/-   FROM  THE BASIC VALUE OF 10%.

INTEREST RATE  PRESENT WORTH
-------------  --------------
    4          1,181,852
    6            787,902
    8            393,951
   10                  0  BASIC VALUE
   12           -393,951
   14           -787,902
   16         -1,181,852
   18         -1,575,803
```

Figure 11.3 (*Continued*).

The cost of coal will present a different story. If our project turns out to be successful, it will be largely due to the fact that coal as a major substitute for oil is proving to be feasible as a primary energy source. Thus an enormous expansion of the coal-producing industry would be in the offing. Our project will be competing intensely for this resource, and the competition will tend to drive prices up. On the other hand, several new technologies will come into existence which, together with economies of scale, will tend to drive prices down. The expansion of the coal industry will be accompanied by widespread use of open-pit mining in the plains states. Coal transportation will expand, even though plants will tend to be located close to sources. The economical way to solve the transportation problem may turn out to be by means of slurry pipelines. Let us assume that exhaustive studies have been made, and the result is that the cost of plant operation will escalate at a rate 1% per year less than the general inflation rate.

The construction costs for such plants will be not quite so favorable. A major trend to the use of coal will certainly lead to serious strains on the capability of the construction industry to build new plant capacity rapidly enough to meet needs. Thus construction costs are expected to escalate 2% faster than general inflation.

Finally, the price of the product output will be governed to a large degree by world market prices of petroleum. As oil supplies diminish, prices will tend to rise. On the other hand, the reduction of demand due to the substitution of coal and nuclear power may be sufficiently offsetting to permit a gradual lowering of the relative price of energy.

This view can be reached by considering the role of energy as a basic component in our standard of living. All production of goods depends, in the end, on three fundamental inputs—material resources, energy resources, and labor. If we assume that standards of living on a world-wide scale will rise in the future as they have in the past (i.e., greater production), and if we further assume that the ratio of materials to energy is technologically constant, it follows that the labor input must decline. A declining relative labor content must mean a higher relative price for labor, or conversely a lower relative price for energy. On the basis of this reasoning and the exhaustive study, alluded to above, we will assume that the price of the plant output will escalate at a rate of $\frac{3}{4}$% per year less than the general inflation rate.

Finally, we must determine the OCC. If the real OCC has the value we assumed in Section 11.1.2 above, then we logically could add the long-term trend of inflation to it. The inflation rates of the 1970s might well be considered atypical of the long-term trend. A value of 3% would be more representative of the 40-year average. Thus the OCC would be the previous 5% plus 3%, that is, 8%. But how can we rationalize an OCC less than the bond rate? Clearly, even with a riskless OCC, which would make the risk in bonds and stocks equivalent, the stockholder would not be expected to accept a lower return than the bondholder. The same inflationary expectations would influence both classes of investor alike. Thus the reasonable riskless OCC would be 10%. This is not to contend that the stockholder should not receive a higher return than the bondholder. His return should clearly be higher to compensate him for the higher risk he assumes. However, this higher return will be realized from the greater cash flow expected than that which was used in the evaluation. Recall that there is no satisfactory way to incorporate risk in the rate of return. It is preferable to factor the cash flow for risk. Let us assume that the cash-flow estimates have already been adjusted appropriately for risk.

If we now use the revenue-requirements approach and the above rates in conjunction with a long-term inflationary trend of 3%, we obtain the solution tabulated in Figure 11.3. The price for the revenue-requirements solution in the computer program is obtained by multiplying the original price assumed, $40.00 per barrel, by the answer given by the program. This is so because the revenue input was not expressed in barrels of fuel, but rather in dollars of $40.00 oil. The value from the solution is shown as $0.704, which translates into a price of $0.704 \times 40 = \$28.16$ per barrel. Furthermore, this price is that obtaining at the time of project startup. This is 10 years from now and will be expected to rise steadily from that time at the rate of 2.25% per year.

This still leaves the question as to what is a valid comparative price in present-day dollars. Should we move back to the present date at this same inflation rate or at some other adjusted rate? If we take the price-rise rate of 2.25%, the price needed to justify the project will be $\$28.16 \times (P/F, 2.25, 10) = \$22.54/\text{bl}$. This value looks quite attractive. Compare it with the price of $28.04 obtained using an evaluation based on constant dollars.

11.2 THE PROBLEM OF REPORTED EARNINGS

The foregoing evaluation indicates that the project would be worthwhile over the long run provided the price at which sales were to commence is at least $26.08—or, adjusted for inflation during the ten-year investment phase, in terms of present day values, $20.88/bl. These prices are below the current market prices for competitive fuels. Therefore why might a decision to accept the project be rejected? The answer is clear from examination of reported annual rates of return (Table II of Figure 11.1). The individual investor is not willing to wait for fifteen years for the return to reach a value of 11.27%, just surpassing the average value over the life of the project. This means that he does not perceive his time–utility function to be represented by the usual negative exponential, which we have used. The only way he can be persuaded to invest his money on such a long-range venture is to provide some mechanism whereby he can realize a suitable return for each year, starting almost from the inception of the project. Since this cannot under any circumstances occur from the sale of fuel, there must be a societal decision to transfer the long-run expected return to him in the early years. In other words, there must be subsidies.

An investment that is small, relative to the size of the firm making it, may be justified by the firm even if the cash flow is negative in the early years. The already profitable existing investments will mask the negative returns of early years of any one seemingly unprofitable venture. No firm, however, can justify a large investment that has the effect of causing stated earnings to be negative. The example project could be justified by a very large firm if its stated earnings could be positive in the first or second year after start-up. We might achieve such a situation if we were to utilize a sufficiently high discount rate. If, for example, we specified a minimum acceptable rate of return of 15% over the inflation rate (i.e., 18%), we would then obtain a price for revenue requirements of $1.239 \times 40 = 49.56, without adjustment for inflation during the investment phase.

11.3 SENSITIVITY ANALYSIS

We have demonstrated the evaluation of this example problem, using a variation of parameters. In the process, we have indirectly demonstrated the sensitivity of the decision to a variation in parameters. Because of the highly subjective nature of selection of parameters, it is desirable to show the systematic variation over a range of parameter changes for each parameter in turn. Table III of Figure 11.3 shows these sensitivities. They are plotted in Figure 11.4 to show the degree of sensitivity of present worth to changes in the OCC, the debt interest rate, and inflation. In all three cases the present worth was based first on the revenue requirements for the baseline value of the parameter. Thus the baseline present worth is always zero.

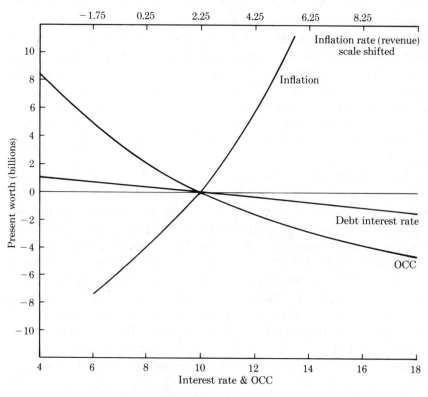

Figure 11.4 Sensitivity.

It will be observed that the desirability of the project declines with increasing interest and opportunity cost of capital rates, but rises with inflation.

11.4 THE DILEMMA OF THE PLANNING PERIOD

The concept of a planning horizon, discussed briefly in Chapter 1, presents a dilemma for such a long-term program as in this example. Clearly, we cannot see what the future holds in store beyond the next 10 years. This time span just covers the capital investment phase, with no consideration for any return flow. We are forced into using the concept of an aspiration. We cannot help depending on self-fulfilling prediction. While a single firm may gamble on an ultimately successful outcome, the essential nature of the aspiration for eventually developing a viable synfuels industry depends on society. It must be a societal aspiration.

If we take the cash-return-flow phase to be a conditional projection based on an aspiration of eventual success of the industry, we still have the question: how far into the future should we go? Traditionally the life of the debt has been taken as this planning period. However, there is no need to do this. We might just as reasonably take the time for the cash flow to stabilize.

Whatever the time we choose, we should give some consideration to the question of terminal value. The use of interest-only repayment schedules would imply that the terminal value is at least as large as the debt. At the same time, if the project is successful, it represents merely the precondition for expansion investments. In general the investment decision is not very sensitive to the terminal value. One important consideration in considering an estimate of the terminal value is that of inflation.

To show the effect of the terminal value on the conclusion, two computer solutions have been obtained with a foreshortened planning period. Both are based on exactly half the operating life of the previous solutions: 15 years in place of 30 years. One solution has the same terminal value as before (i.e., the magnitude of the debt), and the other has twice this value. One of these solutions is shown in Figure 11.5; the other resulted in an index value of 0.823 in place of 0.884.

REPORT ON THE ECONOMIC EVALUATION OF:

SYNFUELS PROJECT

DATE: 10/10/1983

THE MAGNITUDES ARE IN THOUSANDS OF DOLLARS

THE ECONOMIC EVALUATION IS BASED ON THE REVENUE REQUIREMENTS APPROACH WITH THE CONDITIONS OF THE PROJECT AS FOLLOWS:

1. THE RATE OF RETURN IS 10% PER YEAR. (THIS IS QCC OR IRR.)
2. THE DEBT FINANCING AMOUNTS TO $2,985,000 AT 10%, REQUIRING AN ANNUAL PAYMENT OF $298,500 AND THE LIFE OF THE LOAN IS 15 YEARS.
3. THE INCOME TAX RATE IS 30% AND THE CAPITAL GAINS RATE IS 0%.
4. THE METHOD OF DEPRECIATION IS STRAIGHT LINE
5. THE TERMINAL VALUE OF THE PROJECT IS $2,985,000 AND THE FINAL BOOK VALUE IS $3,349,554.
6. THE CAPITAL GAIN IS $-364,554.
7. THE RATES OF PRICE ESCALATION FOR CAPITAL COST, OPERATING COST, AND REVENUES ARE 5%, 3% & 2.25% RESPECTIVELY.
8. OTHER DATA ARE PROVIDED IN THE TABLES BELOW:

TABLE I

CASH FLOW EVALUATION

YEAR	CAPITAL INVESTMENT	REVENUE	OPERATING COSTS	INTEREST	DEPR.	BEFORE-TAX PROFIT	INCOME TAXES **	NET PROFIT	CASH FLOW	DCF
-9	300								-300	-707
-8	315								-315	-675
-7	11,025								-11,025	-21,485
-6	11,576								-11,576	-20,508
-5	12,155								-12,155	-19,576
-4	638,141								-638,141	-934,302
-3	871,062								-871,062	-1,159,384
-2	1,196,035								-1,196,035	-1,447,203
-1	1,403,583								-1,403,583	-1,543,941
0	1,551,328								-1,551,328	-1,551,328
0								...FUTURE WORTH OF CAPITAL IS -6,699,109 *		
1		112,902	283,422	298,500	223,304	-692,324	-207,697	-484,627	-261,323	-237,566
2		577,211	197,378	298,500	223,304	-141,971	-42,591	-99,380	123,924	102,416
3		1,180,396	319,488	298,500	223,304	340,104	102,031	238,073	461,376	346,639
4		1,810,432	424,375	298,500	223,304	864,253	259,276	604,977	828,281	565,727
5		2,468,222	538,667	298,500	223,304	1,407,751	422,325	985,426	1,203,729	750,526
6		2,523,757	548,408	298,500	223,304	1,453,545	436,063	1,017,481	1,240,785	700,391
7		2,580,541	558,249	298,500	223,304	1,500,488	450,147	1,050,342	1,273,645	653,582
8		2,638,603	574,997	298,500	223,304	1,541,803	462,541	1,379,262	1,302,566	607,657
9		2,697,972	592,247	298,500	223,304	1,583,922	475,177	1,108,745	1,332,049	564,919
10		2,758,676	610,014	298,500	223,304	1,626,859	488,058	1,138,801	1,362,105	525,150
11		2,820,747	628,314	298,500	223,304	1,670,629	501,189	1,169,440	1,392,744	488,148
12		2,884,213	647,164	298,500	223,304	1,715,246	514,574	1,200,672	1,423,976	453,723
13		2,949,108	666,579	298,500	223,304	1,760,726	528,218	1,232,508	1,455,812	421,697
14		3,015,463	686,576	298,500	223,304	1,807,083	542,125	1,264,958	1,488,262	391,906
15		3,083,311	707,173	298,500	223,304	1,854,334	556,300	1,298,034	1,521,337	364,196

AFTER-TAX CAPITAL GAIN IS $-364,554
PRESENT WORTH OF CASH REALIZED ON SALE

THE PRICE OF THE PRODUCT TO GENERATE THE REQUIRED REVENUE IS   NET PRESENT WORTH IS   0

Figure 11.5 Solutions with shortened planning period.

328

* NOTE: THE REFERENCE ZERO TIME IS 9 YEARS FROM START OF CAPITAL INVESTMENT PHASE.
THE VALUES SHOWN ARE END OF YEAR AMOUNTS IF DISCRETE DISCOUNTING IS USED,
BUT DISTRIBUTED OVER THE YEAR FOR CONTINUOUS DISCOUNTING.

** NOTE: THE TAX MAY BE NEGATIVE ON THE ASSUMPTION THAT THERE IS OFFSETTING REVENUE FROM OTHER SOURCES.

TABLE II

YEAR	BOOK VALUE	NET PROFIT	RETURN ON EQUITY RETURN ON INVESTMENT
1	6,475,805	-484,627	-7.48
2	6,252,501	-99,380	-1.59
3	6,029,198	238,073	3.95
4	5,805,894	604,977	10.42
5	5,582,591	985,426	17.65
6	5,359,287	1,017,481	18.99
7	5,135,983	1,050,342	20.45
8	4,912,680	1,079,262	21.97
9	4,689,376	1,108,745	23.64
10	4,466,072	1,138,801	25.5
11	4,242,769	1,169,440	27.56
12	4,019,465	1,200,672	29.87
13	3,796,162	1,232,508	32.47
14	3,572,858	1,264,958	35.4
15	3,349,554	1,298,034	38.75

Figure 11.5 (*Continued*).

It will be seen that by cutting the time in half and leaving everything else the same, the price for revenue requirements has not been affected as much as one might expect. The price is adjusted from an index value of 0.704 to 0.884, an increase of 25.6%. This is without making any adjustment for estimating a more realistic terminal value in 15 years. When we increase the terminal value by a factor of four, the present-worth increase amounts to $2,144 million. The computer program does not show the effect on the price but this present worth is in the vicinity of that for a change in the OCC from 10% to 8%.

It is suggested that the reader study the various solutions in detail to develop some feel for the effects of changing parameters.

11.5 THE EVALUATION FROM THE PUBLIC VIEWPOINT

Even though some of the foregoing solutions might appear to make the overall return satisfactory, the short-term objectives of individual investors would almost certainly foreclose any possibility of making a go-ahead decision. Therefore, if it is attractive from an overall societal viewpoint, then government must provide subsidies to encourage the private sector to make the best decision from an overall societal perspective. These subsidies can take many forms, from investment tax credits to direct grants. We will not discuss the ramifications of such possibilities here, but rather will examine some of the basic principles that should be considered.

The effect of subsidies is to reduce the cash-flow inputs of private investors during the investment phase and amplify the return cash flows to them during the early return phase. This might not mean any higher return to these investors in the long run, but it does have the effect of inducing a sharing of the venture between private and public interests. This can cause sufficient shifting of returns to induce the private decision to invest.

The government, in providing a subsidy, is, in effect, creating a supplementary cash-flow stream. The present worth of this stream must also show a positive value for this to be a justifiable societal investment. The difficulty here however is that the return cash-flow component accruing to society is far less definitive than that component allocated to the private partner in the enterprise. In fact, the very indefiniteness of public benefits associated with public investment has led to their being described in noncash terms. Their values must, of necessity, remain imputed values rather than market values. In part, this tends to obscure, though it does not alter, the basic principle of discounting cash flows.

A further characterization of societal benefits is that the risk tends to be transferred from the private to the public share in the undertaking. This is to be expected. The larger the participation in the risk associated with an enterprise, the more diluted the risk effect becomes. This is just the basic principle of insurance. Society as a whole may be quite willing to accept the risk of a synfuels program, but it could be a totally unacceptable level of risk for a company to accept.

The main effect of such sharing is to shift the cash-flow effects to an earlier return time for the private component and to a later return time for the public. This in turn, means that the level of aspiration is more a public aspiration than it is a private one.

While this discussion has focused on the differentiation between public- and private-sector viewpoints, it is essentially the same as what we have come to accept as a normal differentiation of investment interests between bondholder and stockholder. The bondholder invests his money in the enterprise and demands an interest return almost immediately, long before the project financed by those bonds begins to produce a return flow. Furthermore, the significant distinction between a bond and a share of stock is one of risk category. This is far more important from an investment viewpoint than the legal distinction of lender and owner. By deciding to finance with bonds, the stockholder is shifting income to an earlier return time for the bondholder and thereby accepting a later risky return for himself.

In the case of a very large-scale long-term program as in our example, a third subdivision is needed to take care of the component that the stockholder finds too remote and too risky for his liking. This third subdivision can only be society at large, or in other words the government.

11.6 PROBLEMS

1. Extend the synfuels-project example to show the effects of a number of discount rates, debt interest rates, and inflation rates (of your choosing) on the result.

2. Show how different income-tax and depreciation schedules can influence the decision.

3. Construct three hypothetical cash flows that together add up to the total cash flow for the project. These three will be the contributions of the three participants: private stock investors, bond investors, and the government. Structure these so that each will arrive independently at his own positive decision and thereby jointly determine a go-ahead decision for the project. In other words, if any one party could not see that the venture promised to be profitable to it, its choice would be to reject participation. However, if one party saw promise of more than a sufficient return for its participation, it might be willing to surrender some of its promised benefits in order to induce a positive decision from the others. The government, for example, could offer a just-sufficient subsidy to induce the desired mix of debt and equity participation.

Annuity

A uniform (constant) cash flow expressed in dollars per unit time (usually per year).

Balance sheet

The summary equation of state of the enterprise.

A summary statement balancing the assets on one side and the liabilities (equity) on the other.

Call

An option to buy a security at a stipulated price up to a specified date.

Capital

Storage of value within the production system or the consumption system.

The tools of production.

A potential function: a function having the potential for generating a future flow of value.

Capital goods

Intermediate products used within the production process.

Capital recovery factor

The factor that, multiplied by the principal or investment, gives the amount of a constant payment of interest and principal needed to recover the investment.

The factor $(A/P, i, n)$ that determines an annuity, given a principal sum.

Capitalization

The financial structure of the firm.

Capitalize

Accounting: To list an asset in a capital account by original cost.

Financial: To structure the debt and equity of the enterprise (the issuance of stocks and bonds).

Capitalized value (capitalized cost)

An expenditure for which a decision is made to enter it into a capital account and so allocate its cost over a number of years in the future.

The present worth of an infinite cash flow.

Cash flow

An expenditure or revenue stream (in dollars per unit time). Net cash flow is the difference between the revenue and expenditure streams.

Challenger

An asset considered for replacement of an existing asset (the defender).

Constant dollar

A monetary unit consisting of a dollar adjusted for inflation.

Credit money (debt money)

The principal money device in the modern world for facilitating exchange—contrasted with commodity money, which can serve only a limited monetary purpose.

Debenture

A bond not secured by real assets.

Defender

An asset that is being considered for replacement.

Depreciation

In a physical sense, the wearing out of an asset. In an accounting sense, the time-allocation expense of a past expenditure against future income.

Depreciation allowance

An allocation of depreciation expense to a specific time period.

Depreciation reserve (reserve for depreciation)

The sum of all previous depreciation allowances.

Discount function

A function that establishes the equivalence of the value or utility between a future and a present amount—usually taken to be the negative exponential e^{-rt}, or in discrete form $1/(1 + i)^n$.

Discount rate

The parameter, r or i, used in the discount function.

Economic unit

An individual, household, firm, or agency that acts as an individual in a value exchange.

Effective interest rate

The interest rate per year when stated for some period other than a year.

Equity

Ownership of assets, net of any debt obligation secured by those assets.

Expense

Cost represented either by an expenditure or by an allocation such as a depreciation allowance.

External rate of return

A rate of return determined by assuming reinvestment of the cash flow at the OCC.

Externalities

Costs or benefits imposed on others as a consequence of one's economic actions to increase one's own gain.

Finance

The management of money, in particular the raising of funds through issuance of stocks and bonds, for implementing the investment decision.

Financial investment

The allocation of savings for the purchase of financial instruments (paper), such as stocks or bonds.

Forecast

An estimate of the future based on extrapolation of past data.

Free goods

Goods that are not scarce and so can command no power in exchange.

Gross national product

A measure of overall economic activity based on counting, in dollar terms, the total annual product output of society.

Horizon time

The time in the future beyond which outcomes are not foreseeable (like its physical analogy, does not limit planning).

Imputed price

A calculated price not based on actual exchange of goods but presumed to represent what that price would be if an exchange could occur.

Infrastructure

The underlying societal investment necessary for establishing the conditions for private profitable enterprise (social overhead capital).

Interest

Business: The money paid for the use of borrowed funds.
Economics: The marginal return on all capital whether borrowed or owned.

Internal rate of return

The discount rate at which the present worth of a projected cash flow, with no consideration for reinvestment, equates to zero.

Investment

The allocation of resources in the present in anticipation of a greater subsequent return.

Levelized cash flow

The transformation of a cash flow into an annuity.

Leverage

The amplification of profit due to fixing some costs such as bond interest.

Macroeconomics

The subdivision of economics dealing with aggregated effects of the economic interactions between economic units.

Margin

The proportion of debt used for the purchase of an asset (usually stock).

Microeconomics

The subdivision of economics dealing with relationships between economic units, particularly with respect to the exchange of goods.

Money

An instrument for facilitating the exchange of goods and services. It serves the additional function of preserving value over time.

Money illusion

The macroeconomic illusion that money has value in excess of that required to clear the market of all goods and services.

Moneyness

The degree of liquidity of various debt instruments, determining how well such instruments serve as money.

Net worth

The book value of an enterprise—total assets less total debt. On the other side of the accounting equation it is the book value of equity.

Nominal interest rate

A "named" interest rate representing an approximate measure of the true interest rate.

Numeraire

A commodity or good chosen as a reference value for comparing the prices of all other goods and services.

Opportunity cost

The cost of not taking advantage of an available opportunity.

Opportunity cost of capital

The rate of return on some external but unspecified opportunity for investing capital.

Planned life

The period used for the planning of future cash flows in connection with a project evaluation.

Portfolio

A set of various investments.

Prediction

The estimate of future events based on forecasts as well as on all other knowledge, information, or judgment.

Present worth

The discounted value of a future amount or of a projected cash flow.

Price

A unit measure of value, in dollars per unit quantity of goods.

Private goods

Goods that satisfy individual needs exclusively, as contrasted with collective goods.

Profit

Business: The excess of revenues over costs.

Economics: Surplus or excess return realized from a business that is not operating at the margin. It is the return on capital in excess of economic interest.

Public goods (collective goods, social goods)

Goods that are not exclusively for the use of one individual but are enjoyed in common (e.g., a park).

Put

An option to sell a security at a specified price up to a specified date.

Real investment

Physical capital, such as buildings, plant and equipment, as contrasted with financial investment.

Short sale

A sale of a security that is not owned. (It requires that the security be borrowed in order to deliver it.)

Sinking fund

A real or hypothetical fund into which payments are made to accumulate at a specified interest rate.

Sinking-fund factor

The factor $(A/F, i, n)$ that, multiplied by the principal or investment, gives the amount of the payment required to accumulate the investment at the specified interest rate.

Stock

A share in the ownership of a corporation.

Sunk cost

A past expenditure.

Surplus (earned)

Accumulated past profits reinvested in the enterprise.

Transfer payments

Payments to individuals, having the effect of transferring wealth without an increase in GNP.

Utility

A personalized measure of worth.

Value

The worth of a good or service in exchange.

Warrant

An option to convert a security.

Working capital

The capital required for the day-to-day operations of a firm, generally identified as the difference between current assets and current liabilities.

○

○

○ *List of Symbols*

○

A	The periodic end-of-year payment into an annuity.
F	The future sum of a cash flow.
H	The horizon time of future planning period.
I	The amount of an investment.
P	The present worth of a cash flow.
Q	Quantity of output.
S	Price of product in revenue-requirements approach; future amount.
T	The finite time limit on a cash flow.
V	Variance.
a	A rate parameter; coefficient in regression function.
b	A rate parameter; coefficient in regression function.
g	The rate of growth of cash flow.
i	Discrete interest or discount rate.
j	Monthly rate of interest; term index in a function.
k	Term index in a function.
n	The number of time periods for discrete discounting.
q	A probability number.
r	The continuous interest or discount rate.

t	Time.
x	A variable for portfolio allocation; shifted time.
Λ	The Lagrange multiplier.
α	The alpha term in portfolio theory; a discount rate.
β	The beta term in portfolio theory.
γ	The gamma term in portfolio theory.

Discrete Compounding

Discrete compounding came into use as a natural outgrowth of the formulation of debt contracts. Interest was calculated at the end of the specified period at the appropriate rate. If that interest was not paid then, it in turn accumulated interest at the appropriate rate. Thus an initial sum A' would become

$$F_1 = A'(1 + i) \qquad \text{in one period.}$$

At the end of a second period, it would become

$$F_2 = F_1(1 + i) = A'(1 + i)^2,$$

and so on:

$$F_3 = A'(1 + i)^3,$$
$$F_4 = A'(1 + i)^4,$$
$$\vdots$$
$$F_n = A'(1 + i)^n.$$

The sum accordingly is

$$F = A'\left\{(1 + i) + (1 + i)^2 + (1 + i)^3 + \cdots + (1 + i)^n\right\}. \qquad \text{(C1)}$$

Multiplying through by $(1 + i)$ results in

$$(1 + i)F = A'\{(1 + i)^2 + (1 + i)^3 + \cdots + (1 + i)^{(n+1)}\}. \quad \text{(C2)}$$

Subtracting equation C1 from C2,

$$iF = A'\{(1 + i)^{n+1} - (1 + i)\}, \quad \text{(C3)}$$

from which

$$F = A'\frac{(1 + i)\{(1 + i)^n - 1\}}{i}. \quad \text{(C4)}$$

This represents a formula for a constant payment A', made at the beginning of each period (typically one year) into a fund F.

However, if we wanted the payment to be made at the end of the period instead of the beginning, then each payment would grow for a year, so that the end-of-period payment would become

$$A = A'(1 + i). \quad \text{(C5)}$$

Substituting A into equation C4 results in

$$F = A\frac{(1 + i)^n - 1}{i}. \quad \text{(C6)}$$

Rearranging,

$$A = F\frac{i}{(1 + i)^n - 1}. \quad \text{(C7)}$$

But a future amount in n periods is equivalent to

$$F = P(1 + i)^n. \quad \text{(C8)}$$

Thus by substituting into equation C7,

$$A = \frac{P(1 + i)^n i}{(1 + i)^n - 1}. \quad \text{(C9)}$$

These equations will be observed to be the exact equivalent of those for continuous compounding, where $1 + i = e^r$.

APPENDIX D

Table of Factors Using Discrete Interest Rates

n	INTEREST RATE 1%			INTEREST RATE 2%			INTEREST RATE 3%		
	(P/F,i,n)	(A/P,i,n)	(A/F,i,n)	(P/F,i,n)	(A/P,i,n)	(A/F,i,n)	(P/F,i,n)	(A/P,i,n)	(A/F,i,n)
1	0.9901	1.01	1	0.9804	1.02	1	0.9709	1.03	1
2	0.9803	0.5075	0.4975	0.9612	0.515	0.495	0.9426	0.5226	0.4926
3	0.9706	0.34	0.33	0.9423	0.3468	0.3268	0.9151	0.3535	0.3235
4	0.961	0.2563	0.2463	0.9238	0.2626	0.2426	0.8885	0.269	0.239
5	0.9515	0.206	0.196	0.9057	0.2122	0.1922	0.8626	0.2184	0.1884
6	0.942	0.1725	0.1625	0.888	0.1785	0.1585	0.8375	0.1846	0.1546
7	0.9327	0.1486	0.1386	0.8706	0.1545	0.1345	0.8131	0.1605	0.1305
8	0.9235	0.1307	0.1207	0.8535	0.1365	0.1165	0.7894	0.1425	0.1125
9	0.9143	0.1167	0.1067	0.8368	0.1225	0.1025	0.7664	0.1284	0.0984
10	0.9053	0.1056	0.0956	0.8203	0.1113	0.0913	0.7441	0.1172	0.0872
11	0.8963	0.0965	0.0865	0.8043	0.1022	0.0822	0.7224	0.1081	0.0781
12	0.8874	0.0888	0.0788	0.7885	0.0946	0.0746	0.7014	0.1005	0.0705
13	0.8787	0.0824	0.0724	0.773	0.0881	0.0681	0.681	0.094	0.064
14	0.87	0.0769	0.0669	0.7579	0.0826	0.0626	0.6611	0.0885	0.0585
15	0.8613	0.0721	0.0621	0.743	0.0778	0.0578	0.6419	0.0838	0.0538
16	0.8528	0.0679	0.0579	0.7284	0.0737	0.0537	0.6232	0.0796	0.0496
17	0.8444	0.0643	0.0543	0.7142	0.07	0.05	0.605	0.076	0.046
18	0.836	0.061	0.051	0.7002	0.0667	0.0467	0.5874	0.0727	0.0427
19	0.8277	0.0581	0.0481	0.6864	0.0638	0.0438	0.5703	0.0698	0.0398
20	0.8195	0.0554	0.0454	0.673	0.0612	0.0412	0.5537	0.0672	0.0372
21	0.8114	0.053	0.043	0.6598	0.0588	0.0388	0.5375	0.0649	0.0349
22	0.8034	0.0509	0.0409	0.6468	0.0566	0.0366	0.5219	0.0627	0.0327
23	0.7954	0.0489	0.0389	0.6342	0.0547	0.0347	0.5067	0.0608	0.0308
24	0.7876	0.0471	0.0371	0.6217	0.0529	0.0329	0.4919	0.059	0.029
25	0.7798	0.0454	0.0354	0.6095	0.0512	0.0312	0.4776	0.0574	0.0274
26	0.772	0.0439	0.0339	0.5976	0.0497	0.0297	0.4637	0.0559	0.0259
27	0.7644	0.0424	0.0324	0.5859	0.0483	0.0283	0.4502	0.0546	0.0246
28	0.7568	0.0411	0.0311	0.5744	0.047	0.027	0.4371	0.0533	0.0233
29	0.7493	0.0399	0.0299	0.5631	0.0458	0.0258	0.4243	0.0521	0.0221
30	0.7419	0.0387	0.0287	0.5521	0.0446	0.0246	0.412	0.051	0.021

347

n	(P/F,i,n)	(A/P,i,n)	(A/F,i,n)	(P/F,i,n)	(A/P,i,n)	(A/F,i,n)	(P/F,i,n)	(A/P,i,n)	(A/F,i,n)
1	0.9259	1.08	1	0.9091	1.1	1	0.8929	1.12	1
2	0.8573	0.5608	0.4808	0.8264	0.5762	0.4762	0.7972	0.5917	0.4717
3	0.7938	0.388	0.308	0.7513	0.4021	0.3021	0.7118	0.4163	0.2963
4	0.735	0.3019	0.2219	0.683	0.3155	0.2155	0.6355	0.3292	0.2092
5	0.6806	0.2505	0.1705	0.6209	0.2638	0.1638	0.5674	0.2774	0.1574
6	0.6302	0.2163	0.1363	0.5645	0.2296	0.1296	0.5066	0.2432	0.1232
7	0.5835	0.1921	0.1121	0.5132	0.2054	0.1054	0.4523	0.2191	0.0991
8	0.5403	0.174	0.094	0.4665	0.1874	0.0874	0.4039	0.2013	0.0813
9	0.5002	0.1601	0.0801	0.4241	0.1736	0.0736	0.3606	0.1877	0.0677
10	0.4632	0.149	0.069	0.3855	0.1627	0.0627	0.322	0.177	0.057
11	0.4289	0.1401	0.0601	0.3505	0.154	0.054	0.2875	0.1684	0.0484
12	0.3971	0.1327	0.0527	0.3186	0.1468	0.0468	0.2567	0.1614	0.0414
13	0.3677	0.1265	0.0465	0.2897	0.1408	0.0408	0.2292	0.1557	0.0357
14	0.3405	0.1213	0.0413	0.2633	0.1357	0.0357	0.2046	0.1509	0.0309
15	0.3152	0.1168	0.0368	0.2394	0.1315	0.0315	0.1827	0.1468	0.0268
16	0.2919	0.113	0.033	0.2176	0.1278	0.0278	0.1631	0.1434	0.0234
17	0.2703	0.1096	0.0296	0.1978	0.1247	0.0247	0.1456	0.1405	0.0205
18	0.2502	0.1067	0.0267	0.1799	0.1219	0.0219	0.13	0.1379	0.0179
19	0.2317	0.1041	0.0241	0.1635	0.1195	0.0195	0.1161	0.1358	0.0158
20	0.2145	0.1019	0.0219	0.1486	0.1175	0.0175	0.1037	0.1339	0.0139
21	0.1987	0.0998	0.0198	0.1351	0.1156	0.0156	0.0926	0.1322	0.0122
22	0.1839	0.098	0.018	0.1228	0.114	0.014	0.0826	0.1308	0.0108
23	0.1703	0.0964	0.0164	0.1117	0.1126	0.0126	0.0738	0.1296	09.6E-03
24	0.1577	0.095	0.015	0.1015	0.1113	0.0113	0.0659	0.1285	08.5E-03
25	0.146	0.0937	0.0137	0.0923	0.1102	0.0102	0.0588	0.1275	07.5E-03
26	0.1352	0.0925	0.0125	0.0839	0.1092	09.2E-03	0.0525	0.1267	06.7E-03
27	0.1252	0.0914	0.0114	0.0763	0.1083	08.3E-03	0.0469	0.1259	05.9E-03
28	0.1159	0.0905	0.0105	0.0693	0.1075	07.5E-03	0.0419	0.1252	05.2E-03
29	0.1073	0.0896	09.6E-03	0.063	0.1067	06.7E-03	0.0374	0.1247	04.7E-03
30	0.0994	0.0888	08.8E-03	0.0573	0.1061	06.1E-03	0.0334	0.1241	04.1E-03

n	(P/F,i,n)	(A/P,i,n)	(A/F,i,n)	(P/F,i,n)	(A/P,i,n)	(A/F,i,n)	(P/F,i,n)	(A/P,i,n)	(A/F,i,n)
1	0.8696	1.15	1	0.8333	1.2	1	0.8	1.25	1
2	0.7561	0.6151	0.4651	0.6944	0.6545	0.4545	0.64	0.6944	0.4444
3	0.6575	0.438	0.288	0.5787	0.4747	0.2747	0.512	0.5123	0.2623
4	0.5718	0.3503	0.2003	0.4823	0.3863	0.1863	0.4096	0.4234	0.1734
5	0.4972	0.2983	0.1483	0.4019	0.3344	0.1344	0.3277	0.3718	0.1218
6	0.4323	0.2642	0.1142	0.3349	0.3007	0.1007	0.2621	0.3388	0.0888
7	0.3759	0.2404	0.0904	0.2791	0.2774	0.0774	0.2097	0.3163	0.0663
8	0.3269	0.2229	0.0729	0.2326	0.2606	0.0606	0.1678	0.3004	0.0504
9	0.2843	0.2096	0.0596	0.1938	0.2481	0.0481	0.1342	0.2888	0.0388
10	0.2472	0.1993	0.0493	0.1615	0.2385	0.0385	0.1074	0.2801	0.0301
11	0.2149	0.1911	0.0411	0.1346	0.2311	0.0311	0.0859	0.2735	0.0235
12	0.1869	0.1845	0.0345	0.1122	0.2253	0.0253	0.0687	0.2684	0.0184
13	0.1625	0.1791	0.0291	0.0935	0.2206	0.0206	0.055	0.2645	0.0145
14	0.1413	0.1747	0.0247	0.0779	0.2169	0.0169	0.044	0.2615	0.0115
15	0.1229	0.171	0.021	0.0649	0.2139	0.0139	0.0352	0.2591	09.1E-03
16	0.1069	0.1679	0.0179	0.0541	0.2114	0.0114	0.0281	0.2572	07.2E-03
17	0.0929	0.1654	0.0154	0.0451	0.2094	09.4E-03	0.0225	0.2558	05.8E-03
18	0.0808	0.1632	0.0132	0.0376	0.2078	07.8E-03	0.018	0.2546	04.6E-03
19	0.0703	0.1613	0.0113	0.0313	0.2065	06.5E-03	0.0144	0.2537	03.7E-03
20	0.0611	0.1598	09.8E-03	0.0261	0.2054	05.4E-03	0.0115	0.2529	02.9E-03
21	0.0531	0.1584	08.4E-03	0.0217	0.2044	04.4E-03	09.2E-03	0.2523	02.3E-03
22	0.0462	0.1573	07.3E-03	0.0181	0.2037	03.7E-03	07.4E-03	0.2519	01.9E-03
23	0.0402	0.1563	06.3E-03	0.0151	0.2031	03.1E-03	05.9E-03	0.2515	01.5E-03
24	0.0349	0.1554	05.4E-03	0.0126	0.2025	02.5E-03	04.7E-03	0.2512	01.2E-03
25	0.0304	0.1547	04.7E-03	0.0105	0.2021	02.1E-03	03.8E-03	0.2509	09E-04
26	0.0264	0.1541	04.1E-03	08.7E-03	0.2018	01.8E-03	03E-03	0.2508	08E-04
27	0.023	0.1535	03.5E-03	07.3E-03	0.2015	01.5E-03	02.4E-03	0.2506	06E-04
28	0.02	0.1531	03.1E-03	06.1E-03	0.2012	01.2E-03	01.9E-03	0.2505	05E-04
29	0.0174	0.1527	02.7E-03	05.1E-03	0.201	01E-03	01.5E-03	0.2504	04E-04
30	0.0151	0.1523	02.3E-03	04.2E-03	0.2008	08E-04	01.2E-03	0.2503	03E-04

TABLE OF FACTORS USING DISCRETE INTEREST RATES **349**

Computer Programs

Each program is first shown with a print out of the screen formats, followed by the program listing.

JRUN FACTORS

```
**************************
*                        *
*                        *
*    INTEREST FACTORS    *
*                        *
*          BY            *
*                        *
*    J. MORLEY ENGLISH   *
*                        *
*            10/10/1983  *
**************************
```

THIS PROGRAM GIVES ALL THE
RELATIONSHIPS THAT MAY BE
USEFUL FOR TIME VALUE COMPUTATIONS

```
    MENU
    ----
```

1. FACTORS ALONE

2. GIVEN ONE VALUE,
    FIND THE OTHER

3. DETERMINE INTEREST

4. DETERMINE TIME

5. TABLE OF FACTORS

6. EXIT

```
 INDICATE WHICH BY NUMBER
?1
```

IS THE COMPUTATION TO BE BY USING

CONTINUOUS OR DISCRETE DISCOUNTING

```
            (I.E., INTEREST RATE)?
    ANSWER 'C' OR 'D'
?D
```

WHAT IS THE DISCOUNT (INTEREST) RATE
            AND NUMBER OF PERIODS?

INPUT THE DATA AND SEPARATE BY A COMMA
    EXAMPLE: 13,25

?13,17
        TABLE OF FACTORS

FOR AN INTEREST RATE OF   13%
AND TIME OF 17 PERIODS

                NAME   FACTOR
                ----   ------

PRESENT LUMP SUM OF $1.00........0.1252

FUTURE LUMP SUM OF $1.00.........7.9861

ANNUITY PAYMENT FOR $1 PRINCPAL..0.1486

SINKING FUND FOR F = $1.00.......0.0186

PRESENT VALUE OF ANNUITY.........6.7291

FUTURE VALUE OF ANNUITY.........53.7391

DO YOU WISH ANOTHER RATE OR TIME (Y/N)?
?N

THIS PROGRAM GIVES ALL THE
RELATIONSHIPS THAT MAY BE
USEFUL FOR TIME VALUE COMPUTATIONS

            MENU
            ----

        1. FACTORS ALONE

        2. GIVEN ONE VALUE,
            FIND THE OTHER

        3. DETERMINE INTEREST

        4. DETERMINE TIME

        5. TABLE OF FACTORS

        6. EXIT

    INDICATE WHICH BY NUMBER

```
1   HOME : PRINT : PRINT : PRINT
3   PRINT  TAB( 10)"**************
    **********"
4   PRINT  TAB( 10)"*
            *"
5   PRINT  TAB( 10)"*
            *"
6   PRINT  TAB( 10)"*    INTEREST F
    ACTORS   *"
7   PRINT  TAB( 10)"*
            *"
8   PRINT  TAB( 10)"*            BY
            *"
9   PRINT  TAB( 10)"*
            *"
10  PRINT  TAB( 10)"*   J. MORLEY
    ENGLISH  *"
11  PRINT  TAB( 10)"*
            *"
12  PRINT  TAB( 10)"*            1
    0/10/1983 *"
13  PRINT  TAB( 10)"*************
    **********"
14  SPEED= 50: FOR N = 1 TO 200:H
    H = LOG (2)
15  NEXT N: SPEED= 255
20  HOME : PRINT : PRINT : PRINT

30  PRINT "THIS PROGRAM GIVES ALL
    THE "
40  PRINT "RELATIONSHIPS THAT MAY
    BE"
50  PRINT "USEFUL FOR TIME VALUE
    COMPUTATIONS"
60  PRINT : PRINT "      MENU"
65  PRINT "          ---- "
70  PRINT : PRINT "        1.  F
    ACTORS ALONE
75  PRINT : PRINT "        2.  G
    IVEN ONE VALUE,
80  PRINT "              FIND THE
    OTHER
85  PRINT : PRINT "        3.  D
    ETERMINE INTEREST
```

```
90   PRINT : PRINT "         4.  D
     ETERMINE TIME
92   PRINT : PRINT "         5.  T
     ABLE OF FACTORS"
95   PRINT : PRINT "         6.  E
     XIT"
97   PRINT : PRINT " INDICATE WHIC
     H BY NUMBER"
98   INPUT Q
99   IF Q = 6 THEN  END
100  IF Q > 6 THEN 175
102  HOME : PRINT : PRINT : PRINT
     : PRINT "IS THE COMPUTATION
     TO BE BY USING  "
103  PRINT : PRINT "CONTINUOUS OR
     DISCRETE DISCOUNTING      (
     I.E., INTEREST RATE)?"
104  PRINT : PRINT " ANSWER 'C'O
     R 'D'
106  INPUT C$
120  IF Q = 1 THEN 200
125  IF Q = 5 THEN 200
140  GOTO 600
175  HOME : PRINT " WRONG NUMBER;
     TRY AGAIN"
180  GOTO 60
182  REM  **** SUB FOR COMMA LOCA
     TION
183  W$ =  STR$ (W):WY$ =  RIGHT$
     (W$,2): IF  LEN (W$) > 5 THEN
     188: IF  LEN (W$) < 3 THEN 1
     86
185  WZ$ =  LEFT$ (W$, LEN (W$) -
     2):W$ = WZ$ + "." + WY$: RETURN
186  W$ = "0." + WY$: RETURN
188  WX$ =  MID$ (W$, LEN (W$) - 4
     ,3)
189  IF ( LEN (W$) = 6 AND W < 0)
     THEN 191
190  WZ$ =  LEFT$ (W$, LEN (W$) -
     5): GOTO 192
191  WZ$ =  LEFT$ (W$ LEN (W$) - 6
     )
192  W$ = WZ$ + "," + WX$ + "." +
     WY$: RETURN
200  HOME : PRINT : PRINT : PRINT
     "WHAT IS THE DISCOUNT (INTER
     EST) RATE AND NUMBER OF PERI
     ODS?"
210  PRINT : PRINT "INPUT THE DAT
     A AND SEPARATE BY A COMMA"
225  PRINT : PRINT "    EXAMPLE:
     13,25
230  PRINT : INPUT I,N
235  I = I / 100
240  IF Q = 5 THEN 900
250  HOME : PRINT  TAB( 10)"TABLE
     OF FACTORS"
252  PRINT : PRINT " FOR AN INTER
     EST RATE OF    ";I * 100;"%"
255  PRINT " AND TIME OF  ";N;" P
     ERIODS"
256  PRINT " --------------------
     -------------"
257  PRINT "        NAME   "," F
     ACTOR"
258  PRINT "        ----   "," -
     -----"
259  PRINT : GOSUB 260: GOTO 262
260  IF C$ = "C" THEN I =  LOG (1
     + I)
261  RETURN
262  GOSUB 265
263  GOTO 280
265  FS = (1 + I) ^ N:PP = 1 / FS
270  CRF = I / (1 - PP):PV = 1 / C
     RF
275  SF = CRF - I:FV = 1 / SF
276  RETURN
280  PRINT "PRESENT LUMP SUM OF $
     1.00........0" INT (PP * (10
     ^ 4) + .5) / (10 ^ 4)
281  PRINT
282  PRINT "FUTURE LUMP SUM OF $1
     .00........"; INT (FS * (10
     ^ 4) + .5) / (10 ^ 4)
```

```
283 PRINT
284 PRINT "ANNUITY PAYMENT FOR $
    1 PRINCPAL..O"; INT (CRF * (
    10 ^ 4) + .5) / (10 ^ 4)
285 PRINT : PRINT "SINKING FUND
    FOR F = $1.00.......O";
286 PRINT  TAB( 32) INT (SF * (1
    0 ^ 4) + .5) / (10 ^ 4)
288 PRINT : PRINT "PRESENT VALUE
    OF ANNUITY........."; INT (
    PV * (10 ^ 4) + .5) / (10 ^
    4)
289 PRINT
290 PRINT "FUTURE VALUE OF ANNUI
    TY........."; INT (FV * (10 ^
    4) + .5) / (10 ^ 4)
291 PRINT
292 PRINT : PRINT "DO YOU WISH A
    NOTHER RATE OR TIME (Y/N)?"
293 INPUT Y$
294 IF Y$ = "Y" THEN 298
296 IF Y$ < > "Y" THEN 20
298 PRINT : INPUT "  RATE,TIME
    ";I,N
300 I = I / 100
310 GOTO 252
600 REM   DETERMINE VARIABLES
605 IF Q = 4 GOTO 615
610 HOME : PRINT : PRINT : INPUT
    "THE NUMBER OF PERIODS? ";N
612 IF Q = 3 GOTO 710
615 PRINT : INPUT " INTEREST RAT
    E IS? ";I
616 I = I / 100: IF Q = 4 THEN 71
    0
617 GOSUB 260: HOME
620 PRINT : PRINT " WHICH TWO VA
    RIABLES? "
630 PRINT : PRINT "   1. A GIVE
    N P"
640 PRINT : PRINT "   2. A GIVE
    N F
650 PRINT : PRINT "   3. P GIVE
    N A

660 PRINT : PRINT "   4. F GIVE
    N A
670 PRINT : PRINT "   5. P GIVE
    N F
680 PRINT : PRINT "   6. F GIVE
    N P
690 PRINT : INPUT " INDICATE NUM
    BER ";Z
692 IF Q = 3 THEN 710
693 IF Q = 4 THEN 710
700 GOSUB 265
702 IF Q = 2 THEN 800
710 HOME : PRINT
715 PRINT : PRINT " WHAT PAIR O
    F VARIABLES DO YOU WISH? "
716 PRINT : PRINT "   1. P AN
    D F
717 PRINT : PRINT "   2. A AN
    D F
718 PRINT : PRINT "   3. A AN
    D P
719 PRINT : PRINT " INDICATE WHI
    CH ";: INPUT ZZ
720 PRINT : PRINT " INPUT DATA
    AND SEPARATE BY A COMMA"
723 PRINT : PRINT "   EXAMPLE:
    A AND P = 123,987"
725 PRINT : IF ZZ = 1 THEN  INPUT
    " P AND F ";P,F
730 PRINT : IF ZZ = 2 THEN  INPUT
    " A AND F ";A,F
740 PRINT : IF ZZ = 3 THEN  INPUT
    " A AND P ";A,P
750 HOME : PRINT : PRINT
770 HOME : PRINT : PRINT : PRINT
    : PRINT
780 IF Q = 3 THEN 1000
785 IF Q = 4 THEN 2000
800 HOME : PRINT : PRINT : PRINT

801 IF Z = 3 THEN 825
802 IF Z = 4 THEN 840
803 IF Z = 5 THEN 850
804 IF Z = 6 THEN 860
```

```
805  IF Z = 1 THEN  INPUT " P IS?
     ";P
806  IF Z = 2 THEN 815
807  W = INT (P * CRF * (10 ^ 2) +
     .5)
808  GOSUB 183
810  IF Z = 1 THEN  PRINT "  THE
     ANNUITY IS $";W$
811  IF Z = 1 THEN 870
815  INPUT " F IS? ";F
817  W = INT (F * SF * (10 ^ 2) +
     .5): GOSUB 183
820  IF Z = 2 THEN  PRINT " THE A
     NNUITY IS $";W$
821  IF Z = 2 THEN 870
825  INPUT " A IS ";A
827  W = INT (A / CRF * (10 ^ 2) +
     .5): GOSUB 183
830  PRINT " PRESENT VALUE OF ANN
     UITY IS $";W$
831  IF Z = 3 THEN 870
840  INPUT " A ";A
842  W = INT (A / SF * (10 ^ 2) +
     .5): GOSUB 183
845  IF Z = 4 THEN  PRINT " FUTU
     RE VALUE OF ANNUITY IS $";W$
846  IF Z = 4 THEN 870
850  INPUT " F ";F
852  W = INT (F / FS * (10 ^ 2) +
     .5): GOSUB 183
855  IF Z = 5 THEN  PRINT " PRESE
     NT VALUE OF FUTURE SUM IS $"
     ;W$
856  IF Z = 5 THEN 870
860  INPUT " P ";P
862  W = INT (P * FS * (10 ^ 2) +
     .5): GOSUB 183
865  IF Z = 6 THEN  PRINT " FUTUR
     E VALUE OF SUM IS $";W$
870  PRINT : PRINT : PRINT " DO Y
     OU WISH ANOTHER VALUE?"
875  PRINT : INPUT ZQ$: IF ZQ$ =
     "Y           " THEN 620

880  HOME : GOTO 60
900  REM  FACTOR TABLE
901  HOME : PRINT "DO YOU WISH A
     PRINT OUT?": INPUT Z$
902  HOME : IF Z$ = "Y" THEN  PR#
     1
903  PRINT "INTEREST RATE IS ";I *
     100;"%": PRINT
905  PRINT "N";
906  PRINT  TAB( 6)"(P/F,I,N)";
908  PRINT  TAB( 18)"(A/P,I,N)";
910  PRINT  TAB( 31)"(A/F,I,N)"
912  PRINT "----------------------
     -----------------"
913  M = N
914  N = 1: GOSUB 265
915  PRINT N; TAB( 6)"0"; INT (1 /
     FS * (10 ^ 4) + .5) / (10 ^
     4);
916  PRINT  TAB( 18) INT (CRF * (
     10 ^ 4) + .5) / (10 ^ 4);
917  PRINT  TAB( 31) INT (SF * (1
     0 ^ 4) + .5) / (10 ^ 4)
918  FOR N = 2 TO M
920  GOSUB 265
925  PRINT N;
927  PRINT  TAB( 6)"0"; INT (1 /
     FS * (10 ^ 4) + .5) / (10 ^
     4);
929  PRINT  TAB( 18)"0"; INT (CRF
     * (10 ^ 4) + .5) / (10 ^ 4)
     ;
931  PRINT  TAB( 31)"0"; INT (SF *
     (10 ^ 4) + .5) / (10 ^ 4)
940  NEXT N
950  PR# 0
952  VTAB 24
955  PRINT "PRESS ANY LETTER TO C
     ONTINUE";
956  GET Z$
958  HOME
960  GOTO 60
990  END
1000 REM  FIND INTEREST
```

```
1010  IF ZZ = 2 THEN 1100
1020  IF ZZ = 3 THEN 1400
1030  IF ZZ = 1 THEN 1600
1100  X = A / F:I = .1
1102  HOME : PRINT : PRINT : PRINT
      "  PLEASE WAIT!"
1105  I1 = I
1110  GOSUB 265:SF(1) = SF
1140  I = .15: GOSUB 265
1150  SF(2) = SF
1155  I2 = I
1160  I = ((SF(1) - X) / (SF(1) -
      SF(2))) * (I2 - I1) + I1
1170  IF INT (I * (10 ^ 5) + .5)
      / (10 ^ 5) = INT (I2 * (10
      ^ 5) + .5) / (10 ^ 5) THEN
      1190
1171  GOTO 1190
1172  I2 = I
1175  GOSUB 265: GOTO 1150
1180  GOSUB 260
1190  GOSUB 260
1191  I = INT (I * (10 ^ 5) + .5)
      / (10 ^ 3)
1192  HOME : PRINT : PRINT : PRINT

1193  HOME :W = A * 100: GOSUB 18
      3: PRINT : PRINT "FOR AN ANN
      UITY OF $";W$;",":W = F * 10
      0: GOSUB 183: PRINT "A FUTUR
      E SUM OF $";W$;
1194  PRINT " AND ";N;" PERIODS"
1195  PRINT : PRINT " THE INTERES
      T RATE IS ";I;"%"
1196  GOSUB 1642
1199  GOTO 1650
1400  REM  FIND I FOR P/A
1405  HOME : PRINT : PRINT : PRINT
      "  PLEASE WAIT!"
1410  I = A / P - 1 / N
1415  SF = .1 * (10 ^ - 5)
1420  GOSUB 265
1425  I1 = I
1430  I = A / P - SF
1440  IF INT (I * (10 ^ 5) + .5)
      / (10 ^ 5) = INT (I1 * (10
      ^ 5) + .5) / (10 ^ 5) THEN
      1454
1450  GOTO 1420
1453  W = A * 100
1454  HOME : PRINT : PRINT "FOR A
      N ANNUITY OF $";W$;",":W = P
      * 100: GOSUB 183: PRINT " A
      ND PRESENT SUM OF $";W$
1455  IF C$ = "C" THEN  GOSUB 260

1456  PRINT " AND ";N;" PERIODS,"

1460  PRINT : PRINT " THE INTERES
      T RATE IS ";: INVERSE : PRINT
      INT (I * (10 ^ 5) + .5) / (
      10 ^ 3);"%": NORMAL
1465  GOSUB 1642
1470  GOTO 1650
1600  REM   I GIVEN F &P
1610  X = F / P
1620  I = EXP ( LOG (X) / N) - 1
1625  GOSUB 260
1630  I = INT (I * (10 ^ 5) + .5)
      / (10 ^ 3)
1631  HOME :W = P * 100: GOSUB 18
      3: PRINT : PRINT "FOR A PRES
      ENT SUM OF $";W$;",":W = F *
      100: GOSUB 183: PRINT " AND
      FUTURE SUM OF $";W$
1632  PRINT " AND ";N;" PERIODS,"

1633  PRINT
1640  PRINT " THE INTEREST RATE I
      S ";: INVERSE : PRINT I;"%":
      NORMAL
1641  GOSUB 1642: GOTO 1650
1642  PRINT
1645  IF C$ = "C" THEN  PRINT " (
      CONTINUOUS INTEREST)"
```

```
1646  IF C$ < > "C" THEN  PRINT
      "  (DISCRETE INTEREST)"
1647  RETURN
1650  VTAB 20: PRINT " DO YOU WIS
      H TO CONTINUE? ";
1660  INPUT Y$: IF Y$ = "Y" THEN
      60
1665  END
2000  REM  FIND TIME
2005  IF F = 0 THEN 2200
2010  IF P = 0 THEN 2400
2020  X = F / P
2030  N = LOG (X) / LOG (1 + I)
2040  HOME : PRINT : PRINT : PRINT
      " THE NUMBER OF PERIODS IS "
      ;: INVERSE : PRINT  INT (N *
      100 + .5) / 100: NORMAL
2050  GOTO 1650
2200  X = A / P
2210  N =  - LOG (1 - (I / X)) /
      LOG (1 + I)
2220  GOTO 2040
2400  X = A / F
2420  N = LOG (1 + (I / X)) / LOG
      (1 + I)
2430  GOTO 2040
```

```
JRUN CASH FLOW ANALYSIS
        ****************************
        *                          *
        *                          *
        *    CASH-FLOW ANALYSIS    *
        *                          *
        *                          *
        *                          *
        *    J. MORLEY ENGLISH     *
        *                          *
        *            11/10/1983    *
        ****************************
```

HIT ANY KEY TO CONTINUE.
 MENU

```
1. CONSTANT CASH FLOW.

2. EXPONENTIAL CASH FLOW.

3. YEAR-BY-YEAR C.F. INPUTS.


SELECT ONE.   1

WHICH TYPE OF SOLUTION DO YOU WANT:

    1. PRESENT WORTH

    2. INTERNAL RATE OF RETURN
       I.E., RETURN ON INVESTMENT


SELECT ONE   1

WHAT IS THE  DISCOUNT RATE?   12

IS THE DISCOUNT RATE

    <D> DISCRETE

  OR <C> CONTINUOUS

SELECT ONE?D

IS THE RATE BASED ON A YEAR
?Y

WHAT IS THE CASH FLOW? 1000

HOW MANY YEARS (PERIODS) FOR THE C.F.

10
THE PRESENT WORTH OF $1,000.00/YEAR

        AT 12%/YEAR IS
        $5,650.22
DO YOU WISH TO CONTINUE?N
```

```
]LIST

1  HOME : VTAB (8): PRINT  TAB( 1
   0)"*************************
   *"
2  PRINT  TAB( 10)"*
                          *"
3  PRINT  TAB( 10)"*
                          *"
4  PRINT  TAB( 10)"*   CASH-FLOW
   ANALYSIS  *"
5  PRINT  TAB( 10)"*
                          *"
7  PRINT  TAB( 10)"*
                          *"
8  PRINT  TAB( 10)"*    J. MORLEY
   ENGLISH  *"
9  PRINT  TAB( 10)"*
                          *"
10 PRINT  TAB( 10)"*
   11/10/1983 *"
11 PRINT  TAB( 10)"*************
   *************"
12 PRINT : PRINT : PRINT : PRINT
   " HIT ANY KEY TO CONTINUE."
13 GET ZX$
25 DIM A(40),A$(40)
40 ONERR  GOTO 500
76 GOTO 2000
78 F = F * 100
79 F$ =  STR$ ( INT (F + .5))
80 FY$ =  RIGHT$ ((F$),2)
81 IF  LEN (F$) < 3 THEN 83
82 IF ( LEN (F$) = 3 AND F < 0) THEN
   85
83 GOTO 87
84 F$ = "0." + FY$: RETURN
85 F$ = "-0." + FY$: RETURN
87 IF  LEN (F$) > 5 THEN 92
88 IF ( LEN (F$) = 4 AND F < 0) THEN
   99
89 IF  LEN (F$) > 6 THEN 92
91 F$ = FZ$ + "." + FY$: RETURN

92 IF ( LEN (F$) = 6 AND F < 0) THEN
   97
93 FZ$ =  LEFT$ (F$, LEN (F$) - 5
   )
94 FX$ =  MID$ (F$,( LEN (F$) - 4
   ),3):FZ$ =  LEFT$ (F$, LEN (
   F$) - 5): GOTO 98
95 FX$ =  MID$ (F$,( LEN (F$) - 5
   ),3):FZ$ =  LEFT$ (F$, LEN (
   F$) - 6): GOTO 97
97 FX$ =  MID$ (F$,( LEN (F$) - 5
   ),3):F$ = "-" + FX$ + "." +
   FY$: RETURN
98 F$ = FZ$ + "," + FX$ + "." + F
   Y$
99 RETURN
100 REM  *** DISCOUNT SUB ***
105 V = 0
110 FOR J = 1 TO N
120 V = V + (A(J) / ((1 + R) ^ J)
   )
130 NEXT J
135 P = V - IN
140 RETURN
500 HOME : PRINT : PRINT "YOU HA
   VE EXCEEDED THE LIMITS OF PR
   OGRAM"
510 PRINT : PRINT "ARE YOU SURE
   YOU ENTERED THE DATA      C
   ORRECTLY. TRY AGAIN!"
520 A = 0:Y = 0:R = 0
525 GET XZ$
530 GOTO 2000
2000 REM  **** DESCRIPTION
2001 HOME : VTAB (5)
2010 PRINT " MENU"
2020 PRINT " ----"
2030 PRINT : PRINT "    1. CONST
   ANT CASH FLOW."
2035 PRINT : PRINT "    2. EXPON
   ENTIAL CASH FLOW."
2045 PRINT : PRINT "    3. YEAR-
   BY-YEAR C.F. INPUTS."
```

```
2050  PRINT : PRINT : PRINT "SELE      2097  R = Y - G
      CT ONE.   ";: INPUT "";Z       2100  REM ****CONSTANT CF
2051  HOME : PRINT : PRINT "WHICH     2105  HOME : PRINT : PRINT "WHAT
      TYPE OF SOLUTION DO YOU WAN           IS THE CASH FLOW?";: INPUT "
      T:"                                   ";A
2052  PRINT : PRINT "     1. PRES     2110  F = A: GOSUB 78:A$ = F$
      ENT WORTH"                      2120  PRINT : PRINT "HOW MANY YEA
2053  PRINT : PRINT "     2. INTE           RS (PERIODS) FOR THE C.F.": PRINT
      RNAL RATE OF RETURN "                 : INPUT "";N
2054  PRINT "         I.E., RETURN    2180  IF ZZ = 2 THEN 2300
      ON INVESTMENT"                  2185  IF R = 0 THEN 2194
2055  PRINT : PRINT "SELECT ONE       2190  P = A * (1 - ((1 + R) ^ ( -
      ";: INPUT "";ZZ                        N))) / R
2056  IF ZZ = 2 THEN 2058            2192  GOTO 2195
2057  PRINT : PRINT "WHAT IS THE      2194  P = A * N
      DISCOUNT RATE? ";: INPUT "      2195  F = P: GOSUB 78:P$ = F$
      ";Y:Y = Y / 100:R = Y           2200  HOME : VTAB (12)
2058  PRINT : PRINT "IS THE DISCO     2205  IF Z = 3 THEN 2216
      UNT RATE": PRINT : PRINT "      2209  PRINT "THE PRESENT WORTH OF
      <D> DISCRETE"                         $";A$;"/";NA$
2059  PRINT : PRINT " OR <C> CON      2210  IF Z = 2 THEN 2214
      TINUOUS": PRINT : PRINT "SEL    2211  PRINT : PRINT  TAB( 10)"AT
      ECT ONE";: INPUT Y$                    ";Y * 100;"%/";NA$;" IS"
2062  PRINT : PRINT "IS THE RATE      2213  GOTO 2219
      BASED ON A YEAR": INPUT C$: IF  2214  PRINT "WITH A GROWTH RATE O
      C$ = "Y" THEN 2064                    F ";G1;"%/";NA$;" AND": PRINT
2063  NA$ = "PERIOD": GOTO 2069            : PRINT  TAB( 10)"AT ";Y * 1
2064  NA$ = "YEAR"                          00;"%/";NA$;" IS"
2069  IF Y$ < > "C" THEN 2076        2215  GOTO 2219
2070  R = LOG (1 + Y)                 2216  PRINT "THE PRESENT WORTH OF
2076  IF Z = 2 THEN 2080                   THE CASH FLOW": PRINT : PRINT
2077  IF Z = 3 AND ZZ = 2 THEN 23          TAB( 10)"AT ";Y * 100;"%/";
      00                                   NA$;" IS"
2078  IF Z = 3 AND ZZ = 1 THEN 25    2219  HTAB (13)
      00                             2220  VTAB (17): PRINT "$";P$
2079  GOTO 2100                      2225  VTAB (24)
2080  PRINT : PRINT "WHAT IS THE      2230  GOTO 2455
      GROWTH RATE OF THE EXPONENTI    2300  REM ***INTERNAL RATE OF RET
      AL  ";: INPUT G                       URN
2090  G1 = G:G = G / 100             2310  PRINT : PRINT " WHAT IS THE
2092  IF Y$ = "C" THEN 2097                INVESTMENT";: INPUT INV
2094  R = (1 + Y) / (1 + G) - 1      2312  IF Z = 3 AND ZZ = 2 THEN 25
2095  GOTO 2100                            00
```

```
2315 B = A / IN
2320 R1 = B - (1 / N)
2330 V = R / (((R1 + 1) ^ N) - 1)

2335 R = B - V
2340 R2 = INT (R * (10 ^ 4) + .5
     ) / (10 ^ 4)
2350 IF R2 = INT (R1 * (10 ^ 4)
     + .5) / (10 ^ 4) THEN 2400
2365 R1 = R
2370 GOTO 2330
2400 HOME
2405 VTAB (10): HTAB (6):
2410 PRINT "THE INTERNAL RATE OF
     RETURN IS"
2420 VTAB (13): HTAB (12)
2430 Y = R + G: IF Y$ = "C" THEN
     Y = EXP (Y) - 1
2440 Y = INT (Y * (10 ^ 4) + .5)
     / 100
2450 PRINT Y;"% PER PERIOD. "
2455 IF Y$ < > "C" THEN 2470
2456 VTAB 20: PRINT "NOTE: BASED
     ON A CONTINUOUS DISCOUNTING
     ."
2470 VTAB 23: PRINT "DO YOU WISH
     TO CONTINUE";: INPUT QQ$: IF
     QQ$ = "Y" THEN 2000
2475 END
2500 REM ** YEAR BY YEAR INPUT
     OF CASH FOW
2502 PRINT : PRINT "HOW MANY YEA
     RS OR PERIODS FOR THE C.F.";
     : INPUT N
2503 HOME
2505 PRINT "YEAR OR PERIOD   INP
     UT CASH FLOW"
2506 PRINT "--------------   ---
     --------------"
2510 FOR J = 1 TO N
2520 HTAB (8): PRINT J;" . . . .
     . . ."
2525 NEXT J

2530 FOR J = 1 TO N
2540 HTAB (22): VTAB (J + 2): INPUT
     A(J)
2550 NEXT J
2560 IF ZZ = 2 THEN 2700
2600 REM **** PRESENT WORTH
2610 FOR J = 1 TO N
2620 P = P + (A(J) / ((1 + R) ^ J
     ))
2630 NEXT J
2640 GOTO 2195
2700 REM **** IRR ****
2705 FOR J = 1 TO N:U = U + A(J)
     : NEXT
2706 P = U - IN
2710 R = P / N / IN
2720 GOSUB 100
2730 P1 = P:R1 = R
2740 R = 1.1 * R: GOSUB 100
2750 R2 = R:P2 = P
2760 R = (R - R1) * P / (P1 - P) +
     R
2770 IF INT (R * (10 ^ 5) + .5)
     = INT (R1 * (10 ^ 5) + .5)
     THEN 2800
2780 R1 = R2:P1 = P2: GOSUB 100: GOTO
     2750
2800 GOTO 2400
```

```
*************************
*                       *
*                       *
*        BONDS          *
*                       *
*         BY            *
*                       *
*  J. MORLEY ENGLISH    *
*                       *
*         10/10/1983    *
*************************
---------------
```

THIS PROGRAM WILL SOLVE

MOST BOND PROBLEMS FOR YOU.

MENU
-----

    1. YIELD TO MATURITY

    2. PRICE, GIVEN THE YIELD

    3. YIELD TO CALL

    4. PRICES FOR VARIABLE LIFE

    5. EXIT

SELECT ONE BY NUMBER
?2

DO YOU WISH TO CONSIDER TAXES? (Y/N)?Y

WHAT IS THE INCOME TAX RATE (%) ?33

WHAT IS THE CAPITAL GAINS RATE (%) ?12

    DO YOU WISH EXACT DATES? (Y/N)
?N

  IN THAT CASE ENTER THE
  NUMBER OF YEARS TO MATURITY ?7

WHAT IS THE COUPON RATE? 5.25

    WHAT IS THE YIELD? 12.75

THE PRICE SHOULD BE 53.04%

    OF FACE VALUE

    DO YOU WISH TO EXIT? (Y/N)
?Y

]LIST

```
1  HOME : PRINT : PRINT : PRINT
2  PRINT  TAB( 10)"**************
   **********"
3  PRINT  TAB( 10)"*
            *"
4  PRINT  TAB( 10)"*
            *"
5  PRINT  TAB( 10)"*         BOND
   S       *"
6  PRINT  TAB( 10)"*
            *"
7  PRINT  TAB( 10)"*          BY
            *"
8  PRINT  TAB( 10)"*
            *"
9  PRINT  TAB( 10)"*  J. MORLEY E
   NGLISH  *"
10 PRINT  TAB( 10)"*
            *"
11 PRINT  TAB( 10)"*            1
   0/10/1983 *"
12 PRINT  TAB( 10)"**************
   **********"
14 SPEED= 50: FOR N = 1 TO 200:H
   H = LOG (2)
15 NEXT N: SPEED= 255
20 PRINT "--------------"
30 REM  TIME COMPUTATION
32 F = 1
40 HOME
41 PRINT : PRINT : PRINT " THIS
   PROGRAM WILL SOLVE"
42 PRINT : PRINT " MOST BOND PR
   OBLEMS FOR YOU."
50 GOSUB 170
52 HOME : PRINT : PRINT : PRINT
   "DO YOU WISH TO CONSIDER TAX
   ES? (Y/N)";
```

```
54   INPUT QQ$                              200  PRINT : PRINT "          3. Y
56   IF QQ$ = "Y" THEN  GOSUB 700                IELD TO CALL"
57   IF QQ$ < > "Y" THEN T = 1             202  PRINT : PRINT "          4. P
60   IF Z = 4 GOTO 140                           RICES FOR VARIABLE LIFE"
70   HOME : PRINT : PRINT : PRINT          204  PRINT : PRINT "          5. E
                                                 XIT "
71   PRINT : PRINT : PRINT "      D        210  PRINT : PRINT "SELECT ONE BY
     O YOU WISH EXACT DATES? (Y/N               NUMBER   ": INPUT Z
     ) ": INPUT Q$                         212  IF Z = 5 THEN  END
72   IF Q$ = "Y" THEN 80                   215  RETURN
74   PRINT : PRINT " IN THAT CASE          220  IF Z = 1 GOTO 300
     ENTER THE";                           225  IF Z = 2 GOTO 400
75   PRINT : PRINT "   NUMBER OF Y         230  IF Z = 3 GOTO 500
     EARS TO MATURITY ";                   240  IF Z > 5 THEN 245
78   INPUT N:N = N * 2                     245  PRINT "TRY AGAIN": PRINT : GOTO
79   GOTO 140                                   210
80   PRINT : PRINT : PRINT "    EN         300  REM  YIELD TO MATURITY
     TER TODAY'S DATE (MONTH,DAY,          301  LET F = 1
     YEAR)"                                302  HOME : PRINT : PRINT : INPUT
82   PRINT : PRINT "      EXAMPLE               "   THE SELLING PRICE IS ";
     : 11,4,82"                                 P
85   PRINT : INPUT M,D,YE                  305  P = P / 100
86   PRINT : PRINT "ENTER MATURITY         310  Y = C / P
     DATE"                                 312  GOTO 320
100  PRINT : INPUT MD,DD,YD                315  Y = Y1
102  IF YD < 50 THEN YD = YD + 10          320  PI = - C * T * ((1 + Y) ^ ( -
     0                                          N) - 1) / Y
110  N = (YD - YE)                         330  PF = P - PI
120  ND = (MD - M) * 30 + DD - D           333  GOTO 800
130  N = ND / 180 + N * 2                  365  HOME : PRINT : PRINT : PRINT
140  HOME                                       "THE AFTER-TAX YIELD TO MATU
142  IF N < = 1 THEN G = 1 - T                  RITY IS "
150  PRINT : PRINT : PRINT : INPUT         368  INVERSE
     "WHAT IS THE COUPON RATE? ";          370  PRINT : PRINT "<< ";Y2 * 2;"
     C                                          % >>": NORMAL
160  C = C / 200                           371  PRINT : PRINT " THE INCOME T
165  IF Z = 4 THEN 600                          AX RATE IS ";(1 - T) * 100;"
166  GOTO 220                                   %"
170  PRINT : PRINT "    MENU"              372  PRINT : PRINT "    AND CAPIT
180  PRINT "   -----  "                         AL GAINS TAX RATE IS ";G * 1
190  PRINT : PRINT "          1. Y              00;"%"
     IELD TO MATURITY "                    373  PRINT : PRINT "         THE
195  PRINT : PRINT "          2. P              PRICE IS ";P * 100;"%"
     RICE, GIVEN THE YIELD"                374  PRINT : PRINT : PRINT : PRINT
```

```
        : PRINT                              " HOW MANY YEARS?"
375  PRINT "DO YOU WISH TO CONTIN       611  INPUT X
     UE";                                612  PRINT : PRINT "  WHAT IS THE
377  INPUT Q$: IF Q$ < > "Y" THEN            YIELD?"
     END                                 614  PRINT : INPUT Y:Y = Y / 200
378  HOME : GOTO 50                      615  PRINT "DO YOU WISH A PRINT O
400  REM  PRICE                               UT? (Y/N) ": INPUT Q$
410  HOME : PRINT : PRINT : INPUT        616  HOME : PRINT : PRINT : PRINT
     "        WHAT IS THE YIELD? "       617  IF Q$ = "Y" THEN  PR# 1
     ;Y                                  618  PRINT " TABLE OF PRICES AS A
420  Y = Y / 200                              FUNCTION OF N": PRINT " ---
422  GOTO 430                                 ----------------------------
428  Y = Y1                                   ------"
430  P =  - C * T * (((1 + Y) ^  -       619  PRINT " FOR A COUPON RATE OF
     N) - 1) / Y + ((1 + Y) ^  -              ";C * 200;"%S"
     N) * F                              .20  PRINT " AND A YIELD TO MATUR
432  CGTAX = (F - P) * G                      ITY OF ";Y * 200;"%S"
434  P = P - CGTAX                       621  PRINT " ====================
440  P =  INT (P * 10000 + .5) / 1           ============";:: PRINT
     00                                  622  PRINT "NUMBER OF YEARS   PRI
450  HOME : PRINT : PRINT : PRINT            CE"
     : PRINT " THE PRICE SHOULD B        624  PRINT "----------------   ---
     E  ";                                    --"
451  INVERSE : PRINT P;"%": NORMAL       630  X = 2 * X
                                         640  FOR N = 1 TO X
452  PRINT : PRINT "        OF FAC       650  P =  - C * T * (((1 + Y) ^ ( -
     E VALUE "                               N) - 1) / Y + (((1 + Y) ^ ( -
460  PRINT : PRINT : PRINT : PRINT           N)) * F))
     "  DO YOU WISH TO EXIT? (Y/N        652  CGTAX = (F - P) * G
     )                                   654  P = P - CGTAX
462  INPUT Y$: IF Y$ = "Y" THEN  END     660  P =  INT (P * 10000 + .5) / 1
                                             00
465  HOME : GOTO 50                      670   IF (N / 2 =  INT (N / 2)) THEN
500  REM  YIELD TO CALL                       PRINT  TAB( 8)N / 2; TAB( 1
510  HOME : PRINT : PRINT : PRINT            9)P
     " WHAT IS THE CALL PREMIUM          680  NEXT N
     "                                   682  IF QQ$ = "Y" THEN  PRINT "TA
515  PRINT : PRINT " AS A PERCEN             X RATE--";(1 - T) * 100;"% &
     T OF FACE VALUE? ";                      CAPITAL GAINS--";G * 100;"%
520  INPUT F                                 "
525  F = 1 + (F / 100)                   683  IF QQ$ < > "Y" THEN  PRINT
530  GOTO 302                                " TAXES ARE NOT CONSIDERED"
600  REM  SERIES OF PRICES               685  PR# 0
610  HOME : PRINT : PRINT : PRINT        688  PRINT
```

```
690 PRINT " DO YOU WISH TO END?
    (Y/N) ";
692 INPUT Y$: IF Y$ = "Y" THEN  END

694 HOME : GOTO 50
700 REM  TAXES
710 HOME : PRINT : PRINT : PRINT
    "WHAT IS THE INCOME TAX RATE
    (%) ";
720 INPUT T
730 T = 1 - T / 100
740 PRINT : PRINT " WHAT IS THE
    CAPITAL GAINS RATE (%) ";
750 INPUT G:G = G / 100
790 RETURN
800 REM   ITERATION

810 P(1) =  - C * T * (((1 + Y) ^
    ( - N) - 1) / Y + (((1 + Y) ^
    ( - N)) * F)
812 P(1) = P(1) - G * (F - P(1))
820 Y1 = 1.1 * Y
830 P(2) =  - C * T * ((1 + Y1) ^
    ( - N) - 1) / Y1 + (((1 + Y1
    ) ^ ( - N)) * F)
831 P(2) = P(2) - G * (F - P(2))
832 IF P = INT (P(2) * 10000 +
    .5) / 10000 THEN 880
840 DI = P(2) - P(1)
850 Y1 = ((P - P(1)) / DI * (Y1 -
    Y)) + Y
855 PRINT Y1
860 GOTO 830
880 Y2 = INT (Y1 * (10 ^ 5) + .5
    ) / 1000
890 GOTO 365
900 HOME : PRINT : PRINT "DO YOU
    WISH TO CONTINUE (Y/N) ";
910 INPUT Q$: IF Q$ = "Y" THEN 5
    0
```

]RUN DEPREE{ATION

```
****************************
*                          *
*                          *
* DEPRECIATION SCHEDULE *
*                          *
*             BY           *
*                          *
*      J.MORLEY ENGLISH    *
*                          *
*             3/25/1983  *
****************************
```

PRESS ANY KEY TO CONTINUE
THIS PROGRAM WILL LIST
THE DEPRECIATION SCHEDULE
AND BOOK VALUES FOR A NUMBER
OF DEPRECIATION METHODS.

SELECT THE METHOD DESIRED BY NUMBER

    1. STRAIGHT LINE.

    2. DECLINING BALANCE.

    3. SUM OF THE DIGITS.

    4. DECLINING BALANCE WITH A
        CROSS OVER TO STRAIGHT LINE.

    5 .GENERALIZED DEPRECIATION

        (I.E., TO YIELD A CONSTANT ROI)

    6. EXIT

?4
HOW MANY YEARS? ?15

WHAT IS THE DEPRECIABLE AMOUNT
OF THE ASSET?

?10000

DO YOU WANT:

  1. DOUBLE DECLINING BALANCE?

  2 1.75 TIMES DECLINING BALANCE?

  3 1.5 TIMES DECLINING BALANCE?
?2
 DO YOU WISH HARD COPY?

?Y
 DEPRECIATION SCHEDULE USING
D.B. WITH CROSS OVER TO S.L.

N	BOOK VALUE	DEPR. ALLOWANCE
0	10,000.00	
1	8,833.33	1,166.67
2	7,802.78	1,030.56
3	6,892.45	910.32
4	6,088.33	804.12
5	5,378.03	710.31
6	4,750.59	627.44
7	4,196.36	524.54
8	3,671.81	524.54
9	3,147.27	524.54
10	2,622.72	524.54
11	2,098.18	524.54
12	1,573.63	524.54
13	1,049.09	524.54
14	524.54	524.54
15	0.0	524.54

]LIST

```
8   HOME
10  REM   MATRIX INVERSION
11  PRINT "      **************
    ***********"
12  PRINT "          *
              *"
13  PRINT "          *
            *
14  PRINT "          * DEPRECIATION
    SCHEDULE *
15  PRINT "          *
          *
16  PRINT "          *          BY
          *
17  PRINT "          *
          *
18  PRINT "          *   J.MORLEY
    ENGLISH   *
19  PRINT "          *
          *
20  PRINT "          *          3
    /25/1983  *
21  PRINT "      **************
    ***********"
22  PRINT : PRINT : PRINT : PRINT
    " PRESS ANY KEY TO CONTINUE"
    : GET Z$
23  HOME
38  DIM I$(40),Z(40),U(40),V(40)
40  DIM BAL(40),DEPR(40),BA$(40),
    DE$(40),YY(40),Y(40)
100 PRINT " THIS PROGRAM WILL LI
    ST "
110 PRINT " THE DEPRECIATION SCH
    EDULE "
120 PRINT " AND BOOK VALUES FOR
    A NUMBER "
130 PRINT " OF DEPRECIATION METH
    ODS.
140 PRINT : PRINT : PRINT " SELE
    CT THE METHOD DESIRED BY NUM
    BER"
145 PRINT : PRINT "    1. STRAIG
    HT LINE."
150 PRINT : PRINT "    2. DECLIN
    ING BALANCE."
155 PRINT : PRINT "    3. SUM OF
```

```
                THE DIGITS."          315  PRINT : PRINT "         1. DO
160  PRINT : PRINT "    4. DECLIN          UBLE DECLINING BALANCE?"
     ING BALANCE WITH A "          316  PRINT : PRINT "         2 1.
165  PRINT "        CROSS OVER TO          75 TIMES DECLINING BALANCE?"
     STRAIGHT LINE."
167  PRINT : PRINT "    5 .GENERA     317  PRINT : PRINT "         3 1.
     LIZED DEPRECIATION                    5 TIMES DECLINING BALANCE?"
          (I.E., TO YIELD A CONS     319  INPUT Q
     TANT ROI)"                      321  IF Q = 1 THEN Q = 2
168  PRINT : PRINT "    6. EXIT       322  IF Q = 2 THEN Q = 1.75
170  PRINT : INPUT Z: IF Z = 6 THEN   323  IF Q = 3 THEN Q = 1.5
     END                             325  A = 1 / N * Q
171  HOME : PRINT " HOW MANY YEAR     330  FOR I = 0 TO N
     S? ";                           335  DEPR(I + 1) = BAL(I) * A
172  INPUT N                         337  BAL(I + 1) = BAL(I) - DEPR(I +
173  PRINT : PRINT " WHAT IS THE           1): NEXT I
     DEPRECIABLE AMOUNT ": PRINT     338  IF Z = 4 THEN  GOSUB 500
     "    OF THE ASSET? ",           340  FOR I = 0 TO N
174  PRINT : PRINT : INPUT BAL(0)    341  BA(I) =  INT (BA(I) * 100 + .
                                           5)
175  SL = BAL(0) / N                 342  DE(I) =  INT (DE(I) * 100 + .
176  IF Z = 1 THEN 200                     5)
180  IF Z = 2 THEN 300               343  W = BA(I): GOSUB 400:BA$(I) =
185  IF Z = 3 THEN 600                     W$
190  IF Z = 4 THEN 300               344  W = DE(I): GOSUB 400:DE$(I) =
192  IF Z = 5 THEN 1000                    W$
194  IF Z > 6 THEN 100               350  NEXT
200  REM  STRAIGHT LINE              360  GOTO 800
210  FOR I = 0 TO N                  400  REM  *** COMMAS IN NUMBER FO
220  BAL(I + 1) = BAL(I) - SL             RMAT
222  DEPR(I) = SL                    410  W$ =  STR$ (W):WY$ =  RIGHT$
223  BA(I) =  INT (BA(I) * 100 + .        (W$,2): IF  LEN (W$) > 5 THEN
     5)                                   488
224  DE(I) =  INT (DE(I) * 100 + .   420  IF  LEN (W$) < 3 THEN 486
     5)                              430  GOTO 485
225  W = BA(I): GOSUB 400:BA$(I) =   485  WZ$ =  LEFT$ (W$, LEN (W$) -
     W$                                   2):W$ = WZ$ + "." + WY$: RETURN
226  W = DE(I): GOSUB 400:DE$(I) =
     W$                              486  W$ = "0." + WY$: RETURN
230  NEXT I: GOTO 800                488  WX$ =  MID$ (W$, LEN (W$) - 4
300  REM  DECLINING BALANCE               ,3)
310  HOME : PRINT : PRINT "DO YOU    489  IF ( LEN (W$) = 6 AND W < 0)
     WANT:"                               THEN 491
```

```
490 WZ$ = LEFT$ (W$, LEN (W$) -
    5): GOTO 492
491 WZ$ = LEFT$ (W$, LEN (W$) -
    4): GOTO 493
492 W$ = WZ$ + "," + WX$ + "." +
    WY$: RETURN
493 W$ = "-" + WX$ + "." + WY$: RETURN

500 REM  CROSS OVER TO SL
501 FOR I = 1 TO N - 1
502 NSL = BAL(I) / (N - I)
510 IF DEPR(I) < NSL GOTO 530
520 NEXT I
530 NSL = BAL(I - 1) / (N - I + 1
    ): FOR I = I - 1 TO N
532 BAL(I + 1) = BAL(I) - NSL
533 DEP(I) = NSL
540 NEXT I: RETURN
600 REM  SUM OF THE DIGITS
610 S = N * (N + 1) / 2
620 FOR I = 1 TO N
625 DEPR(I) = (N - I + 1) / S * B
    AL(0)
628 NEXT I: FOR I = 0 TO N
630 BAL(I + 1) = BAL(I) - DEPR(I +
    1): NEXT I: FOR I = 0 TO N
631 BA(I) = INT (BA(I) * 100 + .
    5)
632 DE(I) = INT (DE(I) * 100 + .
    5)
633 W = BA(I): GOSUB 400:BA$(I) =
    W$
634 W = DE(I): GOSUB 400:DE$(I) =
    W$
635 NEXT I
640 GOTO 800
800 REM  PRINT
810 HOME : PRINT " DO YOU WISH H
    ARD COPY? "
815 PRINT : PRINT : INPUT Y$
820 IF Y$ = "Y" THEN PR# 1
830 HOME
840 PRINT " DEPRECIATION SCHEDUL
    E USING "
845 IF Z = 1 THEN PRINT "     S
    TRAIGHT LINE "
850 IF Z = 2 THEN PRINT "     D
    ECLINING BALANCE"
855 IF Z = 3 THEN PRINT "     S
    UM-OF-DIGITS"
860 IF Z = 4 THEN PRINT "D.B. W
    ITH CROSS OVER TO S.L."
862 IF Z = 5 THEN PRINT "   GE
    NERALIZED DEPRECIATION"
864 PRINT
865 PRINT "N";: HTAB 5: PRINT "B
    OOK VALUE";: HTAB 20: PRINT
    "DEPR. ALLOWANCE"
870 PRINT "----------------------
    ----------------"
872 BA$(N + 1) = "0"
878 PRINT TAB( 2)"0";: HTAB (14
    - LEN (BA$(0))): PRINT BA$
    (0)
880 FOR I = 1 TO N
882 X = LEN (BA$(I))
884 Y = LEN (DE$(I))
891 I$(I) = STR$ (I):Z = LEN (I
    $(I))
892 HTAB (3 - Z): PRINT I;: HTAB
    (14 - X): PRINT BA$(I);: HTAB
    (29 - Y): PRINT DE$(I)
900 NEXT I
905 PR# 0: PRINT "PRESS ANY KEY
    TO CONTINUE"
906 GET ZZ$
907 HOME : GOTO 140
910 END
1000 REM *** GENERALIZED
1010 HOME : PRINT " THIS WILL DE
     PEND ON THE SHAPE OF THE
     CASH-FLOW FUNCTION. YOU HAV
     E SEVERAL     CHOICES:"
1020 PRINT : PRINT "     1. CO
     NSTANT CASH FLOW.
1025 PRINT : PRINT "     2. EX
```

```
PONENTIAL CASH FLOW."
1030  PRINT : PRINT "       3. IN
      PUT YEAR TO YEAR C.F."
1035  PRINT : PRINT " SELECT ONE
      BY NUMBER"
1040  PRINT : PRINT : PRINT : PRINT

1045  INVERSE : PRINT "NOTE:";: NORMAL
      : PRINT " IN THE CASE OF A C
      ONSTANT C.F.,        THE DE
      PRECIATION FUNCTION IS THE
              SINKING FUND DEPRECIA
      TION."
1050  PRINT : INPUT ZX
1060  HOME : PRINT : PRINT "WHAT
      IS THE EXPECTED RATE OF RETU
      RN      FOR THE ENTERPRISE";
1065  INPUT R:R = R / 100
1066  IF ZX = 1 THEN 1100
1068  IF ZX = 2 THEN 1500
1070  IF ZX = 3 THEN 1800
1100  REM  *** SINKING FUND DEPR.
      ***
1102  Y = BAL(0) * ((R / (1 - (1 +
      R) ^  - N)))
1110  HOME : PRINT : PRINT : PRINT

1115  HOME : PRINT : PRINT : PRINT
      "PLEASE WAIT A MOMENT."
1140  FOR I = 1 TO N
1150  Y(I) = Y: NEXT I
1200  FOR I = 0 TO N
1230  X = 0
1240  FOR J = 1 TO N - I
1250  YY(J) = Y(J + I) / ((1 + R) ^
      J)
1260  X = X + YY(J)
1270  NEXT J:BA(I) = X: NEXT I
1275  FOR I = 1 TO N
1278  DEPR(I) = Y(I) - (R * BA(I -
      1)): NEXT I
1279  FOR I = 0 TO N:BA(I) =  INT
      (BA(I) * 100 + .5)

1280  DE(I) =  INT (DE(I) * 100 +
      .5)
1284  W = BA(I): GOSUB 400:BA$(I) =
      W$
1285  W = DE(I): GOSUB 400:DE$(I) =
      W$
1290  NEXT I
1300  GOTO 800
1500  REM  **** EXPONENTIAL
1510  HOME : PRINT : PRINT : PRINT
      "WHAT IS THE GROWTH RATE OF
      CASH FLOW";
1515  XZ = 0
1520  INPUT G:G = G / 100
1525  IF R = G THEN 210
1530  FOR I = 1 TO N
1540  U(I) = (1 + G) ^ I
1550  XZ = XZ + (((1 + G) ^ I) / (
      (1 + R) ^ I))
1560  NEXT I
1570  A = BAL(0) / XZ
1575  IF R = G THEN 1595
1580  R = (1 + R) / (1 + G) - 1
1590  GOTO 1102
1800  REM  **** SPECIFIC CASH FLO
      W
1810  HOME : PRINT : PRINT : PRINT

1822  PRINT : PRINT : PRINT
1840  PRINT : PRINT "THE CASH FLO
      W PROJECTED WILL BE ADJUSTED
      TO MAKE THE RATE OF RETURN C
      OMPATIBLE  WITH THE INITIAL
      INVESTMENT.     YOU WILLENTE
      R EACH YEAR'S C.F. IN TURN F
      OR THE  PLANNED LIFE OF THE
      ASSET."
1850  PRINT : PRINT "HIT ANY KEY
      TO CONTINUE": GET ZX$
1860  HOME : PRINT "INPUT THE CAS
      H FLOWS YEAR BY YEAR"
1865  PRINT : PRINT  TAB( 10)"YEA
      R      CASH FLOW"
```

```
1870  PRINT  TAB( 10)"----
      --------"
1880  FOR I = 1 TO N
1890  HTAB 12: PRINT I;: HTAB (22
      ): INPUT U(I)
1900  NEXT I
1910  PRINT : PRINT "ARE THESE TH
      E CORRECT VALUES (Y/N)";
1920  INPUT Y$: IF Y$ <  > "Y" THEN
      1880
1930  XZ = 0: FOR I = 1 TO N
1940  V(I) = U(I) / ((1 + R) ^ I)
1950  XZ = XZ + V(I): NEXT I
1960  A = BA(0) / XZ
1970  FOR I = 1 TO N
1972  Y(I) = U(I) * A
1974  NEXT I
1975  HOME : PRINT : PRINT : PRINT
      "PLEASE WAIT A MOMENT."
1980  GOTO 1200
2000  PR# 6
```

]RUN

```
**************************
*                        *
*  REPLACEMENT ECONOMY   *
*          BY            *
*    J.MORLEY ENGLISH    *
*         3/25/1983  *
**************************
```

DO YOU WISH HARD COPY? ?Y

PRESS ANY KEY TO CONTINUE

WHAT IS THE DISCOUNT RATE? ?10

WHAT IS THE CAPITAL INVESTMENT?
?10000

WHAT IS THE INITIAL CASH FLOW?
?2500

WHAT IS THE RATE OF TECHNICAL ADVANCE?
?12

WHAT IS THE RATE OF INCREASE OF
OPERATING EXPENSE? ?15

WHAT IS THE PROBABILITY OF
SUDDEN OBLSOLESCENCE? (0<P<1)?.3

IF IT OCCURS, WHAT DOES THE VALUE
OF THE ASSET BECOME?
?1000

WHAT IS THE RATE OF DECLINE OF THE
TERMINAL VALUE? (%)
?15

        PLEASE WAIT

TABLE OF COSTS
----- -- -----

YEAR	OPERATING COST	LEVELIZED OP. COST	CAPITAL COST*	COST OF SUDDEN OBS.	TOTAL COST/YEAR
1	2,875	2,750	12,320	16,400	31,470
2	3,306	2,881	7,228	13,850	23,959
3	3,802	3,016	5,649	11,682	20,347
4	4,373	3,155	4,964	9,840	17,959
5	5,028	3,297	4,649	8,274	16,220
6	5,783	3,444	4,532	3,471	11,447

7	6,650	3,595	4,541	2,906	11,041	
8	7,648	3,749	4,641	2,425	10,815	
9	8,795	3,907	4,815	2,016	10,738	
						OPTIMUM VALUE
10	10,114	4,069	5,055	1,669	10,792	

* NOTE: THE CAPITAL COST INCLUDES THE OPPORTUNITY COST
OF TECHNOLOGICAL IMPROVEMENT.

THE DATA FOR PROJECT ARE AS FOLLOWS:

INITIAL CAPITAL INVESTMENT IS..$10,000
INITIAL CASH FLOW IS $2,500
DISCOUNT RATE IS 10%
RATE OF TECHNOLOGY CHANGE IS 12%
THE RATE OF DECLINE IN TERMINAL VALUE IS 15% AND
 THE VALUE IN EVENT OF SUDDEN OBSOLESCENCE IS $1,000.
RATE OF INCREASE OF OPERATING COST..15%
PROBABILITY OF OBSOLESCENCE IS 0.3

THE ECONOMIC LIFE IS 9 YEARS
AND THE ANNUALIZED COST CORRESPONDING WITH THIS LIFE IS $10,738.
DO YOU WISH TO CHANGE PARAMETERS?
?N

```
]LIST

8  HOME
10 REM   MATRIX INVERSION
11 PRINT "        **************
   **********"
12 PRINT "         *
              *"
13 PRINT "         *
                 *
14 PRINT "         *     REPLACEMENT
   ECONOMY  *
15 PRINT "         *
                 *
16 PRINT "         *         BY
                 *
17 PRINT "         *
                 *

18 PRINT "         *     J.MORLEY
   ENGLISH  *
19 PRINT "         *
                 *
20 PRINT "         *          3
   /25/1983  *
21 PRINT "         **************
   **********"
22 PRINT : PRINT : PRINT : PRINT
   " PRESS ANY KEY TO CONTINUE"
   : GET Z$
23 HOME
40 DIM A(30),CF(30),CS(30),R(30)
   ,CP(30),CAP$(30),J$(50),COC(
   30),AOC(30),AOC$(30),OC(30)
42 DIM CS$(30),CP$(30),COC$(30),
   OC$(30)
```

```
45  DIM A$(30),U(30),V(30),TC(30)
    ,TC$(30),CAP(30),CF$(30)
48  GOTO 100
50  REM ++++ COMMAS AND DECIMALS

55  W$ = STR$ (W):WY$ = RIGHT$ (
    (W$),3)
57  IF LEN (W$) < 4 THEN 75
58  IF LEN (W$) > 6 THEN 70
64  WZ$ = LEFT$ ((W$), LEN (W$) -
    3)
66  W$ = WZ$ + "," + WY$: RETURN
70  WZ$ = LEFT$ ((W$), LEN (W$) -
    6)
72  WX$ = MID$ ((W$), LEN (W$) -
    5,3)
74  W$ = WZ$ + "," + WX$ + "," + W
    Y$: RETURN
75  RETURN
100 REM  DATA INPUT
130 PRINT : PRINT " WHAT IS THE
    DISCOUNT RATE? ";
140 INPUT I:I = I / 100
142 PRINT : PRINT " WHAT IS THE
    CAPITAL INVESTMENT? "
143 INPUT CAP
144 PRINT : PRINT " WHAT IS THE
    INITIAL CASH FLOW? "
149 INPUT CFO
150 PRINT : PRINT " WHAT IS THE
    RATE OF TECHNICAL ADVANCE?"
152 INPUT B:B = B / 100
155 PRINT : PRINT " WHAT IS THE
    RATE OF INCREASE OF"
156 PRINT "  OPERATING EXPENSE?
    ";: INPUT A
157 A = A / 100
162 PRINT : PRINT " WHAT IS THE
    PROBABILITY OF "
163 PRINT "  SUDDEN OBLSOLESCE
    NCE? (0<P<1)";
164 INPUT P:
165 PRINT : PRINT "  IF IT OCCUR
    S, WHAT DOES  THE VALUE OF T
    HE ASSET BECOME? "
166 INPUT TV
167 PRINT : PRINT " WHAT IS THE
    RATE OF DECLINE OF THE
    TERMINAL VALUE? (%) ": INPUT
    C:C = C / 100
170 W = CAP: GOSUB 50:CAP$ = W$
171 W = TV: GOSUB 50:TV$ = W$
172 W = CFO: GOSUB 50:CFO$ = W$
180 HOME : PRINT  TAB( 10)"PLEAS
    E WAIT"
184 FOR L = 5 TO 35 STEP 5
185 FOR J = 1 TO L:CAP(J) = CAP *
    ((1 + B) ^ J)
187 OC(J) = (CAP * ((1 - C) ^ J))
    - TV * P
188 OC(J) = INT (OC(J) + .5)
190 FOR K = 1 TO J:COC(J) = OC(J
    ) * ((1 + I) ^ - K) + COC(J
    )
192 NEXT K:AOC(J) = COC(J) * I /
    (1 - (1 + I) ^ - J)
194 NEXT J
200 REM  CASH FLOW
202 J = 0:CF(0) = CFO:A(0) = CFO
205 TC(0) = 1000000000000
210 FOR J = 1 TO L
215 U(J) = (1 + A) ^ J:V(J) = (1 +
    I) ^ J
220 CF(J) = CFO * U(J) + OC
225 IF A = I THEN 231
230 A(J) = I / (I - A) * ((V(J) -
    U(J)) / (V(J) - 1)) * CFO
231 A(J) = J * I * V(J) / (V(J) -
    1) * CFO
232 CP(J) = CAP(J) * I / (1 - ((1
    + I) ^ - J))
234 TC(J) = CP(J) + A(J) + AOC(J)

238 IF EL > 0 THEN 240
239 IF TC(J) > TC(J - 1) THEN EL
    = J - 1
```

```
240  NEXT J
241  IF EL = 0 THEN  NEXT L
242  FOR J = 1 TO EL + 1
243  A(J) = INT (A(J) + .5)
244  CP(J) =  INT (CP(J) + .5)
245  TC(J) =  INT (TC(J) + .5)
246  CF(J) =  INT (CF(J) + .5)
247  AOC(J) =  INT (AOC(J) + .5)
248  OC(J) =  INT (OC(J) + .5)
249  W = OC(J): GOSUB 50:OC$(J) =
     W$
250  W = AOC(J): GOSUB 50:AOC$(J) =
     W$
251  W = CF(J): GOSUB 50:CF$(J) =
     W$
252  W = TC(J): GOSUB 50:TC$(J) =
     W$
253  W = CP(J): GOSUB 50:CP$(J) =
     W$
254  W = A(J): GOSUB 50:A$(J) = W$

255  NEXT J
259  HOME
260  PRINT : PRINT : PRINT : PRINT

300  REM  PRINT OUT
310  HOME : PRINT " DO YOU WISH H
     ARD COPY? ";
320  INPUT Y$: IF Y$ = "Y" THEN 9
     00
327  HOME : PRINT  TAB( 18)"TABLE
      OF COSTS"
328  PRINT  TAB( 18)"----- -- ---
     --"
330  PRINT : PRINT "YEAR OPERATIN
     G LEVELIZED CAPITAL  TOTAL "
335  PRINT "         COST    OP. CO
     ST   COST     COST"
340  PRINT "----!---------!------
     --!---------!------"
350  FOR J = 1 TO EL + 1
354  J$(J) =  STR$ (J)

360  HTAB (3 - LEN (J$(J))): PRINT
     J$(J);: HTAB (12 - LEN (CF$
     (J))): PRINT CF$(J);: HTAB (
     22 - LEN (A$(J))): PRINT A$
     (J);
362  HTAB (31 - LEN (CP$(J))): PRINT
     CP$(J);
363  IF J = EL THEN 366
364  HTAB (39 - LEN (TC$(J))): PRINT
     TC$(J)
365  NEXT J: GOTO 376
366  POKE 36,41: PRINT "**": GOTO
     364
367  IF Y$ <  > "Y" THEN  GET XZ$

368  PRINT : PRINT "* NOTE: THE C
     APITAL COST INCLUDES THE OPP
     ORTUNITY COST": PRINT "
        OF TECHNOLOGICAL IMPROVEME
     NT."
369  PRINT : PRINT " THE DATA FOR
      PROJECT ARE AS FOLLOWS:"
370  PRINT : PRINT "  INITIAL CAP
     ITAL INVESTMENT IS..$";CAP$
372  PRINT "  INITIAL CASH FLOW I
     S .........$";CF0$
374  PRINT "  DISCOUNT RATE IS ..
     .............."; INT (I * 10
     000 + .5) / 100;"%"
376  PRINT "  RATE OF TECHNOLOGY
     CHANGE IS ....";B * 100;"%"
377  PRINT "  THE RATE OF DECLINE
      IN TERMINAL VALUE IS ";C *
     100;"% AND": PRINT "   THE V
     ALUE IN EVENT OF SUDDEN OBSO
     LESCENCE IS $";TV$;"."
378  PRINT "  RATE OF INCREASE OF
      OPERATING COST..";A * 100;"
     %"
379  P$ =  STR$ (P)
380  PRINT "  PROBABILITY OF OBSO
     LESCENCE IS  0";P$
382  PRINT : PRINT " THE ECONOMIC
```

```
            LIFE IS ";EL;" YEARS"        780  IF ZZ = 3 THEN  INPUT I:I =
383  PRINT " AND THE ANNUALIZED C             I / 100
     OST CORRESPONDING WITH THIS     785  IF ZZ = 4 THEN  INPUT P
     LIFE IS $";TC$(EL)"."          796  PRINT : PRINT " ANY OTHER "
385  GET XZ$                        800  INPUT Y$: IF Y$ = "Y" THEN 7
390  GOTO 675                            40
400  GET ZX$                        805  EL = 0
600  REM   INTERPOLATE              810  GOTO 184
650  PRINT : PRINT  INT (ECL * 10   900  REM  PRINT OUT FORMAT
     0 + .5) / 100;" YEARS "        910  PR# 1
660  ECL =  INT (ECL + .5)          927  HOME : PRINT  TAB( 18)"TABLE
665  PRINT : PRINT " THE ANNUALIZ        OF COSTS"
     ED COST FOR A LIFE OF ";ECL"   928  PRINT  TAB( 18)"----- -- ---
                                         --"
675  HOME : PRINT " DO YOU WISH T   930  PRINT : PRINT "YEAR OPERATIN
     O CHANGE PARAMETERS? "              G LEVELIZED CAPITAL   COST
680  INPUT YY$: IF YY$ = "Y" THEN        OF      TOTAL "
     740                            935  PRINT "         COST    OP. C
682  PR# 0                               OST   COST*  SUDDEN OBS.
685  GOTO 1000                           COST/YEAR"
700  REM  TOO SLOW A RISE           940  PRINT "----!---------!------
710  HOME : PRINT : PRINT                ----!---------!-----------!-
720  PRINT " THIS WILL NOT GIVE A        ----------"
     SOLUTION FOR"                  950  FOR J = 1 TO EL + 1
730  PRINT : PRINT " ECONOMIC LIF   954  J$(J) =  STR$ (J)
     E BELOW 30 YEARS."             960  HTAB (3 -  LEN (J$(J))): PRINT
740  PRINT : PRINT " TRY A NEW S         J$(J);: HTAB (14 -  LEN (CF$
     ET OF PARAMETERS!"                  (J))): PRINT CF$(J);: HTAB (
745  PRINT : PRINT "      1. OPER        24 -  LEN (A$(J))): PRINT A$
     ATING COST RATE"                    (J);
750  PRINT : PRINT "      2. TECH   962  HTAB (35 -  LEN (CP$(J))): PRINT
     NOLOGY RATE   "                     CP$(J);
760  PRINT : PRINT "      3. DISC   964  POKE 36,(46 -  LEN (AOC$(J))
     OUNT RATE    "                      ): PRINT AOC$(J);
765  PRINT : PRINT "      4. PROB   975  POKE 36,(59 -  LEN (TC$(J)))
     ABILITY OF OBSOLESCENCE"             : PRINT TC$(J)
770  PRINT : INPUT ZZ               976  IF J = EL THEN 979
771  PRINT " INPUT NEW RATE PARAM   978  NEXT J: GOTO 368
     ETER                          979  POKE 36,60: PRINT "OPTIMUM V
772  IF ZZ = 1 THEN  INPUT A:A =         ALUE": GOTO 978
     A / 100                        1000  GET ZX$: PR# 6
775  IF ZZ = 2 THEN  INPUT B:B =
     B / 100
```

JRUN PROJECT EVALUATION

```
*****************************
*                           *
*                           *
*    PROJECT EVALUATION      *
*                           *
*           BY               *
*                           *
*    J. MORLEY ENGLISH       *
*                           *
*              10/10/1983    *
*****************************
```

HIT ANY KEY TO CONTINUE.

THIS PROGRAM EVALUATES THE FEASIBILITY
    OF A PROPOSED PROJECT

IT TAKES INTO CONSIDERATION
    TAXES, DEBT FINANCING & INFLATION.

IT UTILIZES SEVERAL EVALUATION
    TECHNIQUES.

THE EVALUATION WILL BE RECORDED
    TO THE NEAREST WHOLE DOLLAR.

 HIT ANY KEY TO CONTINUE

WHAT IS THE NAME OF PROJECT?

 ?POTLINE

DATE?
?12/13/1983

WHAT IS EVALUATION TECHNIQUE DESIRED?

    1. NET PRESENT WORTH.

    2. INTERNAL RATE OF RETURN.

    3. REVENUE REQUIREMENTS.

    4. EXTERNAL RATE OF RETURN.

 INDICATE BY NUMBER.

?1
WHAT IS YOUR OPPORTUNITY COST OF
    CAPITAL (OCC%)?10

IS THIS CONTINUOUS OR DISCRETE C/D)?
?D

 WILL THE QUANTITY BE IN DOLLARS OR
    1000S OF DOLLARS?

 IF IN DOLLARS ENTER D, OTHERWISE T
?T

WHAT IS YOUR MARGINAL INCOME
    TAX RATE(%)?40

WHAT IS CAPITAL GAINS RATE(%)?16

WHAT IS THE PLANNED LIFE OF PROJECT
?8

CAPITAL INVESTMENT SCHEDULE

OVER HOW MANY YEARS IS THE INVESTMENT
    SPREAD OUT?
?3
YEAR   AMOUNT
----   -------
1   ?1000
2   ?20000
3   ?25000
```
```

CHECK TO SEE IF CORRECT AND IF OK
        INDICATE BY Y Y
COST SCHEDULE
---- --------

HOW MANY YEARS WILL IT TAKE FOR THE
OPERATING COST TO STABILIZE?
?3

YEAR	AMOUNT
1	?1234
2	?2345
3	?4321
4	4321
5	4321
6	4321
7	4321
8	4321

    CHECK TO SEE IF CORRECT AND IF OK
          INDICATE BY Y Y
REVENUE SCHEDULE
------- --------

HOW MANY YEARS DOES IT TAKE FOR REVENUE
  TO REACH CAPACITY LIMITS?4

YEAR	AMOUNT
1	?12000
2	?23000
3	?29000
4	?29500
5	29500
6	29500
7	29500
8	29500

    CHECK TO SEE IF CORRECT AND IF OK
          INDICATE BY Y Y
    WHAT IS THE DEPRECIABLE LIFE?

    ?15

WHAT IS METHOD OF DEPRECIATION?

1. STRAIGHT LINE

2. DECLINING BALANCE

3. SUM OF DIGITS

4. CROSS OVER -- DB TO SL
?4

WHAT IS THE NON DEPRECIABLE VALUE OF
    THE INVESTMENT?   ?19000

CHOOSE THE DECLINING BALANCE RATE:

     1) 1.5 TIMES   2) DOUBLE.
?1

WHAT IS THE TERMINAL VALUE
    OF THE PROJECT?10000

WHAT IS AMOUNT OF DEBT FINANCING
    AT PROJECT START UP?2000

WHAT IS THE INTEREST RATE ON DEBT?12

WHAT IS THE LIFE OF LOAN?30

WHAT IS THE METHOF OF REPAYMENT

    1. AMORTIZATION (1.E.,ANNUITY).

    2. INTEREST ONLY.

    INDICATE WHICH BY NUMBER
?1
NOW FOR INFLATION!

    WE WLL CONSIDER THREE SEPARATE RATES
    CAPITAL INVESTMENT PHASE
    FOR THE OPERATING COST AND
    FOR REVENUES.

```
DO YOU WISH TO USE CONSTANT DOL      6   29,500    4,321      234   1,944
I.E., NO INFLATION, Y/N)             7   29,500    4,321      232   1,652
?Y                                   8   29,500    4,321      230   1,405
PLEASE WAIT                          OPERATING CASH FLOW
ANNUAL PAYMENT IS  $248              ----------------------
---- --------
                                     YEAR TAXES  PROFIT  CASH FLOW  DCF
DEBT SCHEDULE: ANNUAL PAYMENT ON THE  1  2,458    3,687     8,068   7,335
     DEBT IS  $                       2  6,677   10,015    13,739  11,355
                                      3  8,510   12,765    15,931  11,969
                                      4  8,901   13,351    16,042  10,957
<< 248 >>                             5  9,063   13,594    15,881   9,861
 CAPITAL SCHEDULE                     6  9,200   13,801    15,745   8,888
------- --------                      7  9,318   13,977    15,629   8,020
                                      8  9,418   14,127    15,531   7,245

YEAR  INVESTMENT  CAPITALIZED VALUE
----  ----------  ----------- -----
                                     THE NET PRESENT WORTH OF THE PROJECT IS
  1        1,000        1,210               <<< $32,465 >>>
  2       20,000       22,000
  3       25,000       25,000
                     ---------------

                        48,210               DO YOU WISH TO TRY A DIFFERENT OCC?
  INCOME SCHEDULE                    ?N
  ====== ========
                                     DO YOU WISH TO FIND IRR? (Y/N)
YEAR  REVENUE  COST  INTEREST  DEPR.
----  -------  ----  --------  -----  ?N
  1   12,000   1,234     240   4,382
  2   23,000   2,345     239   3,724
  3   29,000   4,321     238   3,166  DO YOU WISH A PRINT OUT? (Y/N) ?Y
  4   29,500   4,321     237   2,691
  5   29,500   4,321     235   2,287 REPORT ON THE ECONOMIC EVALUATION OF:
```

POTLINE

DATE: 12/13/1983

THE MAGNITUDES ARE IN THOUSANDS OF DOLLARS

THE ECONOMIC EVALUATION IS BASED ON THE NET PRESENT WORTH APPROACH WITH THE
CONDITIONS OF THE PROJECT AS FOLLOWS:

1. THE RATE OF RETURN IS 10% PER YEAR. (THIS IS OCC OR IRR.)
2. THE DEBT FINANCING AMOUNTS TO $2,000 AT 12%, REQUIRING AN ANNUAL PAYMENT
   OF $248 AND THE LIFE OF THE LOAN IS 30 YEARS.
3. THE INCOME TAX RATE IS 40% AND THE CAPITAL GAINS RATE IS 16%.

4. THE METHOD OF DEPRECIATION IS BASED ON A CROSS-OVER FROM DECLINING-BALANCE TO STRAIGHT-LINE.
5. THE TERMINAL VALUE OF THE PROJECT IS $10,000 AND THE FINAL BOOK VALUE IS $26,959.
6. THE CAPITAL GAIN IS $-16,959.
7. THE RATES OF PRICE ESCALATION FOR CAPITAL COST, OPERATING COST, AND REVENUES ARE 0%, 0% & 0% RESPECTIVELY.
8. OTHER DATA ARE PROVIDED IN THE TABLES BELOW:

TABLE I

CASH FLOW EVALUATION

YEAR	CAPITAL INVESTMENT	REVENUE	OPERATING COSTS	INTEREST	DEPR.	BEFORE-TAX PROFIT	INCOME TAXES **	NET PROFIT	CASH FLOW	DCF
-2	1,000								-1,000	-1,210
-1	20,000								-20,000	-22,000
0	25,000								-25,000	-25,000
0	....FUTURE WORTH OF CAPITAL IS									-48,210 *
1		12,000	1,234	240	4,382	6,144	2,458	3,687	8,068	7,335
2		23,000	2,345	239	3,724	16,692	6,677	10,015	13,739	11,355
3		29,000	4,321	238	3,166	21,275	8,510	12,765	15,931	11,969
4		29,500	4,321	237	2,691	22,252	8,901	13,351	16,042	10,957
5		29,500	4,321	235	2,287	22,657	9,063	13,594	15,881	9,861
6		29,500	4,321	234	1,944	23,001	9,200	13,801	15,745	8,888
7		29,500	4,321	232	1,652	23,295	9,318	13,977	15,629	8,020
8		29,500	4,321	230	1,405	23,544	9,418	14,127	15,531	7,245

AFTER-TAX CAPITAL GAIN IS $-14,246
PRESENT WORTH OF CASH REALIZED ON SALE

NET PRESENT WORTH IS   32,465

* NOTE: THE REFERENCE ZERO TIME IS 2 YEARS FROM START OF CAPITAL INVESTMENT PHASE.
THE VALUES SHOWN ARE END OF YEAR AMOUNTS IF DISCRETE DISCOUNTING IS USED,
BUT DISTRIBUTED OVER THE YEAR FOR CONTINUOUS DISCOUNTING.

** NOTE: THE TAX MAY BE NEGATIVE ON THE ASSUMPTION THAT THERE IS OFFSETTING REVENUE FROM OTHER SOURCES.

TABLE II

RETURN ON EQUITY

YEAR	BOOK VALUE	NET PROFIT	RETURN ON INVESTMENT
1	43,829	3,687	8.41
2	40,104	10,015	24.97
3	36,939	12,765	34.56
4	34,249	13,351	38.98

5	31,961	13,594	42.53
6	30,017	13,801	45.98
7	28,364	13,977	49.28
8	26,959	14,127	52.4

N

DO YOU WISH TO TEST FOR SENSITIVITY?
?N

DO YOU WISH TO CHANGE DATA?
?N

YOU HAVE NOW EXITED THE PROGRAM.

LIST

```
10   HOME : PRINT : PRINT : PRINT
     : PRINT  TAB( 10)"*********
     ****************"
20   PRINT   TAB( 10)"*
                     *"
30   PRINT   TAB( 10)"*
                     *"
40   PRINT   TAB( 10)"*    PROJECT E
     VALUATION    *"
50   PRINT   TAB( 10)"*
                     *"
60   PRINT   TAB( 10)"*
     BY           *"
70   PRINT   TAB( 10)"*
                     *"
80   PRINT   TAB( 10)"*    J. MORLE
     Y ENGLISH   *"
90   PRINT   TAB( 10)"*
                     *"
100  PRINT   TAB( 10)"*
     4/10/1984 *"
110  PRINT   TAB( 10)"*************
     **************"
120  PRINT : PRINT : PRINT : PRINT
     " HIT ANY KEY TO CONTINUE."
130  GET ZX$
140  DIM K(10),K$(10),KC$,FW$(10)
     ,FW(10)
150  DIM I(30),I$(30),DB(30),DB$(
     30),Y(30),Y$(30),YY$(30)
160  DIM BV(32),BV$(32),DP(30),DP
     $(30),REV(30),REV$(30),C(30)
     ,C$(30),CC(30),RC(30)
170  DIM BP(30),BP$(30),PRO(30),P
     R$(30),CF(30),CF$(30),DCF(30
     ),DC$(30),TX(30),TX$(30),PAY
     (30),PAY$(30)
180  REM ** IF  GOSUB  SYMBOLS **
     ***
190  REM    N = PROJECT PLANNING L
     IFE:REM ND  =  LIFE OF DEBT
     : NL = DEPRECIATION LIFE:
200  REM  BV = BOOK VALUE :REM DP
     = DEPR.:REM FK=TOTAL CAPITA
```
```
     L COST:REM NDP = NON  DEPREC
     IABLE ASSET VALUE:REM SL = S
     TRAIGHT LINE DEPR AMOUNT: RE
     M A = RATE OF DB DEPR.
210  REM    R = DEBT INTEREST RATE
     : REM I = DISCOUNT RATE: REM
     I1 = INFLATION RATE FOR CAP
     ITAL, I2 FOR COSTS, I3 FOR R
     EVENUES
220  REM   T = INCOME TAX RATE, CG
     CAPITAL GAINS TAX RATE
230  REM    KC= CAPITAL INVESTMEN
     T,  K = INFLATED CAPITAL
240  REM  CC = COST,  C = INFLATE
     D COST:REM  RC= REVENUE,REV
     = INFLATE REVENUE:REM
250  GOTO 1740
260  FY$ =  RIGHT$ (F$,3):FZ$ = LEFT$
     (F$, LEN (F$) - 3): IF  LEN
     (F$) > 6 THEN 350
270  IF Z = 1 THEN Z$ = "NET PRES
     ENT WORTH"
280  IF Z = 2 THEN Z$ = "INTERNAL
     RATE OF RETURN"
290  IF Z = 3 THEN Z$ = "REVENUE
     REQUIREMENTS"
300  IF Z = 4 THEN Z$ = "EXTERNAL
     RATE OF  RETURN"
310  RETURN
320  F$ =   STR$ ( INT (F + .5)):FY
     $ =  RIGHT$ ((F$),3): IF  LEN
     (F$) < 4 THEN 430
330  IF ( LEN (F$) = 4 AND F < 0)
     THEN 430
340  IF  LEN (F$) > 6 THEN 370
350  FZ$ =  LEFT$ (F$, LEN (F$) -
     3)
360  F$ = FZ$ + "," + FY$: RETURN
370  IF ( LEN (F$) = 7 AND F < 0)
     THEN 410
380  FZ$ =  LEFT$ (F$, LEN (F$) -
     6)
390  FX$ =  MID$ (F$,( LEN (F$) -
     5),3):FZ$ =  LEFT$ (F$, LEN
     (F$) - 6): GOTO 420
400  FX$ =  MID$ (F$,( LEN (F$) -
     5),3):FZ$ =  LEFT$ (F$, LEN
     (F$) - 6): GOTO 410
410  FX$ =  MID$ (F$,( LEN (F$) -
     5),3):F$ = "-" + FX$ + "," +
     FY$: RETURN
420  F$ = FZ$ + "," + FX$ + "," +
     FY$
430  RETURN
440  REM  *** DISCOUNT FUNCTION
450  PW = 0
```

```
460  FOR J = 1 TO N
470  PW = PW + (CF(J) * ((1 + Y) ^
     - J))
480  NEXT J
490  PW$ = STR$ ( INT (PW + .5))
500  RETURN
510  REM  **** FUTURE WORTH ***
520  FK = 0
530  FOR J = 1 TO M
540  FW(J) = K(J) * (1 + Y) ^ (M -
     J)
550  F = K(J): GOSUB 320:K$(J) = F
     $
560  F = FW(J): GOSUB 320:FW$(J) =
     F$
570  FK = FK + FW(J)
580  NEXT J
590  F = FK: GOSUB 320:FK$ = F$
600  RETURN
610  REM  **** DEPR ... SL ****
620  BV(0) = FK
630  FOR J = 1 TO NL
640  DP(J) = (FK - LV) / NL
650  F = DP(J): GOSUB 320:DP$(J) =
     F$
660  BV(J) = BV(J - 1) - DP(J)
670  NEXT J
680  IF NL > = N THEN 710
690  FOR J = NL + 1 TO N
700  BV(J) = LV: NEXT J
710  FOR J = 1 TO N
720  F = BV(J): GOSUB 320:BV$(J) =
     F$
730  NEXT J
740  RETURN
750  REM  ***DEPR ... DB***
760  BV(0) = FK
770  FOR J = 1 TO N
780  BV(J) = (BV(J - 1) - LV) * (1
     - A) + LV
790  DP(J) = (BV(J - 1) - LV) * A
800  DP$(J) =  STR$ ( INT (DP(J) +
     .5))
810  F = DP(J): GOSUB 320:DP$(J) =
     F$
820  NEXT J
830  REM  *** DEPR ..SUM OF DIGIT
     S ****
840  BV(0) = FK
850  SL = (1 + NL) * NL / 2
860  FOR J = 1 TO NL
870  DP(J) = (NL - J + 1) / SL * (
     FK - LV)
880  F = DP(J): GOSUB 320:DP$(J) =
     F$
890  BV(J) = BV(J - 1) - DP(J)
900  F = BV(J): GOSUB 320:BV$(J) =
     F$
910  NEXT J
920  IF NL > = N THEN 950
930  FOR J = NL + 1 TO N
940  BV(J) = LV: NEXT J
950  FOR J = 1 TO N
960  F = BV(J): GOSUB 320:BV$(J) =
     F$
970  NEXT J
980  RETURN
990  REM  **** DEPR .... DB/SL***
1000 BV(0) = FK
1010 F = BV(0): GOSUB 320:BV$(0) =
     F$
1020 FOR J = 1 TO NL
1030 BV(J) = (FK - LV) * ((1 - A)
     ^ J) + LV
1040 F = BV(J): GOSUB 320:BV$(J) =
     F$
1050 SL = (BV(J) - LV) / (NL - J)
1060 IF J > N THEN 1130
1070 DP(J) = (BV(J - 1) - LV) * A
1080 F = DP(J): GOSUB 320:DP$(J) =
     F$
1090 IF SL = > DP(J) THEN 1110
1100 NEXT J
1110 FOR J = J TO NL
1120 DP(J) = SL:BV(J) = BV(J - 1)
     - SL: NEXT J
1130 FOR J = 1 TO N
1140 F = DP(J): GOSUB 320:DP$(J) =
     F$
1150 F = BV(J): GOSUB 320:BV$(J) =
     F$
1160 NEXT J
1170 RETURN
1180 REM  *** DEBT SCHEDULE***
1190 REM  *** AMORTIZATION***
1200 PAY = DEBT * (R / (1 - (1 +
     R) ^ - ND))
1210 F = PAY: GOSUB 320:PAY$ = F$
1220 DB(0) = DEBT
1230 FOR J = 1 TO ND
1240 DB(J) = DB(J - 1) * (1 + R) -
     PAY
1250 F = DB(J): GOSUB 320:DB$(J) =
     F$
1260 I(J) = DB(J - 1) * R
1270 F = PAY(J): GOSUB 320:PAY$(J
     ) = F$
1280 F = I(J): GOSUB 320:I$(J) =
     F$
1290 NEXT J
1300 RETURN
1310 REM  INTEREST ONLY****
1320 PAY = DEBT * R
1330 F = PAY: GOSUB 320:PAY$ = F$
1340 FOR J = 1 TO ND
1350 I(J) = DEBT * R
1360 F = I(J): GOSUB 320:I$(J) =
     F$
1370 DB(J) = DEBT
1380 F = DB(J): GOSUB 320:DB$(J) =
     F$
1390 NEXT J
1400 RETURN
1410 REM  *** INFLATION ***
1420 FOR J = 1 TO M
1430 K(J) = (1 + I1) ^ (J - 1) *
     KC(J)
1440 F = K(J): GOSUB 320:K$(J) =
     F$
```

```
1450  NEXT J
1460  FOR J = 1 TO N
1470  C(J) = (1 + I2) ^ (M + J) *
      CC(J)
1480  F = C(J): GOSUB 320:C$(J) =
      F$
1490  REV(J) = (1 + I3) ^ (M + J) *
      RC(J)
1500  F = REV(J): GOSUB 320:REV$(J
      ) = F$
1510  NEXT J
1520  RETURN
1530  REM  **** TAXES ****
1540  REM  *** INCOME ***
1550  FOR J = 1 TO N
1560  TX(J) = T * (CF(J) - DP(J))
1570  F = TX(J): GOSUB 320:TX$(J) =
      F$
1580  PROFIT(J) = (1 - T)(CF(J) -
      DP(J))
1590  F = PRO(J): GOSUB 320:PRO$(J
      ) = F$
1600  NEXT J
1610  RETURN
1620  REM *** CHECK DATA***
1630  PRINT : PRINT " CHECK TO SE
      E IF CORRECT AND IF OK": INPUT
      "      INDICATE BY Y ";OK$
1640  RETURN
1650  REM  **** CAPITAL GAINS***
1660  GAIN = TV - BV(N)
1670  F = GA: GOSUB 320:GA$ = F$
1680  NCG = GAIN * (1 - CG)
1690  F = NCG: GOSUB 320:NCG$ = F$
1700  PCASHREALIZED = (TV - DB(N) -
      (GAIN * CG)) * ((1 + Y) ^ ( -
      N))
1710  P = PW - FK + PC
1720  F = P: GOSUB 320:P$ = F$
1730  RETURN
1740  REM  **** PROJECT DESCRIPTI
      ON
1750  HOME
1760  PRINT : PRINT : PRINT "THIS
      PROGRAM EVALUATES THE FEASI
      BILITY          OF A PROPOSED P
      ROJECT"
1770  PRINT : PRINT "IT TAKES INT
      O CONSIDERATION"
1780  PRINT "     TAXES, DEBT FINAN
      CING & INFLATION."
1790  PRINT : PRINT "IT UTILIZES
      SEVERAL EVALUATION
         TECHNIQUES."
1800  PRINT : PRINT "THE EVALUATI
      ON WILL BE RECORDED
         TO THE NEAREST WHOLE DOLL
      AR."
1810  PRINT : PRINT : PRINT " HIT
      ANY KEY TO CONTINUE "
1820  GET A$
1830  HOME : PRINT
1840  PRINT "WHAT IS THE NAME OF
      PROJECT?"
1850  PRINT : INPUT "";NA$
1860  PRINT : PRINT : PRINT "DATE
      ?  ";: INPUT "";DA$
1870  HOME : PRINT : PRINT "WHAT
      IS EVALUATION TECHNIQUE DESI
      RED?"
1880  RR = 0
1890  PRINT : PRINT "     1. NET P
      RESENT WORTH."
1900  PRINT : PRINT "     2. INTER
      NAL RATE OF RETURN."
1910  PRINT : PRINT "     3. REVEN
      UE REQUIREMENTS."
1920  PRINT : PRINT "     4. EXTER
      NAL RATE OF RETURN."
1930  PRINT : INVERSE : PRINT " S
      ELECT ";: NORMAL
1940  PRINT : INPUT "";Z: HOME
1950  IF Z > 4 THEN 1870
1960  PRINT "WHAT IS YOUR OPPORTU
      NITY COST OF CAPITAL (OCC%)"
      ;
1970  INPUT "";Y:Y = Y / 100
1980  PRINT : PRINT "IS THIS CONT
      INUOUS OR DISCRETE C/D)?"
1990  INPUT "";C$: IF C$ = "C" THEN
      Y = EXP (Y) - 1
2000  PRINT : PRINT " WILL THE QU
      ANTITY BE IN DOLLARS OR
      1000S OF DOLLARS?"
2010  PRINT " IF IN DOLLARS ENTER
      D, OTHERWISE T": INPUT "";D
      O$
2020  PRINT : PRINT "WHAT IS YOUR
      MARGINAL INCOME
      TAX RATE(%)";
2030  INPUT "";T:T = T / 100
2040  PRINT : PRINT "WHAT IS CAPI
      TAL GAINS RATE(%)";
2050  INPUT "";CG:CG = CG / 100
2060  IF QQ = 1 THEN 2110
2070  PRINT : PRINT "WHAT IS THE
      PLANNED LIFE OF PROJECT? ":
      INPUT "";N
2080  IF N < = 30 THEN 2110
2090  PRINT " YOU CANNOT HAVE > .
      30 YEARS BECAUSE": PRINT " T
      HAT IS ALL THAT CAN BE HANDL
      ED BY PROGRAM"
2100  GOTO 2070
2110  HOME
2120  IF QQ = 1 THEN 2570
2130  PRINT : PRINT "CAPITAL INVE
      STMENT SCHEDULE"
2140  PRINT : PRINT " OVER HOW MA
      NY YEARS IS THE INVESTMENT
         SPREAD OUT?"
2150  INPUT "";M
2160  IF M < = 10 THEN 2190
2170  PRINT " TOO LONG A PERIOD."
      : PRINT "MUST BE LESS THAN 1
      1 YEARS."
2180  GOTO 2130
2190  PRINT "YEAR";: HTAB (15): PRINT
      "AMOUNT"
2200  PRINT "----";: HTAB (15): PRINT
      "_____ "
2210  FOR J = 1 TO M: PRINT J;
```

```
2220  HTAB (15): INPUT "";KC(J)
2230  NEXT J
2240  GOSUB 1620
2250  HOME : IF OK$ < > "Y" THEN
      2190
2260  HOME : PRINT "COST SCHEDULE
      "
2270  PRINT "---- --------"
2280  PRINT : PRINT "HOW MANY YEA
      RS WILL IT TAKE FOR THE":
      PRINT"OPERATING COST TO
      STABILIZE ?"
2290  INPUT "";NN
2300  PRINT "YEAR";: HTAB (15):
      PRINT"AMOUNT"
2310  PRINT "----";: HTAB (15):
      PRINT "------"
2320  FOR J = 1 TO NN
2330  PRINT J;: HTAB (15): INPUT
      "";CC(J)
2340  IF J > N THEN 2400
2350  NEXT J
2360  FOR J = NN + 1 TO N
2370  CC(J) = CC(J - 1)
2380  PRINT J;: HTAB (16): PRINT
      CC(J - 1)
2390  NEXT J
2400  GOSUB 1620
2410  HOME : IF OK$ < > "Y" THEN
      2260
2420  HOME : PRINT "REVENUE SCHED
      ULE"
2430  PRINT "------- --------"
2440  PRINT : PRINT "HOW MANY YEA
      RS DOES IT TAKE FOR REVENUE"
      : PRINT " TO REACH CAPACITY
      LIMITS? ";: INPUT "";NR
2450  PRINT "YEAR";: HTAB (15):
      PRINT"AMOUNT"
2460  PRINT "----";: HTAB (15):
      PRINT "------"
2470  FOR J = 1 TO NR
2480  PRINT J;: HTAB (15): INPUT
      "";RC(J)
2490  IF J > = N THEN 2550
2500  NEXT J
2510  FOR J = NR + 1 TO N
2520  RC(J) = RC(J - 1)
2530  PRINT J;: HTAB (16): PRINT
      RC(J - 1)
2540  NEXT J
2550  GOSUB 1620
2560  IF OK$ < > "Y" THEN 2420
2570  HOME : IF QQ = 1 THEN 2630
2580  PRINT " WHAT IS THE DEPREC
      IABLE LIFE?"
2590  INPUT "";NL
2600  IF NL < = 30 THEN 2630
2610  PRINT " YOU CANNOT HAVE > .
      30 YEARS BECAUSE": PRINT " T
      HAT IS ALL THAT CAN BE HANDL
      ED          BY PROGRAM"
2620  GOTO 2580
2630  PRINT : PRINT "WHAT IS METH
      OD OF DEPRECIATION?"
2640  PRINT : PRINT "        1. ST
      RAIGHT LINE

2650  PRINT : PRINT "        2. DE
      CLINING BALANCE
2660  PRINT : PRINT "        3. SU
      M OF DIGITS
2670  PRINT : PRINT "        4. CR
      OSS OVER -- DB TO SL
2680  INPUT "";ZZ: HOME
2690  PRINT : PRINT "WHAT IS THE
      NON DEPRECIABLE VALUE OF ":
      PRINT"  THE INVESTMENT?    ";
2700  INPUT "";LV: HOME
2710  F = LV: GOSUB 320:LV$ = F$
2720  IF ZZ = 1 THEN 2780
2730  IF ZZ = 3 THEN 2780
2740  PRINT : PRINT "CHOOSE THE D
      ECLINING BALANCE RATE:"
2750  PRINT : PRINT "      1) 1.5
      TIMES    2) DOUBLE. "
2760  INPUT "";A: IF A = 1 THEN A
      = 1.5
2770  A = A / 10
2780  IF ZZ > 4 THEN 2630
2790  HOME : PRINT : PRINT "WHAT
      IS THE TERMINAL VALUE
            OF THE PROJECT";
2800  INPUT "";TV
2810  F = TV: GOSUB 320:TV$ = F$
2820  PRINT : PRINT "WHAT IS AMOU
      NT OF DEBT FINANCING
      AT PROJECT START UP? ";:
      INPUT"";DEBT
2830  IF DEBT = 0 THEN 2990
2840  F = DEBT: GOSUB 320:DEBT$ =
      F$
2850  PRINT : PRINT "WHAT IS THE
      INTEREST RATE ON DEBT? ";:
      INPUT"";R
2860  R = R / 100
2870  IF QQ = 1 THEN 2930
2880  PRINT : PRINT "WHAT IS THE
      LIFE OF LOAN? ";: INPUT "";N
      D
2890  IF QQ = 1 THEN 2930
2900  IF ND < = 30 THEN 2930
2910  PRINT " YOU CANNOT HAVE >
      30 YEARS BECAUSE": PRINT " T
      HAT IS ALL THAT CAN BE HANDL
      ED          BY PROGRAM"
2920  GOTO 2880
2930  PRINT : PRINT "WHAT IS THE
      METHOF OF REPAYMENT"
2940  PRINT : PRINT "        1. AMOR
      TIZATION (1.E.,ANNUITY).
2950  PRINT : PRINT "        2. INTE
      REST ONLY.
2960  PRINT : PRINT "   INDICATE W
      HICH BY NUMBER"
2970  INPUT "";ZX: HOME
2980  IF ZX > 2 THEN 2930
2990  HOME : PRINT "NOW FOR INFLA
      TION!"
3000  PRINT : PRINT " WE WLL CON
      SIDER THREE SEPARATE RATES"
3010  PRINT "     CAPITAL INVESTME
      NT PHASE",: PRINT "    FOR T
      HE OPERATING COST AND ": PRINT
      "    FOR REVENUES. "
```

```
3020  PRINT : PRINT "DO YOU WISH        3450  HOME : PRINT " CAPITAL SCHE
      TO USE CONSTANT DOLLARS":             DULE"
      PRINT "I.E., NO INFLATION,      3460  PRINT "------- --------"
      Y/N)"                           3470  PRINT : PRINT "YEAR  INVEST
3030  INPUT "";VY$: IF VY$ = "Y"            MENT  CAPITALIZED VALUE"
      THEN 3060                       3480  PRINT "----  ----------  --
3040  PRINT : INPUT "INPUT THE TH          --------- -----"
      REE RATES IN %,SEPARATED BY     3490  FOR J = 1 TO M
      COMMAS ";I1,I2,I3               3500  HTAB (3 - LEN ( STR$ (J)))
3050  I1 = I1 / 100:I2 = I2 / 100:          : PRINT J;: HTAB (18 - LEN
      I3 = I3 / 100                        (K$(J))): PRINT K$(J);
3060  GOSUB 3080                      3510  HTAB (30 - LEN (FW$(J))):
3070  GOTO 3370                             PRINT FW$(J)
3080  REM  **** CALCULATE ****        3520  NEXT J
3090  HOME : PRINT "PLEASE WAIT"       3530  HTAB (20): PRINT "---------
3100  GOSUB 1410                            -----"
3110  GOSUB 510                        3540  HTAB (30 - LEN (FK$)): PRINT
3120  IF DEBT = 0 THEN 3150                 FK$
3130  IF ZX = 1 THEN  GOSUB 1190      3550  GET Z$
3140  IF ZX = 2 THEN  GOSUB 1310      3560  HOME : PRINT " INCOME SCHED
3150  IF ZZ = 1 THEN  GOSUB 610             ULE "
3160  IF ZZ = 2 THEN  GOSUB 750       3570  PRINT " ====== ========"
3170  IF ZZ = 3 THEN  GOSUB 830       3580  PRINT "YEAR REVENUE  COST
3180  IF ZZ = 4 THEN  GOSUB 990             INTEREST  DEPR."
3190  REM  *** PROFIT CALCULATION     3590  PRINT "---- --------  ----
                                            -------- ------"
3200  REM  **** CALCULATION OF PR     3600  FOR J = 1 TO N
      OFITS***                        3610  HTAB (3 - LEN ( STR$ (J)))
3210  FOR J = 1 TO N                        : PRINT J;
3220  BPROFIT(J) = REV(J) - C(J) -    3620  HTAB (12 - LEN (REV$(J))):
      I(J) - DP(J)                         PRINT REV$(J);: HTAB (22 -
3230  F = BP(J): GOSUB 320:BP$(J) =        LEN (C$(J))): PRINT C$(J);:
      F$                                   HTAB (31 - LEN (I$(J))):
3240  PROFIT(J) = BPROFIT(J) * (1 -        PRINT I$(J);
      T)                              3630  HTAB (40 - LEN (DP$(J))):
3250  F = PRO(J): GOSUB 320:PRO$(J         PRINT DP$(J)
      ) = F$                          3640  NEXT J
3260  TX(J) = BPROFIT(J) * T          3650  GET Z$
3270  F = TX(J): GOSUB 320:TX$(J) =   3660  HOME : PRINT "OPERATING CAS
      F$                                   H FLOW"
3280  CF(J) = PROFIT(J) + DP(J)       3670  PRINT "--------------------
3290  CF$(J) = STR$ ( INT (CF(J) +         -"
      .5))                            3680  PRINT "YEAR TAXES  PROFIT
3300  F = CF(J): GOSUB 320:CF$(J) =        CASH FLOW  DCF"
      F$                              3690  FOR J = 1 TO N
3310  NEXT J                          3700  HTAB (3 - LEN ( STR$ (J)))
3320  FOR J = 1 TO N:DCF(J) = CF(          : PRINT J;
      J) * ((1 + Y) ^  - J)          3710  HTAB (10 - LEN (TX$(J))):
3330  F = DCF(J): GOSUB 320:DCF$(J         PRINT
      ) = F$                               TX$(J);: HTAB (18 - LEN (PR
3340  NEXT J: GOSUB 440                    O$(J))): PRINT PRO$(J);: HTAB
3350  RETURN                               (28 - LEN (CF$(J))): PRINT
3360  REM  ***** DATA FORMAT****           CF$(J);: HTAB (36 - LEN (DC
3370  FOR J = 1 TO N                       F$(J))): PRINT DCF$(J)
3380  PAY(J) = PAY - I(J)             3720  NEXT J
3390  F = PAY(J): GOSUB 320:PAY$(J    3730  GET Z$
      ) = F$                          3740  REM  **** RECAP ****
3400  NEXT J                          3750  REM  **** PRESENT WORTH ***
3410  PRINT "ANNUAL PAYMENT IS   $          *
      ";PAY$                          3760  GOSUB 1650
3420  PRINT "---- --------- "         3770  IF Z = 1 THEN 3810
3430  HOME : PRINT "DEBT SCHEDULE     3780  IF RR = 1 THEN 3810
      : ";                            3790  IF Z = 2 THEN 4840
3440  PRINT "ANNUAL PAYMENT ON TH     3800  IF Z = 3 THEN  GOSUB 5070: GOTO
      E DEBT IS $": PRINT : PRINT          5210
      "<< ";PAY$;" >>"                3810  HOME :
```

```
3820   PRINT : PRINT "THE NET PRES
       ENT WORTH OF THE PROJECT IS"
       : PRINT "        <<<  $";P$;"
       >>>
3830   P(1) = P
3840   IF RR = 1 THEN 3960
3850   PRINT : PRINT : PRINT : PRINT
       "     DO YOU WISH TO TRY A D
       IFFERENT OCC?"
3860   INPUT "";Y$: IF Y$ < > "Y"
       THEN 3900
3870   PRINT : PRINT : INPUT "NEW
       RATE  ";Y:Y = Y / 100
3880   GOSUB 3200: GOSUB 1650
3890   GOTO 3450
3900   REM  *** ITERATE FOR IRR **
       **
3910   IF Z = 4 THEN 5230
3920   PRINT : PRINT " DO YOU WISH
       TO FIND IRR? (Y/N) ";
3930   PRINT : INPUT "";Y$
3940   IF Y$ = "Y" THEN 4810
3950   IF RR < > 1 THEN 3970
3960   PRINT : PRINT " THE PRICE O
       F THE PRODUCT IS ": PRINT :
       PRINT "     << $"; INT (S *
       1000 + .
       5) / 1000;" >>"
3970   PRINT : PRINT " DO YOU WISH
       A PRINT OUT? (Y/N) ";
3980   INPUT "";Y$: IF Y$ = "Y"
       THEN 4000
3990   GOTO 5320
4000   REM  *** PRINT OUT FORMAT *
       **
4010   PR# 1
4020   PRINT  CHR$ (15)
4030   GOSUB 270
4040   HOME : PRINT  TAB( 7)"REPOR
       T ON THE ECONOMIC EVALUATION
       OF:"
4050   PRINT : POKE 36,(60 -  INT
       (( LEN (NA$) / 2))): PRINT
       CHR$(14)NA$
4060   POKE 36,86: PRINT "DATE: ";
       DA$
4070   IF DO$ = "D" THEN 4090
4080   PRINT : PRINT "THE MAGNITUD
       ES ARE IN THOUSANDS OF DOLLA
       RS": PRINT
4090   PRINT : PRINT  TAB( 7)"THE
       ECONOMIC EVALUATION IS BASED
       ON THE ";Z$;" APPROACH WITH
       THE CONDITIONS OF THE PROJE
       CT AS FOLLOWS:"
4100   PRINT : HTAB (10): PRINT "1
       . THE RATE OF RETURN IS ";:
       HTAB(13): PRINT  INT (Y *
       10000 +.5) / 100;"% PER
       YEAR.";
4110   PRINT " (THIS IS OCC OR IRR
       .)
4120   IF DEBT = 0 THEN 4150
4130   HTAB (10): PRINT "2. THE DE
       BT FINANCING AMOUNTS TO  $";
       DEBT$;" AT ";R * 100;"%, REQ
```

```
       UIRING AN ANNUAL PAYMENT OF
       $";PAY$;"  AND"
4140   HTAB (13): PRINT "THE LIFE
       OF THE LOAN IS ";ND;" YEARS.
       ": GOTO 4160
4150   HTAB (10): PRINT "2. THERE
       IS NO DEBT FINANCING."
4160   HTAB (10): PRINT "3. THE IN
       COME TAX RATE IS ";T * 100;"
       % AND THE CAPITAL GAINS RATE
       IS ";CG * 100;"%."
4170   HTAB (10): PRINT "4. THE ME
       THOD OF DEPRECIATION IS ";
4180   IF ZZ = 1 THEN ZZ$ = "STRAI
       GHT LINE"
4190   IF ZZ = 2 THEN ZZ$ = "DECLI
       NING BALANCE."
4200   IF ZZ = 3 THEN ZZ$ = "SUM O
       F THE DIGITS."
4210   IF ZZ = 4 THEN ZZ$ = "BASED
       ON A CROSS-OVER FROM DECLIN
       ING-BALANCE TO STRAIGHT-LINE
       ."
4220   PRINT ZZ$
4230   HTAB (10): PRINT "5. THE TE
       RMINAL VALUE OF THE PROJECT
       IS $";TV$;" AND THE FINAL BO
       OK VALUE IS $";BV$(N);"."
4240   IF DEBT = 0 THEN  GOTO 4250
       : HTAB (10): PRINT "THE MORT
       GAGE BALANCE IS $";DB$(N);".
       "
4250   PRINT  TAB( 10)"6. THE CAPI
       TAL GAIN IS $";GA$;"."
4260   PRINT  TAB( 10)"7. THE RATE
       S OF PRICE ESCALATION FOR CA
       PITAL COST, OPERATING COST,
       AND REVENUES ARE ";I1 * 100;
       "%, ";I2 * 100;"% & ";I3 * 1
       00;"% RESPECTIVELY."
4270   PRINT  TAB( 10)"8. OTHER DA
       TA ARE PROVIDED IN THE TABLE
       S BELOW:"
4280   PRINT
4290   POKE 36,59: PRINT  CHR$ (14
       )"TABLE I"
4300   POKE 36,59: PRINT "--------
       -----"
4310   POKE 36,48: PRINT  CHR$ (14
       )"CASH FLOW EVALUATION": PRINT
4320   HTAB (16): PRINT "CAPITAL";
       : HTAB 38: PRINT "OPERATING"
       ;: POKE 36,71: PRINT "BEFORE
       -TAX";: POKE 36,82: PRINT "I
       NCOME";: POKE 36,94: PRINT "
       NET"
4330   PRINT  TAB( 10)"YEAR INVEST
       MENT  REVENUE      COSTS
       INTEREST      DEPR.      PROF
       IT     TAXES **    PROFIT
       CASH FLOW     DCF"
4340   PRINT  TAB( 10)"----!------
       ----------!----------!------
       ----------!----------!------
       ----!----------!----------!
       ----------!----------"
```

```
4350  FOR J = 1 TO M
4360  HTAB (12 - LEN ( STR$ (J))
      ): PRINT J - M;
4370  HTAB (26 - LEN (K$(J))):
      PRINT K$(J);: POKE 36,(113 -
      LEN (K$(J))): PRINT "-";K$
      (J);: POKE 36,(124 - LEN
      (FW$(J)): PRINT "-";FW$(J)
4380  NEXT J
4390  HTAB 12: PRINT "0 .........
      ...........................
      ...........................
      ..........FUTURE WORTH OF CA
      PITAL IS";: POKE 36,(124 -
      LEN (FK$)): PRINT "-";FK$;" *"
4400  FOR J = 1 TO N
4410  HTAB (13 - LEN ( STR$ (J))
      ): PRINT J;
4420  HTAB (37 - LEN (REV$(J))):
      PRINT REV$(J);: POKE 36,(46
      - LEN (C$(J))): PRINT C$(J
      );: POKE 36,(57 - LEN (I$(J
      ))): PRINT I$(J);
4430  POKE 36,(68 - LEN (DP$(J))
      ): PRINT DP$(J);: POKE 36,(8
      1 - LEN (BP$(J))): PRINT BP
      $(J);: POKE 36,(92 - LEN (T
      X$(J))): PRINT TX$(J);
4440  POKE 36,(103 - LEN (PR$(J)
      )): PRINT PR$(J);: POKE 36,(
      114 - LEN (CF$(J))): PRINT
      CF$(J);: POKE 36,(125 - LEN
      (DCF$(J))): PRINT DCF$(J)
4450  NEXT J
4460  PRINT  TAB( 10)"-----------
      ----------------------------
      ----------------------------
      ----------------------------
      ----------------------------"
4470  POKE 36,51: PRINT "AFTER-TA
      X CAPITAL GAIN IS $";NCG$
4480  POKE 36,51: PRINT "PRESENT
      WORTH OF CASH REALIZED ON SA
      LE ";: POKE 36,(125 - LEN (
      PC$)): PRINT (PC$)
4490  POKE 36,117: PRINT "-------
      -----"
4500  POKE 36,93: PRINT "NET PRES
      ENT WORTH IS";
4510  POKE 36,(125 - LEN (P$)):
      PRINT P$
4520  IF RR <  > 1 THEN 4590
4530  IF QQ = 0 THEN 4570
4540  PRINT " THE PRICE OF THE PR
      ODUCT TO GENERATE THE REQUIR
      ED REVENUE IS ";
4550  PRINT : PRINT "  << "; INT
      (S * 1000 + .5) / 1000;" >>
      TIMES THE PRICE USED ORIGINA
      LLY"
4560  PRINT " IF THE ORIGINAL INP
      UT WAS QUANTITY, THEN THIS N
      UMBER IS THE PRICE. ": GOTO
      4590
4570  PRINT " THE PRICE OF THE PR
      ODUCT TO GENERATE THE REQUIR
      ED REVENUE IS "
4580  PRINT : PRINT "   << $"; INT
      (S * 1000 + .5) / 1000;" >>"
4590  PRINT : PRINT  TAB( 10)"* N
      OTE: THE REFERENCE ZERO TIME
      IS ";M - 1;" YEARS FROM STA
      RT OF CAPITAL INVESTMENT PHA
      SE."
4600  PRINT  TAB( 18)"THE VALUES
      SHOWN ARE END OF YEAR AMOUNT
      S IF DISCRETE DISCOUNTING IS
      USED,": PRINT  TAB( 18)"BUT
      DISTRIBUTED OVER THE YEAR F
      OR CONTINUOUS DISCOUNTING."
4610  PRINT : PRINT  TAB( 10)"**
      NOTE: THE TAX MAY BE NEGATIV
      E ON THE ASSUMPTION THAT THE
      RE IS OFFSETTING REVENUE FRO
      M OTHER SOURCES."
4620  REM  **** RETURN ON EQUITY*
      ***
4630  FOR J = 1 TO N
4640  IF BV(J) = 0 THEN 4680
4650  Y(J) =  INT (PRO(J) / BV(J) *
      10000 + .5) / 100
4660  Y$(J) =  STR$ (Y(J))
4670  YY$(J) =  STR$ ( INT (Y(J)))
4680  NEXT J
4690  POKE 36,58: PRINT  CHR$ (14
      )"TABLE II"
4700  POKE 36,58: PRINT "--------
      -------"
4710  POKE 36,49: PRINT  CHR$ (14
      )" RETURN ON EQUITY "
4720  PRINT  TAB( 12)"YEAR";: HTAB
      22: PRINT "BOOK VALUE";"
      NET PROFIT";"     RETURN ON
      INVESTMENT"
4730  PRINT  TAB( 10)"-----------
      ----------------------------
      ----------------------------"
4740  FOR J = 1 TO N
4750  HTAB (15 - LEN ( STR$ (J))
      ): PRINT J;
4760  HTAB (28 - LEN (BV$(J))):
      PRINT BV$(J);
4770  POKE 36,(45 - LEN (PR$(J))
      ): PRINT PR$(J);
4780  POKE 36,(62 - LEN (YY$(J))
      ): PRINT Y$(J)
4790  NEXT J
4800  GOTO 5310
4810  REM  *** INTERNAL RATE OF R
      ETURN
4820  HOME : PRINT " THE PRESENT
      WORTH, WITH ROI = "; INT (Y *
      10000 + .5) / 100;"%,": PRINT
      "    IS "; INT (P + .5);"."
4830  Y(1) = Y:P(1) = P
4840  INPUT "MAKE A GUESS FOR IRR
      ";Y:Y = Y / 100
4850  IF Y = 0 THEN Y = .00000000
      1
4860  GOSUB 3080
```

```
4870  GOSUB 1650
4880  PRINT :P1 = P
4890  Y = (Y - Y(1)) * P / (P(1) -
      P) + Y
4900  Y(1) = Y
4910  PRINT : PRINT "THE NET PRES
      ENT VALUE IS NOW ": PRINT  INT
      (P + .5);","
4920  PRINT : PRINT "THE FIRST TI
      ME IT WAS "; INT (P(1) + .5)

4930  PRINT : PRINT "MAKE A  SECO
      ND GUESS FOR": PRINT "  THE
      INTERNAL RATE OF RETURN "
4940  INPUT "";Y:Y = Y / 100
4950  IF Y = 0 THEN Y = .00000000
      1
4960  P(1) = P:Y(1) = Y(2)
4970  GOSUB 3190: GOSUB 1650
4980  Y(2) = Y
4990  Y = (Y - Y(1)) * P / (P(1) -
      P) + Y
5000  IF  INT (P * 10 + .5) / 100
      = 0 THEN 5040
5010  Y(1) = Y(2)
5020  P(1) = P
5030  GOTO 4970
5040  REM  FINALIZE THE ITERATION

5050  HOME : PRINT : PRINT " THE
      INTERNAL  RATE OF RETURN IS
      ": PRINT : PRINT  TAB( 12)"<
      < "; INT (Y * 10000 + .5) /
      100;"% >>"
5060  GOTO 3970
5070  REM  **** REVENUE REQUIREME
      NTS ****
5080  FOR J = 1 TO N
5090  U = U + ((REV(J) * ((1 + Y) ^
      - J)))
5100  V = V + (((C(J) + I(J)) * ((
      1 + Y) ^  - J)))
5110  W = W + ((DP(J) * ((1 + Y) ^
      - J)))
5120  NEXT J
5130  S = - (PC - FK + (T * W) -
      ((1 - T) * V)) / ((1 - T) *
      U)
5140  FOR J = 1 TO N
5150  RC(J) = RC(J) * S
5160  REV(J) = REV(J) * S
5170  F = REV(J): GOSUB 320:REV$(J
      ) = F$
5180  NEXT J
5190  GOSUB 3190
5200  RETURN
5210  RR = 1
5220  GOTO 3560
5230  REM *** EXTERNAL RATE OF RE
      TURN ****
5240  FOR J = 1 TO N
5250  FUND = FUND + (CF(J) * ((1 +
      Y) ^ (N - J + 1)))
5260  NEXT J
5270  P1 = (FUND * ((1 + Y) ^  - N
      )) + PC

5280  X = Y - ((1 / N) * ( LOG (FK
      / P1)))
5290  HOME : PRINT "THE EXTERNAL
      RATE OF RETURN IS ": PRINT
      TAB(12)"<< "; INT (X * 10000
      + . 5) / 100;"% >>"
5300  GOTO 3970
5310  PR# 0
5320  QQ = 1
5330  HOME : PRINT : PRINT "DO YO
      U WISH TO USE SAME DATA WITH
      "
5340  PRINT : PRINT "      REVISED
      PARAMETERS?"
5350  INPUT "";QQ$: IF QQ$ = "Y"
      THEN 1870
5360  PRINT : PRINT " DO YOU WISH
      TO TEST FOR SENSITIVITY?
5370  INPUT "";UU$: IF UU$ < > "
      Y" THEN 6650
5380  HOME : PRINT : PRINT " SELE
      CT THE PARAMETER TO BE TESTE
      D:"
5390  PRINT : PRINT "       1.  T
      HE DISCOUNT RATE"
5400  PRINT "       2.   THE INFLA
      TION RATE"
5410  PRINT "       3.   DEBT INTE
      REST RATE"
5420  PRINT "       4.   EXIT THE
      PROGRAM"
5430  INPUT "";UU
5440  Z = 1
5450  IF UU = 1 THEN 5510
5460  IF UU = 2 THEN 5850
5470  IF UU = 3 THEN 6230
5480  IF UU = 4 THEN 6690
5490  IF UU = 5 THEN 6570
5500  IF UU = 6 THEN  END
5510  REM  *** SENSITIVITY TO OCC
      ***
5520  Y = Y * .2:C = Y
5530  FOR K = 1 TO 8
5540  GOSUB 6570
5550  Y = Y + C
5560  GOSUB 510: GOSUB 3320
5570  GOSUB 1650
5580  P(K) = P
5590  Y(K) = Y:YY(K) =  INT (Y(K) *
      100)
5600  P$(K) =  STR$ ( INT (P(K) +
      .5))
5610  F$ = P$(K): GOSUB 320:P$(K) =
      F$
5620  YY$(K) =  STR$ (YY(K))
5630  Y$(K) =  STR$ ( INT (Y(K) *
      10000 + .5) / 100)
5640  PRINT P$(K)
5650  NEXT K
5660  Y = Y(4):P = P(4)
5670  IF Y$ = "Y" THEN  PR# 1
5680  PRINT : POKE 36,55: PRINT
      CHR$(14)"TABLE IIIA"
5690  PRINT : POKE 36,54: PRINT
      CHR$(14)"SENSITIVITY": PRINT
5700  HOME : PRINT "THE TABLE SHO
```

```
                WS THE VARIATION DUE TO A CH        6100  P = P(4):I1 = O1:I2 = O2:I3 =
                ANGE IN OCC IN INCREMENTS OF              O3
                20%+/-    FROM   THE BASIC VA   6110  IF Y$ = "Y" THEN  PR# 1
                LUE OF ";Y$(4);"%."             6120  HOME : PRINT : POKE 36,55:
5710  DV$ = " PRESENT WORTH "                         PRINTCHR$ (14)"TABLE IIIB"
5720  PRINT : PRINT "  OCC       ";D    6130  PRINT : POKE 36,54: PRINT
      V$                                            CHR$(14)"SENSITIVITY": PRINT
5730  PRINT "------------ -------   6140  HOME : PRINT "TABLE SHOWS I
      -------"                                       NFLATION EFFECT ON PW.":
5740  FOR K = 1 TO 3                                 PRINT"   INFLATION RATES (%)
5750  HTAB (5 - LEN (YY$(K))):                       ": PRINT" CAPITAL COST PRICE
      PRINT Y$(K);: HTAB (20 - LEN              PRESENT WORTH"
      (P$(K))): PRINT P$(K)             6150  PRINT "  -------  ----  ----
5760  NEXT K                                     -  -------  -----"
5770  HTAB (5 - LEN (YY$(K))):          6160  FOR K = 1 TO 8
      PRINT Y$(K);: HTAB (20 - LEN      6170  HTAB (6 - LEN (IA$(K))):
      (P$(K))): PRINT P$(K);"                     PRINTI1$(K);: HTAB (13 -
      BASIC VALUE"                                LEN (IB$(K))): PRINT I2$(K)
5780  FOR K = 5 TO 8                                 ;: HTAB (19 - LEN (IC$(K)))
5790  HTAB (5 - LEN (YY$(K))):                       : PRINTI3$(K);: HTAB (35 -
      PRINTY$(K);: HTAB (20 - LEN                LEN (P$(K))): PRINT P$(K)
      (P$(K))): PRINT P$(K)             6180  NEXT K
5800  NEXT K                            6190  I1 = O1:I2 = O2:I3 = O3:
5810  PR# 0                                     GOSUB1410: GOSUB 3110: GOSUB
5820  Y = Y(4)                                  1650
5830  GET ZX$                           6200  GET ZX$
5840  GOTO 5360                         6210  PRINT : PRINT "DO YOU WISH
5850  REM     *** INFLATION ****             TO TEST FURTHER? ": INPUT ""
5860  HOME : PRINT " WHICH RATE?"            ;UU$: IF UU$ = "Y" THEN 5360
      : PRINT : PRINT  TAB( 10)"1.
      CAPITAL   ": PRINT  TAB( 10)    6220  GOTO 6650
      "2. COST ": PRINT  TAB( 10)"    6230  REM *** DEBT SENSITIVITY***
      3.PRICE   "                       6240  R = R * .2:C = R
5870  PRINT : PRINT " SELECT ";:        6250  FOR K = 1 TO 8
      INPUT "";WZ                        6260  GOSUB 6570
5880  IF WZ = 1 THEN C1 = .02           6270  R = R + C
5890  IF WZ = 2 THEN C2 = .02           6280  GOSUB 3110: GOSUB 1650
5900  IF WZ = 3 THEN C3 = .02           6290  P(K) = P
5910  IF WZ = 1 THEN I1 =  - .02        6300  R(K) = R:RR(K) =  INT (R(K)
5920  IF WZ = 2 THEN I2 =  - .02              100)
5930  IF WZ = 3 THEN I3 =  - .02        6310  P$(K) =  STR$ ( INT (P(K) +
5940  O1 = I1:O2 = I2:O3 = I3                 .5)
5950  FOR K = 1 TO 8                    6320  F$ = P$(K): GOSUB 320:P$(K)
5960  GOSUB 6570                              = F$
5970  I1 = I1 + C1:I2 = I2 + C2:I3      6330  RR$(K) =  STR$ (RR(K))
      = I3 + C3                          6340  R$(K) =  STR$ ( INT (R(K) *
5980  GOSUB 1410                              10000 + .5) / 100)
5990  GOSUB 3110: GOSUB 1650            6350  NEXT K
6000  P(K) = P                          6360  R = R(4):P = P(4)
6010  I1(K) = I1:IA$(K) =  STR$ (       6370  IF Y$ = "Y" THEN  PR# 1
      INT(I1(K) * 100))                  6380  PRINT : POKE 36,55: PRINT
6020  I2(K) = I2:IB$(K) =  STR$ (             CHR$(14)"TABLE IIIC"
      INT(I2(K) * 100))                  6390  PRINT : POKE 36,54: PRINT
6030  I3(K) = I3:IC$(K) =  STR$ (             CHR$(14)"SENSITIVITY": PRINT
      INT(I3(K) * 100))                  6400  HOME : PRINT "THE TABLE SHO
6040  P(K) =  STR$ ( INT (P(K) +             WS THE VARIATION IN        D
      .5))                                    EBT INTEREST IN INCREMENTS O
6050  F$ = P$(K): GOSUB 320:P$(K) =          F 20%+/-    FROM   THE BASIC V
      F$                                       ALUE OF ";R$(4);"%."
6060  I1$(K) =  STR$ ( INT (I1(K) *     6410  DV$ = " PRESENT WORTH "
      10000 + .5) / 100)                 6420  PRINT : PRINT "INTEREST RAT
6070  I2$(K) =  STR$ ( INT (I2(K) *           E ";DV$
      10000 + .5) / 100)                 6430  PRINT "------------- -----
6080  I3$(K) =  STR$ ( INT (I3(K) *           ---------"
      10000 + .5) / 100)                 6440  FOR K = 1 TO 3
6090  NEXT K
```

```
6450  HTAB (6 - LEN (RR$(K))):        6580  PRINT " PLEASE HAVE PATIENC
      PRINTR$(K);: HTAB (20 - LEN            E."
      (P$(K))): PRINT P$(K)           6590  PRINT : PRINT
6460  NEXT K                          6600  IF UU = 1 THEN  PRINT Y * 1
6470  FOR K = 4 TO 8                        00,P
6480  HTAB (6 - LEN (RR$(K))):        6610  IF UU = 2 THEN  PRINT I3 *
      PRINT R$(K);: HTAB (20 - LEN          100,P
      (P$(K))): PRINT P$(K);" BASIC   6620  IF UU = 3 THEN  PRINT R * 1
      VALUE"                                00,P
6490  FOR K = 5 TO 8                  6630  RETURN
6500  HTAB (6 - LEN (RR$(K))):        6640  NEXT K
      PRINT R$(K);: HTAB (20 - LEN    6650  PRINT "DO YOU WISH TO CHANG
      (P$(K))): PRINT P$(K)                 E DATA?"
6510  NEXT K                          6660  INPUT "";Y$: IF Y$ < > "Y"
6520  R = R(4)                              THEN 6690
6530  GET ZX$                         6670  RR = 0
6540  PRINT : PRINT "DO YOU WISH      6680  QQ = 0: GOTO 140
      TO TEST FURTHER? ": INPUT ""    6690  PRINT : PRINT " YOU HAVE NO
      ;UU$: IF UU$ = "Y" THEN 5360          W EXITED THE PROGRAM."
                                      6700  PR# 0
6550  GOTO 6650                       6710  GET ZX$: PR# 6
6560  -                               6720  END
6570  HOME : PRINT " THIS IS GOIN
      G TO TAKE TIME."
```

This bibliography is subdivided by chapter. However, Chapters 4 and 5 deal largely with the same subject matter and so are combined.

References cited throughout the text are included, as well as suggestions for additional reading.

CHAPTER 1

English, J. Morley, ed., *Cost Effectiveness: Economic Evaluation of Engineered Systems*, John Wiley and Sons, New York, 1968.

Fish, J. C. L., *Engineering Economics*, McGraw Hill, New York, 1923 (1st ed., 1915).

Grant, Eugene L., *Principles of Engineering Economy*, Ronald Press, New York, 1930.

Grant, Eugene L., W. Grant Ireson, & Richard S. Leavenworth, *Principles of Engineering Economy*, John Wiley and Sons, New York, 7th ed., 1982.

Wellington, A. M., *The Economic Theory of Railway Location*, John Wiley and Sons, New York, 2nd ed., 1887.

CHAPTER 2

Baumol, W. J., *Economic Theory and Operations Analysis*, Prentice-Hall, Englewood Cliffs, 4th ed., 1977.

Bohm-Bawerk, *The Positive Theory of Capital*, Trans. by W. Smart, London, 1891.

Boulding, Kenneth, *Economic Analysis, Vol. I: Microeconomics*, Harper and Row, New York, 4th ed., 1966.

Fisher, Irving, *The Theory of Interest*, Reprints of Economic Classics, New York, 1961 (original publication, 1930).

Georgescu-Roegen, Nicholas, *Energy and Economic Myths*, Pergamon Press, New York, 1976.

Henderson, James B. and Richard E. Quandt, *Microeconomic Theory: A Mathematical Approach*, McGraw-Hill, New York, 1958.

Hicks, J. R., *Value and Capital*, Clarendon Press, Oxford, 2nd ed., 1946.

Hirshleifer, Jack, *Price Theory and Applications*, Prentice Hall, Englewood Cliffs, N.J., 1976.

Lind, Robert C., Optimal Resource Allocation, Markets, and Public Policy, in *Economics of Engineering and Social Systems*, J. M. English, ed., John Wiley and Sons, New York, 1972.

Lloyd, Cliff, *Microeconomic Analysis*, Richard D. Irwin, Homewood, Ill., 1967.

Meiselman, David, *The Term Structure of Interest Rates*, Prentice-Hall, Englewood Cliffs, N.J., 1962.

Oser, Jacob, *The Evolution of Economic Thought*, Harcourt, Brace & World, New York, 1963.

Rima, I. H., *Development of Economic Analysis*, Richard D. Irwin, Homewood, Ill., 1967.

Samuelson, Paul A., *Foundation of Economic Analysis*, Harvard University Press, Cambridge, Mass., 1947.

Shackle, G. L. S., *Epistemics and Economics*, Cambridge University Press, Cambridge, England, 1972.

Stigler, George J., *Essays in the History of Economics*, University of Chciago, Chicago, Ill., 1965.

Walras, Leon, *Elements of Pure Economics (1879)*, Trans. by W. Jaffe, Richard D. Irwin, Inc., Homewood, Ill., 1954.

CHAPTER 3

Adam Smith, *Paper Money*, Dell, New York, 1981.

Allen, R. G. D., *Macro-Economic Theory, A Mathematical Treatment*, Macmillan, St. Martins Press, New York, 1968.

Boulding, Kenneth E., *Economic Analysis, Vol. II: Macroeconomics*, Harper and Row, New York, 4th ed., 1955.

Carlson, Keith M., The Mix of Monetary and Fiscal Policies: Conventional Wisdom vs. Empirical Reality, *Federal Reserve Bank of St. Louis*, Vol. 6, #8, Oct. 1982.

Collery, Arnold, *National Income and Employment Analysis*, John Wiley and Sons, New York, 1966.

English, J. Morley, ed., *Economics of Engineering and Social Systems*, John Wiley and Sons, New York, 1972.

Friedman, Milton & Anna J. Schwartz, *A Monetary History of the United States*, Princeton University Press, Princeton, 1963.

Hafer, R. W. & Scott E. Hein, Monetary Policy and Short-Term Real Rates of Interest, *Federal Reserve Bank of St. Louis*, Vol. 65, #3, Mar. 1982.

Horwich, George, *Money, Capital, and Prices*, Richard D. Irwin, Homewood Ill., 1964.

Kendrick, John W., *The Formation and Stocks of Total Capital*, National Bureau of Economic Research, New York, 1976.

Keynes, John Maynard, *The General Theory of Employment Interest and Money*, Harcourt, Brace, New York, 1936.

Laidler, David L. W., *The Demand for Money, Theories and Evidence*, International Textbook Co., Scranton, Pa., 1969.

Lutz, Freidrich A. & Lloyd W. Mints, eds., *Readings in Monetary Theory*, Richard D. Irwin, Homewood, Ill., 1951.

Patinkin, Donald, *Money, Interest, and Prices*, Harper and Row, New York, 1965.

Ritter, Lawrence S. & William L. Ritter, *Principles of Money, Banking, and Financial Markets*, Basic Books, New York, 1974.

Spero, Herbert & Lewis E. Davis, *Money and Banking*, Barnes and Noble, New York, 1970.

Steiner, H. M., *Public and Private Investments—Socioeconomic Analysis*, John Wiley and Sons, New York, 1980.

Teigen, Ronald L., *Readings in Money, National Income and Stabilization Policy*, Richard D. Irwin, Homewood, Ill., 1965.

Thorn, Richard S., *Monetary Theory and Policy*, Random House, New York, 1966.

Thornton, Daniel L., Simple Analysis of the Money Supply Process and Monetary Control, *Federal Reserve Bank of St. Louis*, Vol. 6, #8, Oct. 1982.

Thurow, Lester C., *Dangerous Currents*, Random House, New York, 1982.

Timberlake, Richard H. & Edward B. Selby, *Money and Banking*, Wadsworth Publishing Co., Belmont, Calif., 1972.

Weintraub, Robert E., *Introduction to Monetary Economics*, Ronald Press Co., New York, 1970.

CHAPTERS 4 AND 5

AT & T Co., *Engineering Economy*, American Telephone and Telegraph, New York, 2nd ed., 1963.

Barish, Norman N. & Seymour Kaplan, *Economic Analysis for Engineering Decision Making*, McGraw-Hill, 2nd ed., New York, 1978.

Bierman, H. & S. Smith, *The Capital Budgeting Decision*, The Macmillan Co., New York, 4th ed., 1975.

Bussey, Lynn E. *The Economic Analysis of Industrial Projects*, Prentice-Hall, Englewood Cliffs, N.J., 1978.

Canada, John R. & J. A. White, *Capital Investment Decision Analysis for Management and Engineering*, Prentice-Hall, Englewood Cliffs, N.J., 1980.

Dean, Joel, *Capital Budgeting*, Prentice-Hall, Englewood Cliffs, N.J., 1951.

Degarmo, E. P., J. R. Canada, & W. G. Sullivan, *Engineering Economy*, The Macmillan Co., New York, 6th ed., 1979.

English, J. Morley, Some Investment Concepts in Engineering Systems with Particular Emphasis on Long-Range Investment in *Economics of Engineering and Social Systems*, J. M. English, ed., John Wiley and Sons, New York, 1972.

English, J. Morley, A Perceptual-Time Scale for Determination of a Discount Function, in *Trends in Engineering Decision-making*, Caes Van Dam, ed., Martinus Nijhoff, Leiden/Boston, 1978.

Fabrycky, W. J. & G. J. Thueson, *Economic Decision Analysis*, Prentice-Hall, Englewood Cliffs, N.J., 2nd ed., 1980.

Fish, J. C. L., *Engineering Economics*, McGraw-Hill, New York, 1915.

Fisher, Gene H., *Cost Considerations in Systems Analysis*, Rand Corp., Santa Monica, Calif., 1972.

Fleischer, G. A., *Capital Allocation Theory*, Appleton-Century-Crofts, New York, 1969.

Grant, Eugene, L., W. Grant Ireson, & Richard S. Leavenworth, *Principles of Engineering Economy*, John Wiley and Sons, New York, 7th ed., 1982.

Hanssman, Fred, *Operations Research Techniques for Capital Investment*, John Wiley and Sons, New York, 1962.

Hillier, F. S. & G. J. Lieberman, *Introduction to Operations Research*, Holden-Day, San Francisco, 2nd ed., 1974.

Hoffman, Fred S., The Analysis and Evaluation of Public Expenditures: The PPB System, in *The Economics of Engineering and Social Systems*, J. M. English, ed., John Wiley and Sons, New York, 1972.

Jeynes, P. H., *Profitability and Economic Choice*, Iowa State University Press, Ames, Iowa, 1968.

Massé, Pierre, *Optimal Investment Decisions*, Prentice-Hall, Englewood Cliffs, N.J., 1962.

McKean, R. N., *Efficiency in Government through Systems Analysis*, John Wiley and Sons, New York, 1958.

Morris, W. T., *The Analysis of Managerial Decisions*, Richard D. Irwin, Homewood, Ill., 1964.

Newnan, Donald G., *Engineering Economic Analysis*, Engineering Press, San Jose, Calif., 1980.

Oakford, Robert V., *Capital Budgeting: A Quantitative Evaluation of Investment Alternatives*, John Wiley and Sons, New York, 1970.

Riggs, James I., *Economic Decision Models for Engineers and Managers*, McGraw Hill, New York, 1977.

Smith, Gerald W., *Engineering Economy: The Analysis of Capital Expenditures*, Iowa State University Press, Ames, Iowa, 1973.

Solomon, Ezra, *The Management of Corporate Capital*, The Free Press, New York, 1966.

Swalm, Ralph O., Capital Expenditure Analysis—A Bibliography, *The Engineering Economist*, Vol. 13, #2, Winter 1968.

Tarquin, A. J. & L. T. Blank, *Engineering Economy: A Behavorial Approach*, McGraw-Hill, New York, 1976.

Taylor, G. A., *Managerial and Engineering Economy*, Van Nostrand Reinhold Co., New York, 3rd ed., 1980.

Thuesen, H. G., W. J. Fabrycky, & G. J. Thuesen, *Engineering Economy*, Prentice-Hall, Englewood Cliffs, N.J., 5th ed., 1977.

Wagner, Harvey M., *Principles of Management Science: With Applications to Management Decisions*, Prentice-Hall, Englewood Cliffs, N.J., 2nd ed., 1977.

Weingartner, A. M., *Mathematical Programming and the Analysis of Capital Budgeting Problems*, Prentice-Hall, Englewood Cliffs, N.J., 1963.

CHAPTER 6

Merrill Lynch, Pierce, Fenner and Smith, *How to Read a Financial Report*, Merrill Lynch, Pierce, Fenner and Smith, New York, 1979.

CHAPTER 7

Ball, Richard, ed., *Readings in Investments*, Allyn and Bacon, Boston, 1964.

Cohen, Jerome B. & Edward D. Zinbarg, *Investment Analysis and Portfolio Management*, Richard D. Irwin, Homewood, Ill., 1967.

Cootner, Paul, ed., *The Random Character of Stock Market Prices*, The MIT Press, Cambridge, Mass., 1964.

Davidson, Lawrence S. & Richard T. Froyen, Monetary Policy and Stock Returns: Are Stock Markets Efficient?, *Federal Reserve Bank of St. Louis*, Vol. 64, #3, 1982.

Eisner, Robert, *Factors in Business Investment*, Ballinger Publishing Co., Cambridge, Mass., 1978.

Hester, Donald D. & James Tobin, *Financial Markets and Economic Activity*, John Wiley and Sons, New York, 1967.

Malkiel, Burton G. & Richard E. Quandt, *Strategies and Rational Decisions in the Security Options Market*, The MIT Press, Cambridge, Mass., 1969.

Riley, William B. & Austin H. Montgomery, Jr., *Guide to Computer-Assisted Investment Analysis*, McGraw-Hill, New York, 1982.

CHAPTER 8

Abel, Andrew B., Taxes, Inflation, and Durability of Capital, *Journal of Political Economy*, May–June 1981.

Phillips, A. W., *The Relationship between Unemployment and the Rate of Change of Money Wages in the U.K.*, Economica, U.K., 1958.

English, J. Morley, *Inflation: An Entropy Explanation*, Bedrijfskunde, Holland, Jrg 46, #1, 1974.

CHAPTER 9

Bernhard, Richard H., On the Park–Thuesen Index and the Value of Earlier Uncertainty Resolution, *The Engineering Economist*, Winter 1981.

Bernhard, Richard H., Avoiding Irrationality in the Use of Two-Parameter Risk–Benefit Models for Investment under Uncertainty, *Financial Management*, Spring 1981.

Francis, Jack Clark & Stephan H. Archer, *Portfolio Analysis*, Prentice-Hall, Englewood Cliffs, N.J., 1971.

Hester, Donald D. & James Tobin, *Risk Aversion and Portfolio Choice*, John Wiley and Sons, New York, 1967.

Hillier, Fredrick S., *The Evaluation of Risky Interrelated Investments*, Elsevier North-Holland Publishing Co., New York, 1969.

Malkiel, Burton G., *A Random Walk Down Wall Street*, W. W. Norton & Co., New York, 1973.

Markowitz, Harry, The Utility of Wealth, *Jour. of Political Economy*, 60:151–158, April 1952.

Markowitz, Harry, *Portfolio Selection: Efficient Diversification of Investments*, John Wiley and Sons, 1959.

Oakford, Robert, Mathematics, Computation and Practical Capital Budgeting Decisions, *Proceedings, Institute of Industrial Engineers*, 1982.

Sharpe, William F., A Simplified Model for Portfolio Analysis, *Management Science*, 9:277–293, January, 1963.

Smith, Keith V., *Portfolio Management*, Holt Rinehart and Winston, New York, 1971.

CHAPTER 10

English, J. Morley and Nabil El Ramly, Economic Evaluation of Desalting Sub-System as a Part of a Total Water System, *Desalination*, 3:308–317, 1967.

Grobecker, Allen, et al., Climatic Impact Assessment Program, U.S. Department of Transportation, 1974.

Terborgh, George, *Business Investment Policy*, Machinery and Allied Products Institute, Washington D.C., 1958.

Index